Francis Bacon
Poet, Prophet, Philosopher

Francis Bacon
Poet, Prophet, Philosopher

By
W. F. C. Wigston

Athens ‡ Manchester

Francis Bacon. Poet, Prophet, Philosopher

Published by: Old Book Publishing Ltd

Book Cover Design: Old Book Publishing Ltd

Copyright © 2012 Old Book Publishing Ltd
All rights reserved.

Title of original: Francis Bacon. Poet, Prophet, Philosopher.
Versus Phantom Captain Shakespeare

Originally published in 1891, London, Kegan Paul, Trench, Trubner & Co, Ltd.

ISBN–10: 1-78107-155-1
ISBN–13: 978-1-78107-155-7

EDITOR'S NOTE

Old Book Publishing Ltd takes care in preserving the wording and images of the original books. For this reason we have invested in technology that enables us to enhance the quality of such reproduction. This investment helps overcome problems encountered when reproducing old books, such as stains, coloured paper, discolouration of ink, yellowed pages, see-through and onion skin type paper.

This reproduction book, produced from digital images of the original, may contain occasional defects such as missing pages or blemishes due to the original source content or were introduced by the scanning process.

These are scanned pages and the quality of print represents accurately the print quality of the original book, though we may have been able to enhance it.

As this book has been scanned and/or reformatted from the original we cannot guarantee that it is error-free or contains the full content of the original.

However, we believe that this work is culturally important, and despite its imperfections, have elected to bring it back into print as part of our commitment to the preservation of printed works.

Old Book Publishing

QVOD FELICITER VORTAT REIP: LITERARIAE.
V.C. FRAN: DE VERVLAMIO PHILOSOPH: LIBERTATIS
ASSERTOR AVDAX, SCIENTIARV REPARATOR FELIX
IUCUNDI MENTISQ. MAGNUS ARBITER INCLYTIS
MAX: TERRARUM ORBIS ACAD: OXON: CANTAB.Q. HANC
SUAM INSTAUR: VOTO SUSCEPTO VIVUS DECERNEBAT
OBIIT V NON: APRIL: II D.N: KAROLI. I
PP AVG: cIɔIɔc xxvI.

FRANCIS BACON

POET, PROPHET, PHILOSOPHER

VERSUS

PHANTOM CAPTAIN SHAKESPEARE

THE ROSICRUCIAN MASK

BY

W. F. C. WIGSTON

AUTHOR OF "A NEW STUDY OF SHAKESPEARE," "BACON, SHAKESPEARE, AND THE ROSICRUCIANS," "HERMES STELLA."

"Orpheus himself was torn to pieces by the women in their fury, and his limbs scattered about the fields: at whose death, HELICON (*river sacred to the Muses*), *in grief and indignation, buried his waters under the earth to reappear elsewhere.*" (Bacon's "Wisdom of the Ancients," Orpheus.)

LONDON
KEGAN PAUL, TRENCH, TRÜBNER & CO., Ltd.
1891

This Work is dedicated

TO

IGNATIUS DONNELLY

IN TOKEN

OF RESPECT AND ADMIRATION

BY

THE AUTHOR.

PREFACE.

It may interest those who are already converts to the Baconian theory of the authorship of the Plays, to learn that Mr Donnelly has made further discoveries. He writes under date 12th July 1890: "I am still at work, in all leisure moments, upon the Cipher, and am working out the complete and perfect story, and hope to publish something before long that will end the controversy."

CONTENTS.

PAGE

INTRODUCTION xv

Preliminary Remarks—Lithograph Facsimile Copy of pages 52, 53, "CONFESSIO FRATERNITATIS, or Confession of the Laudable Order of the Rosy Cross," published at Frankfort, 1617, showing how a Stage Player is held up to contempt as an impostor—Michael Maier publishes three works immediately after his return from a visit to England in 1616—In his "Examination and Exposure of Drones and False Alchymists," he re-echoes the "Confessio," and identifies Poetry with Alchymy, giving hints for the Rosicrucians themselves—His Serio Comic Dialogue, "*Lusus Serius*," written also with regard to his stay in England—Contains the story of the "Waking Man's Dream," repeated in the Induction of the "Taming of the Shrew," by the incident of the substitution of Christopher Sly in the place of a Lord—Bacon's Fragment upon Fame—Paraphrase from Virgil—His Fable of Perseus twice repeated—The Perseus myth a Rosicrucian myth centre.

CHAPTER I.

HISTORY OF KING HENRY THE SEVENTH 1

Bacon's History of "King Henry the Seventh"—Missing Link in the orderly succession of Chronicle Plays—Bacon writes this sole History—Parallels—Cipher connection between Bacon's "Henry the Seventh" and the 1623 Folio Plays.

CHAPTER II.

BACON'S ESSAYS APPLIED TO THE PLAYS 25

Ambition, Envy, and Deformity—Richard III.—Thersites—Edmund—Don John—Philip the Bastard—Cassius and Cæsar—Cicero.

CONTENTS.

CHAPTER III.

BACON'S ESSAYS APPLIED TO THE PLAYS—*continued* . . 42

Suspicion—Malice—Cunning—Othello and Iago.—Vain-Glory—Achilles and Ajax.—Boldness—Bardolph, Nym, Pistol.—Parasites and Trencher Friends—Timon and Apemantus.—Usury—Revenge—Shylock.—Riches—The Three Caskets.—Friendship—Parents and Children.—Followers and Friends.

CHAPTER IV.

DIVINATION AND PREDICTION 70

Augury—Perspective—Reflection—Glass Mirror—Rosicrucian Ideas—The World as Theatre—The Theatre as Nature—The Music of the Spheres—Another Rosicrucian Doctrine.

CHAPTER V.

BACON'S "GEORGICS OF THE MIND" 99

Quotations showing Shakespeare employs the word *weed* for vice—Our Bodies compared to a Garden—Abandoned since the Fall—King Lear a neglected piece of ground, crowned with furrow weeds and darnel—The Microcosm the reflection of the Macrocosm—Diseases of the Mind—The Parable of the Talents illustrated by "Measure for Measure."

CHAPTER VI.

BACON AND SENECA 13

Poem by Powell, comparing Bacon to Seneca the Dramatist—Evidently written by one who knew Bacon's poetic side—Resemblance of Bacon to Seneca—His self-comparison with him—Both sacrifices of Faction.

CHAPTER VII.

"ANTITHETA" IN BACON'S WRITINGS 139

Find their reflection in the antithetical style of Shakespeare—Evidence of an impersonal philosophical mind trained in the schools—Bacon's Collection of Antitheta simply Texts for his

CONTENTS.

Essays—Antitheta found in the "De Augmentis," under the "Wisdom of Private Speech," and as part of the Delivery of Secret knowledge or Tradition—Colours of Good and Evil—The Antitheta really the Colours of the Dramatic Artist—Strange introduction of Bacon's Works in the "De Augmentis" as deficients.

CHAPTER VIII.

HISTORY, POETRY, PHILOSOPHY 153

Bacon's suspicious definition of History and Poetry—Their close relationship as past history made present or visible—The number of Chronicle Histories in the 1623 Folio—Bacon's tripartite foundations of Learning, or Faculties of the Soul—Memory—Imagination—Reason—Makes Poetry one of the emanations of the Soul, on which Science is based—Nevertheless confesses, "Poetry is not a knowledge, but a play of wit"—Enigmatic character of "The Advancement of Learning"—Bacon identifies History with Custody or Memory—His art of Tradition or Delivery or transferring those things laid up in the memory to others, &c.

CHAPTER IX.

VERULAM AND CYMBELINE 172

Old Verulam seat of Cassibulan, uncle to Cymbeline—Imogen and her two brothers parallels for Helen, Castor, and Pollux—The Lion's Whelp — Curious MSS. written by Sir Tobie Matthews.

CHAPTER X.

TEMPLE AND VERULAM HOUSE 186

Aubrey's descriptive details—Paintings from classical subjects—Ceres—Jupiter and Apollo represented on the walls of Verulam House—The Fish Ponds.

CHAPTER XI.

PARALLELS 192

Hamlet—Bacon's "Wisdom of the Ancients" refound in the Plays—Horticultural Parallels — Custom, Habit, Use — Love—Falconry—Swans—Duke Humphrey—Music.

BACON, SHAKESPEARE, AND THE ROSICRUCIANS.

CHAPTER I.

BACON AND THE ROSICRUCIANS 271

De Quincey's statements misleading—Rosicrucians not gold-seekers — Rosicrucians reveal Baconian ends — Their Book of Nature reflected in Bacon's "Sylva Sylvarum"—Maier visits England—On his return to Germany seeks to found a Society—Bacon was enlisting the services of learned men beyond the seas for some secret purpose unknown to us—History of the Royal Society mixed up with the history of the Rosicrucian Campanella—Testimony of Des Cartes, Liebnitz, Helmont, showing the Rosicrucian Society did not exist abroad—Parallels between Bacon's writings and Fludd's—Allusions to Solomon, Persian Magic, and the Star in the East, both by Fludd and Bacon in identical language—Bacon adopted the Rosicrucian emblem or type of Architecture and Agriculture.

CHAPTER II.

NOTES ON ROSICRUCIAN LITERATURE 299

Strange correspondence between Rosicrucian literature and the date of Shakespeare's death, 1616—The controversy is at its height in 1617, when the Englishman Robert Fludd defends the Order against the attacks of foreigners—Bacon's term INSTAURATION also used by the Rosicrucians in the sense of RESTORATION of Arts and Sciences—Burton's evidence in his "Anatomy of Melancholy," 1621—Statement that the founder of the Rosicrucian Order was then living—"*Omnium artium et scientiarum instaurator*"—In England only Rosicrucianism took root, showing its origin—Fludd receives money from abroad, and publishes at Frankfort—Receives letters from foreigners—His own words prove originality—Parallels.

CHAPTER III.

ROSICRUCIAN PARALLELS TO BACON'S WRITINGS 312

Air, Soul, Spirit—Bees and Roses—Rose and Lily—The Raven and Dove—Weapon-salve—The Chain of Nature—Pan—Orpheus—Strife and Friendship—The giving of Names—Foundations—*Nil nisi Parvulus*—Signets or Seals—Magnalia or Marvels—The

CONTENTS. xiii

Lion's Whelp—Rosicrucian Curiosities—Everlasting Lamps—The Pythagorean number Thirty-six—Heydon's "Land of the Rosicrucians" identical line for line with Bacon's "New Atlantis."

CHAPTER IV.

GENERAL REMARKS 357

Bacon's "Restoration of Knowledge" connected with his "New Atlantis," the seat of the "Secret Doctrine"—The six days of Creation—Hint for the Creative Cycles connected with the Naros—Fondness of Rosicrucians for the week as a type—Bacon's extraordinary predilection for Solomon—Bacon and Campanella—The City of the Sun—Parallels presented in the play of the "Tempest"—Ben Jonson's "Fortunate Isles"—Allusions to Rosicrucians.

CHAPTER V.

BACON'S "HOLY WAR" 381

The Templar origin of the Rosicrucians—Bacon writes in the spirit of a Knight Templar, urging a Crusade—Though only a peaceable one with pens—Suspicious references to different Orders—Bacon refers to the Temple and its rebuilding—The House of Wisdom—Bacon's Anti-Papal and Anti-Mahommedan Spirit—Bacon's allusions to Sacrifice—His renunciation and complete self-effacement—These were Rosicrucian doctrines.

CHAPTER VI.

HERMES STELLA 397

Bacon's Astrological MSS. Notes, 1603, with strange Parallels from the Rosicrucian, Robert Fludd—The German text of the sixth chapter of Fludd's "Tractatus Apologeticus," 1617, showing how in 1603 the planet Jupiter was in conjunction with Saturn.

APPENDIX 419

Cipher Tables—Notes upon the mispaging in the 1640 "Advancement of Learning"—English words in the text of the first edition of the "Chymical Marriage of Christian Rosy Cross," 1616—Maier's locality of the Rosicrucians—Plainly the Hesperides or Atlantis.

INTRODUCTION.

THIS work is the result of some few months' close study. It is certain anybody giving himself up to complete devotion to this work, might easily double or treble the number of parallels I adduce. The chief difficulty is the recognition of parallelism, for a student must have Shakespeare or Bacon by heart first, since we cannot read the two authors at the same time, and an ordinary remembrance of the chief passages in the plays is not sufficient for discovery. The works have to be read and re-read thousands of times, and recognition of the same thoughts disguised under different language requires practice and a quick eye to detect them. It is certain there is hardly a line, certainly not a simile, illustration, or metaphor, which may not be found repeated by both writers. This may seem a bold assumption, but let any one doubting it, read Mr Donnelly's parallels, then the vast collection adduced by Mrs Pott, and the Journal of the Bacon Society, together with mine, and it is not too much to say they must amount to thousands—certainly to at least five hundred complete and perfect ones. Those who refuse to acknowledge this evidence must be prejudiced, and are determined evidently to defend Shakespeare's prescriptive claim to the authorship of the plays, at the point of the bayonet. They belong to a class who would have the star Lyra rise and set by authority. But how long will fashion, passion, and prejudice hold out against Truth?

It is indeed astonishing to find both Mr Aldis Wright and Dr

Abbott, in their editions of the "Advancement of Learning" and "Essays," filling their notes and glossaries with illustrations from Shakespeare to parallel the English of Lord Bacon's prose writings!

I have endeavoured to avoid repeating parallels already published by others, but it is quite impossible to entirely escape a charge of plagiarism on this point. It is impossible to guard against repetition of parallels which are daily being discovered, or to be acquainted with the entire range of Bacon-Shakespeare literature, which threatens to become enormous. Some of my parallels already have appeared, but I hope they are illustrated anew, and I think the greater part are original; I may truly say, all have been independently arrived at.

Professor Fowler points out in his work, the "Novum Organum," the marvellous resemblance in style, thought, and literary genius in every direction, in all which no other author can be compared to Bacon, except it be Shakespeare. Testimonies of this sort, without any theory or thought behind to suggest that Bacon wrote the plays and is Shakespeare's double, are highly valuable on account of their perfect immunity from any suspicion of bias or prejudice. We find Dr Kuno Fischer pointing out in like manner how the "Want of ability to take an historical survey of the world is to be found alike in Bacon and Shakespeare together, with many excellences common to them both. To the parallel between them, which Gervinus with his peculiar talent for combination has drawn in the concluding remarks to his 'Shakespeare,' and has illustrated by a series of appropriate instances, belongs the similar relation of both to antiquity, their affinity to the Roman mind, and their diversity from the Greek.

"The great interest that Bacon took in portraits of character is proved by the fact that he attempted to draw them himself. With a few felicitous touches he sketched the characters of Julius and Augustus Cæsar, and his view of both was similar to that of Shakespeare. In Julius Cæsar he saw combined all that the

Roman genius had to bestow in the shape of greatness, nobility, culture, and fascination, and regarded his character as the most formidable that the Roman world could encounter. And giving what always serves as the proof of the calculation in the analysis of a character, Bacon so explains the character of Cæsar, as to explain his fate also. He saw, like Shakespeare, that Cæsar was naturally inclined to a despotic feeling, that governed his great qualities and also their aberrations, rendering him dangerous to the Republic and blind with respect to his enemies. He wished, says Bacon, 'not to be eminent amongst great and deserving men, but to be chief among inferiors and vassals. He was so much dazzled by his own greatness that he no longer knew what danger was.' This is the same Cæsar into whose mouth Shakespeare puts the words—

> ——— 'Danger knows full well
> That Cæsar is more dangerous than he.
> We were two lions litter'd in one day,
> And I the elder and more terrible.'
>
> ('Julius Cæsar,' act ii. sc. 2.)

"When Bacon, at last, attributes the fate of Cæsar to his forgiveness of enemies, that by this magnanimity he might impose upon the multitude, he still shows the dazzled man, who heightens the expression of his greatness at the expense of his security" ("Francis Bacon of Verulam," Kuno Fischer, p. 207).

The *Standard* of the 31st December 1888 concludes its summary of the year's literature thus: "By dint of copious advertising, Mr Ignatius Donnelly's labours to prove that Bacon was the author of the plays attributed to Shakespeare had attracted considerable attention. But when 'The Great Cryptogram' appeared, in two huge volumes, it was clear that the 'Baconian theory' was no more than a colossal mare's nest, scarcely worth the trouble of serious examination."

Of the writer of this article I know nothing. Whoever he is I can only exclaim with Prince Hal, "Thou art a blessed fellow to think as every man thinks; never a man's thought in the world keeps the roadway better than thine." Archdeacon Farrar in the *Forum* for May, under the title, "Literary Criticism," writes: "The very demigods of literature—Dante and Shakespeare, and Bacon and Milton—have not escaped these methods. Horace Walpole called Dante 'extravagant, absurd, disgusting; in short, a Methodist parson in Bedlam!' Samuel Pepys, Esq., thought 'Othello' 'a mean thing,' and 'Midsummer Night's Dream' 'the most insipid, ridiculous play I ever saw in my life.' Bacon's 'Instauratio Magna' was described by an eminent contemporary as 'the silliest of printed books.' Hacket, in his 'Life of Lord Keeper Williams,' calls Milton 'a petty schoolboy scribbler'; and another contemporary spoke of him as 'the author of a profane and lascivious poem called 'Paradise Lost.'"

To this list I might add the names of Mesmer derided as a charlatan, Galileo, Harvey, Newton, for the hostile criticism the theory of gravitation met with lasted twenty years, even Leibnitz opposing it. If such great names as these passed through the fiery ordeal of criticism not unscathed, their discoveries at first derided, to be finally universally accepted as commonplace matter of course, surely the Bacon theory can wait profounder consideration and a better verdict at the hands of the public? The criticism quoted from the *Standard* must indeed amuse Mr Donnelly, recalling Goethe's description of literary Philistines:—

> Daran erkenn ich den gelehrten herrn,
> Was ihr nicht tastet, steht euch meilenfern;
> Was ihr nicht fasst, das fehlt euch ganz und gar
> Was ihr nicht rechnet, glaubt ihr, sei nicht wahr
> Was ihr nicht wägt war für euch kein gewicht,
> Was ihr nicht münzt, das meint euch, gelte nicht.

It is astonishing how little general, or even private interest as yet is excited around this Bacon-Shakespeare problem, seeing it promises more real romance than all the wildest fiction ever written. It is a common remark to hear said, "What, after all, if Bacon did write these plays?" If the problem ended here with

INTRODUCTION.

simply a claim to authorship, I confess I should not care much either whose name the plays carried. But it is certain this is perhaps the least part of the problem, and only the entrance to a complete system of cipher revelatory matter. Any doubt as to the existence of a cipher in the 1623 Folio plays can only remain in minds who have not studied the problem. It is the fashion to laugh at this theory, as it is miscalled, in the same way Harvey and Mesmer's discoveries were laughed at by incredulous and ignorant critics, who cannot imagine such a thing being done at all. But *it is certain* (and I write the word *certain* with a full sense that it is wise not to be too sure or confident whilst an element of doubt exists) *the Rosicrucians are at the bottom of the mystery.* In this work the reader will find a few I think striking parallels pointing this way, and I am certain the first earnest student who has access to the genuine writings of the Fraternity will discover a great many more, and that easily. For myself I can trace the influence of Lord Bacon throughout the works of the great English Rosicrucian, Thomas Vaughan. All the curious and recondite doctrines held by the Rosicrucians are repeated by Bacon, and are also to be found in the plays. One is the Music of the Spheres, another that the *Mind of man is a mirror or glass reflecting Nature.** A third a *Restoration of Knowledge* is repeated by Bacon and the Rosicrucians as a leading or opening object they had in view. The comparison of Nature to a *Book or Volume* of God's creatures, with its *alphabet of particulars*, is repeated frequently by Bacon and the Rosicrucians; also hinted at in the plays. The participation of *Matter with Form* in the sense of seal and imprint, as "*signatura rerum*," is a favourite simile of Bacon's and the Rosicrucians. Bacon's theory of Fascination and Divination is entirely borrowed from the great Rosicrucian forerunner and authority Paracelsus, and his disciple, Petrus Severinus. Bacon attributed to the Seven Chief Planets or Stars an occult and extraordinary

* Der Makrokosmus ist der spiegel, in welchem der Mikrokosmus geschant wird. Beide sind eins und dasselbe dem Wesen und der innern Form nach; in der äusseren Form sind sie verschieden " (p. 53, "Joh. Val. Andreas und sein Zeitalter," Wm. Rossbach, 1819).

influence in the dispensation of things. This is a leading Rosicrucian tenet, and is repeated by Fludd almost in identical words in context with Pan as by Bacon.

The Rosicrucians *deduced everything from Light*, and I leave those acquainted with Bacon's writings to judge how far this idea enters into his style and governs the "Novum Organum." A philosophical or ideal Republic, imitated from Plato's "Atlantis," was a Rosicrucian dream, and betrays one of their ends to be the reformation of society. Campanella's "City of the Sun," and John Valentine Andreas' "Christianopolitanæ Reipublicæ," are examples of these Utopias, and Bacon, as the Solomon of the Order, writes his "New Atlantis." The proofs pointing to Bacon as the head of the Society are far more abundant and striking to those who choose to seek for them or to reflect over what we adduce than is supposed. It is no ingenious theory caught from some fancied parallels or imaginary resemblances I bring forward.

This work had almost gone through the printer's hands, when I received from Germany a collection of rare and genuine Rosicrucian works of the early part of the seventeenth century. I am therefore under the necessity of introducing here evidence otherwise intended for the body of this work, which I venture to think is important. It may therefore as well stand first as last, although not strictly belonging to the character of an introduction. This work as a whole is a painstaking attempt to furnish commonplace rather than startling evidence of Bacon's authorship of the plays and of his connection with the Rosicrucian fraternity. Readers who do not care about the somewhat wearisome investigation of parallels may be interested in the second part of my work, in which I have collected some evidence as to the affinity existing between Bacon's writings and the tenets of the Rosicrucians. This is such a difficult subject, so wrapped in mystery, the literature so scarce and obscure, that the indulgence of the reader is begged for the subject, which is only in its infancy. Space forbids my doing bare justice to the subject, but I am sure the impartial critic will see that there is more in my theory than fanciful ingenuity or desire to adduce eclectic ideas.

Before me lays open an original copy of the "FAMA FRATERNITATIS oder Entdeckung der Bruderschafft dess löblichen Ordens des Rosen Creutses, beneben der CONFESSION oder Bekenntniss derselben FRATERNITET, an alle Gelehrte und Haupter in Europa geschrieben" (Franckfurt am Mayn, bey Joh. Bringern, 1617). Upon pages 52, 53 we read the accompanying reference to a *stage-player*, whom I most thoroughly believe is meant for WILLIAM SHAKESPEARE, who figures as a *stage-player*, in a list of twenty-six actors' names,* attached to the 1623 first edition plays. Upon the Stratford Shakespeare monument we read:—

> Ivdicio Pylivm, genio Socratem, arte Maronem,
> Terra tegit, popvlvs mæret, Olympvs habet.

> Stay, passenger, why goest thov by so fast?
> Read, if thov canst, whom enviovs Death hath plast
> Within this monvment, Shakspeare; with whome
> Quick natvre dide; whose name doth deck ye tombe

---

* Facsimile from the Folio Shakespeare, 1623.

The Workes of William Shakespeare,

containing all his Comedies, Histories, and Tragedies: Truely set forth, according to their first *ORIGINALL*.

The Names of the Principall Actors in all these Plays.

William Shakespeare.	*Samuel Gilburne.*
Richard Burbadge.	*Robert Armin.*
John Hemmings.	*William Ostler.*
Augustine Phillips.	*Nathan Field.*
William Kempt.	*John Underwood.*
Thomas Poope.	*Nicholas Tooley.*
George Bryan.	*William Ecclestone.*
Henry Condell.	*Joseph Taylor.*
William Slye.	*Robert Benfield.*
Richard Cowly.	*Robert Goughe.*
John Lowine.	*Richard Robinson.*
Samuel Crosse.	*John Shancks.*
Alexander Cooke.	*John Rice.*

INTRODUCTION.

> Far more then cost ; sieh (sith) all y^t he hath writt
> Leaves living art bvt page to serve his witt.
>
> Obiit Año Doⁱ 1616,
> Ætatis 53, die 23 Ap.

This monument * was erected whilst the widow of Shakespeare was alive, his daughters and his son-in-law, Dr Hall, also accessories to the erection. *Here then is proof Shakespeare died in his fifty-third year.* As has been already by others pointed out, we do not know the exact date of Shakespeare's birth. All we possess is the record of his baptism upon the 26th day of April 1564. This has given rise to the tradition he died on his birthday anniversary.† The testimony of a monument erected by his surviving relatives must outweigh auricular traditions, based on no evidence whatever, beyond repetition of a blunder or guess, perpetrated by unenquiring minds. Now the passage I am about to quote from the "Fama Fraternitatis" of 1617 is upon pages 52 and 53, corresponding with Shakespeare's full age and the age he had just entered when he died, 1616 !

The reference to the *stage-player* is upon page 53. I cannot believe this coincidence only. The reflective reader will, I am sure, find this reference to a *stage-player or actor by the Rosicrucians, as an impostor highly suspicious,* because the Fraternity was a deeply religious sect, and it is difficult to imagine their connection with the stage at all. The question also propounds itself—how was this *stage-player* an impostor ?

The context of this passage points to a BOOK, *in connection with a stage-player or actor !* It is evident this stage-player (*Histrio und*

---

* As to the time of the erection of this monument Dyce writes :—" A monument to his memory, said to be from the chisel of Gerard Johnson, was subsequently erected against the north wall of the chancel, at what time is not known, but earlier than 1623, as it is mentioned in the verses by Leonard Digges, prefixed to the folio of Shakespeare's dramatic works published in that year.

† " William Shakspere was born in April 1564. Upon what day we cannot be certain ; but upon the 26th he was baptised ; and there is a tradition that the day of his death was the anniversary of his birthday. Allowing for the difference between old style and new, 23rd April corresponds with our 3rd of May " (Dowden's " Shakespeare," p. 13).

Comediant) *is connoted with some published work! And I think it is plainly implied his fraud is therefore connected with writings!*

I now give Mr Waite's translation: "For conclusion of our Confession we must earnestly admonish you, that you cast away, if not all, yet most of the worthless books of pseudo chymists, to whom it is a jest to apply the Most Holy Trinity to vain things, or to deceive men with monstrous symbols and enigmas, or to profit by the curiosity of the credulous ; our age doth produce many such, one of the greatest being a stage-player, a man with sufficient ingenuity for imposition ; such doth the enemy of human welfare mingle among the good seed, thereby to make the truth more difficult to be believed, which in herself is simple and naked, while falsehood is proud, haughty, and coloured with a lustre of seeming godly and humane wisdom" (p. 96, "Real History of the Rosicrucians").

The reader will note the date of the edition of the "Confession" (from which I quote) is 1617—*the year following Shakespeare's death, and that it was published at Frankfort on the Maine, where Robert Fludd was at the same date*, 1617, *publishing his defence of the Rosicrucian Fraternity (against the attacks of Libavius) in his* "*Tractatus Apologetici*" (Frankfort, 1617), of which I possess an original copy. Here is instantaneous and irrefutable evidence, connecting England and Germany with these manifestoes. Mr Waite states: "The 'Confessio Fraternitatis' appeared in the year 1615 in a Latin work, entitled, '*Secretioris Philosophiæ Consideratio Brevis à Phillipo à Gabella, philosophiæ conscripta ; et nunc primum unà cum Confessione Fraternitatis R. C. in lucem edita, Cassellis, excudebat. G. Wesselius à* 1615, *Quarto.*'" *

The same year Shakespeare died, 1616, Michael Maier published at Frankfort a work entitled "Examen FUCORUM PSEUDO-

---

The Latin text of this edition runs : "*Unum iis præcipuum* AMPHITHEA-TRALEM HISTRIONEM, *hominem ad imponendum satis ingeniosum*, etc.," page 61. (Bacon was born in 1561.)

* I should like to know who *Phillipo à Gabella* was ? In John Blackbourne's edition of Lord Bacon's works, amongst the characters of Lord Bacon

CHYMICORUM DETECTORUM, *et in Gratiam veritatis amantium succincte refutatorum*" (Francof. Typis Nicolai Hoffmanni, sumptibus Theodori de Brii. Anno MCDXVII.). At the conclusion of the preface we read, "*Vale, Dabam Francofurti Mœnum, Mense Septembri Anno 1616.*" So we find he wrote this five months after Shakespeare's death, which occurred April 23, 1616. This work, as its title demonstrates, is an examination and exposure of the different claims of false alchymists, briefly refuted for the benefit of lovers of truth. Evidently it was *inspired by Maier's visit to England;* for in the preface he writes: "*Cum aliquando in Anglia paucis ab hinc annis nonnihil,* bilis in ejusmodi fucos Alchymicos, aut potius Pseudo-Chymicos, collegerim, non potui quiescere, quin eorum delineationum, calamo arrepto, instituerem, tum ut animo meo pro tempore indulgerem, tum ut bonis omnibus hanc quasi facem incenderem, ne facilè in tenebricosis illorum cryptis pedem lapidi, aut verticem trabi illiderent, hoc est, se circumveniri ab illis hirudinibus et crabonibus (qui non solum sanguinem, opumque substantiam exugere, sed et dolores acerrimos animo corporique infligere tentant) paterentur " (page 4). The reader may gather from this the purpose of the author, whose feelings being stirred with wrath at the memory of certain alchymical drones or pseudo-alchymists he had encountered in England, he determines to undertake their description and portraiture with his pen, partly

we come upon the following unexplainable panegyric upon Bacon by one *Burrhus,* who calls Bacon—Phillip Bacon !

BURRHI. IMPETUS JUVENILES, p. 72.
LECTORI.

"PHILLIPUS BACONUS mortuus est. Esto, inquies, quid hoc ad me ? Imo ad te quisquis quisquis es. PHILLIPUS ille Baconus claris ortis majoribus ; ab ineunte ætate sancte institutus ; ad bonarum artium apicem provectus. Adolescens moribus niveis ; virtute præstans ; religioni parens: Cui musæ in pectore, in vultu gratiæ, in ore suada : Cui vegetum corpus ; mens vivida ; ætas florida ; qui numen, homines, seipsum novit : Quo nemo unquam sanctius amicitiam coluit," &c. ("Characters of the Lord Bacon," p. 201, vol. i., Blackbourne's edition of Bacon's works, 1730).

There were four Frankfort editions of the "Fama Fraternitatis" by 1617, the "*Confessio*" being bound up with the former. (Waite's "Real History of the Rosicrucians," p. 64.)

to relieve his feelings or mind, and partly in order to light a torch for others, lest in dark obscurity they may slip over the same stumbling block, or break their head against the same beam, therefore they are to allow themselves to be fortified from these horseleeches and wasps, who not only *suck up the blood and substance of others, but even endeavour to inflict the acutest sufferings in the mind as well as the body.* At first, on reading this, as well as the caution in the "Fama Fraternitatis," already quoted, the term *pseudochymist* seemed to possess little that was pertinent or applicable to Shakespeare. But great was my astonishment upon commencing this tract, to find Maier opening with poetry, and evidently, by his allusions to Helicon and Parnassus, pointing at the society of the Rosicrucians themselves. Presently I found him *identifying Poetry under the title Chymistry*, in most unmistakable terms. I cannot therefore do better than give the Latin text itself, by which the reader will be convinced Maier *wrote this tract to expose some impostor POET, AS A DRONE* (Fucus) *living upon the work of others.* The Preface commences:—

"Quod Poetæ antiqui de suo HELICONE finxerunt, quod ex diversis hominum generibus ad ejus apicem tendentibus paucissimi eo, quo destinarint, perveniant, multi in medio hæreant, desperantes ad summa ascendere. Maxima autem pars, ad radices imas subsidens, ne cogitet quidem pedem altius efferre, id de Chymica arte revera absque ulla translatione aut figura intelligi debet. Est enim HELICON mons Bœotiæ, non procul à Parnasso, Musis sacer, in quo LAPIS ille à Saturno pro Iove devoratus, ejectus, PRO MONUMENTO perpetuo servatus est, ut testatur Hesiodus: Ad Hunc LAPIDEM videndum et pro summo miraculo amplectendum contendunt ad dictum montem multa hominum millia: verum vix unus ex myriade ad istum pervenit, ceteris, ut ante relatum, circa media et ima occupatis. Causa vero tam difficilis adscensus in hunc montem est multiplex, de qua alias. De artificibus, qui evictis difficultatibus omnibus verticem superarunt, dictum est in SYMBOLIS AUREÆ MENSÆ. Illis, qui circa media latera morantur, et viam ignorant, cui insistant,

xxvi   *INTRODUCTION.*

VIATORUM, instar Ariadnes Philosophicæ, dicavimus, utpote Philosophis, et doctis viris, qui extra septem illas portas, seu montes planetarum non evagantur: *Cæteri, qui ad infima loca abjecti, circa planitiem existentes, partim otiosi lurcones, pigrique ventres, partim nebulones ineptis nugis, et dolis satagentes, excurrunt in aliorum res et bona genio prædatorio, aut certe ingenio proditorio, ad hunc tractatum reservati sunt.* Primis, Gloria et honos pro artis documentis, veluti didactron debitum, cessit. *Secundis,* Instrumentum vel filum non inconcinnum ad artis penetralia viam monstrans à nobis administratum est, ut quasi à carceribus ad calcem, ab initio ad finem, feliciter perveniant. *Ultimis,* utpote fucis admonitio et castigatio in EXAMINE præscribitur. *Fucos* autem eos omnes vocatos velim, non qui in arte simpliciter errant et decepti sunt ab aliis, sed qui alios animo decipiendi invadunt, tentant, irretiunt, et fallaciis captant, sua cum utilitate et illorum damno. Quod genus hominum cum tam Reipublicæ, quam Chymicæ sit valde noxium, inprimis agnoscendum et præcavendum erit " (p. 10, " Examen Fucorum Pseudochymicorum," 1617).

The reader will now be surprised to find Maier classing Poetry and Poets under the head of Chymistry and Chymists (upon page 15), with the marginal note "*Chymico necessaria Poetica*":—
"Absque omni dubio, qui velit et speret ex doctrina propria indagare hanc artem et non tumultuaria quadam materiarum experimentatione, ille opus habebit *artibus dicendi et linguis, quarum ambitu ars Chymica comprehenditur: ac inprimis Poetica, quæ de nullo alio subjecto, quam de Chymicis allegoriis et figmentis primitus introducta est, quemadmodum in nostris Hieroglyphicis* per omnes libros et fabulas demonstravimus. Nam qui corticem rerum inclusarum non penetrat, is minime ad has perveniet, sed semper hærebit in superficie et literali interpretatione, quæ etiamsi satis nota esset, tamen non prodesset, nisi et figuras et allegorias, seu metaphoras dicendi, quibus sæpissime utuntur authores, omnes perspectas habeat." The reader will see that Maier *includes Poetry under the title of Alchymistry, and refers to his Hieroglyphicis* ("*Arcana Arcanissima hoc est Hieroglyphica Ægyptio-Græca*"), in which he expounds

INTRODUCTION.

the allegories concealed behind the gods of Egypt and Greece in a profound manner, closely resembling Lord Bacon's "Wisdom of the Ancients." (This book, of which I possess a copy, is very curious and rare. It treats of Osiris, Isis, Apis, &c., and the whole Greek Pantheon, most abstrusely.)

In September 1616, again,—that is, five months after Shakespeare's death,—I find Michael Maier published also a humorous dialogue entitled "LUSUS SERIUS, quo Hermes sive Mercurius REX, Mundanorum omnium sub homine existentium, post longam disceptationem in concilio Octovirali habitam, homine rationali arbitro, Judicatus et constitutus est" (Oppenheim, Sumptibus Lucæ Iennis. *Bibliop.*, 1616). It is dedicated to—

- Dn. Francisco Antonio, Londin. Anglo, Seniori.
- Dn. Jacobo Mosano, Illustris Mauritii Hassiæ Landgravii, Archiatro digniori.
- Dn. Christiano Rumphio Electrolai Palatino ad Rhenum Med. ordinario circumspecto.

The Dedicatory Epistle to these three persons is as follows: —"Viri, Virtute, Doctrinâ veráq; animi Nobilitate longè conspicui, cum usu receptum sit inter verè amicos, ut alter alteri donaria, etiam quoad precium exigua, uti sunt poma, nuces, aliáve esculenta, potulenta seu utensilia, non tàm propter se, suámve dignitatem, quàm grati animi, nullo loci vel temporis spacio interrupti, significationem, mittat et ab invicem recipiat, hinc non dubitavi, vobis nonnihil ex vernis meis, et quasi raptim ex ingenii lusu (dum in Anglia aliquando in hujusmodi mentem post seria Chymica inciderem) natum et productum, non quidem instar Minervæ (Phidiæ) ex Jovis Cerebro prosilientis, sed potius Hebes (quam Juventutem Latini appellant, quasi jucunditati præfectam et Jovi à poculis) ex Junonis citta, pica seu malacia, hoc est, esu lactucæ agrestis, cum ab Apolline convivio accepta esset, absque ullo cum mare concubitu, monstrosè editæ, mittere et offerre; quod scriptionis genus, si seriis indulgens studiis, ut ludibundum, si animi recreationi, ut non minus serium, pro Vestro in me amore, meóque in vos candore mutuo, recipiatis, etiam atque etiam rogo. Nec vero velim, ut tam doni precium, quod quia chartaceum, vile est nimis, quàm donantis animum, qui vobis nunquam non addictus, respiciatis et veluti nuces aut poma, ab amica manu profecta, æstimetis. Interim quomodocunque sit, me vobis Regem et preciosissima ferè mundi omnia dedicasse et obtulisse, si non quoad formam, tamen materiam, agnoscetis, méque inter Vestri amantissimos, ut hactenus (quod ego vicissim) numerabitis. Valete, dabam Francofurti ad Mœnum, *ipso ex Anglia reditu*, Pragam abituriens; Anno 1616, Mense, Septembri."

This epistle demonstrates the fact Maier had written or conceived this tract whilst in England. The work is disposed in the form of a dialogue, and might be called a serio-comic play. The Cow, the Sheep, the Goose, the Bee, the Silkworm, the Oyster, together with Mercury, as representatives of the animal, vegetable, and mineral kingdoms, appear before an appointed judge, and respectively lay claim to be selected kings of the world. Each recounts the benefits conferred by its species upon man. The cow supplies milk, the goose pens, the bee wax and honey, the silkworm silk, the flax cloth, and so on; all this being argued at length and in detail by each, very plausibly in his own favour. That there is some undermeaning implied in this fable cannot be questioned. But what, indeed, is important and most striking is, when the silkworm comes to recount the services it renders humanity, the story of the *Waking Man's Dream* (which is repeated in the Induction of the "Taming of the Shrew" by the supposed Shakespeare, in the humorous character of Christopher Sly), is repeated verbatim. It is given by Maier exactly as Hazlit gives the story of Phillip, Duke of Burgundy, in his Shakespeare Library.

The Silkworm (*Bombyx*) boasts of the splendour of the silks it spins, and how indebted man is to his works, and (upon page 35) thus addresses the judge before whom it is speaking :—

"Tu ipse optimè novisti, vel doctissimum in literis et scientiis absolutissimum virum in nullo vel saltem exiguo haberi precio, si non bene vestitus fuerit, nec ut talem decebat, se præbuerit; Ac quemcunque vis semihominem, si mentem spectes, serico indutum magnificè, literatissimo illi ante ferri. Tantum tela nostri operis præstare potest, de quo si dubites, vel verâ historiâ rem tibi ob oculos ponam. Phillipus Bonus Burgundiæ Dux aliquando noctu invenit quendam ex infima plebe cerdonem Grandavi in foro somno vinóque sepultum, quem à ministris suis attolli et gestari secum in aulam Ducalem, ubi hominem vestibus suis vilissimis et immundis exui, et indutum indusio lineo in Ducalem lectum reponi jussit, donec villum, quod biberat, edomiret. Manè adfuerunt ipsi pueri Nobiles eleganti facie et vestitu, qui expectarent, dum homo evigilaret, quem interrogârunt, ut ipsum Ducem soliti errant, gestibus et dictis ad blanditias et reverentiam compositis, quo modo vellet vestiri, et simul diversa genera vestium ipsi, ut inde delectum haberet, proposuerunt. Homo multis modis de statu suo ab initio dubitavit, ut et de loco, secumque diu disputavit, an esset ille, qui haberetur, an verò alius ille, qui fuerat. Cum verò animadvertisset et nobile viros adesse, qui sibi ad nutum adstarent et quærerent; An non vellet surgere et ad consueta officia redire, *facile sibi persuaderi passus, sese esse Ducem, qui haberetur. Indutus itaque vestibus ducalibus, cum hac sibi convenientes sentiret, non aliter putavit, quam sese esse tot famulorum Dominum et (necio, quo fato, factum) totius regionis potentissimum Principem.* Ducitur magno comitatu ad viridaria aulæ proxima, hinc ad vivaria piscium, deinde ad jentaculum; à quo tempus teritur ambulando ad alia diversa loca, confabulando de rebus variis, in quibus omnibus, homo, quoad corpus et habitum, se præbuit (qui non erat) Ducem, quoad mentem et cætera omnia (qui erat) cerdonem. Post ad prandium adducitur, in quo ipsi pulcherrimæ fœminæ adjunguntur et optimates aulæ quicunque. Hinc ad venationem ferarum cum equis et canibus, multisque aulicis contendit, unde ad cœnam, in qua cum opiparis et varii generis ferculis tractaretur, ac interim in sanitatem ipsius ab omnibus optimi vini pocula propinarentur, facilimè, cur id genus vini impensè amaret, iterum inebriatus est, ut prius, ac in profundissimum somnum conjectus. Tum ipse Dux Phillipus (qui hactenus inter aulicos fictitio inserviverat hunc hominem, qui huc usque Principis personam sustinuerat, iterum pristino suo loco in medium fori, unde desumptus fuerat, suis propriis vestibus indutum, reportari mundavit ; ubi cum noctem peregisset, ac manè se eo in loco animadvertisset, diu dubitavit de statu suo ; an esset ille, qui nunc videretur, an, verò dux ille, qui visus erat. Verum cum aliter sibi persuadere non posset, præsentibus omnibus signis, inprimis vestibus laceris et vetustis, quæ cerdonem illum viliorem declararent, et absentibus, quæ ducem, tandem domum rediens, uxori suæ veluti somnium, quod ea nocte viderat, quomodo in ducis aula fuisset et qua ratione tractatus, ambulationi et venationi, reliquisque rebus omnibus operam dederit, narravit. Ex quibus apparet, vestes ex nostris telis confectas maximam vim habere ad persuadendum hominibus illis, qui eas gestant, et aliis, qui eas gestari cernunt, qualis et quantus quisque sit. Nam plerique, qui vident se bombycinis exuviis indutos, etiamsi sint ex infima sorte homines et nullo nobilitatis aut doctrinæ colore imbuti, mox sibi persuadent, quod sint tales, quales habentur (ut ille cerdo) cum videant ab omnibus sibi ad nutum dici, applaudi et faveri. Sic et alii, qui cernunt quendam sericeis filis circumseptum, non illum pro verme bombycino habent, at pro ave, cujus nidum molliores texturæ ornent, imò pro eo, cui, ut fortiori assurgendum, ut formoso abblandiendum, ut erudito in sermonibus concedendum, ut seniori locus commodior relinquendus sit. Tantam vim inesse nostris telis animadvertis, ut magis, quam Magnes ferrum, illæ attrahant hominum oculos ad sese, sibique eos propitios reddunt. Inde versiculi :—

> Hunc homines decorant, quem vestimenta decorant :
> In vili veste nemo tractatur honestè :
> Vir bene vestitus pro vestibus esse peritus
> Creditur à mille, quamvis Idiota sit ille :
> Si careas veste, nec sis vestitus honestè,
> Nullius es laudis, quamvis scis omne, quod audis."

INTRODUCTION.   xxxi

I need hardly translate this extract at length. Briefly paraphrased the Silkworm declares dress to be everything, though only appearance.* To illustrate this he relates how Phillip, the Good Duke of Burgundy, discovered one night a certain tanner (cobbler or artisan) asleep dead drunk on the market-place, whom he caused to be lifted up and carried to his Ducal Palace, his rags taken off, and clothed in a linen shirt, then put in the Duke's bed. A number of noble youths or pages of elegant appearance and dress were present, who, upon his awaking, asked him with the same flattery and reverence of words they were accustomed to use to the Duke, how he would dress, and at the same time proffered him different suits of clothes to dress himself in. The man was at first doubtful as to his own condition or where he was, and for a long time disputed with himself whether he was the person he was considered to be, or truly himself. But indeed when he perceived that there were really noblemen present, who waited upon his pleasure and inquired whether he would not get up and betake himself to his duties, he easily allowed himself to be persuaded that he was the real duke, as he was held. Clothed in the ducal garments, which he felt were agreeable and beseeming him, he soon believed, since he was the lord of so many domestics, he must be a prince of power and importance. Then he is led by a great crowd of courtiers to the ducal garden, next to the fish ponds, and thence to breakfast, after which the time is spent in strolling about to other various spots, conversing upon various things, in all of which the man appeared to be, as far as concerned his dress, the Duke himself (which he was not), but in mind and all other things a tanner (which indeed he was). Later on he is led to dinner, at which the most beautiful ladies and the highest in rank were present. After that he goes out to hunt with horses and dogs, then to a banquet, at which dainties and dishes of various sorts are served

* The reader will recognise in the moral of this passage the "Clothes Philosophy" so abundantly satirised in the plays—"The world is still deceived by ornament."

xxxii *INTRODUCTION.*

to him, and meanwhile is primed easily with wine, drunk in his honour, the result being that he again gets intoxicated as before, and falls into the profoundest slumber. Then Duke Phillip (who hitherto had waited, disguised with the courtiers, upon this man, who up to the moment had played the character of the prince) ordered him to be carried to the same spot in the market-place where he had been first found, and his own clothes restored to him. When he had passed the night, early in the morning perceiving where he was, for a long time he was in doubt as to his own identity, whether indeed he was what he seemed, or the Duke he had appeared to be. But persuaded by outward signs, and by his torn and old clothes, which declared him to be a peasant, he at length returned home and related to his wife what he had seen that night—how he had been to the ducal palace, how treated there, the walking and hunting, and the rest, as if it had been a dream. From which it is manifest the garments spun from our webs possess an extraordinary force in persuading those who wear them, and those who perceive us wearing them, who and what each one is. For very many who see themselves clothed in the skins of the silkworm, even though they be of low extraction, and possessing no colour of nobility or learning, presently persuade themselves that they are those they are held to be (like this tanner), since they behold themselves flattered and applauded by all.

The reader will perceive this is the story of Christopher Sly which Hazlitt long ago pointed out was repeated by this tale of the Duke of Burgundy, entitled the "Waking Man's Dream." Consider Maier conceives this "*Lusus Serius*" in England, and publishes it a few months after Shakespeare's death, dedicating the piece to an Englishman whom *I suspect was Bacon himself ! Who was Dr Francisco Antonio ? Here are the two Christian names of Lord Francis Bacon and his brother Anthony Bacon.* Why is he a Lord (seigniori) ? This story related by Maier is upon pages 35, 36 of the tract, corresponding with the two play numbers, 35, 36 (catalogue and full number) of the 1623 Folio ! The evidence taken

INTRODUCTION.

altogether is considerable. The other piece upon false Chymists is written at the same time exactly, as the preface informs us— September 1616. The "Fama Fraternitatis" was rewritten (the one we cite from), 1617, published at Frankfort, *where Maier and Robert Fludd were also both publishing*. The prefaces to both the "Lusus Serius" and "Examen Fucorum" conclude, *Dabam Francofurti ad mœnum. Anno 1616, Mense Septembri.*" The "Fama" I cite from is also published at Frankfort, 1617, and in the preface it states it has been rewritten and improved. In my work, "Bacon, Shakespeare, and the Rosicrucians," I pointed out how wonderfully adapted the story of Sly, in the "Taming of the Shrew," was to represent a man of low extraction like Shakespeare set up by a nobleman like Bacon in his own place with regard to plays or players. Sly, in "The Taming of the Shrew," remains *unrestored* to his former condition, and the joke is therefore left *unconcluded*, as if to suggest it is still in act of perpetration respecting Shakespeare's false position with regard to the plays.

That the Rosicrucians were closely connected with Poetry can be proved from their writings. Two of the works of John Valentine Andreas, the Rosicrucian Protagonist (which I possess), contain upon the title-page—

"Helicone Juxta Parnassum."

These works are: "Menippus sive Dialogorum Satyricorum Centuria," 1617, and "Turbo, sive Moleste et Frustra per cuncta Divagans Ingenium," 1616. Upon page 158 of Michael Maier's "Themis Aurea", (or "Laws of the Rosicrucian Fraternity," 1618), I find this: " Augur non sum, neque vates, licet laurum aliquando momorderim et in Parnassi umbra paucas horulas dormierim, nihilominus, nisi fallor, eorum characterum R. C. expositionem in ænigmatibus, lib 6, Symbolorum auree, mense satis evolvi : R. n, Pegasum, et C. Julium, si ad mentem non sonum verbi respiciatur: Sit tibi clavis, ARCANORUM COGNITIO: En. dabo Arcanum: d.wmml. zii. w. fgqqhka. x. Si potes aperi: Nec pluribus, nec clarioribus opus est. An non hic est unguiculus Rosei illius Leonis gutta Pegaseæ Hippocrenes ?" (Copied from a genuine and original copy printed at Frankfort, Typis Nicolai Hoffmanni, 1618.) Mr Waite translates this thus:—

" 'I am no augur nor prophet, notwithstanding that once I partook of the laurel, and reposed a few brief hours in the shadow of *Parnassus*; nevertheless, if I err not, I have unfolded the significance of the characters R. C. in the enigmas of the sixth book of the Symbols of the Golden Table. R signifies *Pegasus*, and C, if the sense not the sound be considered, *lilium*. Let the KNOWLEDGE OF THE ARCANA be the key to thee. Lo, I give thee the Arcanum! d. wmml. zii. w. sgqqhka. x. Open if thou canst. . . . Is not this the hoof of the Red Lion * or the drops of the Hippocrene fountain?' Beneath this barbarous jargon we discern, however, an analogy with the Rose symbolism. Classical tradition informs us that the Red Rose sprang from the blood of Adonis, but Pegasus was a winged horse which sprang from the blood of Medusa, and the fountain of Hippocrene was produced by a stroke of the hoof of Pegasus" (Waite's "Real History of the Rosicrucians").

Now compare what the same writer, Michael Maier (who visited England in 1616, and was friends with Robert Fludd), writes in his "Arcana Arcanissima" ("Secret of Secrets," from which I copy), under the marginal note, "*Fons Heliconis unde*":
"*Ejusdem Pegasi ungulá fons Hippocrene in bicipiti Parnasso excitatus traditur, ex quo Musæ, Apollo, poëtæ et omnes literati bibunt et eruditiores evadunt: Sic eruditio poëtarum ex fonte Parnassi, hic ex ungula Pegasi, Pegasus ex cruore Medusæ, Medusa ex monstro marino progenita, à Perseo trucidata, Perseus e Jove, Jupiter è Saturno, Saturnus è Cœlo, tanquam aurea cathena dependet*, &c." (p. 157, Oppenheim, 1616).

The reader, I think, will see the society was probably con-

---

* "This is evidently the Mithraic Lion of Persia (the Lion of the Cherubim of the Chaldees)—the *Red Lion* of the Chaldees. Porphyry names this Lion Perses (Perseus. Brightness, the sun born) or the Sun incarnate as man" (*vide* "Enoch," vol. ii. p. 49, Kenealy). Mr Waite has made the mistake of substituting in his translation "Lilium" for "Julium." "Julium" is evidently a reference to the house of the sun Leo in July. *Pegasus was the seal of the Knight Templars* (p. 189, "The Gnostics," King).

nected with POETRY, and particularly with the fount Helicon, which flowed from Parnassus to the fountains of the muses called Aganippe and Hippocrene. Castalia was also a fountain of Parnassus sacred to the muses and Apollo. It is remarkable to find the *"first heir" of the supposed Shakespeare's invention carrying this motto*—

> Vilia miretur vulgus ; mihi flavus Apollo
> Pocula Castalia plena ministret aqua.
>
> ("Venus and Adonis.")

Here is direct connotation with *Apollo, Parnassus, and the fountain of Castalia, close to Helicon, if not identical with it.* The emblem upon the title-page of Lord Bacon's Collection of Apophthegms (published 1671, "Resuscitatio") *is a winged horse—Pegasus!*

It is again remarkable to find Bacon, in his explanation of the fable of Perseus (VII. "Wisdom of the Ancients"), writing :— "The conclusion of the war is followed by two effects: first the birth and springing up of Pegasus, which obviously enough denotes FAME, flying abroad and celebrating the victory." This he again introduces and repeats in his "De Augmentis" (1623, 1638, 1640), Book II.; the Fable of Perseus being selected by him *to illustrate Parabolical Poesy.* If the reader will turn to the catalogue of "A NEW WORLD OF SCIENCES" (always found at the end of the "De Augmentis"), he will find the *sixth "Deficient,"* entitled "*Sapientia Veterum*, Philosophy according to Ancient Parables." If now he will turn to the *Second Book* of the "De Augmentis," 1623, he will find this *Sixth Deficient* introduced, page 108 (1640), *as an example of the Fables of the Poets in connection with Parabolical or Allusive Poetry, and in touch with the entire subject of the Drama and Stage-Plays upon the previous pages* 106, 107. Let me earnestly entreat the student's attention to this, which is a decided proof, Bacon's "WISDOM OF THE ANCIENTS" was written parabolically, *and in connection with Allusive Poetry or Stage-Plays, —the Theatre.* It is not in merely reading my statements, *but in testing them,* the reader will appreciate the truth and value of what I adduce. He will see, in a moment, why Bacon has reserved the titles of his Deficients for a catalogue at the end of the work,—*evidently with a view to concealment and safety,*—*these Deficients being only coasted along.* "But these are but coastings along the shore *premendo litus iniquum*" (page 123, Book II. "Advancement of Learning," 1605, Wright). This shows Bacon thought these Deficients *dangerous subjects* to do more than hint at. In his "Distribution Preface" he writes: "Wherefore we will not neglect to side along (as it were in passage) the coasts of accepted Sciences and Arts, and *to import thither something useful and profitable*" (p. 22, "Advancement," 1640).

But to return to our citation, it is certainly remarkable to find Bacon connoting *Fame with the springing up of Pegasus*, seeing it is a hint for Poetry, if not for the "*Fama Fraternitatis*" itself.

In Bacon's "Resuscitatio," 1671, is to be found a fragment entitled FAME, this being printed in type of extraordinary and remarkable size, quite out of agreement with the other chapter headings, and advertising itself as a singularity of the work, evidently done to attract notice. Directly we examine this Essay fragment, we find the first part entirely borrowed from Virgil's description of Fame (fourth book, "Æneid," 173 l.).

> Extemplo Libyæ magnas it Fama per urbes ;
> Fama, malum, quo non aliud velocius ullum :
> Mobilitate viget, viresque acquirit eundo.
> Parva metu primo ; mox sese, attollit in auras,
> Ingrediturque solo, et caput inter nubila condit.
> Illam Terra parens, irâ irritata deorum,
> Extremam, ut perhibent, Cœo Enceladoque sororem
> Progenuit, pedibus celerem, et pernicibus alis.
> Monstrum horrendum, ingens ; *cui, quot sunt corpore plumæ,*
> *Tot vigiles oculi subter, mirabile dictu,*
> *Tot linguæ, totidem ora sonant, tot subrigit aures.*
> Nocte volat cœli medio terræque, per umbram.
> Stridens, nec dulci declinat lumina somno.
> Luce sedet custos aut summi culmine tecti,
> Turribus aut altis, et magnas territat urbes.*

"The *Poets* make *Fame* a *Monster*. They describe her in part,

---

* Virgil borrowed his phantom from the Eris of Homer, and lines 176, 177 are directly imitated from the Greek poet ("Anthon's Virgil," 410).

INTRODUCTION. xxxvii

finely and elegantly, and in part gravely and sententiously. They say, look how many *feathers* she hath, so many eyes she hath underneath. So many tongues; so many voices; she pricks up so many ears. This is a flourish: there follow excellent *Parables;* as that she gathereth strength in going; that she goeth upon the ground, and yet hideth her head in the clouds. That in the day time she sitteth in a *watch tower*, and flyeth both by night. That she mingleth things done with things not done: and that she is a terror to great *cities;* but that which passeth all the rest is: they do recount that the *earth*, *mother* of the *giants*, that made war against *Jupiter*, and were by him destroyed, thereupon in anger brought forth *Fame*. For certain it is, that Rebels figured by the *giants* and *Seditious Fames* and libels, are but *brothers* and *sisters; masculine* and *feminine*. But now if a man can tame this *Monster*, and bring her to feed at the hand, and govern her, and with her fly other ravening fowl, and kill them, it is somewhat worth. But we are infected with the style of the Poets. To speak now in a sad and serious manner; there is not in all the politics a place less handled, and more worthy to be handled, than this of *Fame*. We will therefore speak of these *points*. What are false *Fames;* and what are true *Fames;* and how they may be best discerned; how *Fames* may be sown and raised; how they may be spread and multiplied; and how they may be checked and laid dead" (p. 212, "Resuscitatio," 1671, Pars. I.).

The first part is entirely a paraphrase of the passage cited from Virgil. Directly we turn to the Rosicrucian Romance known as the "Chemical Marriage of Christian Rosy Cross," published at Strassburg, 1616, we read at the commencement: "Now the same thing still twiching me several times by the coat, I glanced back and behold it was a fair and glorious lady, whose garments were all skye-colour, and curiously bespangled with golden stars. In her right hand she bare a trumpet of beaten gold, whereon a Name was ingraven which I could well read but am forbidden as yet to reveal. In her left hand she had a great bundle of letters

INTRODUCTION.

reserved the titles of his Deficients for a catalogue at the end of the work,—*evidently with a view to concealment and safety,—these Deficients being only coasted along.* "But these are but coastings along the shore *premendo litus iniquum*" (page 123, Book II. "Advancement of Learning," 1605, Wright). This shows Bacon thought these Deficients *dangerous subjects* to do more than hint at. In his "Distribution Preface" he writes: "Wherefore we will not neglect to side along (as it were in passage) the coasts of accepted Sciences and Arts, and *to import thither something useful and profitable*" (p. 22, "Advancement," 1640).

But to return to our citation, it is certainly remarkable to find Bacon connoting *Fame with the springing up of Pegasus*, seeing it is a hint for Poetry, if not for the "*Fama Fraternitatis*" itself.

In Bacon's "Resuscitatio," 1671, is to be found a fragment entitled FAME, this being printed in type of extraordinary and remarkable size, quite out of agreement with the other chapter headings, and advertising itself as a singularity of the work, evidently done to attract notice. Directly we examine this Essay fragment, we find the first part entirely borrowed from Virgil's description of Fame (fourth book, "Æneid," 173 l.).

> Extemplo Libyæ magnas it Fama per urbes ;
> Fama, malum, quo non aliud velocius ullum :
> Mobilitate viget, viresque acquirit eundo.
> Parva metu primo ; mox sese, attollit in auras,
> Ingrediturque solo, et caput inter nubila condit.
> Illam Terra parens, irâ irritata deorum,
> Extremam, ut perhibent, Cœo Enceladoque sororem
> Progenuit, pedibus celerem, et pernicibus alis.
> Monstrum horrendum, ingens ; *cui, quot sunt corpore plumæ,*
> *Tot vigiles oculi subter, mirabile dictu,*
> *Tot linguæ, totidem ora sonant, tot subrigit aures.*
> Nocte volat cœli medio terræque, per umbram.
> Stridens, nec dulci declinat lumina somno.
> Luce sedet custos aut summi culmine tecti,
> Turribus aut altis, et magnas territat urbes.*

"The *Poets* make *Fame* a *Monster*. They describe her in part,

---

* Virgil borrowed his phantom from the Eris of Homer, and lines 176, 177 are directly imitated from the Greek poet ("Anthon's Virgil," 410).

finely and elegantly, and in part gravely and sententiously. They say, look how many *feathers* she hath, so many eyes she hath underneath. So many tongues; so many voices; she pricks up so many ears. This is a flourish: there follow excellent *Parables;* as that she gathereth strength in going ; that she goeth upon the ground, and yet hideth her head in the clouds. That in the day time she sitteth in a *watch tower*, and flyeth both by night. That she mingleth things done with things not done: and that she is a terror to great *cities;* but that which passeth all the rest is: they do recount that the *earth*, *mother* of the *giants*, that made war against *Jupiter*, and were by him destroyed, thereupon in anger brought forth *Fame*. For certain it is, that Rebels figured by the *giants* and *Seditious Fames* and libels, are but *brothers* and *sisters; masculine* and *feminine*. But now if a man can tame this *Monster*, and bring her to feed at the hand, and govern her, and with her fly other ravening fowl, and kill them, it is somewhat worth. But we are infected with the style of the Poets. To speak now in a sad and serious manner ; there is not in all the politics a place less handled, and more worthy to be handled, than this of *Fame*. We will therefore speak of these *points*. What are false *Fames;* and what are true *Fames;* and how they may be best discerned; how *Fames* may be sown and raised; how they may be spread and multiplied; and how they may be checked and laid dead" (p. 212, "Resuscitatio," 1671, Pars. I.).

The first part is entirely a paraphrase of the passage cited from Virgil. Directly we turn to the Rosicrucian Romance known as the "Chemical Marriage of Christian Rosy Cross," published at Strassburg, 1616, we read at the commencement: "Now the same thing still twiching me several times by the coat, I glanced back and behold it was a fair and glorious lady, whose garments were all skye-colour, and curiously bespangled with golden stars. In her right hand she bare a trumpet of beaten gold, whereon a Name was ingraven which I could well read but am forbidden as yet to reveal. In her left hand she had a great bundle of letters in all languages, which she (as I afterwards understood) was to carry into all countries. She had also large and *beautiful wings, full of eyes throughout*, wherewith she could mount aloft, and fly swifter than any eagle" (p. 100, Waite's "Real History of the Rosicrucians").

Compare Bacon: "The *Poets* make *fame* a *Monster*. They describe her in part finely and elegantly; and in part gravely and sententiously. They say look *how many feathers she hath, so many eyes she hath underneath; so many Tongues; so many voices;* she pricks up so many ears. This is a *flourish*." John Valentine Andreas, in his description of his own life, declared he composed the "Chemical Marriage of Christian Rosy Cross" in 1602 and 1603, and his own words are, "*Ludibrium cum monstrorum fœcundo fœtu*, quod mireris a nonnullis aestimatum et subtili indagine explicatum, plane futile et quod inanitatem curiosorum prodat" (p. 99, "Joh. Val. Andreas und sein Zeitalter," Rossbach, 1819). The reader will see the term *monster* used by both this writer and Bacon in connection with *Fame*. The *trumpet* is constantly introduced in the Rosicrucian manifestoes in connection with *Fame*, as may be seen in the above extract from the "Marriage of Christian Rosenkreutz." Upon the frontispiece engraving of Sir Walter Raleigh's "History of the World," 1614, may be recognised an engraved symbol of this *Fame*—a woman with wings, the latter covered underneath with eyes. She holds a trumpet she is blowing to her lips. Beneath she is described by the title "*Fama Bona*." It may be seen Bacon evidently is describing this allegorical figure. It is very curious Sir Walter Raleigh's "History of the World," containing this highly masonic engraving, bears date 1614—that is the same year the "Fama Fraternitatis of the Meritorious Order of the R. C." saw light.

"And this kind of merit was lively set forth in that famed relation of *Orpheus Theatre*, where all beasts and birds assembled, which, forgetting their proper natural appetites of prey, of game, of quarrels, stood all sociably and lovingly together, listening unto the airs and accords of the harp" (p. 49, "Advancement of Learning," 1640). The next page, 50, is mispaged 52 (Shakespeare's age, 1616), and constitutes the first false page in the work. (The words *Orpheus Theatre* are the 49th and 50th in italics from the top of the page, and the 23rd likewise from the bottom upwards).

P. 49, { *Orpheus*, 49, 24.
1640 "Advancement of Learning," { *Theatre*, 50, 23.

Evidently this connotation of the word Theatre with the number *fifty* is to call attention to the next page *fifty* mispaged *fifty-two*, that is Shakespeare's full years when he died, 1616, and thus to suggest *the Shakespeare Theatre!* Directly we read Bacon's *Fable of Orpheus* (in his "Wisdom of the Ancients") we find the following reference to *Helicon*, which the Rosicrucians called their sacred spring!

"Orpheus himself was torn to pieces by the women in their fury, and his limbs scattered about the fields: *at whose death, Helicon (river sacred to the Muses) in grief and indignation buried his waters under the earth, to reappear elsewhere*" ("Wisdom of the Ancients," XI., Orpheus).

Bacon explains this fable thus: "The singing of Orpheus is of two kinds; one to propitiate the infernal powers, the other to draw the wild beasts and the woods. The former may be best understood as referring to natural philosophy; the latter to philosophy moral and civil. For natural philosophy proposes to itself, as its noblest work of all, *nothing less than the restitution and renovation of things corruptible*, and (what is indeed the same thing in a lower degree) the conservation of bodies in the state in which they are, and the retardation of dissolution and putrefaction.

. . . .

"But howsoever the works of wisdom are among human things the most excellent, yet they too have their periods and closes. For so it is that after kingdoms and commonwealths have flourished for a time, there arise perturbations and seditions and wars; amid the uproars of which, first the laws are put to silence, and then men return to the depraved conditions of their nature, and desolation is seen in the fields and cities. And if such troubles last, it is not long before letters also and philosophy are so torn in pieces that no traces of them can be found but a few fragments, scattered here *and there like planks from a shipwreck; and then a season of barbarism sets in, the waters of Helicon being sunk under the ground, until, according to the appointed vicissitude of things, they break out and issue forth again, perhaps among other nations, and not in the places where they were before*" (Orpheus XI., or Philosophy).

The Latin text runs: " Adeo ut fragmenta tantùm ejus, in paucis locis, tanquam NAUFRAGII TABULÆ, inveniantur et barbara tempora ingruant; Heliconis aquis sub terra mersis; donec debitâ rebus vicissitudine, non iisdem fortasse locis, sed apud alias Nationes erumpant et emanent" (1638, "Opera Moralia").

Upon page 91, ch. vi., "Advancement of Learning," 1640, Bacon again introduces this subject in the same words:—
"*Antiquities*, or the *Remains of Histories*, are, as we said, *tanquam Tabula Naufragii;* when industrious and understanding persons (the memory of things being decayed and almost overwhelmed with oblivion) by a constant and scrupulous diligence, out of Genealogies, Calendars, Inscriptions, Monuments, Coins, *Proper Names and Styles*, &c., &c., recover and save somewhat from the deluge of Time." There are exactly fifty-two words in italics upon this page in the 1640 "Advancement of Learning," as if to suggest some connection with Shakespeare or 1616.

It is very well worthy note, the three ancient fables Bacon introduces in his "De Augmentis" in order to illustrate Parabolical Poesy, are the fables of Pan, Perseus, Dionysus, because these three are closely connected with Rosicrucian mysteries, Pan and Perseus especially being introduced by Robert Fludd ("Tractatus Apol.," 1617) and Michael Maier ("Arcana Arcanissima") in the same way as by Bacon.

The author of "Nimrod" writes: "Roger Bacon's writings are scarcely distinguishable in their character from those of the Rosicrucians, and the latter avow *that the name and fable of Demigorgon conceals the secret of their art*" (*vide* "Echo Colloquii," p. 97; "Nimrod," vol. iv., p. 223). It is very striking to find Lord Bacon *giving this story of Pegasus and Medusa in his "Advancement of Learning"* (upon page 73 of the 1638 edition, and pages 120, 121, "Advancement of Learning," 1640), almost in the same words as it is related by the great Rosicrucian, Michael Maier (upon page 157), in his "Arcana Arcanissima." "Perseus, a Prince of the East, is reported to have been employed by Pallas for the destroying of Medusa, who was very infestious to the western parts of the world, about the uttermost coasts of Iberia. A monster, huge and fierce, of an aspect so dire and horrid, that with her very looks she turned men into stones. Of all the Gorgons this Medusa alone was mortal, the rest not subject to death. Perseus, therefore, preparing himself for this noble enterprise, had arms and gifts bestowed on him by three of the gods. Mercury gave him wings, fitted for his feet, not his arms; Pluto, a helmet; Pallas, a shield and a looking-glass. Notwithstanding, although he was thus well furnished, he went not directly to Medusa, but turned into the Greæ, which, by the mother's side, were sisters to the Gorgon. These Greæ, from their birth, were hoary headed, resembling old women. They had but one only eye, and one tooth among them all,—this eye and tooth they lent to Perseus." Compare Maier: "Dum Perseus parere cogitur, ad iter sese accingit; À Pallade itaque; scutum et speculum, à Mercurio Harpen seu falcatum eusem, a Phitone peram et galeam, a Nymphis talaria seu calceos volucres mutuatus est: quibus instrumentis Perseus instructus ad Medusam, multos homines in saxa convertentem unam Gorgonum contendit. *Primo autem ad Greas Perseus profectus est, quæ erant sorores Gorgonum, munero tres oculum et dentem unicum communem habentes, quos ab illis mutuo acceptos tam diu retinuit donec illæ Nymphas, quæ alatos calceos haberent indicassent, etc.*" (p. 155, "Arcana Arcanissima").

The reader will perceive the singular parallelism of these trifling details, which space forbids my illustrating further. Maier gives all *this in context with the fountain of Helicon*, evidently (as he shows in his "Aurea Themis") *connected with the Rosicrucian fraternity*. Bacon's account of this fable is included in what he calls *the Theatre*, viz., the second book of the "De Augmentis," 1623, which he concludes with the words, "*But we stay too long in the Theatre*, let us now pass on to the palace of the mind" (p. 130, 1640 "Advancement of Learning").

Amongst the few valuable and genuine Rosicrucian works to be found, there is one little known, with the title "CONSPICILIUM NOTITIÆ inserviens OCULIS ÆGRIS qui lumen veritatis Ratione medii subjecti, objecti et finis ferre recusant, oppositum Admonitioni Futili Henrici Neuhusii de Fratribus R. C. An sint? Quales sint? Unde nomen illud sibi asciverent? Etc ab. Euchario Cygnæo." The date is 1614. The author's name is evidently only a pseudonym. I find in this tract some extraordinary parallels to Bacon's writings. For example, in Bacon's Sixth Book of the 1623 "De Augmentis," he obscurely discusses a method of the delivery of secret knowledge, which he entitles "TRADITIO LAMPADIS,* *sive methodus ad Filios.*" "*The delivery of the Lamp, or the method bequeathed to the sons of Sapience.*" If the reader will turn to Bacon's "Redargutio," which is laid at Paris, he will find the address interspersed with the expression "*sons*," which shows Bacon belonged to some brotherhood or craft. Cygnæus, in replying to the question as to the nature of the Rosicrucian brotherhood, writes: "Certitudo et continua series Collegiorum, quæ antiquitus occulta similis artificii et rerum naturalium, non sine admiratione, professionis variis in locis et nationibus floruerunt, et tandem quasi per manus ad nos Germanos pervenerunt, ne haberemus, absit scandalum, incusare Deum, quasi omnia

---

* Michael Maier writes in his "Laws of the Rosicrucian Fraternity" ("Themis Aurea," p. 26):—"Deinde habent successionem ab eodem ad se usque et LAMPADA sibi in cursu traditam acceperunt à noto dictæ Fraternitatis consorte seu fœderis membro legitimo."

INTRODUCTION.

primis Patribus ex Jure primogenituræ donarit, et in ultima ætate manum præcluserit. De qua injuria æque conqueritur Fernel. *in præfat. lib. de. addit. rer.* quasi nostrum seculum tanti stuporis tantæque tarditatis vellemus insimulare, nil novum ut cudere posset, nullarum artium afferre proventum. Ut autem ignorantes ambulatorium illud munus videant, visum mihi est stricte ordinem recensere, *quomodo una natio alteri lampada tradiderit"* (p. 8).

Cygnæus then proceeds to point out that the Egyptians had their secret college; that there followed the Cabiri of Samothrace, the Eleusinians, the Magi of Persia, the Brahmans of India, the Gymnosophists of Æthiopia, the Pythagoreans in Greece, &c., and he concludes with the Rosicrucians themselves as the last link in this chain of tradition. Upon the title page (*bis*) of the 1640 "Advancement of Learning," there is this motto at the foot of the page:—

<blockquote>
Deus Omnia
In mensura, et numero, et ordine
Disposuit.
</blockquote>

(p. 61.)

Now compare Cygnæus: "Nam primus Creator amat harmoniam et odit dissonantiam, *qui omnia in numero, pondere et mensura teste Salomone Sap 7 disposuit,*" &c. (p. 18). Cygnæus tells us the Rosicrucians were a *militia who borrowed their symbol of the Cross from Constantine.* "Verum quod quidam duos characteres R. C. interpretentur Roseam Crucem, non caret ratione: quia inde optimus typus confessionis et professionis elucesit. Nam cruce que est sigillum et symbolum veri Christiani, volunt testari, se militare sub vexillo Christi, contra, mundum, carnem, et Satanam. Et Christus ipse Matth. 10, Mark 8, Luke 9, admonet, si quis vult me sequi, deneget semetipsum, et tollat crucem suam, et sequatur me. Legimus quoque; c. 9, Ezech. in populi clade Dominum curam gessisse eorum, qui litera T, id est, cruce signati erant super frontem, à viro lineis induto, et atramentarium scriptoris in lumbis suis habente. Præterea, hoc symbolum non multum abludit à Lutheri sigillo, in quo continebatur crux in corde, et cor comprehendebatur à Rosa. Quid referam de Constantino, cui dubitanti an Romam duceret exercitum, ostendit Deus illustre signum victoriæ: Nam medio die in clara luce, vidit Constantinus in cœlo igneam crucem, cum literis EN TOYTΩ NIKA (In hoc vinces)," p. 27.

This proves the Society was related to the Templars, who adopted the Red Cross from this vision of Constantine. Moreover, the reader will perceive in Bacon's "Holy War" this motto repeated, and there is no question the Rosicrucians were, *like the Salvation Army of to-day, soldiers of the Cross.* Upon the title page of the "Sendbrieff" (or "Missive to the Fraternity of the Rosicrucians"), by Julian de Campis, published with the "Fama Fraternitatis," 1617, Frankfort, I find this at the bottom, "MILITA BONAM MILITIAM, servans fidem et accipies coronam gloriæ." Bacon's "Holy War" is, I am convinced, entirely written in the spirit of a *Peaceful Soldiery*, and should be studied as a Rosicrucian tract for the initiated alone. Cygnæus, "Quoad Rosas, illæ sunt signum victoriæ: Nam Scipio ex Africa reversus, et primus de Hannibale triumphaturus, militibus octavæ legionis, qui primum Carthaginensium castra oppugnassent, ac Ducis eorum insignia abstulissent fasciculum Rosarum gestandum, imo clypeis depictas Rosas ferendas concessit. Sane apud Homerum Achillis scutum legitur, necnon Cassides Hectoris et Æneæ. Arminius Germaniæ Princeps Rosam in Insignibus habebat. Marchiones Brandenburgenses *Comitesque de Eberstein*, necnon plurimæ familiæ, strenua nobilitate claræ, Rosas inter sua insignia gloriose locatas habent: Nam Rosa principibus merito gestanda videtur. Præterea Rosa Auroræ est dicata, signum habetur silentii, lætitiæ, et omnium florum Regnia. Ex Rosa apis mel, aranea venenum parat, juxta Brisardi emblema—

> Toxica ab hoc carpit sublimis aranea flore,
> Dulcia quo parvæ mella parantur api.

Rosa Cantharides interficit, et juxta allium plantata, odoratior evadit juxta Camerarii emblema:—

> Livor iners stimulos generosis mentibus addit:
> Sic per fœda Rosis allia crescit odor."
>
> (p. 29.)

Those who are acquainted with Baden-Baden and its neighbourhood doubtless will remember the castle of Eberstein in the Murg Thal, *with its stone boar and rose crest*. In Bacon's "Redargutio" I find him introducing this sly hint for the Fraternity:—
"Certe, *filii*, facultates artium et scientiarum omnium consensu aut empiricæ aut rationales sunt. Has autem bene commistas et copulatas adhuc videre non licuit. Empirici enim, formicæ more, congerunt tantum et utuntur. Rationales autem, aranearum more, telas ex se conficiunt. *Apis ratio media est, quæ materiam ex floribus tam horti quam agri elicit, sed simul etiam eam propria facultate vertit et digerit*" ("Redargutio Philosophiarum," p. 583, vol. iii., Phil. Wk., E. and S.).

This emblem of the Bee and honey I find Fludd, Vaughan, and Cygnæus introducing in the same manner. The emblem to Fludd's "Summum Bonum" is a Rose with a Bee alighting upon it, and the motto, *Dat rosa mel apibus*.

This shows the Rosicrucians borrowed from the Essenes. But the reader will note that Bacon has laid the "Redargutio," *with its address to fifty persons, styled sons, at Paris*. It is here again we hear of a great Rosicrucian meeting of thirty-six members in 1623, the date of the Folio Plays and "De Augmentis."

Christopher Murr writes: "The Phœnix is a favourite Rosicrucian idea," and in 1616 we find Michael Maier publishing a work upon his return from England to Bohemia. The title is "Jocus Severus, h, e Tribunal æquum quo Noctua Regina avium, Phoenice arbitro, post varias discentationes et querelas volucrum eam infestantium pronunciatur, etc." Francof., 1617. In the Preface we read: "Dabam Francofurti ad mœnum, mense Septembri a 1616 *transitu ex Anglia in Bohemiam.*" The reader will see Maier actually published three works all bearing date September 1616, *after his return from England*, five months after Shakespeare's death. Consider the last poem of the supposed

INTRODUCTION.

Shakespeare bears the mysterious title "The Phœnix and the Turtle," and is evidently in connection with Chester's "Love's Martyr,"* where a great many more poems upon the same subject may be found. Professor Buhle maintains Maier wrote this work, "Jocus Severus," *during his sojourn in England.*

Buhle points out there were no lodges and no Rosicrucians in Germany, where it never took hold at all, *but the case in England was different, for there it gave rise to Freemasonry.* I maintain Maier obtained inspirations in England, which is proved by his three works, "Lusus Serius," "Examen Fucorum," and "Jocus Severus," all bearing the same date, September 1616, published upon his return home. *They must have been written in England.*

* In this work we find Shakespeare's poem, "The Phœnix and the Turtle." Two pages previous to it there is an Invocation to Apollo and the Muses—"*Invocatio ad Apollinem et Pierides*" (p. 171). An allusion pointing to Helicon and Parnassus.

PART I.

Evelyn (in his Discourse of Medals) describes Bacon with "a spacious *Forehead* and piercing *Eye*, always (as he had been told by one that knew him well) looking upwards, as a soul in sublime contemplation." Osborn (in the second part of his Advice to his Son), writes : "His *majestical carriage struck an awful reverence* in those he questioned."

CHAPTER I.

BACON'S HISTORY OF KING HENRY VII.

De Connubio Rosarum.

Septimus Henricus non aere et marmore vivit ;
Vivit at in chartis, magne Bacone, tuis.
Iunge duas, Henrice, rosas ; dat mille Baconus ;
Quot verba in libro, tot reor esse rosas.—T. P.

THE omission of the History of King Henry VII. in the succession of the Chronicle plays is excessively striking and curious, because this period, of all others, was full of incident, full of discovery, and, in the union of the Roses, marks an epoch and period in the history of England. Bacon wrote only one *complete* prose history,[*] that is the perfect one of King Henry VII., which, for some purpose unexplained, we do not find in the 1623 Folio. Examination of the succession of the Chronicle plays betrays the seeming intention to take the chief reigns from King John in order, and thus carry History up to Henry the Eighth. We have King John, Richard II., Henry IV., Henry V., Henry VI., Richard III., each legitimately following on each other's heels; but after Richard III., Henry VIII. follows, and the one History (perhaps of all the most important) is, as it were, "*ripped out*" of the chronological succession of kings or reigns. It has occurred to us if Bacon wanted to prove his claim to the authorship of the plays, that such an omission might be made an instrument of extraordinary use as evidence, external and internal, for the discovery of truth by posterity ; because there is, of course, much

---

[*] The "History of King Henry VIII.," by Bacon, is only a fragment, just commenced. The Memorials of Queen Elizabeth's reign, entitled the "Felicities of Queen Elizabeth," is not a history, but a general survey of her times and character.

in the history of King Henry VII. interwoven with the history of his predecessor Richard III., and his successor Henry VIII.; these connections might be reflected from Bacon's History to the plays in question as links of evidence, by parallels of treatment.

The claims of Perkin Warbeck arose from his personating the Duke of York, one of the two princes murdered in the Tower by Richard III. Now, in Bacon's account of this incident of rebellion and imposture in his history of the reign of King Henry VII., he writes:—

"To detect the abuse (Perkin Warbeck's claims of legitimacy) there were but two ways; the first to make it manifest to the world, *that the Duke of Yorke was indeed murdered:* the other to prove that were he dead or alive Perkin was a *counterfeit*. For the first thus it stood. There were but four *persons, that could speak upon knowledge to the murder of the Duke of York*, viz.: SIR JAMES TYRRELL (the employed man from King Richard), JOHN DIGHTON and MILES FORREST, his servants (the two butchers or tormentors), and the *Priest* of the *Tower*, that buried them. Of which four *Miles Forrest* and the *Priest* were dead, and there remained alive only *Sir James Tyrrell* and *John Dighton*. These two the King caused to be committed to the Tower, and examined touching the manner of the death of the two innocent *Princes*. They agreed both in a tale (as the King gave out) to this effect: That King Richard having directed his warrant for the putting of them to death to Brackenbury, the Lieutenant of the Tower, was by him refused. Whereupon the King directed his warrant to SIR JAMES TYRRELL, to receive the keys of the *Tower* from the *Lieutenant* (for the space of a night) for the *King's* special service. That *Sir James Tyrrell* accordingly repaired to the Tower by night, attended by his two servants aforenamed, whom he had chosen for that purpose. That himself stood at the stair-foot, and sent these two *villains* to execute the murder. That they smothered them in their bed, and that done called up their master to see their naked dead bodies, which they had laid forth. That they were buried under the *stairs*, and some stones cast upon them. That when the report was made to *King Richard*, that his will was done, he gave *Sir James Tyrrell* great thanks, but took exception to the place of their burial, because too base for them that were King's children. Whereupon another night, by the King's warrant renewed, their bodies were removed by the *Priest of the Tower*, and buried by him in some place, which (by means of the *Priest's* death soon after) could not be known" ("History, King Henry VII.," p. 123, 1622).

If we now turn to the Life and Death of King Richard III. in the 1623 Folio, we find an extraordinary parallel in some of the details to this passage just cited.

K. Rich. Shall we hear from thee, Tyrrel, ere we sleep?
Tyr. Ye shall, my lord.   [*Exit.*

Scene III.

Enter Tyrrel.

Tyr. The tyrannous and bloody deed is done.
The most arch act of piteous massacre
That ever yet this land was guilty of.
Dighton and Forrest, whom I did suborn
To do this ruthless piece of butchery,
Although they were flesh'd villains, bloody dogs,
Melting with tenderness and kind compassion
Wept like two children in their deaths' sad stories.
" Lo, thus," quoth Dighton, " lay those tender babes : "
" Thus, thus," quoth Forrest, " girdling one another
Within their innocent alabaster arms :
Their lips were four red roses on a stalk,
Which in their summer beauty kiss'd each other.
A book of prayers on their pillow lay :
Which once," quoth Forrest, " almost changed my mind ;
But O ! the devil "—there the villain stopp'd ;
Whilst Dighton thus told on : " We smothered
The most replenished sweet work of nature,
That from the prime creation e'er she framed."
Thus both are gone with conscience and remorse ;
They could not speak ; and so I left them both,
To bring this tidings to the bloody king.
And here he comes.

Enter King Richard.

All hail, my sovereign liege !
K. Rich. Kind Tyrrel, am I happy in thy news?

> *Tyr.* If to have done the thing you gave in charge
> Beget your happiness, be happy then,
> For it is done, my lord.
> *K. Rich.* But didst thou see them dead?
> *Tyr.* I did, my lord.
> *K. Rich.* And buried, gentle Tyrrel?
> *Tyr. The chaplain of the Tower hath buried them;
> But how or in what place I do not know.*
> *K. Rich.* Come to me, Tyrrel, soon at after supper,
> And thou shalt tell the process of their death.
> Meantime, but think how I may do thee good,
> And be inheritor of thy desire.
> Farewell till soon. [*Exit Tyrrel.*

Tyrrell, Dighton, Forrest, and the *Chaplain of the Tower* are all introduced as by Bacon in his history. Brackenbury is introduced in the play, but omitted from playing any privy part to the murders. Bacon's "*Priest of the Tower*" is the "*Chaplain of the Tower*" *in the play, and buries the bodies of the Princes,* as Bacon relates, *but where* (Bacon states again) "*could not be known.*"

> The chaplain of the Tower hath buried them;
> But how or in what place I do not know.

This trifling parallel goes far to prove who wrote Richard III. But we have far more convincing evidence to adduce that this "History of Hing Henry the Seventh" was written by Bacon expressly to furnish evidence of connection with the preceding reign of King Richard the Third, in its play form. Bacon writes:— " As for conquest notwithstanding *Sir William Stanley,* after some acclamations of the soldiers in the field, had put a crown of ornament (which Richard wore in the battle, and was found amongst the spoils) upon King Henry's head as if there were his chief title " (page 5, "History King Henry VII.," 1622, 1641). Now compare this scene at the conclusion of the battle of Bosworth ("King Richard III.") and of the play:—

SCENE V. *Another part of the field.*

Alarum. Enter RICHARD *and* RICHMOND; *they fight.* RICHARD *is slain. Retreat and flourish. Re-enter* RICHMOND, DERBY *bearing the crown, with divers other Lords.*

> *Richm.* God and your arms be praised, victorious friends;
> The day is ours, the bloody dog is dead.

> *Dcr.* Courageous Richmond, well hast thou acquit thee.
> Lo, here, this long-usurped royalty
> From the dead temples of this bloody wretch
> Have I pluck'd off, to grace thy brows withal:
> Wear it, enjoy it, and make much of it.

The Earl of Derby * was called also Lord Stanley, and is so described in the list of *Dramatis Personæ* attached to the play.

It is remarkable that Bacon's "History of King Henry the Seventh" takes up almost immediately the cue of the text concluding the play of "King Richard the Third":—

> O now, let *Richmond* and *Elizabeth*,
> The true succeeders of each Royal House,
> By God's fair ordinance *conjoin together:*
> And let their heirs (God if thy will be so)
> Enrich the time to come with smooth-fac'd peace.
>
> (End of Play.)

Upon page 3, "The first the title of the Lady Elizabeth with whom by *precedent pact* with the party that brought *him in he was to marry.*" This was one of Henry the Seventh's claims to the throne, through union to the House of Yorke. Bacon dwells page after page upon Lady Elizabeth, and finally upon page 16 gives us the marriage itself. Many historians would have commenced the history after the union of the two Roses. But Bacon betrays in every line of this work a familiarity with the history of the preceding reigns, which every now and then gives as it were a thread out of the texture of the plays:—"About this time the King called unto his privy council *John Morton* and *Richard Fox*, the one bishop of Ely, the other bishop of Exeter, vigilant men, and secret." In the play of Richard the Third we meet with this *Morton, Bishop of Ely*. "They had been both versed in his affairs before he came to the Crown, and were partakers of his adverse fortune" (p. 16, "History of King Henry VII."). "But whatsoever else was in the man, he deserveth a most happy memory, in that he was *the principal mean of joining the two Roses*" (p. 199).

---

* The poet is not correct in calling Stanley Derby on the field of Bosworth. Stanley was not created Earl of Derby till some weeks after the battle, by Henry VII., viz., upon 27th October 1485.

> Morton is fled to Richmond.
>
> ("Richard III.," iv. 3.)

And King Richard exclaims:—

> Ely with Richmond troubles me more near.
> Than Buckingham and his rash levied strength. (*Ib.*)

Some writers consider that Cardinal Morton was the author of Richard III., written in Latin, and which was translated by Sir Thomas More. It is from this work that the account of Richard has been taken by succeeding chroniclers, to whom the Poet seems indebted for his materials.

In the fourth act the first news of the appearance of Richmond (afterwards Henry VII.) is brought by Ratcliffe and Lord Stanley:—

> *Rat.* Most mighty Sovereign on the western coast
> Rideth a puissant navy: to our shores
> Throng many doubtful hollow-hearted friends,
> Unarm'd and unresolv'd to beat them back,
> 'Tis thought that Richmond is their admiral.
>
> . . . . . .
>
> *Stan.* Stirr'd up by *Dorset, Buckingham, and Morton*
> He makes for England, here to claim the crown.
>
> (Act iv. sc. 4.)

This is upon page 199 of the Folio, and upon page 199 also of Bacon's "History of King Henry the Seventh" is the passage cited about Morton, Bishop of Ely: "He had been by Richard the Third committed (as in custody) to the Duke of Buckingham, whom *he did secretly incite to revolt from King Richard.* But after the Duke was engaged and thought the bishop should have been his chief pilot in the tempest, the bishop was gotten into the cock-boat, and fled over beyond seas. But whatsoever else was in the man, he deserveth a most happy memory, *in that he was the principal mean of joining the two roses*" (p. 199, "History of King Henry the Seventh," 1622, first edition, and also p. 199, 1641).

Ratcliffe and Catesby, who play a considerable part in the play, are mentioned by Bacon upon page 13, together with Lord Lovel and the Duke of Norfolk (also both characters in the Tragedy), as "attainted by parliament" as enemies to the King. Upon page 15 Bacon mentions Dorset. "The King sent forthwith money to redeem the Marquess of Dorset and Sir John Bourchier." All this, of course, is history, but history may be treated many ways, and it is striking to find Bacon, as it were, dwelling upon small points, and upon people introduced in the play. Bacon dwells a great deal upon the relations of the King to Brittany in this history:—

> I know the *Bretagne-Richmond* aims.
> ("Richard III.," act iv. sc. 3.)

Upon page 47 Bacon says: "All things were directed by the Duke of Orleans, who gave audience to the chaplain Urswick." If we look at the list of *Dramatis Personæ* prefixed to the " Tragedy of King Richard the Third," we find one " CHRISTOPHER URSWICK, *a priest*." These are details which two writers not acting in collaboration (or not identical) would hardly both repeat in this way. The affairs of this Duke of Orleans are again mentioned in the play of "King Henry the Eighth." Upon page 62 Bacon writes of a battle of Saint Alban fought in Brittany, where "the Duke of Orleans and the Prince of Orange were taken prisoners."

The play of "King Henry the Eighth" commences upon page 205 of the 1623 Folio (Histories). Upon page 205 also of this " History of King Henry the Seventh," Bacon writes: " There was a doubt ripped up in the times following when the divorce of King Henry the Eighth from the Lady Katharine did so much busy the world, whether Arthur was bedded with his lady or no, whereby that matter in fact (of *carnal knowledge*) might be made part of the case." This is a hint-worthy note, because the play of King Henry the Eighth almost entirely revolves upon the divorce of Katharine of Arragon from the King. Even Wolsey's fall is involved in the secret opposition he set in motion with regard to the King's marriage with Anne Boleyn.

At the commencement of the "History of King Henry the

Seventh," Bacon reviews the life and crimes of Richard the Third. It is very striking to find almost everything repeated that we find in the "Tragedy of King Richard the Third." "The executioner of King Henry the Sixth (that innocent prince) *with his own hands;* the contriver of the Duke of Clarence, his brother; the murderer of his two nephews (one of them his lawful king in the present, the other in the future failing of him), and vehemently suspected to have been the importuner of his wife, *thereby to make vacant his bed afore marriage* within the *degrees forbidden.*" Again, "He was not without secret trains and mines to turn Envy and Hatred upon his brother's government; as having an expectation and a kind of Divination, that the King, by reason of his many disorders, could not be of long life, but was like to leave his sons of tender years; and then he knew well how easy a step it was from the place of a Protector and first Prince of the Blood to the Crown." The words "*degrees forbidden*" are placed in italics. Now all these points are prominently brought forward in the play of "King Richard the Third." In the fourth act (scene 4) Richard proposes to Queen Elizabeth he should wed her daughter, who was niece to King Richard, and therefore the union was "*within the degrees forbidden.*" Elizabeth was Queen to Edward the Fourth, the brother to Richard the Third, who therefore stood as uncle to her issue.

> *Queen Eliz.* What were I best to say? her father's brother,
> Would be her Lord? *or shall I say her uncle?*
>
> (Act iv. sc. 4.)

But we even find the same charge laid by the Queen against Richard as by Bacon, and for the same motive, viz., the making away of his wife Anne to make room for the daughter of Queen Elizabeth:—

> Tell her thou madest away her uncle Clarence,
> Her uncle Rivers; yea and *for her sake,*
> *Madest quick conveyance with her good Aunt Anne.*
>
> (Act iv. sc. 3.)

This parallel is not explained away by ascribing these facts to history. For how many Dramatists put to work to write a play of King Richard the Third's life, would repeat exactly by chance what some Historian was writing upon the same reign? It is evident Bacon introduces these points on purpose to present proofs of his authorship of the play in question, *by means of identity of treatment.* These points are only details of History, not important or leading events, and yet the parallelism is complete, and the play is treated in action, as the History of Richard's life is recorded by Bacon.

> I say again give out
> That Anne my queen is sick, and like to die.
> About it, for it stands me much upon
> To stop all hopes, whose growth may damage me.
> I must be married to my brother's daughter,
> Or else my kingdom stands on brittle glass.
>
> (Act iv. sc. 2.)

In the play of "King Henry the Eighth" we find the Duke of Buckingham on his way to execution speaking as follows:—

> Henry the Seventh succeeding truly pitying,
> My father's loss; like a most royal prince
> *Restor'd me to my honours: and out of ruins
> Made my name once more noble.*
>
> (Act ii. sc. 1.)

In Bacon's "History of King Henry the Seventh":—" The King did also with great nobleness and bounty (which Vertues at that time had their turns in his nature) restore Edward Stafford (eldest son to Henry, Duke of Buckingham, attainted in the time of King Richard) not only to his *dignities,* but to his *fortunes* and *possessions,* which were great, to which he was moved also by a kind of gratitude, for that the Duke *was the man that moved the first stone against the tyranny of King Richard,* and, indeed, made the King a bridge to the Crown upon his own ruins" (p. 15). Compare Buckingham's words ("King Henry VIII.," act ii. sc. 1).

> My noble father Henry of Buckingham,
> *Who first raised head against usurping Richard.*

In the play of "Richard the Third" we find Buckingham presented playing exactly such a part as Bacon ascribes to him,— that is in the second scene of the fourth act—where, after learn ing Dorset has fled to Richmond, and being threatened (on account of his wife's son Stanley) by Richard the Third, exclaims:—

> *Buck.* And is it thus? repays he my deep service
> With such contempt? made I him king for this?
> O let me think on Hastings and be gone
> To Brecknock, while my fearful head is on.

Every point prominent in the play is prominently alluded to by Bacon, and it seems most palpably evident these parallels are purposely introduced to furnish proofs of authorship.

Bacon writes that Richard, when Duke of Gloucester, "was not without secret trains and mines to turn envy and hatred upon his brother's government," and that he reflected upon the King's "*voluptuous life and mean marriage.*"

> *Glou.* Ay, Edward will use women honourably.
> Would he were wasted, marrow, bones and all,
> That from his loins no hopeful branch may spring.
> (Act iii. sc. 2, Third "King Henry Sixth.")

A postscript to a letter (dated September 5th, 1621) addressed to James the First by Bacon, runs as follows:—

"Cardinal Wolsey said, that if he had pleased God as he pleased the King, he had not been ruined. My conscience saith no such thing; for I know not but in serving you, I have served God in one. But it may be, if I had pleased God, as I had pleased you, it would have been better with me."

This is repeated in the play of "King Henry the Eighth," act the third, final scene, where Cardinal Wolsey* exclaims:—

> O Cromwell, Cromwell!
> Had I but served my God with half the zeal
> I served my king, he would not in mine age
> Have left me naked to mine enemies.

One month later Bacon writes again to the King, this time mentioning his intention to write this "History of King Henry the Seventh":—

* Cardinal Wolsey held the revenues of several bishoprics and of the rich Abbey of St Albans.

"To the King.

"It may please your most excellent Majesty,

"I do very humbly thank your Majesty for your gracious remission of my fine. I can now, I thank God and you, die, and make a will.

"I desire to do, for the little time God shall send me life, like the merchants of London, which, when they give over trade, lay out their money upon land. So, being freed from civil business, I lay forth my poor talent upon those things, which may be perpetual, still having relation to do you honour with those powers I have left.

"I have therefore chosen to write the reign of King Henry the VIIth, who was in a sort your forerunner, and whose spirit, as well as his blood, is doubled upon your Majesty.

"I durst not have presumed to intreat your Majesty to look over the book, and correct it, or at least to signify what you would have amended. But since you are pleased to send for the book, I will hope for it.

"[God knoweth, whether ever I shall see you again; but I pray for you to the last gasp, resting.]

"The same, your true beadsman,

"FR. ST ALBAN."

"October 8, 1621."

"One day when King Henry the Sixth (whose innocence gave him holiness) was washing his hands at a great feast, and cast his eye upon King Henry, then a young youth, he said, '*This is the lad that shall possess quietly that that we now strive for*'" (p. 247, "History of King Henry the Seventh,' 1641). This is repeated in the essay of "Prophecies." And in the third part of the play of King Henry the Sixth, the King says to Richmond:—

> Come hither England's hope.   [*Lays his hand on his head.*]
>   If secret powers
> Suggest but truth to my divining thoughts,
> This pretty lad will prove our country's bliss.
> His looks are full of peaceful majesty,
> His head by nature framed to wear a crown,

> His hand to wield a sceptre, and himself
> Likely in time to bless a regal throne.
> Make much of him, my lords, for this is he
> Must help you more than you are hurt by me.
>
> (Act iv. sc. 6.)

This parallel already has been noticed by some other writers; but it cannot be omitted, seeing evidence of this kind is not worth much detached or single. In the play of "Richard the Third," the King says :—

> *Rich.* I do remember me Henry the Sixth
> Did *prophesy*, that Richard should be king,
> When Richmond was a little peevish boy,
> A king perhaps. (Act iv. sc. 2.)

It may be seen that Bacon places this prediction in his Essay of "*Prophecies*," as Richard terms it.

Bacon says of King Henry VII. : "He resteth on the title of Lancaster in the main, using the marriage and victory as supporters." In the third part of "King Henry the Sixth," act iv. scene 6, the Earl of Richmond is introduced under the "*tender care*" of the Duke of Somerset, the last male of the Beauforts, the King's near kinsman, through whom Henry Tudor founded his claims to the throne. Henry VII. adopted for one of his chief badges the cognizance of the Beauforts, a portcullis, with the motto "Altera securitas."* This proves how exactly the study of minute points of History reflected in the plays are reflected again by Bacon. There was no need of introducing the Earl of Richmond in this play at all unless for the sake of the prophecy of King Henry VI. This prophecy, Bacon, as we have said, repeats in his Essay of "Prophecies." It is quite an out-of-the-way study. Dugdale, quoting from Polydore Virgil, says: "Finding Henry, Earl of Richmond, in the custody of William Herbert's widow, he brought him from her, and carried him to King Henry, who, looking upon him prophetically, said, '*This is he who shall quietly possess what we and our adversaries do now contend for.*'"

* See page 195, "Notes on the Characters in Shakespeare's Plays." (Trench, 1869.)

The received opinion that the supposed author of the plays drew his materials entirely and only from Holinshed, Stow, and Grafton is erroneous. The study devoted to the composition of these chronicle plays in by-paths of history is a powerful argument against Shakespeare's authorship; that is, if we are to accept what little we know of his life as correct. Because the more extensive the evidence of wide research and reading, the more difficult is it to reconcile these facts with Shakespeare's life, which was more or less an active struggle for money. For example, the dream of Richard III. before the battle of Bosworth is recounted by the old writers Polydore Virgil, Croyland Chronicle, Hall, &c., that the night before the battle "he had a dreadful and terrible dream."

The whole of the play of "King Henry the Eighth" may be said to comprise the rise of Anne Boleyn, and the divorce of Queen Katharine by the King. We mean, this is the epoch embraced. For in the third scene of the second act Anne Boleyn is created Marchioness, and the play terminates with the birth of Elizabeth, and Cranmer's prophecy of her future reign. The Divorce of Queen Katharine and the Coronation of her rival form not only distinguishing features of the play, but the fall of Wolsey really turns upon his opposing secretly the advancement of Anne Boleyn. In Bacon's "History of King Henry the Seventh" he writes: "The February following, Henry Duke of Yorke was created Prince of Wales and Earl of Chester and Flint. For the Dukedom of Cornwall devolved to him by statute. The King also being fast handed, and loath to part with a second dowry, but chiefly being affectionate both by his nature and out of politic considerations to continue the alliance with Spain, prevailed with the Prince (though not without some reluctation; such as could be in those years, for he was not twelve years of age) *to be contracted with the Princess Katharine. The secret providence of God ordaining that marriage to be the occasion of great events and changes.*" ("Hist., King Henry VII.," p. 207).

It is evident the author of the play of "Henry the Eighth"

thought the same thing (the words we place in italics), for
although Cardinal Wolsey's rise and fall stand prominently out in
the play, nevertheless Queen Katherine and her divorce are really
*the springs and motives upon which the intriguing of parties and
the pleasure and displeasure of the King revolves.* Directly
Henry the Eighth finds Wolsey opposing his marriage with Anne
Boleyn, he disgraces him.

The Dukes of Norfolk and Suffolk, both envious of Wolsey's
power, thus converse:

> *Nor.* Believe it, this is true.
> In the Divorce, his contrary proceedings
> Are all unfolded; wherein he appears
> As I would wish mine enemy.
>   *Sur.*   How came
> His practices to light?
>   *Suf.*   Most strangely.
>   *Sur.*   Oh how? how?
>   *Suf.* The Cardinal's letters to the Pope miscarried,
> And came to th' eye o' th' king, wherein was read
> How that the Cardinal did entreat his Holiness
> To stay the judgment o' th' Divorce, &c.
>
>   (Act iii. scene 2.)

The fall of Wolsey almost immediately follows in this act.
Upon page 227 Bacon introduces Wolsey into his history thus:
"The same year likewise there proceeded a treaty of marriage
between the King and the Lady Margaret, Duchess Dowager of
Savoy, only daughter to Maximilian, and sister to the King of
Castile, and therein was employed for his first piece the King's
then *Chaplain, and after the great Prelate, Thomas Wolsey.*" It is
very curious Bacon should introduce Wolsey like this, and no
more be found written upon his career.

King Henry the Eighth is presented in the play as questioning
the *legitimacy of his daughter Mary* (in scene 4, act ii.), and on
the grounds that he had married his brother's wife Katharine:

>   Now, what moved me
> I will be bold with time and your attention:
> Then mark the inducement. Thus it came; give heed to 't:
> My conscience first received a tenderness,

> Scruple, and prick on certain speeches utter'd
> By the Bishop of Bayonne, then French ambassador:
> Who had been hither sent on the debating
> A marriage 'twixt the Duke of Orleans and
> Our daughter Mary: i' the progress of this business,
> Ere a determinate resolution, he,
> I mean the bishop, did require a respite:
> Wherein he might the king his lord advertise
> *Whether our daughter were legitimate,*
> Respecting this our marriage with the dowager,
> Sometimes our brother's wife.

Bacon devotes an entire page to this subject, and writes upon page 205 (King Henry VIII. commences also page 205, "Histories"): "There was a doubt ripped up in the times following, when the divorce of King Henry VIII. from the Lady Katharine did so much busy the world, whether Arthur was bedded with his lady or no, whereby that matter in fact (of carnal knowledge) might be made part of the case. And it is true that the lady herself denied it, or at least her counsel stood upon it, and would not blanch that advantage, *although the plenitude of the Pope's power of dispensing was the main question.* And this doubt was kept long open, in respect of the two Queens that succeeded Mary and Elizabeth, whose legitimations *were incompatible one with another,* though their succession was settled by Act of Parliament" (p. 206).

In a letter to James the First (dated Feb. 11, 1614, p. 72, "Letters," 1702) Bacon writes:—"And I put the Duke of Buckingham's case, who said, *That if the King* (Henry the Eighth) *caused him to be arrested of treason he would stab him.*" This incident is introduced in the play of King Henry the Eighth.

> *Surv.* After "the Duke his father," with "the knife,"
> He stretched him, and with one hand on his dagger,
> Another spread on 's breast, mounting his eyes,
> He did discharge a horrible oath; whose tenor
> Was,—were he evil used, he would outgo
> His father by as much as a performance
> Does an irresolute purpose.
>   *King*   There's his period,
> To sheathe his knife in us. He is attach'd

> Call him to present trial : if he may
> Find mercy in the law, 'tis his ; if none,
> Let him not seek 't of us : by day and night,
> He's traitor to the height. [*Exeunt.*
> ("Henry VIII.," act i. sc. 2.)

It seems to us the reign of Henry the Seventh suggests some strong parallels to explain its fitness to play the part of evidence for the real authorship of Shakespeare's plays. In the first place, it follows the reign of Richard the Third, *an usurper*. And we must concede the point, if Bacon wrote these plays, and holds a lawful claim to the crown of immortality connected with them, the example, or parallel, presented by the usurpation of the throne by Richard the Third, and his deposition by Henry the Seventh, is a strong one. The impostors or pretenders, Lambert Simnel and Perkin Warbeck, supply fresh samples of the same kind. And it is noteworthy this reign presents not only a remarkable moment in English history, as uniting the Roses, but in the discovery of America and voyages of Columbus is an epoch in the world's civilisation. The impression this event made on Bacon's mind may be estimated by the fact that he adopted the simile of this memorable voyage as an emblem of his own intellectual voyage of discovery. And let no one think it was a casual simile, for it dominates not only the "De Augmentis" and "Novum Organum," but also the "New Atlantis" located across the ocean. The title page engravings of the two former works bear the ship emblem, the two columns of Hercules, and the motto of the perlustration of the globe from Daniel.

Bacon's admiration for Henry the Seventh is unbounded :— "For that Louis the Eleventh, Ferdinando, and Henry, may be esteemed for the *Tres Magi* of those ages." "He was a prince, sad, serious, and *full of thoughts and secret observations*, and full of *notes and memorials* of his own hand, especially touching persons." Bacon resembled him in these details. The first edition of this "History of King Henry VII." (1622) contains a portrait of the King. In the edition of 1641, Bacon's portrait (by Marshall) has taken its place. In his preface Bacon writes :

"For he was *a wise man and an excellent king*. He was of an high mind—one that revered himself, and would reign indeed" (p. 238). "This king (to speak of him in terms equal to his deserving) was one of the best sort of wonders, a wonder for wise men. He had parts (both in his virtues and his fortunes) not so fit for a common-place as for observation. Certainly he was religious, both in his affection and observance. But as he could see clear (for those times) through superstition, so (now and then) he would be blinded by human policy. He built and endowed many religious foundations, besides his memorable hospital of the Savoy. And yet was he a great almsgiver in secret, which showed that his works in public were dedicated rather to God's glory than his own. He professed always *to love and seek Peace;* and it was his usual preface in his treaties, That when Christ came into the world *Peace was sung;* and when He went out of the world, *Peace was bequeathed*" ("Hist.," p. 233).

The play of "Richard the Third" concludes with the prayer of Henry the Seventh *for Peace:*—

> O now let Richmond and Elizabeth,
> The true succeeders of each Royal House,
> By God's fair ordinance conjoin together:
> And let thy heirs (God if thy will be so)
> *Enrich the time to come with smooth-faced Peace,*
> With smiling plenty, and fair prosperous days.
> ("Richard III.," act v. sc. 3.)

Bacon represents him exactly as he is here portrayed as a God-fearing king. "His works in public were dedicated rather to God's glory than his own" (p. 233, "Hist."). See Richmond's prayer before the battle:—

> O Thou! whose captain I account myself,
> Look on my forces with a gracious eye;
> Put in their hands thy bruising irons of wrath,
> That they may crush down with a heavy fall
> The usurping helmets of our adversaries!
> Make us thy ministers of chastisement,
> That we may praise Thee in thy victory!
> To Thee I do commend my watchful soul,

> Ere I let fall the windows of mine eyes;
> Sleeping and waking, O defend me still!
> ("Richard III.," act v. sc. 3.)

It was during the reign of King Henry the Seventh that the expedition to Naples under King Charles the Eighth took place, and England entered into a league with the Italian potentates against France. This league consisted of King Henry of England, Ferdinand and Isabella (King and Queen of Spain), the Duke of Venice, and *Ludovico Sforza, Duke of Milan. Ferdinand of Naples* was also included tacitly in this confederation. Bacon constantly refers to this period, which exercised some peculiar fascination or influence upon him. In the 1671 "Resuscitatio" he frequently introduces this epoch as an example of the happiness of leagues. In the "Advertisement of a Holy War" he introduces Naples and Milan together, and it seems to me that it cannot be entirely accidental that the first play standing in the Folio 1623 (and probably the last written) should point at Milan and Naples, Prospero being presented as the rightful Duke of Milan. It is very curious to find at the period we refer to the names of *Prospero* Colonna, Ludovico Sforza, Duke of Milan (who usurped, like Prospero's brother, the title), Alphonso II., King of Naples, Ferdinand, Sebastian King of Portugal (expedition to Africa)— *being names also in the play of "The Tempest."* This is a period in the History of Europe of extraordinary import, inasmuch as it embraced the Reformation. The Papacy attained the *ne plus ultra* of its infamy under Pope Alexander the Sixth, and it was just at this midnight hour, so to speak, Savonarola began to preach at Florence and foreshadow Luther. This also is the great period of discovery of America by Cabot, Columbus, and of the voyages of Vasco de Gama. It was the period of Lorenzo di Medici, of the revival of learning, and the recovery of the lost world of the classics. No period could possibly better suggest a starting point for modern history, and it is my humble belief the 1623 Folio commences, as it were, with this *Aurora* hour of light, reformation, and letters.

BACON'S HISTORY OF KING HENRY VII. 19

In Bacon's "Felicities of Queen Elizabeth," which is to be refound in the "Resuscitatio" (1671), we find him describing the advancement of Elizabeth's mother, Anne Boleyn, in these words: "For first, from the estate of a gentlewoman only, and no way pretending to noble titles, *he* (Henry VIII.) *raised her to the honour of a marchioness.*" This is repeated in the play of "King Henry the Eighth." In the second act (scene 3) the Lord Chamberlain is introduced:—

> *Cham.* You bear a gentle mind, and heavenly blessings
> Follow such creatures. That you may, fair lady,
> Perceive I speak sincerely, and high note's
> Ta'en of your many virtues, the king's majesty
> Commends his good opinion of you, and
> Does purpose honour to you no less flowing
> Than Marchioness of Pembroke; to which title
> A thousand pound a year, annual support,
> Out of his grace he adds.

How is it all these small historical trifles known to Bacon are prominent points also in the plays? And in the concluding passage spoken by Cranmer upon the birth of Queen Elizabeth we find a prophecy, and many points repeated by Bacon in his memoir upon the great Queen's life.

We present the reader * with a *facsimile* copy of pages twenty-one and twenty three of Lord Bacon's "History of King Henry the Seventh," published in 1622, the year preceding the Great Folio Shakespeare, 1623. It is for the expert and critic to decide whether the mathematical connection (or cipher) we are about to point out between these pages and page 53, "Merry Wives of Windsor" is accidental or the result of design. It will be seen that upon page 53 (col. 106), "Merry Wives of Windsor," we find the word "*Bacon*" the 268th word down the column from the top of the page, and the 95th up from the bottom. Directly we turn to page 21 of the "History of King Henry the Seventh," we find the words "*stage-play*" (in italics) are the 268th and 269th words (counting them as two words) down the page, like·

* See Appendix.

wise counted from the top. They are the 52nd and 53rd words counted up from the bottom of the page, and thus the word "*stage*" agrees with the paging of the "Merry Wives of Windsor," 53, on which we find the word "*Bacon*" also the 268th word counted down. I should hardly be at the trouble of wasting time and ink publishing this discovery if it was not certainly a remarkable coincidence of figures in more ways than one. Upon the Stratford monument to Shakespeare's memory, we read he died in his 53rd year (*ætatis*). And not only is it striking to find the word "*Bacon*" upon page 53, "Merry Wives of Windsor," but this word "*stage-play*" giving us the figures 268, 269, 53, 52; Shakespeare being 52 years old (full years), and in his 53rd year, 1616, when he died.

Page 21, "Hist. { *stage* 268 down, 53 up. { *Bacon*, 268, page 53.
K. H. VII." { *play* 269 down, 25 up. { *I.* 269, "M. W. W."

If the reader will turn to the table of this page 21 of Bacon's "History of King Henry the Seventh," he will find the first column giving the figures 22, 23, which are the numbers of the words in italics and Roman type down the page. Now, the play of "King Richard the Third" is the twenty-third play in the 1623 Folio, and does it not seem as if 22 and 23 refer to 1622, 1623, which are the dates of publication of this "History of King Henry the Seventh" and the Great Folio first collected edition? The play of "Richard the Third" commences upon page 173 of the Folio Histories.

Bacon, 268 down, 95 up, p. 53, "Merry Wives of Windsor."
Deduct $268 - 95 = 173$!

Now the striking point has to come. Upon page 56, or column 107, of the "Histories" (that is the sequent column), the same number 268 gives

heart, 268 down, **173** up.

Which if we deduct $268 - 173 = 95$! The reader will see how curious it is to find the deduction of the numbers in these two cases giving us the *up number of the other*, proving some cipher connection. It is worthy of note in 1595 the third part of the reign of King Henry the Sixth was written, and possibly 95 may stand for this date. At anyrate it is curious that the next play, "King Richard the Third," commences upon page 173 of the 1623 Folio, and is the 23rd play.

Richard the Third was a usurper, and it is quite possible Bacon selected the reign of King Henry the Seventh to represent himself by analogy *as the rightful successor to the usurper William Shakespeare.* There is much to bear this theory out. Henry the Seventh's accession brought the wars of the Roses to an end. As a conqueror by might, and king by right of his Lancastrian claim, he supplanted the unlawful usurper Richard the Third. The reader may see that if we count the plays in succession, "Richard the Third" is the *twenty-third* play in order from the commencement of the catalogue. The reign of King Henry the Seventh, if it had been written, would have formed the twenty-fourth play, therefore there is something singularly striking to find upon page 23 of the "History of King Henry the Seventh," the introduction of the words "*Stage Plays*" and "*Masks*"! Not only this, but (16)23 was the date of the first Folio edition of Shakespeare's supposed plays; and as the omitted play of "King Henry the Seventh" would have followed had there been one the play of "Richard the Third," this introduction upon page 23 is very curious.

Upon page 26 of Bacon's "History of King Henry the Seventh" we read of the Queen Dowager: "After her husband's death she was matter of *Tragedy*, having lived to see her brother beheaded, and her two sons deposed from the crown, bastarded in their blood, and cruelly murdered." Is there not reference here to the *Tragedy play of* "*Richard the Third,*" in which all this is portrayed? The word "*Tragedy*" is the twenty-second word in italics from the top of the page, and the play of the third part of "King Henry the Sixth," in which this Queen plays so large a part, is the twenty-second play in the Folio 1623. If we count the word "HASTINGS" (in Roman type), then the word "*Tragedy*" is the twenty-third word from the top of page 26, in extraordinary letterpress, and the "Tragedy of Richard III." is the twenty-third play in order in the Folio. This word "*Tragedy*" is the 267th, 268th, 269th, or 270th word, all counted down from the top of the page, according as we count hyphenated words ("marriage-bed," "bachelor-king," "issue-male") as single or double words. Upon page 53, "Merry Wives of Windsor," these numbers give "*For Bacon, I warrant.*" Upon page 36 of this "History of King Henry the Seventh" there are fifty-two or fifty-three words in italics ("*Fore-fight*" hyphenated), according as we count the hyphenated word singly or double. This was Shakespeare's age, 1616, when he died.

{ 52 years old, and in his 53rd year.
{ 36 plays in the 1623 Folio.

"*A Tragedy*" are the 225th and 224th words all counted up the page. Upon page 53, "Merry Wives of Windsor," the 225th, 224th words (up and down) are:—

Page 53, { in 225 { the 224
"Merry Wives of Windsor" { nouns 224 { pronoun 225.

This "pronoun," *or name standing in place of another name*, is identified in the accusative case with the word Bacon.

Hang hog is Latin for Bacon, I warrant you.

Upon page 23, Bacon's "History of King Henry the Seventh," we read:—" But yet doubting that there would be too near looking and too much *Perspective* into his disguise, if he should show it here in *England*, he thought good (after the manner of *scenes* in *Stage-Plays* and *Masks*) to show it afar off." The words *Stage-Plays* are the 84th and 85th words down from the top of this page 23. Now the time of action comprehending the play of "King Richard III." is from A.D. 1471 to 1485, and if there had been a play of King Richard VII. it would have commenced from the last date. The numbers of these words are as follows, and we give the corresponding figures from page 53, "Merry Wives of Windsor":—

In		83 down,	225 up	P. 5 3, "M.W.W.,"	pronoun	225 down.
Stage	84	,,	224 ,,	col. 106,	the	224	,,
Plays	85	,,	223 ,,		of	223	,,
and	86	,,	222 ,,		borrowed	222	,,
Masques	87	,,	221 ,,		are	221	,,

The *pronoun* stands *in the place of a proper name*. And if we add the paging 23 to 83 and 84 ("In *Stage*"), we get 106 and 107, which are the numbers of the columns of page 53, "Merry Wives of Windsor," from which we take our figures.

Elizabeth, Queen to King Edward IV.

Fuller says of this lady:—"She got more greatness than joy, height than happiness, by her marriage, for she lived to see the death of her husband, murder of her two sons, and restraint of herself and rest of her children." This agrees with her foreboding language in the play:—

Small joy have I in being England's queen.

Miss Strickland says of her: "There never was a woman who contrived to make more personal enemies." After Richard's usurpation she was styled by him, "Dame Elizabeth Grey, late calling herself Queen of England." She retired to the Monastery of Bermondsey, where she died in the reign of her son-in-law, much neglected by him, June 8, 1492. In only one instance has the compiler met with the time of Elizabeth Woodvile's death, and then it was merely stated to have occurred the Friday before Whitsuntide. As Easter Day in 1492 fell on the 22nd of April, the exact date of her decease was the 8th of June. Her will, dated April 10, 1492, exhibits a touching picture of her maternal affection and her poverty, having nothing but her blessing to bequeath to her children, for "I have no worldly goods" is her mournful confession. She was buried in St George's Chapel, Windsor, where on a flat stone, at the foot of her royal husband's tomb, is inscribed:—

King Edward and his Queen Elizabeth Widvile.

Southey's lines would form an appropriate epitaph:—

> Thou, Elizabeth, art here,
> Thou! to whom all griefs were known,
> Who wert placed upon the bier,
> In happier hour than on a throne.

This is the Queen Bacon refers to as the *Queen Dowager*. We find her in the play urging the Marquis of Dorset to fly to Richmond, and this agrees with Bacon's words, "And in her withdrawing chamber had the fortunate conspiracy for the King against Richard the Third been hatched" (p. 21, "History of King Henry VII."). Compare—

> *Queen.* O Dorset, speak not to me, get thee gone,
> Death and destruction dogs thee at thy heels.
> Thy mother's name is ominous to children.
> If thou wilt out-strip death, go cross the seas,
> And live with Richmond, from the reach of hell.
> ("Richard III.," act i. sc. 3.)

"The Marquis of Dorset was Thomas Grey, eldest son of Elizabeth's first marriage. After the death of King Edward, Dorset, attainted by Richard the Third, escaped to the Earl of Richmond, and assisted in raising him to the throne" ("Notes on the Characters of Shakespeare's Plays," p. 224, by G. R. French, 1868). The reader may see how exactly acquainted Bacon is with the details of the reign of King Richard the Third as they are presented by the supposed Shakespeare.

CHAPTER II.

AMBITION, ENVY, AND DEFORMITY.

"He seems to have written the Essays with the pen of Shakespeare."—ALEXANDER SMITH.

PROFESSOR FOWLER writes: "In vol. i. p. 5 De Maistre makes what appears to me to be a very true criticism on Bacon—'Rarement il résiste à l'envie d'être poète'" (p. 137, Introduction, "Nov. Org.").

RICHARD III.

LET those who would trace Bacon's mind in the characters of the plays, carefully read his Essay on "Deformity," and then study the character of Richard III. as depicted in his self-examining speech (at the opening of the play), and notice how exactly what Bacon remarks upon the compensations of Nature are illustrated in this one portrait.

"Deformed persons are commonly even with nature, for as nature hath done ill by them, so do they by nature, being for the most part (as the Scripture sayeth) void of natural affection, and so have their revenge of nature; *certainly there be a consent between the body and the mind*, and where nature erreth in the one, she ventureth in the other. Whosoever hath anything fixed in his person that doth induce contempt, hath also a perpetual spur in himself to rescue and deliver himself from scorn. Therefore *all Deformed persons are extreme bold*. First, as in their own defence as being exposed to scorn, but in process of time, by a general habit. So that in a great wit Deformity is an advantage to rising. Still the ground is they will, if they be of spirit, seek to free themselves from scorn; which must be, either by *virtue or malice*" ("Deformity," 1625).

> *Richard.* I, that am curtail'd of this fair proportion,
> Cheated of feature by dissembling nature,
> *Deformed, unfinish'd, sent before my time*
> *Into this breathing world, scarce half made up,*
> And that so lamely and unfashionable,
> That dogs bark at me as I halt by them.
> Why I (in this weak piping time of peace)
> Have no delight to pass away the time,
> Unless to see my shadow in the sun,
> And descant on mine own *Deformity.*
> And therefore since I cannot prove a lover,
> To entertain these fair well-spoken days,
> I am determined to prove a villain.

Let the reader next read the Essay on "Boldness," which Bacon has already declared is an attribute of deformed persons. And let us call to mind Richard III., as Duke of Gloucester, making love to Lady Anne over the coffin of her husband, killed by him. "Wonderful like is the case of boldness, in civil business; what first? *Boldness;* what second and third? Boldness. And yet Boldness is a child of ignorance, and *baseness,* far inferior to other parts. But nevertheless *it doth fascinate,* and bind hand and foot, those that are either shallow in judgment, or weak in courage, which are the greatest part; yea, and prevaileth with wise men at weak times. Therefore we see it hath done wonders in popular states, but with senates and princes less. And more even upon the first entrance of Bold Persons into *Action than soon after; for Boldness is an ill keeper of promise*" ("Boldness"). We have already found Bacon writing upon Deformity: "Certainly there is a consent between the body and the mind." Richard III. says :—

> Then since the heavens have shaped my body so,
> *Let Hell make crooked my mind to answer it.*

In Bacon's "Natural History" he writes: "It is an usual observation, *that if the body of one murdered be brought before the murderer, the wounds will bleed afresh*" (Century x., Exp. 958). An illustration of this is given in the play of "King Richard the Third," in the celebrated second scene of the first act, where Richard (as Duke of Gloucester) stops the "corse" of King

AMBITION, ENVY, AND DEFORMITY.

Henry the Sixth, whom he murdered in order to court Lady Anne.

> *Glouc.* Stay you that bear the corse, and set it down.
> *Anne.* What black magician conjures up this fiend,
> To stop devoted charitable deeds?
>
> .   .   .   .
>
> If thou delight to view thy heinous deeds,
> Behold this pattern of thy butcheries.
> O, gentlemen, see, see! *dead Henry's wounds
> Open their congeal'd mouths, and bleed afresh.*
> Blush, blush thou lump of foul deformity;
> *For 'tis thy presence that exhales this blood
> From cold and empty veins, where no blood dwells;
> Thy deed inhuman and unnatural,
> Provokes this deluge most unnatural.*
>
> ("Richard III.," act i. sc. 2.)

THERSITES.

Thersites is described in the list of "*Dramatis Personæ*" prefixed to the play of "Troilus and Cressida" as "*A Deformed and scurrilous Græcian.*" Once more we find him, as we have already found Richard the Third, of an envious, discontented disposition. Achilles addresses him:—

> How now thou *core of envy!*

And Patroclus exclaims:—

> Why, thou damnable *box of envy!*

Bacon concludes his Essay upon "Envy" with the words:—"It is also the vilest affection, and the most depraved; for which cause it is the proper *attribute of the Devil*, who is called the Envious Man that soweth tares amongst the wheat by night." Thersites, in a soliloquy following his quarrel with Ajax, ends:—

> I have said my prayers, and *devil envy,* say Amen.

Bacon writes:—"A man that is *busy*, and inquisitive, is commonly *envious:* for to know much of other men's matters, cannot be, because all that ado may concern his own estate; therefore it must needs be, *that he taketh a kind of play pleasure in looking upon the fortunes of others;* neither can he, that mindeth but his own business, find much matter for envy." How this is exactly reflected in the portrayal of the character of Thersites, may be seen by turning to the play. He is always looking on at others, spying and criticising, full of other people's business and with none of his own, unless this is his especial vocation. He maintains this *rôle* to the very last of *a looker on or spectator*, and at the conclusion of the play, whilst the Greeks and Trojans are fighting hard, exclaims:—

> Now they are clapper-clawing one another, *I'll go looke on.*

Thersites takes no interest in himself, but is for ever depressing others, abusing them, and implying they have no wit or brains; and his *curiosity* is so great, we find him bent upon nothing (during the battle at the finale of the play) but seeing the meeting of Troilus and Diomede. He exclaims, "I would fain see them meet," and although his life is threatened by Hector, immediately the danger is past he recurs to the objects of his insatiable curiosity again in the words:—

What's become of the wenching rogues? I think they have swallowed one another. I would laugh at that miracle—yet in a sort lechery eats itself: I'll seeke them.

Bacon remarks: "*Non est curiosus quin idem sit malevolus.*" That Thersites is malevolent to the backbone cannot be questioned. For malevolence (following a dictionary and not our inspiration) means spiteful, bitter, rancorous, evil-minded, and Thersites is all these, describing himself to Hector as "a scurvy railing knave, a very filthy rogue."

The last time we hear of Thersites in this play he is presented as brought to bay by a *bastard*, and confessing himself a bastard also in order to save his life (or escape combat), on the score of kindred. This is evidently a touch of Bacon's in harmony with his Essay on "Envy," where he says: "*Deformed Persons*, and Eunuchs, and old men, and *Bastards* are envious."

Enter MARGARELON.

Mar. Turn, slave, and fight.
Ther. What art thou?

Mar. A bastard son of Priam's.

Ther. I am a bastard too; I love bastards: I am a bastard begot, bastard instructed, bastard in mind, bastard in valour, in everything illegitimate. One bear will not bite another, and wherefore should one bastard? Take heed, the quarrel's most ominous to us: if the son of a whore fight for a whore, he tempts judgment: farewell, bastard.

Mar. The devil take thee, coward! [*Exit.*

In Bacon's "Antitheta" upon "Beauty" we read: "Deformed Persons commonly have their revenge of Nature." Again, "Deformed Persons seek to rescue themselves from scorn by malice and boldness."

The Bastard Edmund.

("King Lear.")

Bacon in his Essay on "Envy":—"Deformed persons, and eunuchs, and old men, *and bastards are envious:* for he that cannot possibly mend his own case, *will do what he can to impair another's.*" In the Tragedy of "King Lear" we have the *Bastard* Edmund, half brother to Edgar (sons of Gloucester), filled with *envy* of his brother's legitimate birth, forging a letter purposing to be from the latter, and letting his father see it with the express purpose of damaging his brother's fortune and inheritance. As we have already quoted, but must again repeat, "Again *Envy is ever joined with the comparing of a man's self;* and where there is no comparison, no envy." In the case of Cassius in "Julius Cæsar" we shall presently find the text of the play introducing this effect of comparison with wondrous art. And in the case of the bastard Edmund we refind once more a soliloquy of mortified and envious self-comparison with his legitimate brother Edgar:—

Enter Edmund, *with a letter.*

> *Edm.* Thou, nature, art my goddess; to thy law
> My services are bound. Wherefore should I
> Stand in the plague of custom, and permit
> The curiosity of nations to deprive me,
> For that I am some twelve or fourteen moonshines
> Lag of a brother? Why bastard? wherefore base?
> When my dimensions are as well compact,
> My mind as generous, and my shape as true,

As honest madam's issue? Why brand they us
With base? with baseness? bastardy? base, base?
Who, in the lusty stealth of nature, take
More composition and fierce quality
Than doth, within a dull, stale, tired bed,
Go to the creating a whole tribe of fops,
Got 'tween sleep and wake? Well, then,
Legitimate Edgar, I must have your land:
Our father's love is to the bastard Edmund
As to the legitimate: fine word,—legitimate!
Well, my legitimate, if this letter speed,
And my invention thrive, Edmund the base
Shall top the legitimate. I grow; I prosper:
Now, gods, stand up for bastards!

Enter GLOUCESTER.

Glou. Kent banish'd thus! and France in choler parted!
And the king gone to-night! subscribed his power!
Confined to exhibition! All this done
Upon the gad! Edmund, how now! what news?

Edm. So please your lordship, none.   [*Putting up the letter.*

Glou. Why so earnestly seek you to put up that letter?

Edm. I know no news, my lord.

Glou. What paper were you reading?

Edm. Nothing, my lord.

Glou. No? What needed, then, that terrible dispatch of it into your pocket? the quality of nothing hath not such need to hide itself. Let's see: come, if it be nothing, I shall not need spectacles.

Edm. I beseech you, sir, pardon me: it is a letter from my brother, that I have not all o'er-read; and for so much as I have perused, I find it not fit for your o'er-looking.

Glou. Give me the letter, sir.

Edm. I shall offend, either to detain or give it. The contents, as in part I understand them, are to blame.

Glou. Let's see, let's see.

Edm. I hope, for my brother's justification, he wrote this but as an essay or taste of my virtue.

Glou. [*Reads*] "This policy and reverence of age makes the world bitter to the best of our times; keeps our fortunes from us till our oldness cannot relish them. I begin to find an idle and fond bondage in the oppression of aged tyranny; who sways, not as it hath power, but as it is suffered. Come to me, that of this I may speak more. If our father would sleep till I waked him, you should enjoy half his revenue for ever, and live the beloved of your brother,   "EDGAR."

Hum—conspiracy!—"Sleep till I waked him,—you should enjoy half his revenue,"—My son Edgar! Had he a hand to write this? a heart and brain to breed it in?—When came this to you? who brought it?

AMBITION, ENVY, AND DEFORMITY.

Edm. It was not brought me, my lord; there's the cunning of it; I found it thrown in at the casement of my closet.

Glou. You know the character to be your brother's?

Edm. If the matter were good, my lord, I durst swear it were his; but, in respect of that, I would fain think it were not.

Glou. It is his.

Edm. It is his hand, my lord; but I hope his heart is not in the contents.

Glou. Hath he never heretofore sounded you in this business?

Edm. Never, my lord: but I have heard him oft maintain it to be fit, that, sons at perfect age, and fathers declining, the father should be as ward to the son, and the son manage his revenue.

Glou. O villain, villain! His very opinion in the letter! Abhorred villain! Unnatural, detested, brutish villain! worse than brutish! Go, sirrah, seek him; I'll apprehend him: abominable villain! Where is he?

("King Lear," act i. sc. 2.)

If we now turn to Bacon's Essay on "Cunning," we find the *letter trick* of Edmund exactly described: "*Some procure themselves to be surprised at such times, as it is like the party that they work upon, will suddenly come upon them: and to be found with a letter in their hand, or doing somewhat which they are not accustomed with the end, they may be opposed of those things, which of themselves they are desirous to utter.*" This situation is pretty closely approximated, for Edmund allows his father to surprise him with the forged letter expressly that it may be read, and himself catechised as to the contents and bearing thereof. This example of "cunning" is very much after the manner of Iago's practice upon Othello; and Gloucester is, as Edmund exclaims, "a credulous father," without much suspicion. Bacon writes: "For some are begotten of old men, some of young men. Again, some in the fervency of the father's love (*as it is commonly in bastards*); others after the cooling of it as in long married couples" ("Hist. Life and Death," Exp. 32).

> *Bastard.*   Why brand they us
> With base? with baseness? *bastardy?* base, base?
> Who in the lusty stealth of nature, take
> More composition and fierce quality
> Than doth, within a dull, stale, tired bed
> Go to the creating a whole tribe of fops,
> Got 'tween a sleep and wake?
>
> ("Lear," act i. sc. 2.)

The Bastard "Don John."
("Much Ado about Nothing.")

In the play of "Much Ado about Nothing" we are once more presented with a BASTARD in the person of *Don John*, half-brother to Don Pedro, Prince of Arragon. Here again (as in "King Lear") the bastard is depicted as an envious, malevolent villain, who is at the bottom of all the mischief in the play. He is introduced in the first act and third scene with his *two followers*, Conrade and Borachio. These two men are employed as spies, and answer exactly to what Bacon writes in his Essay "Of Followers and Friends." "There is a kind of *Followers* likewise which are dangerous, *being indeed espials; which inquire the secrets of the house, and bear tales of them to others.* Yet such men many times are in great favour; for they are officious, and commonly exchange tales." Almost with the first words Borachio utters and reports himself in the play, we find him fulfilling this *rôle* of an *espial*, and listening to the secrets of the Prince and Claudio, whilst secreted behind the arras.

Bora. Being entertained for a perfumer, as I was smoking a musty room, comes me the prince and Claudio, hand in hand, in sad conference: I whipt me behind the arras: and there heard it agreed upon that the prince should woo Hero for himself, and having obtained her, give her to Count Claudio.
(Act i. sc. 3, "Much Ado about Nothing.")

Don John is first introduced as a melancholy, discontented man, who (as Conrade says to him) "*has of late stood out against his brother.*" Don John, in spite of restored favour ("hath taken you newly into his grace"), is envious of Claudio, who has become Don Pedro's "*right hand*" or favourite. When the Bastard hears of Claudio's engagement to Hero, he determines to cross it.

Enter DON JOHN *and* BORACHIO.

D. John. It is so; the Count Claudio shall marry the daughter of Leonato.
Bora. Yea, my lord; but I can cross it.
D. John. Any bar, any cross, any impediment will be medicinable to me; I am sick in displeasure to him, and whatsoever comes athwart his affection ranges evenly with mine. How canst thou cross this marriage?

AMBITION, ENVY, AND DEFORMITY.

Bora. Not honestly, my lord; but so covertly that no dishonesty shall appear in me.

D. John. Show me briefly how.

Bora. I think I told your lordship a year since, how much I am in the favour of Margaret, the waiting gentlewoman to Hero.

D. John. I remember.

Bora. I can, at any unseasonable instant of the night, appoint her to look out at her lady's chamber window.

"There are conceits that some men that are of an ill and *melancholy nature*, do incline the company into which they come *to be sad and ill-disposed*" ("Sylva Sylvarum," Ex. 941).

Leon. Was not Count John here at supper?

Ant. I saw him not.

Beat. How tartly that gentleman looks! I never can see him but I am heart-burned an hour after.

Hero. He is of a very melancholy disposition.

("Much Ado about Nothing," act ii. sc. 1.)

PHILIP THE BASTARD.
("King John.")

In this play we have the bastard Philip, who is half brother to Robert Faulconbridge, son to Sir Robert Faulconbridge. Philip is the eldest son, but relinquishes his rights as heir in favour of his younger brother, preferring to be knighted by the King, and to be openly reputed the bastard son of Richard Cœur de Lion. In the depicting of this character we see how faithful to his Essays Bacon has been. For we find Philip bitter in words, and, like Thersites, a railer. He finds fault, and abuses Austria and the Dauphin, and confesses in the following speech his complete character, which is to rail, *out of envy*, abuse what he does not possess:—

> And why *rail* I on this Commodity?
> But for because he hath not woo'd me yet:
> Not that I have the power to clutch my hand,
> When his fair angels would salute my palm;
> But for my hand, as unattempted yet,
> Like a poor beggar, raileth on the rich.
> Well, whiles I am a beggar, I will *rail*
> And say there is no sin but to be rich;
> And being rich, my virtue then shall be

> To say there is no vice but beggary.
> Since kings break faith upon commodity,
> Gain, be my lord, for I will worship thee. [*Exit.*
> ("King John," act ii.)

Like Thersites his tongue is scurrilous and spiteful; his description of his half brother Robert is evidently coloured with envy at his legitimacy of birth :—

> *Bast.* Madam, an if my brother had my shape,
> And I had his, sir Robert's his, like him;
> And if my legs were two such riding-rods,
> My arms such eel-skins stuff'd, my face so thin
> That in mine ear I durst not stick a rose
> Lest men should say, "Look, where three farthings goes!"
> (Act i. sc. 1.)

When the Dauphin makes love to Blanch of Spain, niece to King John, the bastard exclaims :—

> In such a love, so vile a lout as he.

And a fine touch is given in the scene laid before Angiers, where the bitterness most at his heart is roused in a moment by the words "*breed,*" "*well-born bloods,*" which reflect upon and remind him of the illegitimacy of his birth :—

> *First Cit.* In brief, we are the King of England's subjects:
> For him and in his right, we hold this town.
> *K. John.* Acknowledge then the king, and let me in.
> *First Cit.* That can we not; but he that proves the king
> To him will we prove loyal: till that time
> Have we ramm'd up our gates against the world.
> *K. John.* Doth not the crown of England prove the king?
> And if not that, I bring you witnesses,
> Twice fifteen thousand hearts of England's breed,—
> *Bast.* Bastards, and else.
> *K. John.* To verify our title with their lives.
> *K. Phil.* As many and as well-born bloods as those,—
> *Bast.* Some bastards too. (Act ii. sc. 1.)

This trifle shows the exquisite delicacy of the painting in this art. The bastard Philip is proud of his father's blood (Richard Cœur de Lion), which speaks in his fearless utterance and spirited renunciation of his claims to his brother's land, so much so that Queen Elinor exclaims :—

> I like thee well: wilt thou forsake thy fortune,
> Bequeath thy land to him, and follow me?
>
> (Act i. sc. 1.)

Nevertheless he never forgets that he is bastard, and it bespeaks a wonderful knowledge of the human heart, how in a moment he is stung by a word into bitter remembrance of what he is, which he seeks to discharge and relieve himself of, by challenging and bitter self-irony.

ENVY.

Bacon, in his Essay upon "Envy," writes: "And it is also noted that *Love* and *Envy do make a man pine*, which other affections do not, because they are not so continual."

In the tragedy of "Julius Cæsar" nothing is drawn with greater art than the characters of *Cassius, Brutus, and Casca*. At the opening of the play we are presented with a scene in which Cassius begins the work of undermining and inflaming the mind of Brutus against Cæsar. He describes how he saved Cæsar's life from drowning in the Tiber, and exclaims:—

> I (as *Æneas*, our great ancestor,
> Did from the flames of Troy, upon his shoulder,
> The old *Anchises* bear), so from the waves of Tiber
> Did I the tired *Cæsar*: and this man
> *Is now become a God, and Cassius is*
> *A wretched creature, and must bend his body,*
> *If Cæsar carelessly but nod on him.* (Act i. sc. 2.)

Apply Bacon's further remarks upon "*Envy*" in this passage:— "Again, Envy is ever joined *with the comparing of a man's self; and where there is no comparison no envy*." Cassius saved Cæsar's life by being a better swimmer, and it is a notable feature in Envy (if not in a great deal of human nature) that if a man surprise others by showing talents or qualities he was not suspected of possessing, he will excite comparison in those points where he has proved himself inferior to those who now envy him. For the mind is easily inclined to judge a man *by one thing*, and from this weakness to claim superiority *in other things*. When therefore one with whom we have been on familiar and intimate terms, whom we have imagined we have measured, and taken exhaustive stock of, all at once surprises us by going to the front, the mind receives a rude shock, and insulted self-comparison falls back at once upon those points where we have proved superior. Cassius continues about Cæsar:—

> He had a fever when he was in Spain,
> And when the fit was on him I did mark
> How he did shake: 'tis true this God did shake,
> His coward lips did from their colour fly,
> And that same eye, whose bend doth awe the world,
> Did lose his lustre: I did hear him groan:
> I, and that tongue of his, that bade the Romans
> Mark him, and write his speeches in their books,
> Alas it cried, "Give me some drink, *Titinius,*"
> As a sick girl: Ye gods it doth amaze me,
> A man of such a feeble temper should
> So get the start of the majestic world,
> And bear the palm alone. (Act i. sc. 2.)

Familiarity breedeth contempt. And, as Bacon admirably remarks:—"A man that hath no vertue in himself ever *envieth* vertue in others. For men's minds will either feed upon their own good, or upon other's evil; *and who wanteth the one will prey upon the other; and who so is out of hope to attain to another's vertue, will seek to come at even hand, by depressing another's fortune.*" In the passage we are about to cite may be found an exact parallel to the words quoted from Bacon as to the *pining or thinning effects of Envy*, in the person of Cassius.

> *Cæsar.* Let me have men about me, that are fat,
> Sleek-headed men, and such as sleep o' nights:
> *Yond Cassius has a lean and hungry look,*
> He thinks too much: such men are dangerous.
>
> (Act i. sc. 2.)

In Plutarch's life of Cæsar we read: "Cæsar too had some suspicion of him (Cassius), and he even said one day to his friends, 'What think you of Cassius? I do not like his pale looks.' Another time, when Anthony and Dolabella were accused of some designs against his person and government, he said, 'I have no apprehensions from those *fat and sleek men;* I rather fear *the pale and lean ones,*' meaning Cassius and Brutus" ("Julius Cæsar," Plut., vol. iv., Langhorne's ed., 1774.)

AMBITION, ENVY, AND DEFORMITY. 37

It is evident Bacon borrowed from this passage. And we can only admire and respect the fidelity with which he has adhered in these particulars to history.

Plutarch, in his life of Brutus, describes Cassius as "a man of violent passions, and an enemy to Cæsar, rather *from personal than political hatred.*" And this is also implied or suggested in the passages from the play quoted. But here we find the expression itself:—

> With full as many signs of deadly hate,
> *As lean-fac'd envy* in her loathsome cave.
>   ("2 King Henry VI.," act iii. sc. 2.)

Cæsar remarks of Cassius:—

> Such men as he be never at heart's ease,
> Whiles they behold a greater than themselves,
> And therefore are they very dangerous.
>   (Act i. sc. 1.)

"The roots of the male-peony, dried, tied to the neck, doth help the *Falling-sickness;* and likewise the *Incubus,* which we call the *Mare*" ("Sylva Sylvarum," Cent. x., Ex. 966).

Cassi. But soft I pray you: what did *Cæsar* swoon?
Casca. He fell down in the market-place and foam'd at mouth, and was speechless.
Brutus. 'Tis very like he hath the *Falling-sickness.*
Cassi. No, *Cæsar* hath it not; but you and I
And honest *Casca,* we have the *Falling-sickness.*
                    ("Julius Cæsar," act i. sc. 2.)

"There was an Ægyptian *Soothsayer* that made *Anthonius* believe that his genius (which otherwise was *brave and confident*) was in the presence of *Octavianus Cæsar, poor and cowardly;* and therefore he advised him *to absent himself* (as much as he could) and remove far from him. This Soothsayer was thought to be suborned by *Cleopatra,* to make him live in Egypt, and other remote places from Rome. Howsoever, the conceit of a *Predominant or Mastering Spirit,* of one man over another, is ancient and received still, even in vulgar opinion" ("Sylva Sylvarum," Cent. x., Ex. 939, 940).

Now compare the following passage from the second act, third scene, of the Play of "Anthony and Cleopatra," and mark how thoroughly and entirely Bacon's prose is reproduced.

> *Soothsayer.* But yet hie you to Egypt again.
> *Anthony.* Say to me, whose Fortunes shall rise higher,
> *Cæsar's* or mine?
> *Soothsayer. Cæsar's.* Therefore (Oh *Anthony*) stay not by his side.
> Thy *Dæmon*, that's thy spirit which keeps thee, is
> Noble, courageous, high, unmatchable,
> Where *Cæsar's* is not. But near him, thy angel
> *Becomes a fear;* as being o'erpowered, therefore
> Make space enough between you.   (Act ii. sc. 3.)

The result of this advice is that *Anthony* exclaims, "*I will to Egypt,*" showing how exactly the play follows the passage we quote from Bacon. We see this in even little trifles like the adherence to the title "*Soothsayer*" and the sequence of narrative. Anthony's character is (apart from Cæsar's) "brave and confident," "noble, courageous;" in *Cæsar's* company it turns "poor and cowardly," and his genius "becomes a fear." An expression of Bacon's is "Mastering Spirits," and we find it in these words of Anthony :—

> No place will please me so, no mean of death,
> As here by Cæsar and by you cut off,
> The choice and *master spirits* of this age.
>
>   (Act iii. sc. 1.)

Macbeth, speaking of Banquo :—

> *Macbeth.* There is none but he,
> Whose being I do fear: and under him
> *My genius is rebuk'd as it is said*
> *Mark Anthony's was by Cæsar.*
>
>   (" Macbeth," act iii. sc. 1.)

Under "Fascination" Bacon writes in the Fourth Book of "The Advancement of Learning" (chapter iii.) :—" Whence the conceits have grown, made almost popular of the *Mastering Spirit; of men ominous and unlucky;* of the strokes of love and envy; and of others of like nature."

> *Cas.* But what of Cicero? shall we sound him?
> I think he will stand very strong with us.
> *Casca.* Let us not leave him out.

AMBITION, ENVY, AND DEFORMITY. 39

Cin. No, by no means.
Met. O, let us have him, for his silver hairs
Will purchase us a good opinion
And buy men's voices to commend our deeds:
It shall be said, his judgment ruled our hands;
Our youths and wildness shall no whit appear,
But all be buried in his gravity.
  Bru. O, name him not: let us not break with him;
For he will never follow any thing
That other men begin.

("Julius Cæsar," act ii. sc. 1.)

What careful and exact study of Cicero's life the author must have given! For Cicero, enquiring of the Oracle of Delphi, by "what means he might rise to the greatest glory, the priestess bade him 'Follow nature, and not take the opinion of the multitude for the guide of his life.'" And Cicero had no share in the conspiracy against Cæsar, though he was one of Brutus' particular friends. Plutarch describes his vanity as disgusting, and no doubt he had too exalted an opinion of himself to follow anyone.

Cassius. Did Cicero say anything?
Casca. I, he spoke *Greek*.
Cass. To what effect?
Casca. Nay, and I tell you that, I'll ne'er look you in the face again. But those that understood him smiled at one another, and shook their heads: but for mine own part, it was *Greek* to me.

("Julius Cæsar," act i. sc. 2.)

This proves the author of this play was a thorough scholar. For Cicero, in fear of Sylla's resentment, retired to Greece, attending the lectures of Antiochus at Athens, and is reported by Plutarch to have declaimed in Greek at Rhodes, where he studied under the rhetorician Apollonius, the son of Molo. The same writer says at first he was called "*a Greek and a scholastic*" at Rome, and later on in life rendered the Greek terms of logic and natural philosophy into the Roman language. Plutarch affirms that Cicero gave Latin terms for these Greek words, *phantasia, syncatathesis, epoche*, &c., &c. (*Vide* Plutarch's "Cicero"). These exquisite studies of character and history, carried out to the minutest particulars, by the author of the plays, are all against

Shakespeare. For if we are to credit Mr Gladstone, Shakespeare only wrote for the common people; and what should the people care whether Cicero knew Greek or no, or whether he was a man who would not follow the leadership of others? Why should an author writing for bread, pressed for leisure and means, enter into all these artistic and exquisite finishing touches, where all is truth?

"It hath been observed *that in anger the eyes wax red*" ("Nat. Hist.," Exp. 872).

> And Cicero
> Looks with such ferret and such *fiery eyes*,
> As we have seen him in the Capitol,
> Being cross'd in conference by some senators.
> ("Julius Cæsar," act i. sc. 2.)

"Kings in ancient times (and at this present in some countries) were wont to put *great trust in Eunuchs;* because they that are envious towards all, are more obnoxious and officious towards one. But yet their trust towards them hath rather been as to *good spials and good whisperers*" ("Deformity"). In "Twelfth Night" we find Viola playing the part of an Eunuch, and becoming the trusted confidant, messenger, spy, and whisperer of Duke Orsino.

> *Cap.* Be you his eunuch, and your mute I'll be.
> (Act i. sc. 2.)
>
> *Duke.* Cæsario,
> Thou know'st no less but all; I have unclasp'd
> To thee the book even of my secret soul.
> (Act i. sc. 3.)

The Eunuch *Mardian* (in "Antony and Cleopatra") is sent to Antony to whisper in his ear the pretended death of Cleopatra, and to play the part of a trusted spy to report the effect:—

> *Cleo.* To the monument!
> Mardian, go tell him I have slain myself;
> Say that the last I spoke was "Antony,"
> And word it, prithee, piteously: hence Mardian
> *And bring me how he takes my death.*
> (Act iv. sc. 13.)

AMBITION, ENVY, AND DEFORMITY.

" There is use also of *Ambitious men* in pulling down the greatness of any subject that overtops " ("Ambition").

The part Cardinal Wolsey plays in "King Henry the Eighth" in pulling down the Duke of Buckingham is a notable illustration of Bacon's words. He writes: "It is counted by some a weakness in Princes to have favourites: *but it is of all others the best remedy against ambitious great ones.*"

The Earl of Surrey exclaims to Cardinal Wolsey:—

> Thy ambition
> (Thou scarlet sin) robb'd this bewailing land
> Of noble Buckingham.
>
> ("Henry VIII.," act iii. sc. 2.)

In the same manner as Wolsey removed Buckingham, Norfolk and Suffolk succeed in pulling down Wolsey.

> Cromwell, I charge thee fling away ambition,
> *By that sin fell the angels:* how can man then
> (The Image of his maker) hope to win by it?
>
> ("Henry VIII.," act iii. sc. 2.)

Compare—"For the *desire of power was the fall of angels*, the desire of knowledge the fall of man" (Preface to the "Instauration," p. 19).

"Men of *Noble birth* are noted to be envious towards new men when they rise. For the distance is altered" ("Envy").

> *Buck.* This butcher's cur is venomed-mouthed, and I
> Have not the power to muzzle him, therefore best
> Not wake him in his slumber. *A Beggar's book
> Out-worths a Noble's blood.*
>
> (Act i. sc. 1.)

Cardinal Wolsey was a man of mean birth, and the envy his rise created amongst the nobility is well illustrated at the commencement of the play of "Henry the Eighth." We are presented with Buckingham, Norfolk, and Abergavenny, each mad with envy and hatred of Wolsey's pride, power, and ambition.

> *Buck.* The devil speed him: no man's fire is freed
> From his ambitious fingers.

CHAPTER III.

BACON'S ESSAYS APPLIED TO THE PLAYS.

SUSPICION, MALICE, CUNNING, ETC.

> That cuckold lives in bliss
> Who, certain of his fate, loves not his wronger;
> But, oh, what damnèd minutes tells he o'er,
> Who dotes, yet doubts, suspects, yet strongly loves!
> ("Othello," act iii. sc. 3.)

IAGO's villainy is chiefly caused *by disappointed ambition*, for the play opens with his complaints against Othello's promotion of Cassio over his head:—

> *Rod.* Thou told'st me thou didst hold him in thy hate.
> *Iago.* Despise me, if I do not. Three great ones of the city,
> In personal suit to make me his lieutenant,
> Off-capp'd to him: and, by the faith of man,
> I know my price, I am worth no worse a place:
> But he, as loving his own pride and purposes,
> Evades them, with a bombast circumstance
> Horribly stuff'd with epithets of war;
> And, in conclusion,
> Nonsuits my mediators; for, "Certes," says he,
> "I have already chose my officer."
> And what was he?
> Forsooth, a great arithmetician,
> One Michael Cassio, a Florentine,
> A fellow almost damn'd in a fair wife;
> That never set a squadron in the field,
> Nor the division of a battle knows
> More than a spinster; unless the bookish theoric,
> Wherein the toged consuls can propose
> As masterly as he: mere prattle, without practice,
> Is all his soldiership. But he, sir, had the election:
> And I, of whom his eyes had seen the proof
> At Rhodes, at Cyprus, and on other grounds
> Christian and heathen, must be be-lee'd and calm'd
> By debitor and creditor: this counter-caster,

> He, in good time, must his lieutenant be,
> And I—God bless the mark !—his Moorship's ancient.
>
> (Act i. sc. 1.)

Bacon's Essay upon "Ambition:"—"*Ambition* is like choler; which is an humour, that maketh men active, earnest, full of alacrity and stirring, *if it be not stopped. But if it be stopped, and cannot have his way, it becometh adust, and thereby malign and venomous.*" How exactly this describes Iago's checked ambition, changed into the poison of the serpent, which has crept into Othello's bosom in order only to sting him to his destruction.

> *Iago.* Why, there's no remedy ; 'tis the curse of service,
> Preferment goes by letter and affection,
> And not by old gradation, where each second
> Stood heir to the first. Now, sir, be judge yourself,
> Whether I in any just term am affined
> To love the Moor.
>   *Rod.*   I would not follow him then.
>   *Iago.* O, sir, content you ;
> I follow him to serve my turn upon him :   (Act i. sc. 1.)

Bacon, in the passage quoted, is undoubtedly *thinking of the serpent*, and it is well worthy reflection that when all Iago's villainy is disclosed at the end of the play, we find the following text in harmony with this idea:—

>   *Lod.*   Where is that *Viper?*
> Bring the villain forth,
>   *Othello. I look down towards his feet ; but that's a fable.*
>
> (Act v.)

How else are we to understand these words of Othello's except by reference to the fable of the serpent of Paradise, crawling in the dust (or "*adust*" as Bacon writes) *at the feet?* Bacon's mind, as we know by his "Wisdom of the Ancients," was fond of rationalizing all fables. The way he interprets the Proverbs of Solomon in the "Advancement" proves this. And we venture to suggest that the vast amount of scriptural allusion, paraphrase, and application to be found in the plays called Shakespeare's may be refound re-echoed in the "Two Books of the Advancement" and the "De Augmentis." A little book called "Shakespeare and the Bible" calls attention to one side of the question. The theological side of Bacon's writings has never really received the attention it deserves. Dr Abbot has certainly devoted a chapter to it in his edition of the Essays. But the extraordinary study Bacon made of the Bible may be estimated from the fact that in the 1623 "De Augmentis" there are *one hundred and fifty quotations, allusions, or references to the Old and New Testaments alone!* And in the Essays there are over seventy of such allusions.

For the play of "Othello" the best commentary are Bacon's Essays on "Suspicion" and "Ambition":—"There is nothing makes a man *suspect much more than to know little:* and therefore men should remedy *suspicion by procuring to know more,* and not to keep their suspicions in *smother."* How exactly this fits the *suspicions of Othello.* And does not Bacon perhaps in this word *"smother"* point at the *smothering* of Desdemona? Othello knew little except what he gathered from Iago, whose truth and honesty he ought to have held in suspense before his wife's. "What would men have? Do they think *those they employ and deal with are saints? Do they not think they will have their own ends, and be truer to themselves, than to them? Therefore there is no better way to moderate suspicions* than to account upon such suspicions as true *and yet to bridle them as false"* ("Suspicion"). If Othello had only obeyed the letter of these injunctions he would have tarried for better evidence, and questioned the integrity of Iago at the same time. "For so far a man ought to make use of *suspicions* as to provide, *as if that should be true that he suspects yet it may do him no hurt.* Suspicions that the mind of itself gathers are but buzzes; *but suspicions that are artificially nourished, and put into men's heads, by the tales and whisperings of others have stings."* This is just the case of Othello, whose suspicions are put into his head and nourished artificially by the tales and whisperings of Iago. The entire moral of this tragedy might be comprised in the words—too much suspicion, too little suspicion. In the play of the "Winter's Tale," the jealousy of Leontes is grounded likewise upon suspicion, but of the *mind itself,* self-created by a suspicious nature. Othello is simple, credulous, passionate, violent. He neither represses his jealousy or *"guards"* (as Bacon suggests in the first lines of his Essay) against the dangers of giving too easy ear to others. Bacon writes:—"They dispose kings to tyranny, *husbands to jealousy.*" These last words, as is also the final Italian proverb, "*Sospetto licentia fede,*" are both pretty direct hints for Othello, whose faith entirely departs with the first breath of suspicion. Ford, in the "Merry Wives of Windsor," is another example of suspicion. It is a fact that suspicious people are often the most credulous and unsuspecting where they ought to be the opposite, and this is nowhere better illustrated than in Othello, who never suspects the one being who deserved it until too late. If this Essay does not apply exactly to the plays of the "Winter's Tale" and "Othello," as forming the "*interior*"* of their action on which the plot revolves, we are indeed at fault. It is to be remarked the villainy of Iago is likewise the outcome of *suspicion.*

> *Iago.* I hate the Moor,
> And it is *thought abroad,* that 'twixt my sheets
> He's done my office. *I know not if 't be true,*
> *But I for mere suspicion* in that kind,
> Will do as if for surety. (Act i. sc. 3.)

Iago's suspicions answer exactly to Bacon's words: "Suspicions that the mind of itself gathers *are but buzzes. But suspicions that are artificially nourished and put into men's heads by the tales and whisperings of others have stings*" ("Suspicion"). Here is exactly the difference between Othello's suspicions and Iago's. The former's are "*put into his head*" on account of the latter's (which are "*buzzes*") in order to be revenged for the suspicion of a wrong. A fine touch is given when Iago exclaims:—

> By *Janus* I think no.

For Bacon describes *Janus* as bifrons—that is, *doubled-faced.*

The next essay of Bacon's which throws a light upon this art is that on "Cunning." The wonderful way in which Iago insinuates the poison of jealousy into the mind of Othello is reflected in this Essay, as we shall show. Iago, after having aroused Othello's suspicions as to Cassio's interview with Desdemona, and his acquaintance with her before Othello's marriage, *cautions*

* One of Bacon's titles for his Essays is "*Interioria Rerum,*" or the *interior of things.*

him against jealousy, which transfers, as it were, the suspicion he is trying to fasten in Othello's mind from any appearance of showing what he is really trying to do. Iago having kindled the first sparks of jealousy, turns the "*cat in the pan*," and strengthens his own ends by disclaiming and laying to Othello the implied charge he is hastily jealous:—

> Oh beware my lord of Jealousy
> It is the green-eyed monster which doth mock
> The meat it feeds on. (Act iii. sc. 3.)

Bacon writes: "There is a *cunning*, which we in England call *the turning of the cat in the pan*, which is when that which a man says to another, *he lays it as if another had said to him*. And to say truth it is not easy, when such a matter passed between two, to make it appear from which of them it first moved and began." If we study the whole of this scene where Iago first begins working upon Othello's mind, we find this exactly illustrated. This caution against jealousy uttered by Iago, reads *as if Othello and not Iago had first started the subject*, and places the latter in the position of a friend endeavouring to disabuse a suspicious mind of jealous fancies. The effect argues for honesty and good faith, and except in minds of great worldly experience and subtlety, produces a contrary result, strengthening the suspicions already harboured. To caution others against what we are trying to insinuate, is a certain rule of cunning often to be remarked in life.

Because in order to fix suspicions in another's mind, the first thing necessary is to disarm suspicion against the interestedness or good faith of our evidence or motives. If we are suspected, our insinuations have no weight. And so it is with Iago. His art is to appear frank, honest, cautious, not too certain of his own suspicions, and in thus acting he goes far to undermine Othello's faith. The play of "Othello" might be briefly expressed as *Suspicion* and disappointed *Ambition*, employing *Cunning* as an instrument of *Malice* upon others. Nothing is so striking as the exhaustive manner in which Bacon's Essays apply both in title and in subject matter to the affections or passions of the human mind as portrayed in the plays falsely attributed to Shakespeare. Bacon concludes this Essay on "Cunning" thus: "Some build rather upon the *abusing of others*, and (as we now say) *Putting tricks upon them*, than upon soundness of their own proceedings." The *trick* of the handkerchief by which Iago convinces Othello of Desdemona's infidelity pretty closely examples this quotation. Be it observed the verb Bacon employs, "*Abusing*" is frequently introduced in the play—

> *Othello.* I am *abus'd*, and my relief
> Must be to loath her.
>
> *Iago.* As I confess it is my nature's plague
> To spy into *abuses*. (Act iii. sc. 3.)

Aldis Wright in his Glossary (Essays) describes this word as meaning "*Deception*," "*Mockery*," and no doubt this is very near what Bacon intends to convey. Bacon writes in his Essay on "Love": "I know not how, *but martial men are given to love:* I think it is, but as *they are given to wine.*" This is well illustrated in the person of Cassio, who *gets drunk*, and whose amorous relations with Bianca assist to further Iago's villainous conspiracy. Then we have Bertram, another "martial man," in "All's Well that Ends Well," pursuing an intrigue with Diana; also Falstaffe and Doll Tear Sheet; and each of these cases illustrate what Bacon means when he adds to this remark, "For perils commonly ask to be paid in pleasures."

VAIN-GLORY.

In his Essay upon "Vain-glory," Bacon says: "In military commanders and soldiers, *vain-glory* is an essential point; for as iron sharpens iron, so by *glory* one courage sharpeneth another." In "Troilus and Cressida" we find Ajax set up as champion of the Greeks against Achilles, on purpose to stimulate and whet the pride of the latter. Hector's challenge to single combat is aimed at Achilles:

> *Ulysses.* This challenge that the gallant Hector sends,
> However it is spread in general name,
> Relates in purpose only to Achilles. (Act i. sc. 3.)

Ulysses and Nestor plot a device by which the result of the lottery is to fall upon Ajax, with the purpose of physicking the pride of the insolent Achilles.

> No, make a lottery,
> And by device let blockish Ajax draw
> The sort to fight with Hector : among ourselves,
> Give him allowance as the worthier man,
> For that will physic the great myrmidon
> Who broils in loud applause, and make him fall
> His crest that prouder than blue Iris bends.
>
> (Act i. sc. 3.)

In short, the vain-glory of each of these leaders of faction in the Græcian tents is employed to special purpose to stir and rouse the other, particularly Achilles, who sulks in his tent. Ajax is described :—

> Ajax is grown self-willed, and bears his head
> In such a rein, in full as proud a place
> As broad Achilles, and keeps his tent like him ;
> Makes faction feasts, rails on our state of war
> Bold as an Oracle, and sets Thersites,
> A slave, whose gall coins slanders like a mint,
> To match us in comparison with dirt. (Act i. sc. 3.)

In these last lines describing Thersites, we find re-echoed Bacon's definition of envious persons : "A man that hath no virtue in himself, ever *envieth* virtue in others. For men's minds will either feed upon their own good, or upon other's evil ; and who wanteth the one will prey upon the other. And who so is out of hope to attain to another's virtue, will seek to come at even hand by depressing another's fortune."

The vain-glory of Ajax is thus pictured by Thersites :—

Ther. A wonder !

Achil. What ?

Ther. Ajax goes up and down the field, asking for himself.

Achil. How so ?

Ther. He must fight singly to-morrow with Hector, and is so prophetically proud of an heroical cudgelling that he raves in saying nothing.

Achil. How can that be ?

Ther. Why, he stalks up and down like a peacock,—a stride and a stand ; ruminates like an hostess that hath no arithmetic but her brain to set down her reckoning : bites his lip with a politic regard, as who should say "There were wit in this head, an 'twould out;" and so there is, but it lies as coldly in him as fire in a flint, which will not show without knocking. The man's undone for ever; for if Hector break not his neck i' the combat, he'll break 't himself in vain-glory. (Act iii. sc. 3.)

BOLDNESS.

The characters of Bardolph, Nym, Pistol, and Falstaffe might be each fairly epitomized *as a mixture of boldness, imposture, and impudence*, which borders closely upon the ridiculous, and excites our laughter at their swashing words and weak performances. The first three are *Mountebanks* unqualified. In Bacon's Essay on "Boldness" he seems to be evidently writing with just such characters in his mind's eye. "Surely as there are *Mountebanks* for the natural body: so are there *Mountebanks* for the politic body. Certainly to men of great judgment *Bold persons are a sport to behold;* nay and to the vulgar also, *Boldness* hath somewhat of the ridiculous. *For if absurdity be the subject of laughter, doubt you not, but great boldness is seldom without some absurdity.* Especially, it is a sport to see, when a bold fellow is out of countenance; for that puts his face into a most shrunken and wooden posture; as needs it must; for in bashfulness, the spirits do a little go and come; but with bold men upon like occasion, they stand at a stay, like a stale at chess, where it is no mate, but yet the game cannot stir" ("Boldness"). Can we not see all this with the visual eye, painted in Falstaffe, who, checkmated by the Prince and Poins in the recital of his exploits with the thieves, must have exhibited just such a countenance as Bacon describes, when discovered in his mountain of falsehoods? The Hostess of the "Boar's Head" remarks when Falstaffe plays the king:—

"O the father, how he holds his countenance."
("1 King Henry IV.," act ii. sc. 4.)

Bacon opens his Essay upon "Boldness" by comparing it to *Action*. And this is a most profound observation. For the essence of boldness in the sense Bacon implies, is the impudence of *playing a rôle*, and assuming a part which, as in the case of Nym, Bardolph, and Pistol is thoroughly theatrical, full of affectation, and belonging to the stage rather than to life. The bravos of a transpontine theatre might be imagined to swagger, bully, and bluster as these mountebanks really do, and their repertory of fustian extravagance and bombast is the reproduction off the stage, of what was once a characteristic of low theatres and poor actors. They are really stage rascals lightened with a touch of humour, but devoid of Falstaffe's good-fellowship and ready wit. In Bacon's "*Antitheta Rerum*," under "Boldness" (xxxiii., Book vi., "Advancement of Learning," 1640, p. 316), we find:—"What action is to an Orator, the same is boldness to a politic; the first, the second, the third virtue. Impudence is good for nothing but imposture."

Parasites and Sycophants.

Bacon writes:—

"Such were those *trencher* philosophers which in the later age of the Roman state were usually in the houses of great persons whom not improperly you may call solemn *parasites*, of which kind *Lucian* makes a merry description of the Philosopher that the great lady took to ride with her in the coach, and would needs have him carry her little dog *Melitæus*, which he doing officiously, and yet uncomely, the page scoffing said, '*I doubt our philosopher of a stoic will turn cynic*'" (page 24, Book i., "Advancement of Learning").

The play of "Timon of Athens" is in great measure taken from the Greek of *Lucian** (Holme's "Authorship of Shakespeare," p. 57). Apemantus in that play is the philosopher and stoic, Bacon describes. And can we not see in the contexts of the words "*parasites*," "*trencher-friends*" in the passage we now quote, Bacon's pen reflected?

---

* "Warburton discovered that the whole of the first speech of Autolycus ("Winter's Tale") is taken from Lucian's book upon astrology" (Ward's "History of Dramatic Literature").

> *Timon.* Live loathed and long,
> Most smiling, smooth, detested *parasites*,
> Courteous destroyers, affable wolves, meek bears,
> You fools of fortune, *trencher-friends*, time's flies,
> Cap and knee slaves, vapours, and minute jacks.
>
> ("Timon of Athens," act iii. sc. 5.)

But what further strengthens the parallel, Apemantus is as much cynic as stoic:—

> *Apemantus' grace.*
>
> Immortal gods, I crave no pelf;
> I pray for no man but myself:
> Grant I may never prove so fond,
> To trust man on his oath or bond;
> Or a harlot, for her weeping;
> Or a dog that seems a-sleeping;
> Or a keeper with my freedom;
> Or my friends, if I should need 'em.
> Amen. So fall to't:
> Rich men sin, and I eat root.   (Act i. sc. 2.)

The fine distinction of characters drawn between Timon and Apemantus is well worthy study. Apemantus is stoic and cynic, but without being misanthrope. He does not shun mankind, though he perfectly penetrates the motives of the flatterers, who, calling themselves Timon's friends, eat him. It is this knowledge of character which makes him cynical. It is Timon's ignorance of the world which upsets his balance with the load of the discovery made too late. Apemantus may be churlish and sour, but like medicine unpalatable to the taste, his physic, if taken in time, would have saved Timon. There can be little doubt Apemantus is introduced as a foil to contrast a stoic and cynic with an epicurean. Timon, with his painters, poets, parasites, jewellers, banquets, and presents, undoubtedly belongs to the latter class of pleasure-seekers. Directly he finds he has been victimized by his flattering friends and trencher companions, he falls into the opposite extreme of misanthropy, and like an overloaded ship capsizes. He becomes, too late, ten times more cynical than Apemantus, who not only had the wisdom to make use of his knowledge of the world, but would not punish himself on account of it. One extreme leads to the other extreme. It is to be remarked that no one unacquainted with the philosophy of the different schools of classical philosophical thought, could have drawn this nice distinction between cynic and epicurean, stoic and misanthrope. The greater part of the Greek of Lucian from which the play is taken would not furnish a sciolist with the necessary distinctions. Plutarch introduces Timon in his lines of Antony and Alcibiades.

> *Alcibiades.* I never did thee harm.
> *Timon.* Yes, thou spok'st well of me.
> *Alcibiades.* Call'st thou that harm?
> *Timon.* Men daily find it.
>
> ("Timon of Athens," act iv. sc. 3.)

"Some men are *praised* maliciously to their hurt, *thereby to stir envy and jealousy towards them; Pessimum genus inimicorum laudantium;* in so much as it was a proverb amongst the Græcians; *that he that was praised to his hurt,* should have a push rise upon his nose" ("Of Praise," 1625).

Apemantus. Heavens! that I were a Lord.
Timon. What wouldst do then, *Apemantus?*
Apemantus. E'en as *Apemantus* does now, hate a Lord with my heart.
Timon. What, thyself?
Apemantus. I.

("Timon," act i. sc. 1.)

"Pride if it ascend *from contempt of others to a contempt of itself,* at last is chang'd into Philosophy" (*Antitheta,* "Pride," xiv.).

"He that seeks his own praise, withal seeks the profit of others" (*Antitheta,* "Vain-Glory," xix.).

This is very nearly the text of the sermon embraced in the play of "Timon of Athens":—

Apem. What a coil's here!
Serving of becks and jutting-out of bums!
I doubt whether their legs be worth the sums
That are given for 'em. Friendship's full of dregs:
Methinks, false hearts should never have sound legs.
Thus honest fools lay out their wealth on court'sies.

Tim. Now, Apemantus, if thou wert not sullen, I would be good to thee.
Apem. No, I'll nothing: for if I should be bribed too, there would be none left to rail upon thee, and then thou wouldst sin the faster. Thou givest so long, Timon, I fear me thou wilt give away thyself in paper shortly: what need these feasts, pomps, and vain-glories?

SUSPICION, MALICE, CUNNING, ETC.

Tim. Nay, an you begin to rail on society once, I am sworn not to give regard to you. Farewell ; and come with better music. [*Exit.*
Apem. So :
Thou wilt not hear me now ; thou shalt not then :
I'll lock thy heaven from thee.
O, that men's ears should be
To counsel deaf, but not to flattery !

("Timon," act i. sc. 2.)

"The deformity of *flattery is comical, but the damage tragical*" ("Flattery," *Antitheta,* xxxviii.).

"He that is flexible comes nearest the nature of Gold" ("Facility," xxix., *Ib.*).

The contrast between Apemantus and Timon of Athens is a very fine study of character. Timon is best summed up in the words of Apemantus :—

The middle of Humanity thou never knew'st, but the extremity of both ends.

The character of Apemantus is pretty well indicated by Bacon. "The lighter sort of malignity turneth but to a *crossness* or frowardness, or *aptness to oppose,* or difficileness or the like ; but the deeper sort to envy and mere mischief. Such men in other calamities are, as it were, in season, and are ever on the loading part (*easque semper aggravant*) ; *not so good as the dogs that licked Lazarus' sores, but like flies that are still buzzing upon anything that is raw*" ("Goodness and Goodness of Nature").

The hint Bacon gives us in the word "*dogs*" seems to indicate the school of *cynics* to which class Apemantus belongs, visiting Timon in his misery only to indulge in the pleasure of telling him the truth, and to lick his sores with "I told you so."

2. Away, unpeaceable dog,
Or I'll spurn thee hence.
  Ape. I will fly like a dog, the heels of the ass.
  1. He's opposite to humanity.

("Timon," act i. sc. 1.)

Timon is epicurean, Apemantus stoical and cynical at the same time.

Happy are they that hear their detractions, and can put them to mending.
("Much Ado about Nothing," act ii. sc. 3.)

"For there is no such flatterer as a man's self, and there is no such remedy against flattery of a man's self as the liberty of a friend" ("Friendship").

Apemantus is such a friend to Timon of Athens, but without effect.

> The *learned pate*
> Ducks to the Golden *Fool*. All's oblique.
> ("Timon," act iv. sc. 3.)
>
> Wise men follow fools. (Essay of "Superstition.")
>
> I am *Misanthropos*, and hate mankind.
> ("Timon," act iv. sc. 3.)

"*Misanthropi*, that make it their practice to bring men to the boughs, and yet have *never a tree* for the purpose in their gardens as *Timon had*" ("Goodness and Goodness of Nature").

Compare—

> I have *a tree* which grows here in my close.
> ("Timon," act v. sc. 2.)

Now both Bacon's quotation and Shakespeare's are taken from Plutarch—

"My Lords of Athens, I have a little yard in my house where there groweth a fig *tree*, on the which many citizens have *hanged* themselves; and because I mean to make some building on the place, I thought good to let you all understand it, that before the fig-tree be cut down if any of you be desperate, you may there in time go hang yourselves" (North's Plutarch, "Antonius," p. 100, 2nd ed., 1595).

> Men shut their doors against *a setting sun*.
> ("Timon," act i. sc. 2.)

"Pompey turned upon again, and in effect bade him be quiet. For that more men adored the sun rising, *than the sun setting*" (Essay on "Friendship," 1625). This is borrowed from Plutarch's "Pompey" (xiv.). It is well worthy deep attention that this passage does not occur in the same Essay, edition 1607-12, or edition 1612. Bacon was evidently rewriting the Essays with a view to the insertion of just those touches in contact with the plays, which so justify the title he gives to them, "*De Interiora Rerum,*" or the "*Interior of Things*" (*Vide* "De Augmentis," Satyra Seria, Liber vii.). In this same Essay we find another quotation from *Plutarch's* lines, touching Calphurnia's dream and Decimus Brutus, illustrated by us, to be refound in the play of "Julius Cæsar." Every moment we come across *Plutarch*. For example, in this Essay: "The parable of *Pythagoras* is dark but true; '*Cor ne edito: eat not the heart.*'" This is quoted by *Plutarch* ("De Educ. Puer.," xvii.). Again (Essay on "Friendship"): "*It was well said by Themistocles to the King of Persia; that speech was like cloth of Arras, opened and put abroad, whereby the imagery doth appear in figure; whereas in thoughts they lie but as in packs*" (1625). This is repeated by Plutarch, "Themistocles" (xxix. 4).

"Plutarch saith well to that purpose, 'Surely I had rather a great deal, men should say, there was no such man at all as Plutarch, than that they should say, that there was one Plutarch that would eat his children as soon as they were born, as the poets speak of Saturn" (Essay on "Superstition," 1625, Brit. Museum copy). Plutarch, "De Superstitione," x., Essay on "Fortune," "*Cæsarem portas et Fortunam ejus,*" "So Sylla chose the name of Felix, and not of Magnus" (Plutarch, "Cæsar," xxxviii.; Plutarch, "Sylla," xxxiv.).*

Plutarch is quoted five times in this Essay ("Timoleon," xxxv. 1; "Sylla," vi. 5).

USURY, REVENGE.

That it is against Nature, *for money to beget money.*

("Usury.")

This idea is repeated in the "Merchant of Venice":—

Antonio. Or is your gold and silver ewes and rams.
Shylock. I cannot tell, I make it *breed* as fast.

(Act i. sc. 3.

"As for Mortgaging or Pawning, it will little mend the matter; for either men will not take pawns without *use;* or if they do,

---

* Bacon is as familiar with Plutarch as Shakespeare,—who took Julius Cæsar, Coriolanus, Antony and Cleopatra almost entirely from North's Plutarch.

SUSPICION, MALICE, CUNNING, ETC.

they will look precisely for the Forfeiture. I remember a cruel moneyed man in the country that would say, 'The Devil take this usury, it keeps us from forfeitures of mortgages and bonds" ("Usury").

The use of the words "*Forfeiture,*"* "*bond,*" is frequent in the "Merchant of Venice" in connection with Shylock. If any one seemed qualified to write this play it was Bacon. He had extensive dealings in his life with the Jews in borrowing money, and was once arrested on his return from the Tower, and thrown into a sponging-house, of which indignity he bitterly complained. Out of these difficulties arising from debts he was assisted by the liberality of his brother *Anthony*, whose name in Italian (*Antonio*) appears in this play, acting just such a part towards *Bassanio*. Mr Donnelly has already drawn attention to this. Shylock, indeed, is one who, in Bacon's words, "*will look precisely for the Forfeiture,*" and as a "*cruel moneyed man*" is represented in the play looking rather to his "*Forfeiture of mortgage*" and his "*bond*" in the pound of flesh to be cut from Antonio's body, than to repayment of the capital:—

> *Shy.* My deeds upon my head, I crave the law,
> The penalty and forfeit of my *bond.*
> *Portia.* Is he not able to discharge the money?
> *Bassanio.* Yes, here I tender it for him in the Court;
> Yea, twice the sum, if that will not suffice,
> I will be bound to pay it ten times o'er,
> On forfeit of my hands, my head, my heart:
> If this will not suffice, it must appear
> That malice bears down truth. And I beseech you
> Wrest once the law to your authority.
> *To do a great right, do a little wrong,*
> And curb this *cruel* devil of his will.
> ("Merchant of Venice," act iv. sc. 1.)

Note how we find in this passage the words "*forfeit,*" "*bond,*" "*cruel,*" as we find them in the passage quoted from "Usury." The three Essays, "*Usury,*" "*Revenge,*" "*Friendship,*" illustrate in their titles the "Merchant of Venice," which play idealises

---

* Bacon writes:—"And that which heightens their fear is that they know they are in danger *to forfeit their flesh*, but are not wise of the payment day" ("Of Death").

"Friendship" and "Revenge," the action of the plot revolving upon "Usury," inasmuch as the friendship of Antonio for Bassanio causes him to fall into Shylock's power. Bacon writes:— "Amongst which that of all others is the most frequent, where the question is of *a great deal of good to ensue of a small injustice*" ("Advt.," Book II., xxi., ii.). Compare the lines already quoted:—

> To do a great right, do a little wrong.

"But then let a man take heed, the *Revenge be such, as there is no law to punish:* else a man's enemy is still beforehand, and it is two for one" ("Revenge").

How exactly the spirit of these words finds reflection in the Revenge *Shylock* seeks upon *Antonio* in the "Merchant of Venice!" For the law steps in, through the reading of Portia, to punish Shylock's revenge.

> *Portia.* The law hath yet another hold on you.
> It is enacted in the laws of Venice,
> If it be proved against an alien,
> That by direct or indirect attempts
> He seek the life of any citizen,
> The party 'gainst the which he doth contrive,
> Shall seize one-half his goods, the other half
> Comes to the prize coffer of the State.
> ("Merchant of Venice," act iv. sc. 1.)

"Certainly in taking *Revenge* a man is but even with his enemies; *but in passing it over he is superior:* for it is a Prince's part to pardon" ("Revenge").

> *Duke.* That thou shalt see the difference of our spirit,
> *I pardon thee thy life before thou ask it.*
> ("Merchant of Venice," act iv. sc. 1.)

The whole of this Essay upon Revenge breeds the same spirit of mercy we refind in the play.

> The quality of mercy is not strain'd,
> It droppeth as the gentle rain from heaven
> Upon the place beneath.
> ("Merchant of Venice," act iv. sc. 1.)

"And Solomon, I am sure, saith, *It is the glory of a man to pass by an offence*" ("Revenge").

> It is twice blest,
> It blesseth him that gives and him that takes;
> 'Tis mightiest in the mightiest, it becomes
> The throned monarch better than his crown.
>
> (Act iv. sc. 1.)

In the Essay on "Usury" we read:—"That *Usurers* should have *Orange-tawney Bonnets*, because they do *Judaize*."

It is curious in a note upon this word "orange-tawney" (Glossary, "Essays," Aldis Wright), to find ourselves brought (through Mr Knight) into contact with Shakespeare and with the *Venetians*.

"Orange-tawney, *adj*. Of a dark orange colour. In Knight's 'Shakespeare' (ii. p. 250) it is said, Vecellio, a Venetian, 'expressly informs us that the *Jews* differed in nothing, as far as regarded dress, from *Venetians* of the same professions, whether merchants, artisans, &c., with the exception of a *yellow bonnet*, which they were compelled to wear by order of the government.' See also Sir W. Scott's description of Isaac of York in 'Ivanhoe,' c. 5: 'He wore a high square yellow cap of a peculiar fashion, assigned to his nation to distinguish them from Christians' (E. xli. p. 168)."

Does Bacon introduce this trifle about the colour of the Jew Usurers' Bonnets to give us a hint *for Shylock and Venice?* Orange-tawney was the colour assigned to the Jews by law. And Mr Wright quotes Vecellio to show that the "*yellow bonnet*" *was compulsory in Venice*.

RICHES.

Both in St Matthew's and St Mark's Gospel reference is made to "the *deceitfulness of riches.*" Bacon repeats this in his Essay upon "Riches:" "For certainly great riches have sold more men than they have bought out." We may see this reflected in the play of "Timon of Athens," and in the parable of the three Caskets, exemplified in the "Merchant of Venice". In the parable of the "Pearl of Great Price" we have something akin to the parable of these caskets. This parable teaches us that

SUSPICION, MALICE, CUNNING, ETC. 59

prior to finding this pearl of great price, men are industriously engaged in the pursuit of objects whose value is deceptive and inferior. Like the Princes of Morocco and Arragon they are seeking "goodly," or as it is expressed in the original "beautiful pearls." Every object which they consider valuable and which promises to yield them felicity, is eagerly sought after. Their views, however, are confined within the narrow limits of this life, and have no reference to the invisible world, or the heavenly judgment of Portia. For to select that, they must give and hazard all they have, deny the lust of the flesh and pride of the eye, and seek that which doth rather threaten than promise aught. It is significant that the following speech is put into the mouth of Bassanio, *who makes the right choice of the Caskets*. In our opinion it touches to the heart the entire ethical tendency and promise of this art when thoroughly revealed.

> *Bass.* So may the *outward shows be least themselves,*
> *The world is still deceiv'd with ornament.*
> In Law, what plea so tainted and corrupt
> But being season'd with a gracious voice,
> Obscures the show of evil? In Religion,
> What damned error, but some sober brow
> Will bless it, and approve it with a text,
> Hiding the grossness with fair ornament;
> There is no vice so simple but assumes
> Some marks of virtue *on his outward parts.*
> ("Merchant of Venice," act iii. sc. 2.)

Inasmuch as Bassanio wins Portia with this speech, we may infer these lines have a profound application to ethics. The entire action of the play and the after judgment of Portia revolves upon this *right choice* of Bassanio, summed up in this speech, which really is a reflection upon the *deceitfulness of Riches*, inasmuch as the Princes who chose the Casket of Gold and Silver *were deceived and chose wrongly*. Nor can it be allowed this incident of the Caskets is but a device and no emblem of something deeper. For that Gold is pointed at as Riches cannot be mistaken:—

> *Bassanio.* Therefore then thou *gaudy gold,*
> Hard food for *Midas,* I will none of thee,

> Nor none of thee, thou pale and common drudge
> 'Tween man and man : but thou, thou meagre lead,
> *Which rather threat'nest than doth promise aught,*
> *Thy paleness* moves me more than eloquence,
> And here choose I, joy be the consequence.
>
> (Act iii. sc. 2.)

Portia is undoubtedly an emblem of the *right life*, that is of the inward and true or unworldly life. We are not at all sure the author in the following lines was not suggesting the terms upon which such a life could only be purchased when he wrote, and perhaps hinting at such men as Bruno, Campanella, Galileo, whose devotion to truth was paid down upon the rack, at the stake, or expiated in prison.

> *Bass.* Let me choose ;
> For as I am, I live upon the rack.
> *Por.* Upon the rack, Bassanio ! then confess
> What treason there is mingled with your love.
> *Bass.* None but that ugly treason of mistrust,
> Which makes me fear the enjoying of my love :
> There may as well be amity and life
> 'Tween snow and fire, as treason and my love.
> *Por.* Ay, but I fear you speak upon the rack,
> *Where men enforced do speak anything.*
>
> (Act iii. sc. 2.)

How all this is re-echoed in Bacon's Essay upon "Riches"! "Hearken also to Solomon, and beware of hasty gathering of riches, *qui festinat ad Divitias non erit insons.*" Again : "Of great riches there is no real use, except it be in the distribution ; the rest is *but conceit.* So saith Solomon. Where there is much there are many to consume it ; and what hath the owner but the sight of it with his eyes ? The personal fruition in any man cannot reach to feel great riches. There is a custody of them, or a power of dole and donative of them ; *or a fame of them, but no solid use to the owner*. Do you not see what feigned prices are set upon little stones and rarities ? And what works of ostentation are undertaken because there might seem to be some use of great riches ? For certainly great riches have sold more men than they have bought out" ("Riches").

How many will subscribe to this doctrine in the present day? Or how many who regard the massing of a vast fortune together as the one thing needful, refrain condemning Bacon as a visionary? These however were the real doctrines of the Rosicrucians.

Mr Donnelly, quoting the Rev. Charles Wordsworth, writes: "Take the entire range of English literature, put together our best authors who have written upon subjects professedly not religious or theological, and we shall not find, I believe, in all united, so much evidence of the Bible having been read and used as we have found in Shakespeare alone" ("Great Cryptogram," ch. v., p. 436, vol. i.).

James Brown, in his "Bible Truths," writes: "In Bacon's Essays, the especial favourites of the author, which he so carefully revised and re-wrote in the ripeness of his age and experience, and which therefore may be considered the very cream and essence of his wonderful genius, this characteristic element obtains a prominence that cannot fail to have struck his most cursory reader. Out of these fifty-eight short essays I have found, in twenty-four of them that treat more exclusively of moral subjects, *more than seventy allusions to Scripture*" (preface to first edition, p. 4).

The enormous quantity of parallels and applications from the Scriptures to be found in the plays has created a special literature of its own (Wordsworth's, Brown's, Selkirk's, &c.), to illustrate it. Brown writes, "*that one of his* (the author of the plays) *great teachers indeed was the Bible.*" Bacon's favourite writer, Solomon, finds endless application in the plays. Solomon is alluded to in "Love's Labour Lost" (act i. sc. 2, and act iv. sc. 3), the Queen of Sheba in "King Henry VIII." (act v. sc. 4). Brown illustrates the plays by hundreds of quotations from the Old and New Testaments. Proverbs, the Psalms, Ecclesiastes, the Book of Wisdom, are especially frequent amonst his citations, and these were also favourite books with Bacon. It is impossible to quote them here, for they fill a volume.

Friendship.

"*That a friend is another himself:* for that a *friend is far more than himself*" (Essay of "Friendship").

"A principal fruit of *Friendship* is the ease and discharge of the fulness and swellings of the heart, which passions of all kinds do cause and induce. We know diseases of stoppings and suffocations are the most dangerous in the body; and it is not much otherwise in the mind. You may take *Sarza* to open the liver; *Steele* to open the spleen; Flower of *Sulphur* for the lungs; *Castoreum* for the brain. But no receipt openeth the heart but a true friend, to whom you may impart griefs, joys, fears, hopes, suspicions, counsels, and whatsoever lieth upon the heart, to oppress it in a kind of civil shrift or confession."

How this high value set upon friendship finds its reflection in the plays over and over again,—Hamlet and Horatio,—Bassanio and Antonio,—Valentine and Proteus!

Study how Hamlet *unburthens* his heart to Horatio, and how Bassanio does the same to Antonio:—

> *Bassanio.* To you, Antonio,
> I owe the most in money and in love,
> And from your love I have a warranty,
> *To unburthen all my plots and purposes.*
> ("Merchant of Venice," act i. sc. 1.)

> *Hamlet.* Dost thou hear,
> Since my dear soul was mistress of my choice,
> And could of men distinguish, her election
> Hath sealed thee for herself. For thou hast been
> As one in suffering all, that suffers nothing.
> Give me that man
> That is not passion's slave, and I will wear him
> In my heart's core: in my heart of hearts,
> As I do thee. ("Hamlet," act iii. sc. 2.)

Parents and Children.

"The *illiberality of parents in allowance towards their children* is a harmful error, makes them base, acquaints them with shifts, *makes them sort with mean company*, and makes them surfeit more when they come to plenty" ("Parents and Children").

SUSPICION, MALICE, CUNNING, ETC.

This seems reflected in "As You Like It," where we find *Orlando* opening the play with these words:—

Orl. As I remember, Adam, it was upon this fashion, bequeathed me by will, *but poor a thousand crowns*, and, as thou sayest, charged my brother on his blessing to breed me well, and there begins my sadness. . . . He lets me feed with his hinds, bars me the place of a brother, and as much as in him lies *mines my gentility with my education*.

The elder brother Oliver enters, and a scene ensues between the two:—

Oli. Let me go, I say.
Orl. I will not, till I please: you shall hear me. My father charged you in his will to give me good education: you have trained me like a peasant, obscuring and hiding from me all gentleman-like qualities. The spirit of my father grows strong in me, and I will no longer endure it: therefore allow me such exercises as may become a gentleman, or give me the poor allottery my father left me by testament.

Bacon writes in his Essay on "Envy":—"Lastly, *near kinsfolk* and fellows in office, and those that are bred together, are more apt to envy their equals when they are raised." Again: "*Cain's envy was the more vile and malignant towards his brother Abel because when sacrifice was better accepted there was nobody to look on*" ("Envy"). "*Whoso is out of hope to attain another's virtue will seek to come at even hand by depressing another's fortune*" ("Envy"). "There be times when a man's virtues may be his ruin." Compare this passage:—

SCENE III. *Before* OLIVER'S *house.*

Enter ORLANDO *and* ADAM, *meeting.*

Orl. Who's there?
Adam. What, my young master? O my gentle master!
O my sweet master! O you memory
Of old Sir Rowland! why, what make you here?
Why are you virtuous? why do people love you?
And wherefore are you gentle, strong and valiant?
Why would you be so fond to overcome
The bonny priser of the humorous duke?
Your praise is come too swiftly home before you.
Know you not, master, to some kind of men
Their graces serve them but as enemies?
No more do yours: your virtues, gentle master,
Are sanctified, and holy traitors to you.

> O, what a world is this, when what is comely
> Envenoms him that bears it!
> *Orl.* Why, what's the matter?
> *Adam.* O, unhappy youth!
> Come not within these doors; within this roof
> The enemy of all your graces lives;
> Your brother—no, no brother; yet the son—
> Yet not the son, I will not call him son
> Of him I was about to call his father—
> Hath heard your praises, and this night he means
> To burn the lodging where you use to lie
> And you within it; if he fail of that,
> He will have other means to cut you off.
> I overheard him and his practices. (Act ii. sc. 3.)

"FOLLOWERS AND FRIENDS," "SUITORS," "FACTIONS."

Bacon's two Essays upon "Followers and Friends" and upon "Suitors" follow each other in succession, as if some connection existed between them. The play of "Titus Andronicus" is remarkable for the divisions and "*factions*" of the "*followers*" of Saturninus and of Titus Andronicus. The play opens with the respective claim and appeal of each of the two sons of the late Emperor of Rome to the throne.

> *Saturnine.* Noble Patricians, Patrons of my right,
> Defend the justice of my cause with arms,
> And countrymen my loving *followers*
> Plead my successive title with your swords.
> *Bassianus.* Romans, *Friends, Followers,*
> Favourers of my Right. . . . (Act i. sc. 1.)

Marcus Andronicus (brother to Titus) enters with a crown, and cries—

> Princes *that strive by Factions and by Friends,*
> Ambitiously for rule and empery;
> . . . .
> Dismiss your *Followers,* and as *Suitors* should
> Plead your deserts in peace and humbleness.
>
> (Act i. sc. 1.)

We quote this to illustrate the introduction of the expressions "Followers and Friends," coupled as by Bacon (with "*Followers*") in close context with "*Suitors.*" Bacon's Essay upon "*Faction*" follows (next to one) the Essay upon "*Suitors.*" Consider how largely these matters enter into the historical plays like the one we cite. For the three chronicle plays of "Henry the Sixth" largely deal with the factions of the Roses, Yorke and Lancaster. "Troilus and Cressida" also present the factions of Ajax and Achilles and their rival quarrels. So that we may perceive Bacon had some good reasons in presenting us with the Essays upon "Faction," "Followers and Friends," "Seditions and Troubles," "Empire," &c., touching as they do a vast deal of the action of these plays.

Bacon writes in this Essay on "Faction":—"The faction, or party, of Antonius and Octavianus Cæsar, against Brutus and Cassius, held out likewise for a time: but when Brutus and Cassius were overthrown, then soon after Antonius and Octavianus brake and subdivided." How exactly and faithfully all this is represented and set forth in the plays of "Julius Cæsar" and "Antony and Cleopatra"! For example, immediately after Mark Antony's funeral oration over the body of Cæsar, and the reading of the will, by which Antony sets the people of Rome into infinite uproar against the murderers, we find Octavius introduced:—

> 2 *Ple.* Go, fetch fire.
> 3 *Ple.* Pluck down benches.
> 4 *Ple.* Pluck down forms.
>
> *Enter* SERVANT.
>
> *Servant.* Sir, Octavius is already come to Rome.
> *Ant.* Where is he?
> *Servant.* He and Lepidus are at Cæsar's house.
> *Ant.* And thither will I straight to visit them.
>
> (Act iii.)

This is at the conclusion of the third act. The next act opens with the introduction of Antony, Octavius, and Lepidus sitting in council as a faction or triumvirate, and the play ends with the overthrow of the other faction of Brutus and his death at Philippi. Bacon writes in his Essay on "Prophecies": "A *phantasm* that appeared to M. Brutus in his tent said to him, *Philippis iterum me videbis* ('Thou shalt see me again at Philippi')."

This is introduced at the end of the fourth act, "Julius Cæsar" (scene 3):—

Enter the GHOST OF CÆSAR.

Brutus. How ill this taper burns ! Ha ! who comes here ?
I think it is the weakness of mine eyes
That shapes this monstrous apparition.
It comes upon me. Art thou anything ?
Art thou some god, some angel, or some devil,
That makest my blood cold and my hair to stare ?
Speak to me what thou art.
Ghost. Thy evil spirit, Brutus.
Bru. Why comest thou ?
Ghost. To tell thee thou shalt see me at Philippi.
Bru. Well ; then I shall see thee again ?
Ghost. Ay, at Philippi.
Bru. Why, I will see thee at Philippi, then.

[*Exit Ghost.*

If we now turn to the play of "Antony and Cleopatra," we find Bacon's remarks about the breaking up of the faction between Antony and Octavius, prominently depicted in the sixth scene of the third act, where Octavius Cæsar is introduced (with Agrippa and Mæcenas), complaining of Antony's conduct at Alexandria with Cleopatra. The rest of the play is but the history of the dismemberment of the Triumvirate, and final war between Cæsar and Antony, resulting in the battle of Actium. In context with the passage quoted on "faction" by Bacon, we read as if a hint for Lepidus:—" And therefore those that are *seconds in factions*, do many times, when the faction subdivideth, prove principals: *but many times also they prove cyphers and cashiered.*" This was the fate of Lepidus, and in the play we find Cæsar saying of Antony:—

Lastly he frets,
That *Lepidus* of the triumvirate *should be deposed*,
And being that, we detain all his revenue.

(Act iii. sc. 6.)

Lepidus is presented throughout the play *as a complete cipher.* Antony, in an interview with Cæsar, thus speaks of him:—

Let this fellow
Be *nothing of our strife;* if we contend,
Out of our question wipe him.

("Antony and Cleopatra," act ii. sc. 2.)

Antony again alludes to Lepidus, who has just been despatched to fetch Cæsar's will:—

> *Ant.* This is a *slight unmeritable man,*
> Meet to be sent on errands: is it fit
> The three-fold world divided, he should stand,
> One of the three to share it?
> *Oct.* So you thought him,
> And took his voice who should be prickt to die
> In our black sentence and proscription.
> *Ant.* Octavius, I have seen more days than you,
> And though we lay these honours on this man,
> *To ease ourselves of divers sland'rous loads,*
> He shall but bear them as the ass bears gold
> To groan and sweat under the business,
> Either led or driven as we point the way.
>
> (Act iv. sc. 1.)

"*In order to divert Envy from themselves,*" Bacon writes:—"the wiser sort of great person, bring in ever upon the stage, *somebody, upon whom to derive the envy, that would come upon themselves; sometimes upon ministers and servants; sometimes upon colleagues and associates*" ("Envy").

It is true that "*sland'rous loads*" is not exactly envy, but envy begets slander, and there is generally very little slander where there is absence of envy. Bacon further explains it: "This envy being in the Latin word *Invidia*, goeth in the modern languages by the name of *discontentment*, of which we shall speak in handling of *sedition.* It is a disease in a state, like to infection."

In Bacon's Essay on "Love":—"You must except nevertheless *Marcus Antonius,* the half partner of the Empire of Rome; and Appius Claudius, the Decemvir and Law-giver: *whereof the former was indeed a voluptuous man and inordinate.*" This is as he is represented in the play of "Antony and Cleopatra," and as he is depicted by Plutarch, from whom so much is borrowed.

"And it is not amiss to observe also how small and mean faculties gotten by education, yet when they fall into great men or great matters, do work great and important effects: whereof we see a notable example in Tacitus of *two stage players*, Percennius and Vibulenus, who by their faculty of playing, put the Pannonian armies into an extreme tumult and combustion. For there arising a mutiny amongst them upon the death of Augustus Cæsar, Blæsus the lieutenant had committed some of the mutiners, which were suddenly rescued; whereupon Vibulenus got to be heard speak, which he did in this manner: *These poor innocent wretches appointed to cruel death, you have restored to behold the light: but who shall restore my brother to me, or life unto my brother, that was sent hither in message from the legions of Germany, to treat of the common cause? And he hath murdered him this last night by some of his fencers and ruffians, that he hath about him for his executioners upon soldiers. Answer, Blæsus, what is done with his body? The mortalest enemies do not deny burial. When I perform my last duties to the corpse with kisses, with tears, command me to be slain besides him; so that these my fellows, for our good meaning and our true hearts to the legions, may have leave to bury us.* With which speech he put the army into an infinite fury and uproar: whereas truth was he had no brother, neither was there any such matter; *but he played it merely as if he had been upon the stage*" (Book II. xix. 3, "Advancement of Learning," 1605).

This is another example of how everything connected with *the stage or with the art of acting* drew Bacon's attention, and held fast his mind, so that what he read in Tacitus of these *two stage players*, Percennius and Vibulenus, he treasures up in his memory and cites here. But what is really far more pertinent than this simple observation of ours, is the extraordinary parallel furnished by the "speech" of Antony, over the body of Cæsar, in "Julius Cæsar," where the arts of the actor are so excellently combined with the arts of oratory:—

> I come to bury Cæsar, not to praise him,
> . . . . . .
> I know not, gentlemen, what you intend,
> Who else must be let blood, who else is rank:
> If I myself there is no hour so fit
> As Cæsar's death hour; nor no instrument
> Of half that worth, as those your swords; made rich

> With the most noble blood of all this world.
> I do beseech you, if you bear me hard,
> Now whilst your purple hands do reek and smoke
> Fulfil your pleasure. Live a thousand years,
> I shall not find myself so apt to die.
> No place will please me so, no mean of death,
> As here by Cæsar, and by you cut off,
> The choice and master spirits of this age.
>
> ("Julius Cæsar.")

The entire speech of Mark Antony is too long to quote here. But the end of his oration over Cæsar's body has the same result as the speech of Vibulenus Bacon quotes. Antony sets the people of Rome into a state of "*infinite fury and uproar*" by his skill in the art of acting, for whilst disclaiming any direct charge against Brutus with the iterated words, "*For Brutus is an honourable man, so are they all; all honourable men,*" he so depicts the virtues of the dead Cæsar, and works upon the feelings of his audience, that a direct denunciation of the murderers could hardly have attained its end better. In the play of "Hamlet," we see the same effect produced by the introduction of the players and Interlude. The art of dissimulation for ends was never more exquisitely illustrated. In Bacon's Essays upon "Dissimulation" and "Cunning" may be refound the arts of which Antony makes use. "For if a man have that penetration of judgment, as he can discern what things are to *be laid open, and what to be secreted, and what to be shown at half lights*, and to whom and when (which indeed are arts of state and arts of life, as Tacitus well calleth them)," &c.

> Is it not monstrous that this *player here*,
> *But in a fiction, in a dream of passion*,
> Could force his soul so to his own conceit,
> That from her working all his visage warm'd,
> Tears in his eyes, distraction in's aspect,
> A broken voice, and his whole function suiting
> With forms to his conceit? And all for nothing!
> For Hecuba!
> What's Hecuba to him or he to Hecuba,
> That he should weep for her?
>
> ("Hamlet," act ii. sc. 2.)

CHAPTER IV.

DIVINATION AND PREDICTION.

UPON Divination or Prediction (Book II. ch. xi. "Advancement of Learning")—that is, Prophecy, Bacon writes: "But the divination which springeth from the internal nature of the soul, is that which we now speak of; which hath been made to be of two sorts, primitive and by influxion. Primitive is grounded upon the supposition, that the mind, when it is withdrawn and collected into itself, and not diffused into the organs of the body, hath some extent and latitude of prenotion; *which therefore appeareth most in sleep, in ecstasies, and near death,* and more rarely in waking apprehensions; and is induced and furthered by those abstinences and observances which make the mind most to consist in itself."

Now I wish to draw attention to the striking parallel, that throughout what is miscalled Shakespeare's art, we refind this prenotion of the mind, introduced either in sleep or before death:—

> Methinks I am a prophet new inspired,
> *And thus expiring do foretell of him.*
>
> ("Richard II.," act ii. sc. 1, 31, 32.)

Let the readers recall the vision of Richard the Third just before his death, or of Brutus before Philippi, in "Julius Cæsar," or of Juliet's presentiment and Romeo's dream:—

> *Jul.* O God, I have an ill-divining soul!
> Methinks I see thee, now thou art below,
> As one dead in the bottom of a tomb:
> Either my eyesight fails, or thou look'st pale.
> *Rom.* If I may trust the flattering truth of sleep
> My dreams presage some joyful news at hand:
> My bosom's lord sits lightly in his throne;
> And all this day an unaccustom'd spirit

DIVINATION AND PREDICTION. 71

> Lifts me above the ground with cheerful thoughts.
> I dreamt my lady came and found me dead.
>
> (Act v. sc. 1.)

Or Clarence's dream just before his death:—

> *Clarence.* O, I have passed a miserable night,
> So full of fearful dreams of ugly sights.
> . . . . . .
> Oh then began the Tempest to my soul
> . . . . . .
> Then came wand'ring by
> A shadow like an angel, with bright hair,
> Dabbl'd in blood, and he shriek'd out aloud,
> "Clarence is come, false fleeting, perjur'd Clarence,
> That stabb'd me in the field by Tewkesbury:
> Seize on him, Furies, take him unto torment."
>
> ("Richard III.," act i. sc. 4.)

Immediately following the relation of this Dream, the two murderers enter. So that we find Bacon's connection of dreams of a prophetic character, with nearness of death, to be strictly carried out in the plays. Hamlet, just before his death, exclaims:—

Hamlet. But thou would'st not think how ill all's here about my heart: but it is no matter.

Horatio. Nay good, my Lord.

Ham. It is but foolery; but it is such a kind of gain-giving as would perhaps trouble a woman.

Hor. If your mind dislike anything, obey it. I will forestall their repair hither, and say you are not fit.

Ham. Not a whit, we defy *Augury*, there's a special Providence in the fall of a sparrow. If it be now, 'tis not to come; if it be not to come, it will be now; if it be not now, yet it will come; the readiness is all.

("Hamlet," act v., last scene.)

Upon the same page Bacon discusses Divination he introduces Augury: "Divination hath been anciently and fitly divided into two parts, artificial and natural. Artificial is of two sorts, one argueth from causes, the other from experiments only, by a blind way of authority; which latter is for the most part superstitious, such was the heathen discipline upon the *inspection of the entrails of beasts, the flight of birds,* and the like" (ch. iii. Book IV. "De Augmentis").

DIVINATION AND PREDICTION.

The reader will see Bacon has *Augury* associated in his mind in context with divination, and we refind Hamlet terming his presentiment *Augury* also. The dream of Calphurnia, just prior to Cæsar's assassination, is another example in point:—

> *Cæs.* Nor heaven nor earth have been at peace to-night:
> Thrice hath Calpurnia in her sleep cried out,
> "Help, ho! they murder Cæsar!" Who's within?
> ("Julius Cæsar," act ii. sc. 2.)

Here again augury is introduced in context with prophetic dreams:—

> *Cæs.* Cowards die many times before their deaths:
> The valiant never taste of death but once.
> Of all the wonders that I yet have heard,
> It seems to me most strange that men should fear:
> Seeing that death, a necessary end,
> Will come when it will come.
>
> *Re-enter* SERVANT.
>
> What say the augurers?
> *Serv.* They would not have you to stir forth to-day.
> Plucking the entrails of an offering forth,
> They could not find a heart* within the beast.
> *Cæs.* The gods do this in shame of cowardice:
> Cæsar should be a beast without a heart,
> If he should stay at home to-day for fear.
> No, Cæsar shall not: danger knows full well
> That Cæsar is more dangerous than he:
> We are two lions litter'd in one day,
> And I the elder and more terrible:
> And Cæsar shall go forth.
>
> ("Julius Cæsar," *Ib.*)

In "Titus Andronicus" we find Augury introduced, and a soothsayer in "Cymbeline." These points reveal profound study of the classics, and it is most improbable Shakespeare had either the leisure or learning to acquaint himself with such niceties. We are now about to point out how well the author was

---

* The absence of the heart was considered a prodigy of extraordinary omen. It was accounted amongst the *Pestifera auspicia cum cor in extis aut caput in jocinore non fuisset* ("Paul," s. v. p. 244). Cicero mentions how Cæsar was in this manner forewarned that his purple robe and golden throne would bring about his death (Cic., "Divin.," ii. 16; Plin., *Ibid.*).

acquainted with Cicero's writings, and with his peculiar scepticism, as to the validity of these following unnatural events, introduced as foreshadowing Cæsar's death :—

> *Casca.* A common slave—you know him well by sight—
> Held up his left hand, which did flame and burn
> Like twenty torches join'd, and yet his hand,
> Not sensible of fire, remain'd unscorch'd.
> Besides—I ha' not since put up my sword—
> Against the Capitol I met a lion,
> Who glared upon me, and went surly by,
> Without annoying me : and there were drawn
> Upon a heap a hundred ghastly women,
> Transformed with their fear ; who swore they saw
> Men all in fire walk up and down the streets.
> And yesterday the bird of night did sit
> Even at noon-day upon the market-place,
> Hooting and shrieking. When these prodigies
> Do so conjointly meet, let not men say
> "These are their reasons ; they are natural ;"
> For, I believe, they are portentous things
> Unto the climate that they point upon.
>
>   *Cic.* Indeed, it is a strange-dispos'd time :
> *But men may construc things, after their fashion,*
> *Clean from the purpose of the things themselves.*
> Comes Cæsar to the Capitol to-morrow ?
>
>   *Casca.* He doth ; for he did bid Antonius
> Send word to you he would be there to-morrow.
>
>   *Cic.* Good night, then, Casca ; this disturbed sky
> Is not to walk in.
>
>   *Casca.*   Farewell, Cicero.
>   ("Julius Cæsar," act i. sc. 3.)

There can be no doubt from the words put in the mouth of Cicero, the author of the plays was well acquainted with Cicero's writings and Cicero's sceptical mind. Cicero belonged to a sect that professed to hold *nothing for certain*, as to Divine matters especially. Saint Augustine is severe upon Cicero for denying the prescience of Providence, whilst allowing the existence of Deity. Almost throughout the entire ninth chapter of his "City of God," he attacks Cicero upon this point. In the person of Cotta (First Book, "Touching the Nature of the Gods"), "I wish I could but as easily find out what's true, as I can confute that which is false." It is just in regard to these omens or portents introduced by Bacon in "Julius Cæsar," that Cicero is made to question their *prescience*, that is, their connection with a foreknowledge of things to come, as tokens of Deity (see Second Book "Divination"). Bacon's predilection for Cicero throughout his "Essays" and "Advancement of Learning" is marked, quoting him almost every dozen pages or oftener. In the "De Augmentis" Cicero is cited thirty-one times. In a letter addressed to Andrews, Lord Bishop of Winchester, written after his disgrace, and prefixed to "An Advertisement touching an Holy War," Bacon compares his fall to Cicero's and Seneca's. This is a hint of the greatest possible importance, implying that Bacon resembled these illustrious men in persecution, as being the victims of their times and the sacrifices of faction. But what study and reflection the passage from "Julius Cæsar" illustrates! A trifle like this is akin to a revelation, for the more we discover the learning of the writer of these plays, the more difficult becomes the Shakespeare myth to believe.

In concluding his Book upon "Divination," Cicero parallels in some measure Lucretius:—"Let us end" (he writes) "with this Divination by Dreams, as with the rest. For, to speak truly, Superstition spread amongst people, has weighed with its yoke upon almost all mankind, and taken by storm the imbecility of humanity. We have already declared so in our books upon the 'Nature of the Gods,' and we there have insisted upon it in the discussions introduced; for we believe we are rendering a great service to ourselves, and to our fellow-citizens, in suppressing it altogether" (Cicero's "Divination," ii. 72, 2).

Again:—"If some dreams are true and some false, I should like to learn how we are to distinguish them. If there is no method, wherefore listen to these interpreters? If there is one I am curious to know what it is; but they will be embarrassed to disclose it" (Cicero's "Divination," ii. 62).

The Latin expressions for these sorts of omens were *prodigium, vortentum, ostentum, monstrum.*

DIVINATION AND PREDICTION.

In "Cymbeline" (last act) we have Jupiter introduced "sitting upon an eagle," with a soothsayer who divines in quite a classically inspired sense. The eagle (ἀετός) was the special messenger of Jupiter, and, according to Homer, was "the most accomplished of birds" ("Iliad," viii. 247; xxiv. 310. *Cf.* Pind., "Isthm.," vi. (v.) 50; Xenoph., "Anab.," vi. 1, 23). Theocritus styles this bird *par excellence* the bird of Divination, a distinction which later on was disputed by the vulture (Theoc., "Idyll," xxvi. 31; "Etymol. Magn.," p. 619, 39).

> *Soothsayer.* For the Roman eagle
> From South to West on wing soaring aloft
> Lessen'd herself, and in the beams of the sun
> So vanish'd; which *foreshadowed* our Princely eagle,
> The imperial Cæsar should again unite
> His favour with the radiant Cymbeline,
> Which shines here in the West.
>
> ("Cymbeline," act v.)

This shows the writer was well versed in the art of Divination, for the Eagle, the Vulture, and the Crow were the three chief birds of Roman Vaticination. During sleep, Posthumus Leonatus has a vision of the descent of Jupiter, and finds himself in possession of a book—"a rare one." Now this shows the extraordinary classical erudition of the author, for there were held to be *messenger dreams* sent by Jupiter or Zeus, as we shall show, amongst the ancients. With Homer dreams are ærial shadows or images (εἴδωλα), which take the shape of forms. Thus the one that appeared to Agamemnon took the likeness of Nestor ("Iliad," ii. 5). Athené appears in a dream to Nausicaa and to Telemachus, and Patroclus thus demanded Achilles to hasten his funeral. (Hom., "Odyss.," vi. 13; xv. 10; "Iliad," xxiii. 65). With Homer dreams are sent by Zeus ("Iliad," i. 63). *Zeus alone possesses the power to summon dreams from afar off.* The Pythagorean mysticism considered dreams as the sons of night and the messengers of the moon, of that moon which crept into the grotto of Latmos, close to Endymion asleep, or which unsealed the prophetic soul of the Sybil. Bacon slyly hints at this when he writes:—"It is said that Luna was in love with the shepherd Endymion, and in a strange and unwonted manner betrayed her affection; for he, lying in a cave framed by nature under the mountain Latmos, she sometimes descended from her sphere to enjoy his company as he slept; and after she had kissed him ascended up again" (Endymion, "Wisdom of the Ancients").

> Peace, how the Moon sleeps with Endymion,
> And would not be awak'd.
>
> ("Merchant of Venice," act v.)

And mark what Bacon quotes (from Philo Jud.):—"For sense, like the Sun, opens and reveals the face of the terrestrial Globe, *but shuts up and conceals the face of the Celestial*" (Preface to the "Instauration"). This is as much as to say it is *at night only* we discover the depths of the stars, and intellect must shut out sense, be blind to externals, to perceive by the mind's eye supernatural truths. The sense's night being the opener of the mind's truths. There is no doubt Bacon introduces the incident of Posthumus' dream, with the strange oracle and "rare book," in "Cymbeline" as an act symbolic of *Divination* in the full classic sense of *inspired truth*. I cannot allow it is fiction, or without relationship to some as yet-to-be-discovered reality. The title Posthumus points to an *after birth*, and is wholly in keeping with all we have to expect of this art, as full of revelatory matter. It is strange to find Sir Toby Matthew affixing his seal to a curious document entitled "*Posthumus, or the Survivor*," in 1640, the date of the first edition of the translation of the "De Augmentis." (See Doctor Neligan's strange manuscript, published by Mr Smith in the little work, which first seriously started the Baconian theory.) The introduction of Jupiter can surprise no one who remembers how Bacon declares, he is going with the ancients *usque ad aras*. "But I going the same road as the ancients."

Bacon once more shows he possessed the knowledge we have refound in the plays, both in "Julius Cæsar" and in "Cymbeline," upon augury.

DIVINATION AND PREDICTION.

> *Scarus.* Swallows have built
> In Cleopatra's sails their nests : the augurers
> Say they know not, they cannot tell ; look grimly,
> And dare not speak their knowledge.
> ("Antony and Cleopatra," act iv. sc. 12.)

Bacon's Essay upon "Friendship :—" *With Julius Cæsar, Decimus Brutus* had obtained that interest as he set him down in his testament, for heir in remainder after his nephew. And this was the man that had power with him, *to draw him forth to his death.* For when *Cæsar* would have discharged the Senate, in regard of some ill presages, and specially a dream of *Calphurnia,* this man lifted him gently by the arm out of his chair, telling him he hoped he would not dismiss the Senate till his wife *had dreamt a better dream.*"

The whole of this is *exactly reproduced in* the play of "Julius Cæsar" (act ii.) :—

> *Deci. Brutus.* Cæsar, all hail ; good morrow, worthy Cæsar,
> I come to fetch you to the Senate house.
> *Cæsar.* And you are come in very happy time,
> To bear my greeting to the Senators,
> And tell them that I will not come to-day.
> *Deci. Brutus.* Most mighty *Cæsar,* let me know some cause,
> Lest I be laught at when I tell them so.
> *Cæsar.* The cause is in my Will, I will not come,
> That is enough to satisfy the Senate,
> But for your private satisfaction,
> Because I love you, I will let you know.
> *Calphurnia* here, my wife, stays me at home ;
> She *dreamt to-night* she saw my statue,
> Which like a fountain with an hundred spouts
> Did run pure blood ; and many lusty Romans
> Came smiling and did bathe their hands in it.

To all this D. Brutus replies:—

> When *Cæsar's* wife shall meet with *better dreams,*
> If *Cæsar* hide himself, shall they not whisper,
> Lo, *Cæsar* is afraid ?

This is exactly as Bacon writes, and the dream is given in the play in detail by *Calphurnia.*

PERSPECTIVE, REFLECTION, GLASS-MIRROR.

"Praise is the *reflection of virtue. But it is glass or body which giveth the reflection*" ("Praise").

Bacon means here (as he points out in "Troilus and Cressida") we cannot obtain fame, praise, or glory until it is seen *reflected by others*. This is endlessly repeated in the plays. When Richard the Second sends for *a glass or mirror* and beholds himself, he exclaims :—

> O flattering glass,
> *Like to my followers in prosperity,*
> *Thou dost beguile me!* (Act iv. sc. i.)

> He was the mark and glass, copy and book
> That fashion'd others.
> ("2 Henry VI.," act ii. sc. 3.)

This is a very profound simile. Because we can never see *ourselves at all in life, as others see us, and a glass is not the same thing as sight.*

> Tell me, good Brutus, can you see your face?
> *Bru.* No, Cassius; for the eye sees not itself,
> But by reflection, by some other things.
> *Cas.* 'Tis just;
> And it is very much lamented, Brutus,
> And you have no such mirrors as will turn
> Your hidden worthiness into your eye
> That you might see your shadow.
> Therefore, good Brutus, be prepared to hear:
> And since you know *you cannot see yourself*
> *So well as by reflection, I, your glass,*
> Will modestly discover to yourself
> That of yourself which you yet know not of.
> ("Julius Cæsar," act i. sc. 1.)

"That window which Momus once requited. He when he saw in the frame of man's heart so many angles and recesses, found fault *there was not a window, through which a man might look into those obscure and crooked windings*" (Lib. VIII., p. 401, "Advancement of Learning," 1640).

PERSPECTIVE, REFLECTION, GLASS-MIRROR.

> Now see what good turns eyes for eyes have done:
> Mine eyes have drawn my shape, and thine for me
> *Are windows to my breast*, where through the sun
> Delights to peep, to gaze therein on thee.
>
> (Sonnet xxiv.)

"Like a true friend to show you *your true shape in a glass*, and that not in a false one to flatter you, nor yet in one that should make you seem worse than you are, and so offend you; but in one made by the *reflection of your own words and actions*" ("Letter lxx. to Lord Chief Justice Coke," 1702.)

"And the more aptly is the mind of a wise man compar'd *to a glass or mirror, because in a glass his own image may be seen together with the images of others, which the eyes cannot do of themselves without a glass*" (Parable xxxiv., Lib. VIII., "Advancement of Learning," p. 397).

> It may do good, pride hath no other glass
> To show itself but pride.
>
> ("Troilus and Cressida," act iii. sc. 3.)

> Methinks you are my glass, and not my brother;
> *I see by you* I am a sweet-faced youth.
>
> ("Comedy of Errors," act v. sc. 1.)

> Come, come, and sit you down; you shall not budge;
> *You go not till I set you up a glass,*
> *Where you may see the inmost part of you.*
>
> ("Hamlet," act iii. sc. 4.)

Your mind is the clearer, Ajax, and your virtues the fairer; he that is proud eats up himself. *Pride is his own glass*, his own trumpet, his own chronicle, and whatever praises itself but in the deed, devours the deed in the praise. ("Troilus and Cressida.")

"Grounded upon the conceit, that the mind *as a mirror or glass*, should take illumination from the foreknowledge of God and spirits" (Book II., "Advancement of Learning," p. 46, 1605).

"God hath framed *the mind of man as a mirror or glass* capable of the image of the universal world" (Book I. p. 6, "Advancement of Learning," 1640).

"The more shame for learned men, if they be for knowledge like *winged angels;* for base desires they be like serpents which crawl in the dust, carrying indeed about them Minds *like a mirror or glass*, but menstruous and distain'd" (Book V., p. 217, "Advancement of Learning," 1640).

"Praises are the reflexed beams of virtue" ("Antitheta," p. 304).

> Yea from the *glass-faced flatterer*
> To Apemantus.
>
> ("Timon of Athens," act i. sc. 1.)

Here again is the perfect and original philosophy of Bacon's, that we *see ourselves in other's faces*, and it is a far profounder simile than at first sight strikes us. For do we not see *by others* whether it goes ill or well with us? And as our own image in a mirror pleases us or no, so does the reflection react upon our self-consciousness.

> 'Tis not her glass but you that flatters her,
> And out of you she sees herself more proper
> Than any of her lineaments can show her.
> ("As you Like It," act iii. sc. 5.)

Essay on "Friendship:—"For as *S. James* saith, they are as men, *that look sometimes into a glass, and presently forget their own shape and favour.*" *

Compare " Richard the Second " (act iv. sc. 3) :—

> *Richard.* Give me that glass, and therein will I read,
>
> . . . . .
>
> Was this the face, the face
> That every day, under his household roof,
> Did keep ten thousand men? Was this the face,
> That like the sun, did make beholders wink?
> Is this the face, which fac'd so many follies,
> That was at last out-fac'd by Bolingbroke?
>
> . . . . .
>
> *How soon my sorrow hath destroy'd my face?*

---

* " The second precept concerning this knowledge is, for men to take good information touching their own person, and well to understand themselves: knowing that, as S. James saith, though men look oft in a glass, yet they do suddenly forget themselves; wherein as the divine glass is the word of God, so the politic glass is the state of the world, or times wherein we live, in the which we are to behold ourselves " (Two Books of "Advancement of Learning," p. 234).

PERSPECTIVE, REFLECTION, GLASS-MIRROR.

> *Bolingbroke.* The shadow of your sorrow hath destroy'd
> The shadow of your face.
>   *Richard.*   Say that again.
> The shadow of my sorrow ; ha, let's see,
> 'Tis very true, my grief lies all within,
> And these external manner of laments
> Are merely shadows to the unseen grief,
> That swells with silence in the tortur'd soul.
>
> (Act iv. sc. 1.)

"For the mind of man is far from the nature of a clear and equal *glass*, wherein the *beams* of things should *reflect* according to their true incidence" ("Advancement of Learning," Bk. II. p. 55).

> May never glorious sun *reflex his beams*.
> ("1 King Henry VI.," act v. sc. 4.)

"I believe well that this your Lordship's absence will rather *be a glass unto you*, to show you many things, whereof you may make use hereafter" ("Letter to the Marquis of Buckingham," March 10, 1622).

"*Organa sensuum cum organis reflectionum conveniunt.* This hath place *in Perspective Art ; for the eye is like to a glass*, or to waters" (Lib. III., p. 135, "De Augmentis," 1640). From the note in the margin, Bacon has taken this from the Arabian writer Alhazen* ("Optics," Vitello).

Alhazen was a Spanish Moor who discovered atmospheric

---

* It is very striking to find Bacon had been studying the works of this extraordinary man, particularly as he makes no further mention of him elsewhere. It shows Bacon's knowledge of the most advanced discoveries and thought, was far deeper than we have any idea of. Draper maintains our debt to the Arabians and Spanish Moors in scientific discoveries to have been enormous and as yet half recognised. In Bacon's "Holy War" there is a curious and suspicious reference to these Moors :—

Pollio. "What say you to the Extirpation of the Moors of Valentia ?" At which sudden question Martius was a little at a stop, and Gamaliel prevented him and said, "I think Martius did well in omitting that action, for *I, for my part, never approved of it ; and it seems God was not well pleased with that deed.*"

It is to the Arabians Alchemy owes its origin, particularly to Geher. Friar Bacon was another writer upon this subject, and we may observe in him the use of induction and observation of facts in nature quite after the Baconian method.

refraction. His date was about A.D. 1100. "He was the first to correct the Greek misconception as to the nature of vision, showing that the rays of light come from external objects to the eye, and do not issue forth from the eye and impinge on external things, as up to his time had been supposed. He determined that the retina is the seat of vision, and that impressions made by light upon it are conveyed along the optic nerve to the brain. With extraordinary acuteness, he applies the principles with which he is dealing to the determination of the height of the atmosphere, deciding its limit as nearly $58\frac{1}{2}$ miles. One of his works is entitled, 'The Book of the Balance of Wisdom.' In this book the weight of the atmosphere is set forth, and he further explains the theory of the balance and steelyards, showing the relations between the centre of gravity and the centre of suspension—when those instruments will set and when they will vibrate. He recognises gravity as a force; asserts that it diminishes with the distance. He knows the relation between the velocities, spaces and times of falling bodies, and has very distinct ideas of capillary attraction. He improves the construction of that old Alexandrian invention the Hydrometus. The determination of the densities of bodies, as given by Alhazen, approach very closely to our own; in the case of mercury they are even more exact than some of those of the last century. I join, as, doubtless, all natural philosophers will do, in the pious prayer of Alhazen, that in the day of judgment, the All-Merciful will take pity on the soul of Abur-Rachân, because he was the first of the race of men to construct a table of specific gravities; and I will ask the same for Alhazen himself, since he was the first to trace the curvilinear path of a ray of light through the air. Though more than seven centuries part him from our times, the physiologists of this age may accept him as their compeer, since he received and defended the doctrine now forcing its way of the progressive development of animal forms" (Draper's "Intellectual Development of Europe," vol. ii. pages 45, 46, 47, 48).

PERSPECTIVE, REFLECTION, GLASS-MIRROR.

The Fable of Narcissus or Self-Love in "The Wisdom of the Ancients" should be read in connection with this subject. Bacon writes that Narcissus, "having espied the shadow of his own face in the water, was so besotted and ravished with the contemplation and admiration thereof, that he by no means possible could be drawn from beholding his image in this *glass*; insomuch, that by continual gazing thereupon, he pined away to nothing, and was at last turned into a flower of his own name, which appears in the beginning of the spring, and is sacred to the infernal powers *Pluto, Proserpine*, and the *Furies*." In the following Sonnet may be found "Perspective" introduced as illusion :—

XXIV.

Mine eye hath play'd the painter and hath stell'd
Thy beauty's form in table of my heart;
My body is the frame wherein 'tis held,
And perspective it is best painter's art.
For through the painter must you see his skill,
To find where your true image pictured lies;
Which in my bosom's shop is hanging still,
That hath his windows glazed with thine eyes.
Now see what good turns eyes for eyes have done:
Mine eyes have drawn thy shape, and thine for me
Are windows to my breast, where-through the sun
Delights to peep, to gaze therein on thee;
  Yet eyes this cunning want to grace their art:
  They draw but what they see, know not the heart.

Like perspectives, which rightly gazed upon
Show nothing but confusion—ey'd awry,
Distinguish form.

("Richard II.," act ii. sc. 2.)

A natural perspective that is and is not.

("Twelfth Night.")

"*Like perspectives which show things inwards when they are but paintings*" (Bacon, "Natural History," Cent. i. 98).

"*Poesy*, in the sense in which I have defined the word, *is also concerned with individuals;* that is, with individuals invented in imitation of those which are the subject of true history; yet with this difference, that it commonly exceeds the measure of nature, joining at pleasure things which in nature would never have come together, and introducing things which in nature would never have come to pass; just as *Painting* likewise does. This is the work of Imagination."

It is most important to observe that Bacon compares *Poesy* to *Painting*, not only in this passage, but abundantly elsewhere, in exactly the same way we find in the Sonnets attributed to Shakespeare.

"*Poesy* composeth and introduceth at pleasure, even as *Painting* doth; which indeed is the work of imagination" (Lib. II. chap. lxxvii. "Advancement of Learning").

"As faces shine in waters, so men's hearts are manifest to the wise" ("Advancement of Learning," Parable xxxiv.; Proverbs xxvii. 19).

"This parable distinguishes between the hearts of wise men and of other men, comparing those *to waters or mirrors* which reflect the forms and images of things, those to earth or rude stone which reflect nothing. The mind of a wise man is aptly compared to a *mirror*, because in it he sees his own image along with those of others, and he endeavours to be no less varied in application than in observation" (Book VIII. "De Augmentis").

It may be remarked here that the mind, like the surface of a lake, or of water, *must be calm and tranquil to reflect truly.* Directly we are influenced by passions or affections, not only does the mind refuse to reflect clearly, but it refracts, that is, disproportions and is prejudiced, even as objects are refracted by water. In the following citations from the Sonnets may be found both "*Glass*" and "*Perspective*" introduced again. It is my belief these are not casual or surface similes, but are very profoundly connected with some very important natural laws applied to art and lying closely at the root of the 1623 Theatre.

"Thus have we now dwelt with two of the three beams of man's knowledge, that is, *radius directus*, which is referred to nature, *radius refractus*, which is referred to God, and cannot report truly, because of the inequality of the medium" ("Two Books of the Advancement," p. 129).

XXII.

> My glass shall not persuade me I am old,
> So long as youth and thou are of one date;
> But when in thee time's furrows I behold,
> Then look I death my days should expiate.
>
> The wrinkles which *thy glass* will truly show,
> Of mouthed graves will give thee memory.
>
> (Sonnet lxxvii.)

I do not think an *hour-glass of Time* is here implied, because "*wrinkles*" are *to be shown* or *reflected*, and it seems to us by "*thy glass*," is meant the generations of men (in the sense that the plays are reflected by others), who pass away praising these works, man being here collectively personified as growing old and wrinkled, for this is one of Bacon's especial ideas, that the past is the youth of the world and the present its old age. " As for antiquity, the opinion touching it which men entertain is quite a negligent one, and scarcely consonant with the world itself. *For the old age of the world is to be accounted the true antiquity; and this is the tribute of our own times, not of that earlier age of the world in which the ancients lived; and which though in respect of us it was the elder, yet in respect of the world it was the younger*" (Book I., "Advancement of Learning")

> If that the World and Love were young,
> And truth in every Shepheard's tongue,
> These pretty pleasures might me move,
> To live with thee and be thy Love.
>
> ("Passionate Pilgrim.")

"That man is, as it were, *the common measure and mirror or glass of nature*" (Paracelsus, Fludd, *passim;* p. 250, "Advancement of Learning," 1640.)

"It seemeth both in ear and eye, the instrument of sense hath a sympathy or similitude with that which giveth the reflection" ("Natural History," Exp. 282).

86 PERSPECTIVE, REFLECTION, GLASS-MIRROR.

In the Fourth Book of the "De Augmentis," Bacon writes in the following reserved and suspicious manner concerning *Perspective*, curiously connecting it with *Sense and Sensibility*. This is be found under the 28th Deficient or Star, entitled " *De Nixibus Spiritus in motu voluntario*," which is rendered " Of the Difference between Perception and Sense " (" Catalogue Deficients "). The subject belongs to the third section of the third chapter. "*The Distribution of the faculties of the sensible Soul. § Into motion. § Into Sense.*" We read, " But of *Sense and Sensibility* there hath been made a far more plentiful and diligent enquiry, both in general treatises about them, and in particular sciences ; as in *Perspective* and *Music ; how truly is not to our purpose to deliver*. Wherefore we cannot set them down as deficients. Notwithstanding there are two noble and remarkable parts, *which in this knowledge we assign to be Deficient ;* the one concerning *the difference of perception and sense ; the other concerning the form of Light*" (p. 212, "Advancement of Learning," 1640).

It may be seen Bacon *reserves* " Perspective," and "Music," as " *not to our purpose to deliver,*" showing by the language he uses that he held some special knowledge upon the subjects, which he mysteriously withholds. It is my opinion, founded upon some very profound reflections in connection with the "Natural History," (where we refind Music treated at great length) that like the "History of the Winds," these subjects belong to the machinery of the fourth part of the "Instauration,"—the plays.

" Are not the organs of the senses of one kind with the organs of reflection, *the eye with a glass*, the ear with a cave or strait, determined and bounded ? Neither are these *only similitudes*, as men of narrow observation may conceive them to be, *but the same footsteps of nature*, treading or printing upon several subjects or matters. ("Two Books of the Advancement," ii. 108.) In the "Novum Organum," ii. 27, the same illustrations are given of what Bacon calls "conformable instances " or "physical similitudes." From these he deduces the principle " *organa sensuum et corpora, quæ pariunt reflexiones ad sensus esse similis naturæ.*"

Bacon, when comparing the *eye with a glass*, means a looking-glass. This is a highly important point to note. Because if the Latin passage did not run "*oculus enim similis, speculo,*" it might be open to doubt whether he did not mean *transparent or common glass*, which is a very different simile altogether. We see at once that the entire force of Bacon's simile, and the similes extracted from the plays, revolve upon *reflection*. Bacon evidently was in possession of some important and extraordinary law with regard to the senses and reflecting bodies, which he intentionally withholds. He calls this consent or respondency in the Architectures and fabrics *of things Natural and things civil*—Persian Magic * ("De Augmentis," III. i.). In the "Two Books of the Advancement" he calls this particular branch of knowledge "*Philosophia prima, sive de fontibus scientiarum,*" and writes against this head:—"This science, therefore (as I understand it), I may justly report as deficient: for I see sometimes the profounder sort of wits in handling some particular argument will now and then draw a bucket of water out of this well for their present use: but the spring-head thereof seemeth to me not to have been visited; being of so excellent use, *both for the disclosing of nature, and the abridgement of art*" (Book II. p. 108). He calls this science "*a common parent.*" "This science being therefore first placed as a common parent like unto Berecynthia which had so much heavenly issue, *omnes cælicolas omnes supera alta tenentes*" (*Ib.*). In the "Novum Organum" he exemplifies as conformable instances:—"Speculum et oculus; et similiter fabrica auris, et loca reddentia echo" (Book ii. 27). There can be no doubt the theory of reflection, or of beams of reflection, hold a most important position in the Baconian primary Philosophy, for in context with all this quoted, and as it were at the opening of the subject of the partition of philo-

* By the "*Persian Magic,*" Bacon probably alludes to the Magian system which was the source of the philosophy of the Ionian Heraclitus, whose influence upon Plato is so conspicuous. The "Thætetus" is entirely devoted to the development of the doctrines of Heraclitus, and its consequences, so well summed up by Plato, "Nothing is, but all becomes."

sophy (Book III. "De Augmentis"), Bacon writes:—"The object of Philosophy is of three sorts—God, Nature, Man: so likewise there is a triple BEAM of Things; for Nature darts upon the understanding with a *direct beam;* God because of the inequality of the medium, which is the Creature, with a *refract beam;* and man represented and exhibited to himself with a *beam reflex*" (Book III. ch. i. § "De Augmentis"). There is some special philosophy in all this, inasmuch as we have found in the plays the last or third of these partitions, viz., the *reflex'd beam* represented as man seen by others. The profound thinker must perceive, that the theory of the *eye as a looking-glass,*—that is as a reflecting and refracting medium,—may be involved in this question. In the Second Book of "The Advancement of Learning" this quotation from the "De Augmentis" is omitted, but finds its parallel, or echo, in these words:—"Thus have we now dealt with two of the three beams of man's knowledge; that is, *radius directus,* which is referred to Nature, *radius refractus,* which is referred to God, and cannot report truly because of the inequality of the medium. There resteth *radius reflexus whereby man beholdeth and contemplateth himself*" (Book II. p. 129). How fond Bacon is of this simile of the *Looking-Glass!* He writes that man may not inquire the nature of God. *But of Angels and Spirits he may.* "But the sober inquiry touching them, which by the gradation of things corporal may ascend to the nature of them, or which may be seen in the soul of man, *as in a looking-glass, is in no wise restrain'd*" ("De Augmentis," Lib. III. ii.). And this at once agrees with Bacon's theory of DIVINATION BY INFLUXION:—"That the mind as a mirror or glass should take a secondary kind of illumination from the foreknowledge of Gods and *Spirits,* unto which the same state and regiment of the body which was to the first doth likewise conduce" (Lib. IV. ch. iii. "De Augmentis"). This and the next paragraph particularly upon "Fascination" *are undoubtedly Rosicrucian doctrines.*

Bacon quotes Paracelsus and Crollius, both Rosicrucians, in

context with the last subject. The great English Rosicrucian, Thomas Vaughan, writes:—

"God in love with his own beauty frames a glass to view it by reflection" ("The Author to the Reader," "Anthroposophia Theomagica," Thomas Vaughan, Waites' edition).

"Truly Nature is much of this strain, for she hath infinite beauteous patterns in herself, and all these she would gladly see beyond herself, *which she cannot do without the matter, for that is her glass*" ("Cœlum Terræ; or the Magician's Heavenly Chaos and First Matter of all Things," Thomas Vaughan, p. 131, Waite).

We find Robert Fludd writing in his "Mosaicall Philosophy" (Book II., p. 172, 1659):—"St Dionysius saith 'That an angel is the image of God, and the shining forth of his hidden light, *a mirror pure and most bright*, without spot, without wemm, and without defiling. And for this cause he calleth the angels, *Algamatha*, that is *most clean mirrors, receiving the light of God;* argueing truely that they are the images of the Catholic emanation, from whence they spring. For scriptures say, that the spirit of wisdom is the brightness of the eternal light, *a glass or mirror of the majesty of God*, without spot, and the image of his goodness.'"

"The quavering upon a stop in music, gives the same delight to the ear that the playing of light upon the water, or the sparkling of a diamond gives to the eye—

Splendet tremulo sub lumine pontus."

("Advancement of Learning," Book III., 135.)

This splendid comparison of one sense with another (*hearing with sight*) is as striking as it is poetical and beautiful.

The quotation from Virgil and its application to waves of sound reveals the philosopher-poet finding analogies and parallels the most apparently remote, and illustrating them by a line from another poet in a moment. Compare—

That strain again, it had a dying fall;
O, it came o'er my ear, like the sweet sound

> That breathes upon a bank of violets;
> Stealing and giving odour.
>
> ("Twelfth Night," act i. sc. 1.)

Mark how *sound* and *smell* are brought in to illustrate each other, the effort of the poet being to pile up delight by identifying or multiplying one pleasurable sense with another. But nevertheless it is a comparison, and the same philosophic spirit is apparent as in Bacon. In the "Natural History" we find Bacon studying profoundly the Consent of Visibles and Audibles, that is seeking a scientific basis in experience, for the relationship of one sense to another—sight to hearing. Of odours he writes:—"That, which above all others, yields the *sweetest smell in the air is the violet*" (Essay on "Gardens"). In the passage quoted from "Twelfth Night," we find the simile of flowers giving forth odours compared to breath—

> That *breathes* upon a bank of violets.

Compare, "And because the *breath* of flowers is far sweeter in the air (where it comes and goes *like the warbling of music*)" (Essay on "Gardens"). Here we have the parallel complete of *scent and sound* brought together as in the play. In the "Sylva Sylvarum" (Century ii. 113)—"There be in music certain figures or tropes; almost agreeing with the figures of rhetoric, and with the *affections of the mind* and other senses. First, the division and quavering which please so much in music, have an agreement with the glittering of light; as the moon-beams playing upon a wave. Again, the *falling from a discord to a concord*, which maketh great sweetness in music, *hath an agreement with the affections*, which are reintegrated to the better after some dislikes; it agreeth *also with the taste which is soon glutted* with that which is sweet alone. The sliding from the close or cadence, hath an agreement with the figure in rhetoric, which they call *præter expectatum;* for there is a pleasure even in being deceived."

Love is an affection of the mind, and we may see how completely this passage applies to the passage already quoted from "Twelfth

Night," even to the "*dying fall*" and to the word "*glutted*" (which finds its fellow in "*surfeiting*") :—

> If *music* be the *food* of Love, play on
> Give me excess of it : that *surfeiting*,
> The appetite may sicken, and so die.

> O, learn to read what silent love hath writ :
> To hear with eyes belongs to love's fine wit.
> (Sonnet xxiii.)

"*To hear with eyes*"—this is a strange simile. Yet directly we turn to Bacon's "Natural History" we find him very seriously and at great length studying the "*Consent*" and "*Dissent*" of "*Visibles and Audibles.*" So much attention does he give to this subject, we believe it touches far more deeply the interpretation of his art than we can as yet even faintly conjecture—"It seemeth both in ear and eye, the instrument of sense, hath a sympathy or similitude with that which giveth the reflection ; as hath been touched before. For as the sight of the eye *is like a Christal, or glass, or water ,* so is the ear a sinuous cane with a hard bone to stop and reverberate the sound" (Exp. 282). Again, "As *Visibles* work upon a looking-glass, which is like the pupil of the eye ; and *Audibles* upon the plane of echo, which resemble in some sort, the cavern and structure of the ear " (Exp. 263).

THE WORLD AS THEATRE—THE THEATRE AS NATURE.

The extreme fondness Bacon has for contemplating the world and Nature in the spirit of the lines, "*All the world's a stage, and all the men and women merely players*" ("As you like it "), is striking.

"That it is one of the aptest particulars that hath come or can come upon the *Stage* for your Lordship to purchase honour upon" ("Letter of Advice to Essex").

> O Lord thou art our home to whom we fly,
> And so hast always been from age to age.

> Before the hills did intercept the eye,
> Or that the frame was up of *Earthly Stage*.
> (Translation, 90th Psalm.)

"But men must know that in this *Theatre* of man's life, it is reserved only for God and Angels to be lookers on" (p. 339, Book VII., "Advancement of Learning").

"It is the speech of a lover, not of a wise man, *Satis magnum alter alteri Theatrum sumus*" (p. 23, Book I., "Advancement of Learning").

"God hath of late raised an occasion, and erected as it were *a stage or theatre*" (Charge against Mr S. W. and H. I. for Scandal, &c., Part I., p. 59, "Resuscitatio," 1671).

"For if a man can be partaker of *God's Theatre*, he shall likewise be partaker of God's rest" (Essay xi., "Of Great Place").

In the Essay upon "Friendship" (1607-12, Harleian MS. 5, 106; also 1612 edition, but omitted in edition of 1625) we read:—"There be some whose *lines are, as if they perpetually played upon a stage, disguised to all others, open only to themselves;* but perpetual dissimulation is painful, and he that is all fortune and no nature is an exquisite hireling." This is a possible hint for "*lines*" in the sense of *verses* (as a play of words), and perhaps refers to the plays. It is striking this passage is omitted from the edition of 1625, as if too dangerous. This quotation finds a parallel in this other hint, "*Certainly, there be whose Fortunes are like Homer's Verses, that have a slide and easiness more than the verses of other poets*" (Essay on "Fortune," 1625).

"But to enumerate these things were endless: I have given the rule where a man cannot fitly *play his own part*; if he have not a friend, he may quit *the stage*" ("Friendship").

> *Antonio.* I hold the world but as the world, *Gratiano*,
> *A stage where every man must play a part.*
> ("Merchant of Venice," act i. sc. 1.)

The motto to the *Globe Theatre* was "*Totus Mundus agit his-*

trionem." It is well worthy note that Bacon's "De Augmentis" is called by him "The Intellectual *Globe.*"

There are two ways of understanding these comparisons of the world to a stage, and man's life with that of an actor's. The one is as a poetical and fanciful simile, the other is *as a philosophical truth.* I venture to maintain the belief the idea is applied by Bacon to the plays in a far deeper sense than perhaps has been yet conceived. And one of the reasons for our so doing, is the profound reflection of the Platonic Philosophy in the Sonnets, and in such plays as the "Midsummer's Night's Dream." This has been universally acknowledged by all students of this art. Now Plato's philosophy is essentially one that contemplates everything as illusive and false, which does not pertain to the *realities of mind.* Phenomena with him are *idols, images, counterfeits, shadows, imitations*—and he uses these actual words to express the relationship of form to matter. One of these words is *mimesis,* or *mimetic,* which is the players' art. In fact with Plato, all we see in this great world are but shows, it is a stage, on which we act before the ages. If the difference obtaining between what we call reality and unreality consists in endurance, then it is certain there is no more reality in life outside mind, memory, and works than in the actor's art, which has no reality outside the theatre or stage he plays on. Everything *which is not real,* but related to something else, carries the character of illusion and imitation about it. A man looking back to his past life, with the exception of what he holds in his hand of it, either of wealth, works, or writings, must feel there is a curious element of the theatre about it. We have acted, looked on at others, gone through infinite scenes, all of which at the time gave the impression of reality even as the present moment; yet, except in memory, nothing substantial remains, and the eternal *now* is but a series of scenes in which we are both actors and spectators at the same time. The invisible mind outlives the visible body. The characters of the plays of Francis Bacon have more reality about them, than even the lives of their originals, such as Julius Cæsar, Anthony, or Brutus.

It is evident from the fifteenth Sonnet the author of the plays took this view seriously and profoundly:—

> When I consider everything that grows
> *Holds in perfection but a little moment,*
> *That this huge stage presenteth nought but shows*
> Whereon the stars in secret influence comment.
>
> ("Sonnet XV.")

This comparison of the world to "shows" or "plays" is repeated exactly by Bacon: "And therefore Velleius the Epicurean, needed not to have asked, why God should have adorned the Heavens with stars, as if he had been an Ædilis: *one that should have set forth some magnificent shows or plays*" ("Advancement of Learning," Book II., p. 162, Wright).

The identification of Nature with the character of *"God's Theatre"* is very striking in this passage, and I think it most essential to point out, Bacon *identifies Nature with Art*, as we refind in the "Winter's Tale." I allude to this because I feel convinced beyond doubt in my own mind, Bacon looked upon the whole world as a *natural theatre*, and therefore it is just as likely when he uses the words "Nature" or "Interpretation of Nature" he is alluding to the 1623 Folio as to real nature. He almost always writes of public life as a stage:—"First, if your Majesty do at any time think it fit for your affairs to employ me again publicly *upon the stage*," &c. ("Memorial of Access to King James," Nov. 13, 1622).

> Life's but a walking shadow, a poor player
> That struts and frets his hour upon the stage
> And then is heard no more: it is a tale
> Told by an idiot, full of sound and fury,
> Signifying nothing.
>
> ("Macbeth," act v. sc. 5.)

"Neither can any man marvel at the play of puppets, *that goeth behind the curtain, and adviseth well of the motion*" (Book I., p. 67, "Advancement of Learning," Wight).

This is the remark of a man who had thoroughly sifted and seen through the clothes philosophy, and penetrated to the secret motives of the human breast. It is the ironical summing up of one who had anatomized Society, and who found it pulled by the mechanical wires of custom and selfishness. The whole of the plays, particularly those pieces which we learn by heart, are pregnant with just this extraordinary side-piercing sight, which lays bare the *nakedness of the mind*, and the vast difference between reality and appearance. The importance of this subject cannot be over-estimated when we reflect how largely Ethics revolve upon the correspondence of appearance to reality—that is, of *the outward man to the inward man !* Bacon gives us a touch of his mind when he writes upon the *Will* and the *Understanding* (in the Fifth Book "De Augmentis"):— "That this Janus is bifronted, and turns faces. For the face towards reason hath the print of truth, but the face towards *action* hath the print of goodness, which nevertheless are faces" (ch. i., Book V.).

In this case he seems to be alluding to his *own Art*. For he places *Imagination* (identified everywhere with poetry) as the common *attorney or nuncius* between the Will (Action or external) and the Understanding (Logic or rationalism of the plays). They have *faces*, but only in appearance. He writes :—"Truth and goodness differ but as the seal and the stamp."

"Your life is nothing but a continual *acting on the stage*" ("Mask for Essex").

> The wide and universal *theatre*
> Presents more woeful pageants than the scene
> Wherein we play.
> ("As you like it," act ii. sc. 6.)

This is evidence that the writer of *the plays* regarded the world as a *theatre*.

"God sends men into this wretched *theatre*, where being arrived, their first language is that of mourning" (Bacon).

> When we are born we cry that we are come
> To this great *stage* of fools.
> ("Lear," act iv. sc. 6.)

"In the meantime I think myself, howsoever it hath pleased God otherwise to bless me, a most unfortunate man, to be deprived of two, a great number in true friendship, of those friends, whom I accounted as *no stage friends, but private friends*, &c." ("Letter to Toby Matthew," cx.).

MUSIC OF THE SPHERES.

"Si Platonis et Cardani opinionibus fidem aliquam adhibeamus, optima harmonia ex sphærarum conglomeratione generatur, quæ auribus nostris propter distantiæ magnitudinem percipi non potest" (ch. vi. "De Naturæ Arcanis Tractatus Apol.," 1617, R. Fludd). "If we place any belief in the opinions of Plato and Cardan, a divine harmony is generated from the intercourse of the spheres, which we cannot hear on account of the greatness of the distance." How exactly this idea is repeated in the "Merchant of Venice."

> There's not the smallest orb which thou behold'st
> But in his motion like an angel sings,
> Still quiring to the young eyed cherubims:
> Such harmony is in immortal souls;
> But whilst this muddy vesture of decay
> Doth grossly clothe it in, *we cannot hear it*.
>
> (Act v. sc. 1.)

"The names of sounds in all probability were derived from the seven stars, which move circularly in the heavens, and compass the earth" ("Nicom. Harm.," c. 3). "The circumagitation of these bodies must of necessity cause a sound" (Macrobius in "Somn. Scip.," ii. p. 82). "Pythagoras first of all the Greeks conceived in his mind, and understood that the spheres sounded something concordant, because of the necessity of proportion, which never forsakes cœlestial beings" (Macrobius). "Those sounds which the seven Planets and the sphere of fixed stars, and that which is above us, termed by them *Antichthon* make, Pythagoras affirmed to be the nine Muses: but the composition and symphony, and, as it were, connexion of them all, whereof as being eternal and unbegotten, each is a part and portion, he named Mnemosyne" ("Porphyry," p. 21). "Pythagoras, by musical proportion, calleth that a tone by how much the moon is distant from the earth, &c." (*vide* "Pliny," l. ii. c. 22).

Continuing the passage from Fludd: "Cum tamen ab effectu, in his inferioribus non modò hujus musicæ consonantiæ symphoniacæ cognoscantur, sed etiam dissonantiæ; nam illæ amorem, symphoniam, et appetentiam amabilem in rebus excitant, hæ odium, discordiam, et exitialem contemptum." This is the doctrine of Pythagoras, *i.e.*, "The Pythagoreans define music as an apt composition of contraries, and an union of many, and consent of differents. Its end is to unite, and aptly conjoin. God is the reconciler of things discordant, and this is his chief work according to music and medicine to reconcile enmities. In music consists the agreement of all things, and aristocracy of the universe; *for what is harmony in the world, in the city is good government, in a family temperance*" ("Theon. Smyr. Matth.," c. i.).

This is endlessly repeated in the plays:—

> Music do I hear?
> Ha! Ha! keep time: how sour sweet music is,
> When time is broke and no proportion kept!
> *So is it in the music of men's lives.*
> And here have I the daintiness of ear
> To check time broke in a disorder'd string;
> *But for the concord of my state and time*
> *Had not an ear to hear my true time broke.*
> ("Richard II.," act v. sc. 5.)

Bacon evidently believed in the music of the Spheres. In his Parable of the Universe, according to the fable of Pan, he writes: "The two engines which Pan bears in his hands, do point the one at Harmony, the other at Empire; for the pipe of seven reeds doth evidently demonstrate the consent and *harmony; or discordant concord of Nature, which is caused by the motion of the seven wandering stars*" * ("De Augmentis," chap. xiii. Book II.).

* "Examinemus diligenter fabulas poëtarum et ingentia arcana sub iis inveniemus. Cur Pan (per quem universa natura significatur) *ex septem syringibus seu calamis fistulam composuit*, per quam harmoniam dulcem edidit, nisi quia spiritus intellectualis, *qui movet cœlos, facit musicam correspondentem in his inferioribus. Nam per compositioné ex septem fistulis*

Compare "Midsummer Night's Dream,"—

> How shall we find the *concord of this discord?*
>
> (Act v. sc. 1).

Compare First Part "King Henry IV." (act i. sc. 2)—

> For we that take purses, go by the moon and seven stars.

This music of the Spheres, which is to be refound in Cicero's "Vision of Scipio," *is an especial subject of the Rosicrucians.* So much is this the case, that Spedding, in a footnote to the above passage cited from Bacon, adds:—"For dreams about the music of the Spheres, see Robert Fludd's work *Utriusque Cosmi majoris scilicet et minoris, metaphysica, physica et technica Historia,* 1617. The third book of the first tract is wholly *De Musicâ mundana,* and is illustrated by an engraving of a bass viol, of which the dimensions extend through the solar system."

"In 'Antony and Cleopatra,' Cleopatra, bewailing Antony's death, compares his voice to the 'tunèd spheres' (act v. sc. 2); and in 'Twelfth Night' Olivia pays the same compliment to the page in disguise, with whom she is in love. Pericles, prince of Tyre, in his ecstasy at finding his daughter Marina, suddenly hears sounds of music unheard by the others, which he calls the music of the spheres" (Paul Stapfer, "Shakespeare and Classical Antiquity," p. 92).

significatur congregatio septem orbium planetarum et mirabili ipsorum harmonia in cælo et in terris, hoc est, ubicunque natura illa universalis se extendit" (Tractatus Apol., Pars iii., De Occultis et admirandis Musices arcana effectibus, p. 178, 1617. Robert Fludd).

CHAPTER V.

BACON'S "GEORGICS OF THE MIND."

"*But to speak the truth, the best Doctors of this knowledge are the Poets*, and *writers of Histories*, where we may find painted and dissected to the life, how affections are to be stirred up and kindled, how still'd and laid asleep; how again contain'd and refrain'd that they break not forth into act" (Book VII., "De Augmentis").

"Another parable put He forth unto them, saying, The kingdom of heaven is likened unto a man which sowed good seed in his field; but while men slept, his enemy came and sowed tares among the wheat, and went his way. But when the blade was sprung up, and brought forth fruit, then appeared the tares also. So the servants of the householder came and said unto him, Sir, didst not thou sow good seed in thy field? from whence then hath it tares? He said unto them, An enemy hath done this. The servants said unto him, Wilt thou then that we go and gather them up? But he said, Nay; lest while ye gather up the tares, ye root up also the wheat with them. Let both grow together until the harvest: and in the time of harvest I will say to the reapers, Gather ye together first the tares, and bind them in bundles to burn them: but gather the wheat into my barn" (Matthew xiii. 24-30).

"And therefore, as Plato said elegantly, *That virtue, if she could be seen, would move great love and affection;* so seeing that she cannot be showed to the sense by corporal shape, the next degree *is to show her to the imagination in lively representation:* for to show her to reason only in subtilty of argument was a thing ever derided in Chrysippus and many of the Stoics, who thought to thrust virtue upon men by sharp disputations and conclusions, which have no sympathy with the will of man" ("Advancement of Learning," ii. 178).

"Nos docet apostolus ad mysterii perfectionem vel sub Agricolæ, vel architecti typo pertingere."—ROBERT FLUDD.

"A MAN'S nature runs either to *herbs or weeds;* therefore let him seasonably water the one, and destroy the other" ("Of Nature in Men").

Iago. Virtue ! a fig ! 'tis in ourselves that we are thus or thus. Our bodies are our gardens, to the which *our wills are gardeners:* so that if we will plant nettles, or sow lettuce, set hyssop and weed up thyme, supply it with one gender of *herbs*, or distract it with many, either to have it sterile with idleness, or manured with industry, why, the power and corrigible authority of this lies in our wills. ("Othello," act i. sc. 3.)

In scene ii. act 5, Othello exclaims to Desdemona:—

> Oh thou *weed:*
> Who art so lovely fair, and smell'st so sweet,
> That the sense aches at thee.

> Oh fie, fie, 'tis an *unweeded garden*,
> That grows to seed: things *rank* and gross in nature
> Possess it merely.

("Hamlet," act i. sc. 2.)

> He's a *rank weed*, Sir Thomas,
> And we must root him out.

("King Henry VIII.," act v. sc. 1.)

There can be very little doubt Bacon has chosen this simile of "Weeds" to express Human Nature in a state of backwardness and vice. In the "De Augmentis" he calls poetry a *luxuriant weed*, and in a prayer ("Resuscitatio," p. 17, 1671) writes:—"I have (though in a *despised weed*) procured the good of all men." "As for poesy (whether we speak of fables or metre, it is, as we have said before, as a *Luxuriant Herb* † (*weed?*) brought forth without seed, and springs up from the strength and *rankness* of the soil" (p. 264, Book VI., "Advancement of Learning"). Note the coupling of the words "*rank weed*," "*unweeded garden*," "*things rank*" (in the quotations from the plays), poesy being a *plant* coming, as it were, from the lust of a *rank soil*" (p. 109, Book II., "Advancement of Learning").

"All flesh is grass" is not only metaphorically but literally true; for "all those creatures we behold are but the herbs of the field digested into flesh in them, or more remotely carnified in ourselves" ("Religio Medici," Browne, 70).

* Iago in this passage *asserts the complete liberty of the will*, and this makes his villainy so much the more villainous and detestable. Bacon writes: "For the purity of Illumination and the Liberty of Will began together, *fell together*" (Fifth Book, "De Augmentis," chap. i.).

† "Luxurians *herba*" ("De Augmentis," 1623). *Herba* in Latin means *weed* as well as Herb—also "*the blade of any corn*" (Ainsworth's Latin Dictionary).

The only light we can throw upon this is the suggestion, Bacon's purpose was ethical instruction for "*the good of all men;*" his theatre has the aim of holding up the vices and passions of men to scorn, as a warning and as a means of eradicating the tares. He writes of the passion "Envy":—"The envious man *that soweth tares amongst the wheat* by night." And we have presented to us the portrait of Lear:—

> Crown'd with *rank fumitor, and furrow weeds*,
> With bur-docks, hemlock, nettles, cuckoo flowers,
> *Darnel*,* *and all the idle weeds that grow
> In our sustaining corn.*
>
> (Act iv. sc. 4.)

Why have these especial weeds, found ever in the corn, been selected? I hope it will not be deemed impertinence to suggest what is *possibly* intended by this awful picture? Lear's madness is the result of the wickedness of his daughters. He may have been generous, credulous, weak, and simple, but, like Othello, he was "great of heart," and his misery is the result of ingratitude —the inhumanity of his own flesh and blood. He is crowned with the tares and with the weeds of degenerate nature, and *like some ruined and abandoned piece of ground*, is an emblem of what neglect by others can produce. He carries on his shoulders and on his head the burthen and crown of a ruined nature, neglected, cast out, and is the most terrible picture of what inhumanity and envy can effect in this world or in literature! Nature alone sympathises with him—the storm, the lightning, the rage, are

* There can be very little doubt Bacon had in his mind *the Parable of the Tares* (Matt. xiii. 24-30) in this portrait of Lear crowned with weeds that grow in corn. The plant representative of tares is *Darnel*. "From the accounts of modern enquirers competent to form an opinion on this point, the reference is (in the Biblical Parable of the Tares) to a kind of weed or poisonous grass called '*darnel*' (*Lolium temulentum*), which is in all respects so like the wheat that before it comes into ear it is hardly possible to observe any distinction between the two plants" ("Picture Lessons," by Peter Grant, p. 30).

> Interque nitentia culta
> Infelix Lolium et steriles dominantur avenæ.
> (Virgil's "First Georgic.")

reflected in himself and in his heart. We are not only *gardeners for ourselves*, but alike *gardeners to and for others*. The words duty, charity, temperance, inculcate this. For we do not stand alone, and we can hardly move in this life without either nourishing tares in others, or helping to eradicate them. A man's life will generally yield on retrospection the dismal record, that he might have been better—*if others had been better*.

The inculcation of the necessity for occupation and work to escape evil is most prominent in the plays:—

> We bring forth *weeds*,
> When our quick minds lie still.
>
> ("Anthony and Cleopatra," act i. sc. 2.)

Still better is evil and its poisonous effects painted in these lines—

> Here is your husband; *like a mildew'd ear*
> *Blasting* his wholesome brother.
>
> (Act iii. sc. 4.)

In this image we have the *corn* and the *tares* again suggested.

> Confess yourself to heaven;
> Repent what's past; avoid what is to come;
> And do not *spread the compost on the weeds*
> *To make them ranker*.
>
> ("Hamlet," act iii. sc. 4.)

In the following lines we have idleness and sloth compared to a fat weed:—

> And duller should'st thou be than the *fat weed*,
> That rots itself in ease on Lethe Wharf,
> Would'st thou not stir in this.
>
> ("Hamlet," act i. sc. 3.)

LXIX.

> Those parts of thee that the world's eye doth view
> Want nothing that the thought of hearts can mend;
> All tongues, the voice of souls, give thee that due,
> Uttering bare truth, even so as foes commend.
> Thy outward thus with outward praise is crown'd;
> But those same tongues that give thee so thine own
> In other accents do this praise confound
> By seeing farther than the eye hath shown.

> They look into the beauty of thy mind,
> And that, in guess, they measure by thy deeds;
> Then, churls, their thoughts, although their eyes were kind,
> *To thy fair flower add the rank smell of weeds:*
> But why thy odour matcheth not thy show,
> The solve is this, that thou dost common grow.

It is evident from this Sonnet the author held "*culture of the mind*" not only in high estimation, but the imagery of *flowers for virtues and weeds for vices* is prominent from first to last in the quotations adduced. The world abandoned to evil and wickedness is "*an unweeded garden, things rank and gross possess it merely.*" "*Our bodies are our gardens, to the which our wills are gardeners.*" Now it is very striking — perhaps startling for sceptics of the Baconian theory of the Plays—to find Bacon entitling his Ethics, "*Georgics of the Mind*," which title he borrows from Virgil's "Observations upon Husbandry." "We will therefore divide Moral Philosophy into two main and principal knowledges; the one concerning the exemplar or image of Good; the other concerning the Regiment and Culture of the Mind, which we are wont to call the GEORGICS OF THE MIND" (p. 335, Book VII., "Advancement of Learning," 1640).

In the following passage from the play of "Richard the Third," we find the young Duke of York presented, quoting his wicked uncle :—

> I, quoth my uncle Gloucester,
> *Small herbs have grace, great weeds do grow apace.*
> And since methinks I would not grow so fast,
> Because sweet flowers are slow, and weeds make haste.
>
> .   .   .   .
>
> I could have given my uncle's Grace a flout,
> To *touch his growth nearer than he touch't me.*
>
> ("Richard III.," act. ii. sc. 4.)

> Now is the spring, and *weeds* are shallow rooted,
> Suffer them now, and they'll o'ergrow the garden,
> And choke the *herbs* for want of husbandry.
>
> ("2 King Henry VI.," act i. sc. 1.)

Compare the above with "A man's nature runs either to *herbs or weeds*," and see how the same words are employed in context—

"*herbs*"—"*weeds*"—in both quotations, one from the phantom captain Shakespeare,—the other from Bacon.

> Two such opposed kings encamp them still,
> *In man as well as herbs, grace and rude will ;*
> And where the worser is predominant,
> Full soon the canker doth eat up that plant.
> ("Romeo and Juliet," act ii. sc. 3.)

It is remarkable how fond the author of the plays is of comparing *plants and flowers* with human nature, and of cankers to illustrate vice. It cannot be called a casual metaphor because so often repeated:—

> *Pro.* Yet writers say, as in the sweetest bud
> The eating canker dwells, so eating love
> Inhabits in the finest wits of all.
> *Val.* And writers say, as the most forward bud
> Is eaten by the canker ere it blow,
> Even so by love the young and tender wit
> Is turn'd to folly, blasting in the bud,
> Losing his verdure even in the prime
> And all the fair effects of future hopes.
> ("Two Gentlemen of Verona," act i. sc. 1.)

> Virtue itself 'scapes not calumnious strokes :
> The canker galls the infants of the spring,
> Too oft before their buttons be disclosed,
> And in the morn and liquid dew of youth
> Contagious blastments are most imminent.
> ("Hamlet," act i. sc. 3.)

That weeds are applied as a metaphor for vices is certain :—

> We have strict statutes and most biting laws,
> The needful bits and curbs to headstrong *weeds*.
> ("Measure for Measure," act i. sc. 2.)

> Twice treble shame on Angelo,
> *To weed my vice* and let his grow.
> ("Measure for Measure," act iii. sc. 2.)

This is the idea of husbandry, or *self-culture* applied to the garden of our bodies and minds, as Georgics. Bacon writes, "*God Almighty first planted a garden,*" and there may be in this remark some implied thought of *Man before the fall, of purity before sin entered the world, and the devil sowed the tares of vice.*

"The primeval curse pronounced upon the earth in consequence of man's sin, was '*Thorns also and thistles shall it bring forth to thee;*' and what the earth then became in a physical sense, that the soul of man became in a spiritual—a wilderness of rank and noxious thorns, and we might add *weeds*" ("Picture Lessons," by Peter Grant).

"The field on which the good seed is sown by Christ, is the world. In the parable it is called His field; and the world is His, though not *by possession yet by right. Meanwhile it is usurped by a rival power—even by the arch-spirit of evil* *—but when Christ comes to take possession of it, He comes whose right it is to reign. The *tares* which were sown in this field along with the wheat, *are the children of the wicked one.* 'Ye are,' saith the Lord, 'of your father the devil; and the lusts of your father ye will do.' Both in the world and in the Church they are like *darnel*, unprofitable in themselves, and positively injurious to the good seed by temptation and by persecution. Even though they may enjoy the benefit of the same soil, and sunshine, and showers, as the good plants, they are *but as noxious weeds* in the field, whose end is to be burned" ("Picture Lessons," p. 32, Parable of the Tares, Peter Grant).

He entered into due consideration how to *weed* out the partakers of the former rebellion. ("History of King Henry VII.")

We find Bacon in his Essays using the same simile to illustrate the extirpation of vice by law. "Revenge is a kind of wild justice, which, the more man's nature runs to, the more ought law *to weed it out*" ("Of Revenge").

And in the following passage, "*Pride*" is expressed as "*seeded*" with the words "*rank*," "*nursery*," used by Bacon to express Poetry.

> The *seeded* pride
> That hath to this maturity blown up
> In *rank* Achilles, must or now be cropt,

* The play of "Hamlet" presents strong parallels to this parable. Prince Hamlet is the *rightful heir to a throne usurped by a king who is the incarnation of evil.*

> Or shedding breed a *nursery* of like evil
> To over-bulk us all.
> > ("Troilus and Cressida," act i. sc. 3.)

One of the "Antitheta" in the Sixth Book of the "De Augmentis" is entitled "Pride." It is these "Antitheta" Bacon introduces with the preliminary words that they are *seeds*, not flowers.

"Afflictions only level those *mole-hills of pride. Plough the heart and make it fit for wisdom to sow her seed, and for grace to bring forth her increase.* Happy is that man, therefore, both in regard of heavenly and earthly wisdom, that is thus wounded to be cured; thus broken to be made straight; thus made acquainted with his own imperfections to be made straight" ("Letter lxx. to Lord Chief Justice Coke," 1702).

"Cast their *seeds* in the minds of others" ("Advancement of Learning," Book I.).

Why your herb-woman; she that sets *seeds and roots of shame and iniquity*. ("Pericles," act iv. sc. 6.)

"After the knowledge of characters follows the knowledge of *Affections and passions, which are the diseases of the mind*, as hath been said. For as the ancient Politiques in popular states were wont to say, *That the people were like the sea, and the orators like the winds*, because as the sea would of itself be calm and quiet, if the winds did not move and trouble it, so the people of their nature would be peaceable and tractable if the seditious orators did not set them in working and agitation. So it may be truly affirmed, that *man's mind*, in the nature thereof, would be temperate and staid, if the *affections as winds did not put it into tumult and perturbation*" (Book VII., "De Augmentis," Trans. 1640, p. 354).

How this is applied in the plays may be seen in a few quotations:—

> Oh no, my dream was lengthened after life;
> Oh then began *the tempest to my soul*.
> > ("Richard III.," act. i. sc. 4.)

Throw up thine eye! see, see what showers arise,
Blown with the windy tempest of my heart.
("3 Henry VI.," act ii. sc. 5.)

But this effusion of such manly drops,
This shower *blown up by tempest of the soul,*
Startles mine eyes.
("King John," act v. sc. 2.)

Belike for want of rain which I could well
Beteem them *from the tempest of my eyes.*
("Midsummer's Night's Dream," act i. sc. 1.)

The identification *of the microcosm of man's soul with the macrocosm of Nature* is very apparent throughout this wondrous art, but particularly in the case of King Lear, where the storm outside is the deep bass counterpoint to the tempest in Lear's heart, forlorn as the desolate heath o'er which the wind blows. Notice also that the affection of Lear's soul is described as a *malady or disease*, which is in keeping with Bacon.

SCENE IV. *The heath. Before a hovel.*

Enter LEAR, KENT, *and* FOOL.

Kent. Here is the place, my lord; good my lord, enter;
The tyranny of the open night's too rough
For nature to endure.   [*Storm still.*
  Lear.   Let me alone.
Kent. Good my lord, enter here.
Lear.   Wilt break my heart?
Kent. I had rather break mine own. Good my lord, enter.
Lear. Thou think'st 'tis much that this contentious storm
Invades us to the skin: so 'tis to thee;
But where the *greater malady* is fix'd,
The lesser is scarce felt. Thou'ldst shun a bear;
But if thy flight lay toward the raging sea,
Thou'ldst meet the bear i' the mouth. When the mind's free,
The body's delicate: the tempest in my mind
Doth from my senses take all feeling else
Save what beats there.
("King Lear," act iii. sc. 3.)

I venture to suggest the play of the "Tempest" borrows its title from the affinity of its subject matter to the creative power or soul power of the poet author, *as breath, life, air, wind in motion.* And the word "Tempest" is allied to the word

Soul. θῦμός—the soul, is derived by Plato ("Cratyl" 419) from θύω, which means to "*rush on*" or "along," as of a mighty rushing wind, and signifies also to storm, rage, also passion and affection in its kindred forms. In Latin *animus* (the soul) is the seat of anger, wrath, *the feelings*. How applicable to one who has stirred the entire breast of man! Upon the same page the piece quoted from Bacon by us already is found; we come upon this in context with it, as a pretty direct hint. "So, likewise, I find some elegant books of some *affections, as of anger*, of tenderness of countenance, and some few others. But to speak the truth, *the best doctors of this knowledge are the poets and writers of histories, where we may find painted and dissected to the life how affections are to be stirred up and kindled, how still'd and laid asleep; how again contained and refrained that they break not forth into Act?*" (Book VII., Ethic, "De Augmentis," Trans. 1640, p. 355.) Why this sentence ends with a note of interrogation we cannot explain, unless it be to invite us to ask what particular poet is pointed at!

We find in "Macbeth" the same treatment *of sin as a disease, an infection* :—

> Canst thou not minister to a *mind diseased*
> Pluck from the memory a rooted sorrow:—
> Raze out the written troubles of the brain.
>
> (Act v. sc. 3.)

And the Doctor exclaims :—

> *Infected minds*
> To their deaf pillows will discharge their secrets.
> ("Macbeth," act v. sc. 1.)

This is all in perfect keeping with what Bacon writes :— "*Affections and passions which are the diseases of the mind*," already quoted. Again :—" First, therefore, in this as in all things which are practical, we ought to cast up our account, *what is in our power and what not :* for the one may be dealt with by way of alteration. Now in the *culture of the mind of man, and the cure of the diseases* thereof, three things fall into consideration: the diverse characters of dispositions, *the affections, and the remedies*"

("Georgics of the Mind, or the Culture of Morals," Book VII., chap. iii.).

In the plays we repeatedly find Love described as an "*infection:*"—

> *Boyet.* If my observation, which very seldom lies,
> By the heart's still rhetoric disclosed with eyes,
> Deceive me not now Navarre is *infected.*
> *Princess.* With what?
> *Boyet.* With that which we lovers entitle *affected.*
> *Princess.* Your reason?
> *Boyet.* Why, all his behaviour did make them retire
> *To the court of his eye peeping through desire.*
> ("Love's Labour Lost," act ii. sc. 1.)

Now compare this by Bacon:—"There be none of the affections which have been noted to *fascinate or bewitch, but love and envy.* They both have vehement wishes; they frame themselves readily into imaginations and suggestions; *and they come easily into the eye;* especially upon the presence of the objects, which are the points that conduce to fascination" ("Of Envy"). In Bacon's "Natural History" he writes:—"Lust causeth a flagrancy in the eyes" (Exp. 722). "The cause of both these is, for that in lust the sight and the touch are the things desired, and *therefore the Spirits resort to those parts which are most effected*" (*Ib.*).

> *for beauty is a witch*
> Against whose charms faith melteth into blood.
> This is an accident of hourly proof.
> ("Much Ado about Nothing," act ii. sc. 1.

"The affections (no doubt) do make the Spirits more powerful and active; and especially those affections *which draw the Spirits into the eyes:* which are two, Love and Envy. And fascination is ever by the eye" ("Natural History," Ex. 944, Cent. x.).

> Methinks I feel this youth's perfections,
> With an invisible and subtle stealth,
> To creep in at mine eyes.
> ("Twelfth Night," act i. sc. 5.)

Bacon terms vices and sins diseases of the mind. In the plays we find the expression "*Infection.*"

> *Anne.* Vouchsafe defined *infection* of a man,
> For these known evils but to give me leave,
> By circumstance to curse, thy cursed self.
> ("King Richard III.," act i. sc. 2.)

> *Anne.* Out of my sight! thou dost *infect* my eyes.
> *Glou.* Thine eyes, sweet Lady, have *infected* mine.
> (*Ib.*)

The use of the expressions "purge," "purging," "purgation," are very frequent in the plays, and betray familiarity with medicine. We refind Bacon frequently using these words in the same sense, viz., as a *cathartic*.

"Yet in our judgment it (Astrology) should rather be *purged* than clean cast away" ("Advancement of Learning," p. 147).

> Till the foul crimes done in my days of nature
> Are burnt and *purged away*.
> ("Hamlet," act i. sc. 4.)

> To take him in the *purging* of his soul.
> ("Hamlet," act iii. sc. 3.)

"The next, that after this example, it is like that judges will fly from anything in the likeness of corruption (though it were at a great distance) as from a serpent, which tendeth to the *purging* of the Courts of Justice" ("Lord Chancellor Bacon to the Lords," Cabala, p. 5, 1654).

> *Ros.* You must be *purged* too, your sins are rack'd,
> You are attaint with faults and perjury.
> ("Love's Labour Lost," act i. sc. 2.)

"I would only ask why the Civil State should be *purged* and restored by good and wholesome laws" ("Life," vol. iii. p. 105).

"Therefore care would be had that (as it fareth in *ill purgings*) the good be not taken away with the bad, which commonly is done when the people is the reformer" ("Superstition").

"And here I will make a request, that for the latter (or at least for a part thereof) I may revive and reintegrate the misapplied and abused name of natural magic; which in the true sense is but natural wisdom, or natural prudence, taken according to the ancient acception *purged from vanity* and superstition" ("Advancement of Learning," Book II. p. 111).

In continuation of the passage cited from Bacon's "Ethics," touching his assertion that "*the best Doctors of this knowledge are the poets*, where we may find *painted and dissected to the life*, how affections are to be stirred up and kindled; how still'd and laid asleep; how again contain'd and refrain'd, that they break not forth into act? Likewise how they disclose themselves, though repressed and secreted? What operations they produce? What turns they take? How they are enwrapt one within another? How they fight and encounter one with another? And other the like particularities. Amongst the which, this last is of special use in Moral and Civil matters. *How I say to set Affection against Affection, and by the help of one to master and reclaim another? After the manner of Hunters and Fowlers, who hunt beast with beast,** *and fly bird with bird*" (Book VII., p. 355, " De Augmentis," Trans. 1640).

The setting of affection against affection in this manner is abundantly portrayed in the plays. In the play of "Troilus and Cressida," the pride of Ajax is set against the pride of Achilles in exactly the way inculcated by Bacon—that is, as preying upon each other:—

> How one man eats into another's pride,†
> While pride is fasting in his wantonness.
> ("Troilus and Cressida," act ii. sc. 3.)

> Two curs shall tame each other: pride alone
> Must tarre the mastiffs on, as 'twere their bone.
> (*Ib.*, act i. sc. 3.)

Space forbids us to illustrate what is really one of the leading motives of this play, viz., the contrast afforded by Ajax and

---

* Give him allowance as the worthier man,
For that will *physic* the great Myrmidon.
("Troilus and Cressida.")

† Humanity must perforce *prey on itself*,
Like monsters of the deep.
("King Lear," act iv. sc. 2.)

Achilles, the former egged on by the plot of Ulysses and Nestor to humble the pride of the latter, and put him into motion.

Or take the "Taming of the Shrew," where *one bad temper* is (in Bacon's words) *master'd and reclaim'd by another bad temper*—a she-devil by a he-devil.

> *Gremio.* A bridegroom say you? 'Tis a groom indeed,
> A grumbling groom, and that the girl shall find.
> *Tranio.* Curster than she? Why 'tis impossible.
> *Gremio.* Why he's a devil, a devil, a very fiend.
> *Tranio.* Why, she's a devil, a devil, the devil's dam.
> *Gremio. Tut, she's a lamb, a dove, a fool to him.*
> ("Taming of the Shrew," act iii. sc. 2).

> *Pet.* Thus have I politicly begun my reign,
> And 'tis my hope to end successfully.
> My falcon now is sharp, and passing empty;
> And till she stoop she must not be full gorged,
> For then she never looks upon her lure.
> Another way I have to man my haggard,
> To make her come and know her keeper's call,
> That is, to watch her, as we watch these kites
> That bate and beat and will not be obedient.
> ("Taming of the Shrew," act iv. sc. 1.)

This is exactly an example of what Bacon writes in his book of Ethics in the "De Augmentis." "But to speak truth, the best Doctors of *this* knowledge are the Poets. . . . *How I say to set affection against affection, and by the help of one to master and reclaim another!* After the manner of Hunters and Fowlers, who hunt beast with beast, and *fly bird with bird*" ("Advancement of Learning," 1640, p. 355).

"In Much Ado About Nothing," we find Benedict and Beatrice brought into a mountain of affection for each other by a trick which might be called a "fowler's," viz.—imitation. Each overhears that the one is madly in love with the other, and just as wild birds are caught by a call bird, find themselves limed in reality in the end. It is characteristic of this entire art that character is set against character, as shadow or contrast, and that Ethic is predominant from first to last in the treatment.

In the "Two Books of the Advancement," 1605, we read:

BACON'S "GEORGICS OF THE MIND." 113

—"It were too long to go over the particular remedies which learning doth *minister to, all the diseases of the mind;* sometimes purging the ill humours, sometimes opening the obstructions, sometimes helping digestion, sometimes increasing appetite, sometimes healing the wounds and exulcerations thereof, and the like; and therefore I will conclude with that which hath *rationem* corrupt the state thereof. For the mind of man is far from the nature of a clear and equal glass, wherein the beams of things should reflect according to their true incidence; nay, it is rather like an enchanted glass, full of superstition and imposture, if it be not delivered and reduced."

Note the words we place in italics, where we refind the three chief words of the line already quoted from "Macbeth":—

Canst thou not *minister to a mind diseased?*

Bacon no doubt borrowed this image from Cicero: "But if the joy of living is interrupted by the afflicting maladies of the body, how much greater must its interruption be from the *Diseases of the Mind?* Now the Diseases of the Mind consist in insatiable and superfluous appetites after Riches, Glory, Power, and even sensual pleasures; add to these disquiet, uneasiness, and melancholy; all of which prey upon and consume with anxiety the spirits of those who are ignorant that the mind ought to have no sensation of pain, for anything that is distinct from the pain of the body, either present or to come. And now I must observe, that there is not a fool in the world who is not sick of some one or other of *these diseases;* and therefore there is not a fool who is not unhappy" ("De Finibus"). Cicero's influence upon Bacon in the matter of morals divides honours with Seneca. Both inculcated doctrines of the noblest morality or unselfishness, and we may guess that the writer who penned the following words, would hold a high place with the author of such plays as "Measure for Measure" and the "Merchant of Venice." "Let me ask you whether you think I won't say an Homer, an Archilochus, a Pindar, even a Phidias, a Polycletus, a Zeuxis,

H

directed their arts to the purposes of sensual pleasures?" ("De Finibus," ii. x.).

"For to this end shall truth be delivered as naked as if yourself were to be *anatomized*" ("Letter to Chief-Justice Coke," lxx. 1702).

> The wise man's folly is *anatomized*.
> ("As you Like It," act. ii. sc. 7.)

> Let them *anatomize* Regan.
> ("Lear," act iii. sc. 6.)

There are eleven entries of the words "*anatomy*," "*anatomized*" in the plays (see Cowden Clarke's "Concordance"). And it is used in the sense of *discovering disease of the soul*, and also in the sense of a skeleton:—

> A mere *anatomy*, a mountebank.
> ("Comedy of Errors," act v. sc. 1.)

Directly we open the Seventh Book of Bacon's "De Augmentis," we find ourselves in contact with the subject of "Morals," or "Ethic," which rightly employed is really the basis of Drama and all Stage Plays. In the Second Book of the "Advancement" (1605), Bacon writes: "And therefore, as Plato said elegantly, *That virtue, if she could be seen, would move great affection and love: so seeing that she cannot be shewed to the Sense, by corporal shape the next degree is to show her to the Imagination in lively representation:* for to show her to *Reason*, only in subtilty of argument, was a thing ever derided in Chrysippus and many of the Stoics, who thought to thrust virtue upon men by sharp disputations and conclusions, which have no sympathy with the will of Man" ("Advancement of Learning," Book II., p. 67, 1605).

This is such an unmistakable allusion or hint for the use of Representative Poetry (the Drama) as means of ethical instruction, that it hardly needs our apology. Bacon is plainly referring to "Virtue" seen or represented upon the Stage in Stage Plays, and we have only to think of Isabella in "Measure for Measure," or of Desdemona, to realise all Bacon writes. We see Bacon is not alluding to *Virtue* in daily life, for he declares, "she cannot be shewed to the sense, by corporal shape." And he condemns argument and persuasions by means of Reason, as of no use and effect. *Imagination* is the faculty of the mind, producing and answering with Bacon to Poetry. "The parts of humane learning have reference to the three parts of Man's understanding, which is the seat of learning: History to his Memory, *Poesie to his Imagination*, Philosophy to his Reason" (p. 7, Book II., "Advancement of Learning," 1605). "*Representative (Poesy) is as a visible history, and is an image of actions as if they were present*" (p. 18, "Advancement of Learning," Bk. II., 1605). "Dramatical or Representative (Poetry) is as it were visible history" ("Advancement of Learning," p. 106, 1640). And that Bacon in the passage quoted (about the *representation of virtue* to the Imagination) is alluding to the value of a right use of the Drama, for purposes of ethical teaching, may be seen in his use of the words "*lively representation*" and "*Imagination.*" In Book II. of the "De Augmentis" (the only page upon which he directly discusses, or alludes to the use and abuse of the Drama): "Dramatical or Representative Poesy, which brings the World upon the Stages, *is of excellent use if it were not abused*. For the instructions and corruptions of the Stage may be great, but the corruptions in this kind abound, the discipline is altogether neglected in our times. For although in modern Common-wealths, Stage Plays be but esteemed a sport or pastime unless it draw from the satyr, and be mordant, yet the care of the Ancients was *that it should instruct the minds of men unto virtue*" (p. 107, "Advancement of Learning," 1640).

If we now return to Bacon's "Ethics" (Seventh Book) in his "De Augmentis" (1623, 1640), we find him again *hinting* at the value of *Representation of Character*, and the uselessness of precepts, arguments, and dry lessons, as instruments of instruction and example in morality. "It is not the disputing that moral virtues are in the mind of man by habit, and not by nature; or formally distinguishing between generous spirits and the obscure vulgar; that those are won by the weight of Reasons; these by reward and punishment; or the witty precept, that to rectify the mind of man, it must like a staff be bowed the contrary way to its inclination, and the like glances scattered here and there. These and the like are far short of being a just excuse of *the Deficience of that thing which now we seek*" (Book VII., p. 334).

For a moment we halt in the quotation of the passage to call attention to the fact, that Bacon is propounding *a Deficience, and seeking something which is to take the place, and better dry rules and arguments, for the instruction of virtue and morality*. What can this be? He then continues: "For writings should be such as should MAKE MEN IN LOVE WITH THE LESSONS, and not with the teachers." How thoroughly this agrees with *the lessons of the Theatre, known as Shakespeare's plays!* And is it not in these plays that we can exclaim, *Virtue is seen and does move great affection and love?* But it is evident to a close student of Bacon's *obscure and private language* (the Seventh Book, "De Augmentis"), he is really driving at *portrayal or portraits of character and characters!* "In handling of this Science, those which have written thereof, seem to me to have done, *as if a man that professed the art of writing should only exhibit fair copies of Alphabets and letters joined, without giving any precepts for the carriage of the hand and framing of the characters*" (Book VII., "Advancement of Learning," p. 333, 1640).

The prominency of the ethical in the construction of the plays is a point which always gathers strength with deeper study. I am myself convinced, although I cannot pretend to furnish evidence of my belief, that the Ethical in these works *amounts to philosophical principle*, which will some day be revealed by Bacon himself, and astonish us by its laying bare the mechanism of morality, as a result of law. No anticipation or bare study of the text will ever bring us to the solution of this problem, except through the application of the "De Augmentis," as *a great key book* to unriddle this problem, with the assistance of Bacon himself. This work is *initiatory and magistral*. It is the prose text, written *in private and obscure language*, of the plays, which grew up side by side with it, as works and keys, or what he terms "*Interpretation of Nature.*" And we can see this in the fact, that as Bacon continued to write plays after 1605, he found it necessary *to rewrite and enlarge* the "Two Books of the Advancement of Learning" into the stately "De Augmentis," which appears side by side with the first collected edition of the plays the same year, 1623. Everything in the "De Augmentis" of 1623, may be refound *in germ* in the 1605 "Two Books of the Advancement of Learning." The fact Bacon repeats the same subjects (only developed and enlarged) in the "De Augmentis" as are to be found in the "Two Books of the Advancement" is proof he was writing with a distinct object in view, and not for the sake of variety or present fame. But the slightest study of the two works reveals their characters at a glance. Setting the ciphers and great book of "*Delivery of Secret Knowledge*" aside, with its methods and distinct affiliation with the Essays (through the "Colours of Good and Evil," "Antitheta," and "Minor Formulæ"), the chapters and sections upon "*Places of suggestion*" or "*Topic,*" "*Literate Experience,*" "*Promptuary Place of Preparation,*" cannot be explained upon any theory at all except as fingerposts of direction, *for something literary in some book and not in nature.* I know how this statement will arouse scepticism and incredulity, but let those who so feel, first rub their eyes a little, and read the third chapter of the Fifth Book of the "De Augmentis" in Latin, or in the English translation by Wats of 1640. Let them suppose themselves to have the question put them, *to what does all this apply, or, indeed, what does it mean?* I venture to think their replies would be curious, and their written statements interesting. I entirely put aside for the moment the leading or basic part History and Poetry play in this work, disguised under the terms "Feign'd History," "Imagination," and "Elocution." I want to know why Rhetoric is part of the "*Wisdom of Private Speech*" and of "*Promptuary,*" or *Suggestive?* And why the examples of this Rhetoric are the kernels, or *pros* and *cons*, of the Essays? Further, why all this

belongs to the art *Traditive*, or "*Delivery of the things Invented*"?
All this we assert deals with *Art*. For Bacon distinctly writes:
—"Invention (Discovery) is of two kinds, much differing, *the one of Arts* and Sciences, the other of arguments and speeches. *The former of these* (Arts) I report to be wholly DEFICIENT, which seems to me such a deficience, as if in the making of an inventory *touching the estate of a Defunct, it should be set down, of ready money nothing;* for as money will fetch all other commodities; so all other arts are purchased by this art." This is a pretty clear hint for the plays. And in the "Two Books of the Advancement" of 1605, the same subject is varied thus :—

"To procure this ready use of knowledge there are two courses, preparation and suggestion. The former of these seemeth scarcely a part of knowledge, consisting rather of diligence than of any artificial erudition. And herein Aristotle wittily, but hurtfully, doth deride the Sophists near his time, saying, *They did as if one that professed the art of shoe-making should not teach how to make up a shoe, but only exhibit in a readiness a number of shoes of all fashions and sizes.* But yet a man might reply, that if a shoemaker should have no shoes in his shop, but only work as he is bespoken, he should be weakly customed. But our Saviour, speaking of divine knowledge, saith, *That the kingdom of heaven is like a good householder, that bringeth forth both new and old store:* and we see the ancient writers of rhetoric do give it precept, that pleaders should have the places, whereof they have most continual use, ready handled in all the variety that may be; as that, to speak for the literal interpretation of the law against equity, and contrary; and to speak for presumptions and inferences against testimony, and contrary. And Cicero himself, being broken unto it by great experience, delivereth it plainly, that whatsoever a man shall have occasion to speak of (if he will take the pains), he may have it in effect premeditate and handled *in thesi*."

It seems to us Bacon is pretty clearly alluding to the *pros* and *cons*, or places of "persuasion and dissuasion," of the Essays,

BACON'S "GEORGICS OF THE MIND." 119

as implied in the "Colours of Good and Evil." And we are not at all sure by the word "*shoes*," he is not playing upon the word "*shows*," or *plays*. In the "De Augmentis" this same passage is varied thus:—"To procure this *ready Provision* for discourse there are two ways; either that it may be designed or pointed out, *as it were, by an index, under what heads the matter is to be sought; and this is what we call topic; or else that arguments may be beforehand framed and stored up about such thing as are frequently incident and come into disceptation, and this we will call promptuary art or of preparation.*" The passage continues from this moment just as the passage quoted from the "Two Books of the Advancement." Bacon is evidently hinting that *examples* are necessary before arguments, and that *Shoes are part of the estate of a shoemaker*, and more to the point *as the things themselves* than mere arguments. All this points, we think, to the Antitheta as promptuary to the plays, Bacon calls this part "*Promptuary Preparation*," belonging to "*Inventive Arts*" as "*Places of Suggestion*," being a branch of Logic, of which this Book V. treats. In the "Platform of the Design," we find this Art of Discovery (Invention) divided into *Arts and Arguments*.

Inquisition or Invention
- Arts into — Literate Experience.
- Arguments into — Interpretation of Nature.

In the "Two Books of the Advancement," 1605, "*De Cultura animi*" is the germ of the "Georgics of the Mind" in the 1623 "De Augmentis." And we find this "husbandry of character" (upon page 202, sec. xxii., Book II. Wright), discussing "*men's natures*" or *characters*, page 206, with hints for the Essays, inasmuch as the subjects we place in italics are the titles of some of Bacon's Essays:—

"A man shall find in the traditions of astrology some pretty and apt divisions of *men's natures*, according to the predominances of the planets; lovers of quiet, lovers of action, lovers of victory, lovers of honour, lovers of pleasure, lovers of arts, lovers of change, and so forth. A man shall find in the wisest sort of these relations which the Italians make touching conclaves, the natures of the several cardinals handsomely and lively painted forth. A man shall meet with in every day's conference the denominations of sensitive, dry, formal, real, humorous, certain, *huomo di prima impressione*, *huomo di ultima impressione*, and the like: and yet nevertheless this kind of observations wandereth in words, but is not fixed in inquiry. For the distinctions are found (many of them), but we conclude no precepts upon them: wherein our fault is the greater; *because both history, poesy, and daily experience are as goodly fields where these observations grow;* whereof we make a few posies to hold in our hands, but no man bringeth them to the confectionery, that receipts might be made of them for use of life.

"Of much like kind are those impressions of nature, which are imposed upon the mind by the sex, by the age, by the region, by health and sickness, by *beauty* and *deformity*,* and the like, which are inherent and not extern; and again, those which are caused by extern fortune; as sovereignty, *nobility*, obscure birth, *riches*, want, magistracy, privateness, *prosperity*, *adversity*, constant *fortune*, variable fortune, rising *per saltum*, *per gradus*, and the like."

Mark the hint Bacon gives us as to "*history*" and "*poesy*" for *the fields where these observations grow*. Amongst Bacon's "Essays" and "Antitheta," we find the subjects "Nobility," "Riches," "Adversity," and "Fortune," and it seems to us Bacon gives us these same titles as hints, fearing to say more in context with poetry. "Sovereignty" is much the same as "Empire," which is one of the essays. It is the context of all this that gives force to our evidence. For Bacon introduces the *affections as part of Ethics*, and blames Aristotle for his omission to do the same:—

"Another article of this knowledge is the inquiry touching

* There are two Essays by Bacon, entitled "Beauty," and "Deformity."

the affections; for as in medicining of the body, it is in order first to know the divers complexions and constitutions; secondly, the diseases; and lastly, the cures: so in medicining of the mind, after knowledge of the divers characters of men's natures, it followeth in order to know the diseases and infirmities of the mind, which are no other than the perturbations and distempers of the affections. For as the ancient politiques in popular estates were wont to compare the people to the sea, and the orators to the winds; because as the sea would of itself be calm and quiet, if the winds did not move and trouble it; so the people would be peaceable and tractable, if the seditious orators did not set them in working and agitation: so it may be fitly said, that the mind in the nature thereof would be temperate and stayed, if the affections, as winds, did not put it into tumult and perturbation. And here again I find strange, as before, that Aristotle should have written divers volumes of Ethics, *and never handled the affections, which is the principal subject thereof;* and yet in his Rhetorics, where they are considered but collaterally and in a second degree (as they may be moved by speech), he findeth place for them, and handleth them well for the quantity; but where their true place is, he pretermitteth them. For it is not his disputations about pleasure and pain than can satisfy this inquiry, no more than he that should generally handle the nature of light can be said to handle the nature of colours; *for pleasure and pain are to the particular affections, as light is to particular colours"* (Book II. "Advancement of Learning," 1605).

Have we not here a hint *for the title and subject matter*, "The *Colours* of Good and Evil," which are attached to the Essays, and were published 1597 with them ?—

"Nothing more variable than faces and countenances: yet men can bear in memory the infinite distinctions of them; nay, a painter with a few *shells of colours*, and the benefit of his eye, and habit of his *imagination*, can imitate them all that ever have been, are, or may be, if they were brought before him" ("Advancement of Learning," 1605, Book II., p. 136).

In this same work Bacon tells us *Poesy is referred to imagination:*—

"The parts of human learning have reference to the three parts of man's understanding, which is the seat of learning: history to his memory, poesy to his imagination, and philosophy to his reason" (p. 85).

And here let us remark, the "Antitheta," given in the Sixth Book "De Augmentis," are affiliated to the "Colours of Good and Evil," and there is a *gradus* of descent evidently, from the "Essays" to the "Colours," "Antitheta," and "Minor Formulæ." What we are suggesting is that the *colours* (in the painter's sense) of the characters of the 1623 theatre, are the "*Antitheta*," viz.:— the affections, passions, whose titles are Pride, Ingratitude, Envy, Vainglory, Constancy, Fortitude, Temperance, Dissimulation, Boldness, Flattery, Love, Friendship, with their conditions, Nobility, Beauty, Youth, Health, Riches, Honours, Praise, &c.

These, we say, are the *Colours of the Theatre*, and the particular treatise "On the Colours of Good and Evil" merely instructions for our unravelling of these colours in the plays, the *pros* and *cons* to instruct us to guard against sophisms, and to show how the same thing may be obscured in the Essays. The strong points are that we find the "Essays" connected with the "Antitheta," or really identified with them as fruit and seed. And these "Antitheta" are given as *promptuary, text, or cues*, and part of the "Wisdom of Private Speech," embraced under the title of Book VI. as *Tradition or Elocution*. It is our conviction all this is only *per gradus ad Theatrum*. In the "Platform of the Design" of the Sixth Book we find ("Advancement of Learning," 1640):—

ILLUSTRATION OF SPEECH OR RHETORIC.
- *The use, office, and application.*
  - Of the dictates of Reason to Imagination.
  - Of Speech respectively to particulars, or the Wisdom of Private Speech.
- *Appendices.*
  - Colours of Good and Evil.
  - Antitheta Rerum.
  - Lesser styles and forms of Speech.

It may be seen how the last three are bracketed together as illustrations of Rhetoric, undoubtedly pointing to the Essays. Nobody can question that, inasmuch as the two first, viz., "Colours of Good and Evil," were published with the Essays, and are only ways of showing us how the same thing may be said many ways, with the sophisms of rhetoric, so to speak, argued, and their fallacies exposed. We say Bacon wrote this expressly to caution us against literal interpretation of the letter* of the Essays, and to give us a hint as to the Theatre also through the Essays applied in the spirit. The "Antitheta" are the kernels of the Essays, or affections and passions of the characters, of which the plays are composed. Archbishop Whately declares the "Antitheta" are identical with the Essays—at least many of them, and Doctor Abbott has followed in the same footsteps, attaching many of the "Antitheta" (if not all) to their respective subjects in the Essays. Therefore this being acknowledged, it behoves the critic to explain why these kernels, or cues of the Essays, are to be found under the all-embracing title of the Sixth Book (where they are introduced) of "Tradition or Elocution." Because "Tradition" is explained by Bacon in these words: "*Now let us come unto the Art of Delivery, or of expressing and transferring those things which are invented, judged, and laid up in the Memory, which by a general name we will call Tradition*" (Book VI., "De Augmentis," p. 258, 1640). Reference to the Platform or Design of this Book will show this title embraces *the entire Sixth Book*. Besides, these "Colours of Good and Evil," "Antitheta," and "Minor Formulæ" come under "*The Wisdom of Private Speech*," and I defy anyone to explain this except as an esoteric doctrine for those who can pierce the veil, and see what

* This is attached to the opening of the "Antitheta"—

Pro verbis legis.

Non est interpretatio, sed divinatio, quæ recedit a litera:
Cum receditur a litera, judex transit in legislatorem.

Pro sententia legis.

Ex omnibus verbis est eliciendus sensus qui interpretatur singula.

Bacon really implies by it. Why should the simple *pros and cons* of Rhetoric be thus attributed *to a secret or reserved method?* Directly we study their titles, our suspicions are doubly aroused, for Pride, Revenge, Envy, Love, Ingratitude, Vain-Glory, Dissimulation, Boldness, Flattery, Friendship, Suspicion, are not only to be refound as Essays, but common-sense tells us are the *Colours, Passions, or Affections at the bottom* of Comedy and Tragedy. *They are the paints in which the Dramatic Artist dips his brush or pen.* And if Bacon wanted to point at the Theatre, either indirectly through the Essays, or directly without them, what indeed could be a deeper hint for the plays called Shakespeare's? It is suspicious enough Bacon selects just these subjects for examples. And it is far more suspicious he calls them "seeds" or "skeins," to be unravelled as *Promptuary Places of Suggestion*. (Book VI., p. 300, "Advancement of Learning," 1640.)

We have elsewhere, in a brief manner, drawn attention to a few of the prominent texts of the Essays, to be refound in the sermons of the plays. No doubt with patience and industry the entire Essays and their cues, the "*Antitheta*," are to be thus unravelled and applied to characters of the Folio Plays, 1623.

Lamartine writes: "It is as a moralist that Shakespeare excels.... His works cannot fail to elevate the mind by the purity of the morals they inculcate. They breathe so strong a belief in virtue, so steady an adherence to good principles, united to such a vigorous tone of honour, as testifies to the author's excellence as a moralist; nay, as a Christian." (Quoted in Donnelly's "Great Cryptogram.")

It is as a moralist that Bacon is pre-eminent in the "De Augmentis," the seventh book treating of morality, the eighth book containing no less than Thirty-Four Parables from the Proverbs of Solomon, with their explications, and the ninth book dealing with Inspired Divinity. The work opens with the idea of sacrifice, springing out of "devout cheerfulness," the work ends with the same spirit of sacrifice and a prayer to God. The "Two Books of the Advancement of Learning" conclude with Divine

Learning—"*The matter revealed*," "*The nature of the revelation.*" And in both these works the Theological element is most evident, and predominates over the profane matter treated therein. Solomon is Bacon's inspired prototype, and we are not at all certain he did not identify himself to some degree with him. For in certain philosophical tracts he repeatedly introduces the expression "*my son,*" which, as he had no sons of his own, must be understood philosophically, or from the standpoint of a brotherhood or craft. He calls his Thirty-seventh Deficient, "The method bequeathed to the *sons of Sapience.*" This at once recalls the Proverbs and language of Solomon:—

1. *My son*, if thou wilt receive my words; and hide my commandments with thee,

2. So that thou incline thine ear unto *wisdom*, and apply thine heart to understanding (Proverbs ii. 1, 2).

The resemblance of some of the plays in plot and incidents to parables of Scripture must have struck every thoughtful reader. The introduction of the three caskets in the "Merchant of Venice" closely resembles the parable of "The Pearl of Great Price" (Matthew xiii. 45, 46). "Measure for Measure" holds some parallel to the Parable of "The Talents." "For the kingdom of heaven is as a man travelling *into a far country*, who called his own servants *and delivered unto them his goods*. And unto one he gave five talents, to another two, and to another one, to every man according to his several ability ; *and straightway took his journey.*" We find the Duke in the play doing exactly this with regard to Angelo—delivering unto him his goods or government—and straightway *pretending to take his journey into a far country.* And this idea is borne out by the interpretation of the parable, which of course is that we must turn our talents and gifts to account. See how this key-note is struck by the Duke in almost the first lines of the play :—

> Thyself and thy belongings
> Are not thine own so proper, as to waste
> Thyself upon thy virtues; they on thee:
> Heaven doth with us, as we with torches do,

> *Not light them for themselves: for if our virtues*
> *Did not go forth of us, 'twere all alike*
> *As if we had them not: Spirits are not finely touch'd*
> *But to fine issues :* nor nature never lends
> The smallest scruple of her excellence,
> But like a thrifty goddess she determines
> Herself the glory of a creditor
> Both thanks and use.
>
> ("Measure for Measure," act i. sc. 1.)

Is not the parable further hinted at in Angelo's reply—we mean *the talent as a piece of money or a coin ?*

> *Angelo.* Now good my Lord,
> Let there be some more test made of *my mettle,*
> Before so noble and so great a figure
> *Be stamp't upon it.*
>
> (Act i. sc. 1.)

The author seems to have had a piece of money in his mind—perhaps *an angel !* But there is the parable both in the text and in the main idea of the plot construction, with the alteration that the Duke, instead of actually going on his journey, plays the part of an invisible, ubiquitous, and all-seeing Providence, who searches out the thoughts and wicked acts of his servants, whilst they imagine him absent; the end being to punish the wicked servant who has misused the trust committed to him, and to reward the good. There can be little doubt the ethical motive of this play, is to teach, that to the all-seeing eye of Providence nothing can be hid. And see how Bacon repeats all this in other forms in his Essays, particularly condemning Selfishness or "Wisdom for a man's self." In this Essay he writes:—
"An ant is a wise creature for itself; but it is a shrewd thing in an orchard or garden. And certainly men that are great lovers of themselves *waste the public. It is a poor centre of a man's actions* HIMSELF. *It is right earth.* For that only stands fast upon his own centre; whereas all things *that have affinity with the heavens move upon the centre of another, which they benefit.*"
Bacon's irony with regard to the ant is pretty severe. The ant makes sad havoc in the garden, whilst seeking only its own

ends. And we may guess what Bacon infers with regard to himself, when he says, "It is a blessed thing to have a mind concentric with the orb of the universe." Again, "But the corrupter sort of politics, that have not their minds instituted and established in the true apprehension of duties, and the contemplation of good in the universality, *refer all things to themselves as if they were the world's centre, and that the concurrence of all lines should touch in them and their fortunes;* never caring in all tempest what becomes of the ship, so they may retire and save themselves in the cockboat of their own fortune" ("De Augmentis," p. 23, 1640).

I would observe that the doctrine of Good being derived out of Evil, and that man's ends are invisibly directed by supreme Providence, seems prefigured in the substitution of Mariana for Isabella, by which the purposed sin of Angelo becomes an instrument of restitution and right. In "All's Well that Ends Well" we find a parallel—Helena (like Mariana) exchanging *rôle* with Diana in order to regain her husband. There can be little doubt in the character of Diana (and in her name), the author intended to picture Chastity and Virtue, just as we refind it in the character of Isabella. *Virtue and Vice* are made, in short, to change parts in both these cases. *Sin or the intention to sin*, bringing good out of evil, man's individual selfish ends being changed to serve the *supreme purposes* of the Almighty, as we perceive in the secret agency of the Duke in "Measure for Measure." Bacon gives us a hint when he writes:— "Also the question controverted with such heat between the schools of Zeno and Socrates, on the one side, who placed Felicity in Virtue simple or attended, which hath a great share in the *Duties of Life:* and on the other side, other sects and professions, as the schools of the Cirenaics and Epicureans, who placed it in pleasure, and made Virtue—*as it is used in some Comedies where the mistress and the maid change habits*—to be but as a handmaid, without which pleasure cannot be well waited and attended upon" (Lib. VII. "De Augmentis," p. 339, 1640).

In the "Two Books of the Advancement" (1605) we read—
"*Some Comedies of Errors.*" This simile we refind in Cicero's
"De Finibus" ("Concerning the Ends of Things Good and Evil").
"In the next place, by the concurrence of the Virtues which
reason terms the *Mistress* of all (though you contend they are
but the *pages and handmaids of pleasure*") ("De Finibus," Book II.
ch. v.). Bacon writes: "Vice itself assumes the shape and
shadow of virtue."

> Sæpe latet vitium proximitate boni.

("Colours of Good and Evil," 4.)

In "Much Ado about Nothing" we have the handmaid (Margaret) of Hero changing places with her—that is, *acting* her mistress. The result is that Hero appears in the eyes of her father, Claudio, as tainted. Virtue has changed places with vice. This play may rightly be entitled a "Comedy of Errors." I venture to think there is something in this idea, which might be further worked out. For by this simple and clever artifice we discover the full workings and effects of *appearance*, or of *acting*, and the disastrous consequences of vice when it takes the place of virtue. Bacon has reversed the process he quotes. Instead of virtue being the handmaid of vice, he has in this Comedy, made vice the handmaid of virtue, to show how supreme and beautiful virtue is if *unattended*. There is another moral seemingly embraced in this change of characters. In this world it is very easy for not only vice to *appear* virtuous, but easier for virtue to *appear* vicious. For appearances go often further than realities, seeing people have neither time, leisure, nor sufficient penetration to always rightly gauge character or motive. An honest character is far more likely to lay itself open to censure and its enemies, than a crafty man of the world who plays his cards well.* King Lear is entirely deceived by the *acting* of Regan and Goneril, and the silence of Cordelia is con-

---

* Poor honest Lord, brought low by his own heart,
  Undone by goodness.
              ("Timon of Athens," act iv. sc. 2.)

strued the opposite way. Othello and Desdemona are the victims of Iago's *acting* in the same way. Timon of Athens is the victim of the flattery of his friends, imagining they possess as generous a nature as his own. The whole of Ethic turns upon the correspondence of the internal to the external—*being and appearance*. Dowden describes the art of the plays thus:—" An indifference to *externals* in comparison with that which is of the *invisible life*" ("Shakespeare's Mind," p. 34).

It is just this preference or predominance of the *invisible, interior life and reality*, which constitutes the splendour and glory of these plays. It is this which establishes these works in our hearts as household words—a second Bible, where those who are in sorrow or distress may find themselves. The acting is the world, but the reality is anatomized, and we may be sure Bacon has carried this print of truth and goodness (for he says, "*they are one*") very much further than we as yet can have the faintest idea. The rationalism of these plays, *which is only a question of time*, and of the application of the Baconian philosophy to them, will reveal the voice of the Dead, speaking to us in no uncertain tones. How fatal the deceitfulness of externals, protestations, and acting are in life, is summed up in the play of "King Lear," who is not the only fool in the world who believes all he hears or what he sees alone.

> *Cord.* What shall Cordelia do? Love and be *silent.*
>
> *Lear.* Let it be so; *thy truth then be thy dower.*
> ("King Lear," act i. sc. 1.)

Bacon, under the heading "Loquacity,"* argues the *pro* and *contra* of *Silence*. The play of "King Lear" may almost be called a tragic sermon on this text. For nothing is more in contrast than the loquacity and protestations of love (towards their father) of Regan and Goneril, with the *silence* of Cordelia. See what Bacon writes of "Ingratitude" (and it may be recalled Goneril *poisons her sister and commits suicide*). "The crime of

* "*Silence is a candidate for Truth*" (xxxi.).

ingratitude is not to be repressed by punishments, *but to be referred over to the Furies* " (Ingratitude, " Antitheta," XV.).

From an early age Bacon seems to have been imbued with these ethical ideas pointing to the common welfare of men. For in one of his earliest compositions we find " *Philautia,*" or *Selfishness*, introduced in a by no means favourable aspect. Bacon's own life with regard to all this has yet to be written—*by himself*. We are convinced he sought power in order to command wits and means * for his literary and philosophical ends rather than for itself or himself. He says in the " Advancement," that the *society self or external self is apart and another thing altogether from the interior (or true) man*. And in this remark we can see he regarded the World of Action as a Stage where every man must *play a part*. And is this not true ? If we refuse to play a part in life (*or suppress say a part*), we very soon find ourselves only lookers-on. For as long as men are men, and life is what it is, to meet those on equal terms who are not better, and perhaps even worse than ourselves, we must carry a mask of reserve, and conform to the world's ways. Bacon, we venture to suggest, conformed to the universal insanity of his age. He tried plain-speaking and honest speech, and found no road to preferment that way. He saw flattery and servility and intrigue were the only paths to honour. He saw a great good might come of a little wrong, and he chose this way. In reflecting upon Bacon's political life and character, critics have written as if he lived in a Palace of Truth. They forget Elizabeth's Court and her successors was full of intrigue, crooked ways, and honesty carried on the sleeve a disqualifier for advancement. Bacon who writes is quite another man from the Bacon who acts. In the former we have *the real man*, in the latter the man of the world playing his part, where all is acting. He probably saw no more immo-

---

* " For good thoughts (though God accept them), yet towards men are little better than good dreams, except they be put in act, *and that cannot be without power and place, as the vantage and commanding ground*" ("Of Great Place ").

rality in this double life than most men do who do not carry windows in their breasts, the question of morality being often more matter of degree than principle. The man of honest heart who finds himself fallen amongst dishonest people or thieves, may be well pardoned playing a rôle to be on fair terms with them.

It seems to us in "Measure for Measure" we have reflected in the person of Angelo, and in the incident of the substitution of Mariana for Isabella, a lesson of extraordinary suggestion and ethical instruction. For it is in the power of Providence to shape "our ends, rough hew them how we will." Evil often is followed by good, even as day follows night, and spring winter.

The *supreme good* is undoubtedly extracted out of things evil, the evil of the present moment being the progenitor of good future.

> Virtue itself turns vice, being misapplied;
> And vice sometimes by action dignified.
> ("Romeo and Juliet," act ii. sc. 3.)

> There is no vice so simple but assumes
> Some mask of virtue on his outward part.
> ("Merchant of Venice," act iii. sc. 2.)

CHAPTER VI.

BACON AND SENECA.

Thomas Powell to Bacon.

To

Trve Nobility and Tryde Learning

Beholden

Francis, Lord Verulam, and Viscount St Albanes.

> O giue me leaue to pull the curtaine by,
>   That clouds thy Worth in such obscurity;
> Good Seneca, stay but a while thy bleeding,
> T'accept what I receiuèd at thy Reading:
>   Here I present it in a solemne strayne:
>   And thus I plucke this curtayne backe againe.

(From "The Attovrney's Academy," by Thomas Powell: 3rd edition, 1630.)

It seems to us these lines were indited, by a *knower of Bacon's real dramatic disguise and concealment, behind the curtain of the Shakespeare Theatre*. The reference to Seneca is striking. Because Gervinus affirms the author of the plays was thoroughly acquainted, and profoundly imbued, with the writings of both Seneca and Plautus. Gervinus maintains Plautus and Seneca were Shakespeare's ideals. "If Shakespeare had had occasion at any time *to name his ideal,* and to denote the highest examples of dramatic art which lay before him, *he would have named none but Plautus and Seneca.*"

The line—

> Let me lodge Lichas on the horns o' the moon,
>   ("Antony and Cleopatra," act iv. sc. 10),

was supposed by Warburton to be taken from Seneca's "Hercules." Certain it is, Seneca's works were an especial study of Bacon's, and it is just in the Seventh Book of the "De Augmentis," which treats of *Ethic*, that he frequently cites from him. For example:—"Veré magnum habere fragilitatem hominis securitatem Dei." "Vita sine proposito languida et vaga est" ("Senec. in Epistles"). "De Partibus vitæ quisque deliberat, de summa nemo" ("De Brev. vitæ") (pages 336, 343, 351, "Advancement of Learning," 1640).

In the Sixth Book of the "Advancement of Learning" (1623 and 1640), we find Bacon giving us a collection of "*Antitheta*," which are forty-seven in number, with each a "pro" and "contra." Bacon writes: "*A collection of this nature* we find in Seneca, but in Suppositions only or Cases of this sort (in regard we have many ready prepared), we thought good to set down some of them for example; these we call *Antitheta Rerum*" (Book VI., p. 300, "Advancement of Learning," 1640). In a collection of the third group of Essays, published 1612, we find one "Of Love," which was altered in the 1625 (British Museum copy) edition. The 1612 Essay opens, "*Love* is the argument always of *Comedies*, and many times of *Tragedies*." In the 1625 Edition this is changed into, "The *Stage* is more beholding to *Love* than the life of man. For as to the *Stage*, Love is ever matter of *Comedies* and now and then of *Tragedies*." In this Essay we read: "It is a poor saying of Epicurus, '*Satis magnum alter alteri Theatrum sumus*'" (we are a sufficiently great Theatre, the one to the other). Seneca quotes this in his Epistle (i. 7), ascribing it to Epicurus. Seneca is repeatedly quoted by Bacon in the "Essays," and thirteen times in the 1640 "Advancement of Learning" (see Index). Directly we recall the Comedies of the Folio, we find them dealing mostly with Love, but it is not so apparent in the Tragedies except in "Othello," "Troilus and Cressida," and "Antony and Cleopatra." It is the main theme of the "Two Gentlemen of Verona," of the "Merry Wives," of "Measure for Measure," of "Much Ado about Nothing," of "Love's Labour's Lost," of "A Midsummer Night's Dream," of "The Merchant of Venice," of "As You Like It," of "The Taming of the Shrew," of "All's Well that Ends Well," of "Twelfth Night," and of "The Winter's Tale," but in the chronicle plays it is only incidentally introduced. In "Timon of Athens," "Julius Cæsar," "Macbeth," "Hamlet," "Lear," it plays hardly any rôle at all, so that Bacon's distinction is pretty correct, and where he studied the differences between Comedy and Tragedy in this respect we should like to know?

In "Hamlet" Polonius makes the speech:—"The best actors in the world, either for Tragedy, Comedy, History, Pastoral, Pastoral-Comical, Historical-Pastoral, Tragical-Historical, Tragical-Comical-Historical-Pastoral, scene indivisible, or Poem unlimited. *Seneca* cannot be too heavy, nor *Plautus* too light." In the Seventh Book of the "De Augmentis" (translation by Gilbert Wats, 1640), which (mark it) treats of *Ethic*, and the "*diverse characters of men's natures or dispositions*" (p. 352), we find a decided parallel to this passage:—"So among the Poets, *Heroical, Satyrical, Tragedians, Comedians*, you shall find everywhere the images of wits, although commonly *with excess, and beyond the bounds of truth*" (p. 352). On the next page (353), "For we see *Plautus* makes it a wonder to see an old man beneficent, *Benignitas quidem hujus oppido ut adolescentuli est*" ("Mil. Glo.").

Bacon evidently was studying character in Plautus pretty closely. How Bacon's observation upon excess finds its parallel in Hamlet's speech to the Players:—"Be not too tame neither, but let your own discretion be your tutor. Suit the action to the word, the word to the action, with this special observance: *that you o'erstep not the modesty of nature.*"

The spirit of Seneca's "morals" is to be refound in Bacon's "Advancement of Learning," "De Augmentis" (Book VII.), and in the Essays. Seneca gives a series of Essays upon "Anger," consisting of twelve chapters, and Bacon gives us an

Essay also upon "Anger." How much Bacon was indebted to Seneca's "Epistles" is evident from the identity of subjects and even terms which he reproduces. For example, one of Seneca's epistles is upon "Custom." Another is "Every Man is the Artificer of his Own Fortune." Bacon's treatment of "Custom," both in his Essay and in the Seventh Book "De Augmentis," shows he had deeply taken to heart Seneca's writings. Another Essay (also introduced in the "De Augmentis") is upon "Fortune," and it seems Sir Nicholas Bacon was fond of quoting the following line :—

"Faber quisque fortunæ propriæ"

("Advancement of Learning," Book II., p. 93, 1605). For in "Fragmenta Regalia," by Naunton, we read (under Sir Nicholas Bacon) he was fond of saying :—

"Unus quisque suæ fortunæ faber."

Seneca's "Epistles" are wonderfully close to the spirit, if not even the style, of much of Bacon's wisdom, and Seneca's entire teaching is *self-sacrifice and philanthropy*, inculcated in just the same religious and philosophical way by Bacon. "It is often objected to me, that I advise people to quit the world, to retire and content themselves with a good conscience. But what becomes of your precepts then (say they) that enjoin us to die in action? To whom I must answer, That I am never more in action than when I am alone in my study; where I have only lock'd up myself in private, to attend the business of the public. I do not lose so much as one day; nay, and part of the night too I borrow for my book. When my eyes will serve me no longer, I fall asleep, and till then I work. I have retired myself, not only from men, but from business also: And my own in the first, *to attend the service of Posterity, in hope that what I now write may, in some measure, be profitable to future generations*" (Epistle VI., "The Blessings of a Virtuous Retirement." "How we come to the Knowledge of Virtue." Seneca's "Morals," 1678). Everyone acquainted with Bacon's writings must recognise in these last words what Bacon is perpetually repeating for himself. "Born for the service of mankind," writes Bacon. And it is always for "After Ages," "Posterity," he writes. In his preface to the "Instauration":—"Some demonstration of his sincere and propense affection to promote the good of mankind" (p. 3, "Advancement of Learning," 1640). "Truly he esteemed other ambition whatsoever inferior to the business he had in hand : for either the matter in consultation, and thus far prosecuted, is nothing, or so much as the conscience of the merit itself, ought to give him contentment, *without seeking a recompense from abroad*" (p. 3, "Advancement of Learning," 1640). This is thoroughly in the style of Seneca. Bacon writes:—"I take *Goodness* in this sense the affecting of the weal of men, which is that the Græcians called *Philanthropia;* and the word *Humanity* (as it is used) is a little too light to express it. *Goodness* I call the habit, and *Goodness of Nature* the inclination. *This, of all virtues and dignities of the mind, is the greatest, being the character of the Deity.** And without it Man is a busy, mischievous, wretched thing, no better than a kind of vermin" ("Of Goodness and Goodness of Nature"). Again, "The inclination to *Goodness* is imprinted deeply in the nature of man, insomuch that, if it issue not towards men, it will take unto other living creatures: as it is seen in the Turks, a cruel people, who, nevertheless, are kind to beasts, and give alms to dogs and birds : insomuch as Busbechius reporteth, a Christian boy in Constantinople had like to have been stoned, for gagging in a waggishness a long-billed fowl" ("Goodness and Goodness of Nature"). See how all this is re-echoed in "Titus Andronicus":—

> Wilt thou draw near the nature of the Gods ?
> Draw near them in being merciful.
> Sweet mercy is nobility's true badge.
>
> (Act i. sc. 1.)

Seneca's letters upon "Cruelty" and upon "Clemency" (or Mercy) are re-echoes of all this. Seneca writes:—"Though

---

* Earthly power doth then show likest God's
When mercy seasons justice.
("Merchant of Venice," act iv. sc. 1.)

Mercy and Gentleness of Nature keeps all in peace and tranquillity, even in a cottage, yet is it much more beneficial and conspicuous in a palace. Clemency does well with all, *but best with Princes.*" Compare with this the clemency of the Prince to Shylock, and the lines:—

<blockquote>The quality of mercy is not strained, &c.</blockquote>

In 1591, when Bacon was thirty-one, he writes to Lord Burleigh: "This, whether it be curiosity or vain glory, or nature, or if one take it favourably, *Philanthropia is so fixed in my mind as it cannot be removed*" ("Letters"). With this should be coupled Bacon's deeply religious spirit, as evinced in his writings and the testimony of Doctor Rawley (" this lord was religious ") to the same effect. Bacon's life had (we suggest) two distinct ends and two distinct phases. One was the real Bacon *himself* (as Dr Abbott puts it), alone like Seneca in his study, writing for Posterity and the service of mankind. This was the contemplative looker on, the true man. The other phase was the man of action, playing a part as means to his great ends.

Bacon in his dedicatory epistle to Andrews (Bishop of Winchester) accompanying his "Holy War," compares himself to *Demosthenes, Cicero,* and *Seneca.* Bacon was the first Orator of his age, as Ben Jonson testifies. "The fear of every man that heard him was, lest he should make an end." And so the comparison with Demosthenes is exact. Cicero was a great Orator also, and a great lawyer like Bacon, also a writer and Philosopher; but Seneca was a great Dramatist, and it is not so easy to see the parallel except in the point of Fortune. " Only one specimen of the talents of the Romans for Tragedy has come down to us. These are the ten tragedies which pass under the name of Seneca " (Donaldson's, 'Theatre of the Greeks," p. 357). It is well worthy study to ask ourselves if Bacon in this comparison of himself with Seneca does not give us a profound hint as to his *dramatic side.* Gervinus (as already quoted by us) declares Seneca to have inspired Shakespeare. And here is the *alter ego* of Shakespeare confessing to self-comparison with this Latin author. "Seneca, indeed, who was condemned for many corruptions and crimes, and banished into a *solitary island* kept a mean; and though his pen did not freeze, yet he abstained from intruding into matters of business; but spent his time in writing *books of excellent argument and use for all ages;* though he might have made better choice (sometimes) of his dedications. *These examples confirmed me much in a resolution to spend my time wholly in writing, and so to put forth that poor talent, or half talent, or what it is, that God hath given me, not as heretofore to particular exchanges, but to banks or mounts of perpetuity which will not break.*"

There is a vast deal in Seneca's morals that we refind in Bacon's works in more ways than one. Seneca: "I could never hear Attalus upon the vices of the age, and the errors of life *without a comparison for mankind*" (ch. v. "Of a Happy Life"). In the "New Atlantis" we read of the Tirsan, "who had an aspect as if he pitied men."

"For we ourselves are our own greatest flatterers" (ch. vi. "Of a Happy Life," Seneca).

"It hath been well said, that the Arch-flatterer with whom all the petty flatterers have intelligence, is a man's self" (Essay, "Love").

"It is every man's duty to make himself profitable to mankind" (ch. vii. "Happy Life").

"The passage to virtue is fair, but the way to greatness is craggy, and it stands not only upon a precipice, but upon ice too: and yet it is a hard matter to convince a great man that his station is slippery" (ch. xii. "Happy Life").

> The art o' the court,
> As hard to leave as keep; whose top to climb
> Is certain falling, *or so slippery that*
> The fear's as bad as falling.
>
> ("Cymbeline," act iii. sc. 3.)

CHAPTER VII.

"ANTITHETA" IN BACON, ETC.

"For who knows not that the doctrine of contraries are the same, though they be opposite in use" (Book VI., p. 209, "Advancement of Learning").

"They that endeavour to abolish vice destroy also virtue, for contraries, though they destroy one another, are yet in life of one another" ("Religio Medici," Browne, p. 113).

HEGEL, in his logic, affirms "*everything is at once that which it is, and the contrary of that which it is.*" Bacon has in his Rhetoric drawn up a collection of "*Antitheta*," or *pros* and *cons*, that give, as it were, the Sophisms of each side of a question or proposition. Most of these subjects are identical with, or touch very nearly the arguments of the Essays. Nothing is so remarkable in the plays as the antithetical style, which gives the supposed Shakespeare at once his depth and peculiar hall mark of distinction from every other writer ancient or modern. *Whether philosophising or illustrating, nothing the author delights in more than antithesis or paradox.* It enters so largely into the text of his Theatre, we must conclude the author's mind was so constituted, *so impersonal and universal, that he could contemplate no subject without at once embracing its negative.* Here are a few examples.

> In poison there is physic.
> ("2 King Henry IV.," act i. sc. 1.)

> These sentences to sugar, or to gall,
> Being strong on both sides are equivocal.
> ("Othello," act i. sc. 3.)

> And do but see his vice,
> 'Tis to his vertue a just equinox.
> *The one's as long as t'other.*
> ("Othello," act ii. sc. 2.)

> Merry and tragical ! Tedious and brief !
> That is hot ice, and wondrous strange snow,
> How shall we find the concord of this discord ?
> ("Midsummer Night's Dream," act v. sc. 1.)

> The better act of purposes mistook,
> Is to mistake again, though indirect,
> *Yet indirection thereby grows direct.*
> ("King John," act i. sc. 1.)

> His humble ambition, proud humility :
> His jarring concord : and his discord dulcet,
> His faith, his sweet disaster.
> ("All's Well that Ends Well, act i. sc. 1.)

> O brawling love ! O loving hate !
> O anything of nothing first create !
> O heavy lightness. Serious vanity ?
> Misshapen chaos of well-seeming forms !
> Feather of lead, bright smoke, cold fire, sick health.
> Still waking sleep, that is not what it is :
> This love feel I, that feel no love in this.
> ("Romeo and Juliet," act. i. sc. 1.)

To quote them all would be to quote a greater part of the 1623 Folio, for we venture to maintain the style of the works known as Shakespeare's, is characterised by profundity of expression, the result of a perfectly-trained mind, holding a peculiar philosophy, and applying it to everything as explanation. What we mean is, that in this iterated Antithesis we hold a powerful key for the locked wards of the mind of whoever wrote these plays. This delight in Antithesis is at once a proof of an intellect matured in the schools, familiar with Aristotle (as Bacon confesses in his letter to Mountjoye), and of a mind always clear, estimating philosophy as master of poetry, not servant. Buffon has declared that "the style is the man" in writing. Style is the outcome of thought. If the thoughts are profound, clear, and philosophic, the style will reveal it. Nothing is more certain, we venture to suggest, than that the mind of the author of this style known as Shakespeare's, delighted in embracing the idea of the contrary or negative of a thing, at the same time as its positive. Excess always brings (in the philosophy of the plays), its direct opposite. Loss brings want, plenty satiety and disgust; *excessive generosity and faith in humanity*, produces *excessive misanthropy and cynicism*, as in the cases of "Timon of Athens," and "King Lear." There is in the plays evidence (both in style and in construction of plot and character), of a mind bent upon illustrating the dangers of excess in anything, and we find it revealed in such passages as the following:—

> The violence of either grief or joy
> Their own enactures with themselves destroy.
> ("Hamlet," act iii. sc. 2.)

"For aught I see, they are as sick *that surfeit with too much as they that starve with nothing; it is no small happiness, therefore, to be seated in the mean.* Superfluity comes sooner by white hairs, but competence lives longer." ("Merchant of Venice," act i.)

Under such passages we may perceive the doctrine pointed, that *proportion or balance* is as much an ingredient in happiness as in Art or Nature. In the Sonnets we find evidence once more of this philosophy of contraries at war, and yet in union or love. Evil with Bacon is not an affirmative, but only a negative, and we find the plays reiterating the words of Gœthe in Faust, that the Devil is he, "*who constantly denies*," and yet "*brings forth the good.*"

> God Almighty!
> There is some soul of goodness in things evil,
> Would men observingly distil it out;
> Thus may we gather honey from the weed,
> And make a moral of the devil himself.
> ("King Henry V.," act iv. sc. 1.)

Amongst Bacon's "Colours of Good and Evil," we find him almost enunciating the same doctrine:—"*That which draws near to Good or Evil, the same is likewise Good or Evil; but that which is remov'd from Good is Evil, from Evil is Good.*" In the Reprehension of this Colour Bacon writes:—"But the colour deceives three ways; first, in respect of *Destitution;* secondly, in respect of *Obscuration;* thirdly, in respect of *Protection.* In regard of

Protection, for things approach and congregate not only for consort and similitude of nature, but even *that which is evil* (especially in Civil matters) *approacheth to Good for concealment and Protection;* so wicked persons betake themselves to the sanctuary of the Gods, *and vice itself assumes the shape and shadow of virtue.*

Sæpe latet vitium proximitate boni."

(P. 214, Lib. VI., "Advancement of Learning," 1640.)

> *There is no vice so simple but assumes*
> *Some mark of virtue on his outward parts:*
> How many cowards, whose hearts are all as false
> As stairs of sand, wear yet upon their chins
> The beards of Hercules, and frowning Mars,
> Who inward search'd have livers white as milk,
> And these assume but valours excrement
> To render them redoubted.
>
> ("Merchant of Venice," act iii. sc. 2.)

Now these repeated "*Antitheta*" cannot be explained upon any ordinary grounds as casual indulgences of thought, and if they were even so, they would remain unexplained. They are so frequent, and play such a profound part in the style of the text, we must conclude not only are they introduced with reference to some philosophical principles underlying the construction and rationalism of these plays, as yet unrevealed to us, but that the author had arrived at some definite and accepted explanation of life as the result of Opposites or Contraries, in some such sense as expounded in the philosophy of Heraclitus. The remarkable point is, we find Bacon re-echoing all this in his Essays, and "Antitheta," and "Colours of Good and Evil." In a letter to Lord Mountjoye prefixed to these colours, or *pros* and *cons*, he confesses he has borrowed them from Aristotle's "Rhetoric." So that we see his mind was perfectly trained and versed in these sophisms, for and against, which he examples as places of *persuasion and dissuasion.* These "Antitheta" are applicable to the Essays. If we read the Essay on Truth (for example) we find two contradictory or antithetical propositions,—one setting forth and inclining to a life of study, and the other a life of active politics. It is this that gives the Essays an impersonality and an impossibility of arriving at any particular teaching, except for good in the main. Dissimulation is praised as politic, yet Bacon elsewhere declares himself "vanquished with an immortal love of truth." Presently he declares "Nakedness of the mind to be as uncomely as nakedness of the body." We desire to point out the parallel that Bacon is universal, impersonal, all-sided, impartial, and we refind exactly the same myriad-minded impassiveness and philosophical treatment in the plays. From Bacon's Essay upon "Cupid, or the Origins and Principles of Things," we are inclined to believe he had adopted some sort of philosophy, founded on what may be permitted us to briefly term, Affirmatives and Negatives, otherwise rendered in such synonyms as Light and Darkness, Love and Hate, Heat and Cold, Attraction and Repulsion, in connection with the philosophy of Participation of Parmenides, and the Atomic theory of Democritus. We find in the Sonnets this philosophy of Opposites very strongly hinted and delivered in the form of paradox. The philosophy of the plays frequently turns upon profound paradox. Everything runs to its opposite,* like an over-loaded ship. Directly we lose a thing we feel its loss, though not before. Excess produces its direct opposite in want. Discord prepares for Concord. Too much sweetness produces bitterness, and so applied to everything in morality and life. I think the reader will grant this is a great characteristic of what is known as Shakespeare's writings. And being so, we are certain it amounted in the writer's mind to something more than chance reflection. It infects the language and compacts it into that condensed form of pithy philosophy and paradox so often hard to follow. Virtue and Vice are treated from this point of view as laws of attraction and repulsion, as effects of light and shadow. If we were asked to characterise the peculiar style of the writing of the plays (apart from plot or

---

* The present pleasure,
By revolution lowering does become
The opposite of itself.
("Antony and Cleopatra," act i. sc. 2.)

character), we should say that it abounded and revelled in antithetical expression and paradox. The writer has always the affirmative and the negative of a proposition in his mind at the same time, and frequently involves one with the other. Even in portrayal of character the same great law is observed. The fools in the plays are really the wise men, and are introduced, as in Lear, always to lighten some dark background. Timon becomes cynic like Apemantus, whom he had never listened to in prosperity. Lear's real madness is set side by side with Edgar's feigned madness. The real and the false are introduced as light and shadow to illustrate each other. We see this again in Hamlet's feigned and Ophelia's real madness. It is particularly prominent in the contrast afforded by Apemantus the cynic, and Timon the misanthrope, the latter becoming a hundredfold more cynical than the former when too late.

Archbishop Tenison in "Baconiana" (pub. 1679) thus alludes to the Essays:—"His Lordship wrote them in the English tongue, and enlarged them as occasion served, and at last added to them the '*Colours of Good and Evil*,' which are likewise found in his book '*De Augmentis*.'" This is a very important point for us to consider, because it at once shows Bacon wrote these Essays with an eye upon Aristotle's Rhetoric, and that he intended to write in an impersonal and philosophic spirit— for the "*Colours of Good and Evil*" are *pros and cons* of both sides of every proposition. But what is far more important, and I think a discovery of some weight, is that in the "De Augmentis," 1623 (and 1640 translation by Wats), we find these " Colours" introduced as part of "*The Wisdom of Private Speech.*" "Surely it will not be amiss to recommend this whereof we now speak to a new *Inquiry*, and to call it by name ' THE WISDOM OF PRIVATE SPEECH,' and to refer it to Deficients; a thing certainly which the more seriously a man shall think on, the more highly he shall value; and whether this kind of *Prudence* should be placed between *Rhetoric* and the *Politics* is a matter of no great consequence. Now let us descend to the *Deficients*

"ANTITHETA" IN BACON, ETC. 145

in this Art, *which (as we have said before) are of such nature as may be esteemed rather Appendices*, than portions of the art itself, and pertain all to the PROMPTUARY PART OF RHETORIC.

"First, we do not find that any man hath well pursued or supplied the wisdom and the diligence also of Aristotle; for he began to make a collection of the *Popular signs and colours of Good and Evil in appearance, both simple and comparative*, which are indeed the *Sophisms of Rhetoric:* they are of excellent use, specially referred to business and *the wisdom of private speech*" (Book VI., p. 210, "Advancement of Learning," 1640).

Upon this follow twelve examples of the "Colours of Good and Evil." Then follow immediately "*Antitheta Rerum*" (or the counterpoint of things, see platform) which Bacon has imitated from Seneca, and which he calls "a second *Provision* or *Preparatory Store*," which are places of Persuasion and Dissuasion. These are forty-seven in number. The first point to note is the place these subjects hold in the "De Augmentis," viz.:—"*Illustrations of Speech or Rhetoric*," which last (mark) is but one of the three great Divisions of Elocution or of Tradition (see table). But the final words of the Fifth Book (introducing us to the Sixth Book) conclude, "Now we descend in order to the *fourth member of Logic, which handles Tradition and Elocution*." In the platform of the design may be seen the heading and the divisions and subdivisions of the Sixth Book, falling or embraced under the chief heading:—

THE PARTITION OR THE ART OF ELOCUTION OR OF TRADITION INTO:—

(And under this falls) "*Illustration of Speech or Rhetoric*." So that these "Colours of Good and Evil" belong *to the Art of Delivery (Tradition) of things (?) invented, and (as we have heard already)* PROMPTUARY and APPENDICES of "*The Wisdom of Private Speech*," but why it should be *private speech* or what it should *prompt to*, we have no instructions except our wits or guesses to assist us! It is plain all this refers to something else,

K

which Bacon has to veil in obscure and private language. Our theory is that he here suggests *the Essays in contact with the Plays.* And we have already discovered some of the examples Bacon gives, evidently in contact with the Plays. In a letter to Prince Henry, dedicating his fourth edition of the Essays 1612 to him, Bacon writes:—"Which I have called *Essays*. The word is late, but the thing is *ancient;* for *Seneca's Epistle to Lucilius*, if you mark them well, *are but Essays*, that is dispersed meditations, though conveyed in the form of epistles." This is important, because we find Bacon introducing his "Forty-seven Examples of Antitheta Rerum" with the words:—"*A collection of this nature* we find in Seneca, but in suppositions only or cases. Of this sort (in regard we have many ready prepared) we thought good to set down *some of them for example;* these we call *Antitheta Rerum*" (p. 300, Book VI., "Advancement of Learning," 1640). Now Gervinus asserts Seneca to have been Shakespeare's (save the mark!) ideal, and that the author of the Plays studied this ancient tragedian more than any other writer. So that to find Bacon alluding to Seneca's Epistles in context with his own Essays is highly suspicious, pointing to the Plays, seeing the *subjects of these Essays* are for a large part devoted to analysis of *human character, passions, or affections of the mind which constitute the motives of Comedy and Tragedy*, viz.:—Love, Anger, Envy, Suspicion, Beauty, Deformity, Ambition, Friendship, Vain-Glory, Cunning, Revenge, Simulation and Dissimulation, Boldness, Seditions, Faction, Empire, Fortune, Usury, all of which enter, in an extraordinary degree, into the composition of the *Dramatis Personæ* and text of the 1623 Theatre attributed to Shakespeare. Each of these titles is the subject of an Essay by Bacon, and we cannot imagine an analysis of the plays resolving itself into anything less than a study of these affections, attributes, and their relationships. The *colours of the Theatre* are given us in these Essays, as on the palette of a dramatic artist waiting to use them.

By examining the (1605) "Two Books of the Advancement of Learning," and collating the Second Book with the 1623 "De

Augmentis," which grew out of it, we can trace the germs or early sketch of what Bacon afterwards developed into eight separate books. In seeking this particular point in the Sixth Book, we find in the 1605 "Advancement" this:—"Now we descend to that part which concerneth the ILLUSTRATION OF TRADITION *comprehended in that science*, which we call *Rhetoric or art of Eloquence*." This is confirmation of what we already have suggested. "The duty and office of *Rhetoric* is *To apply Reason to Imagination* for the better moving of the will; for we see *Reason* is disturbed in the administration thereof by three means; by *illaqueation*, or *sophism*, which pertains to *Logic*; by *imagination or impression*, which pertains to *Rhetoric*; and by *Passion or Affection*, which pertains to *Morality*" (p. 66, Book II., 1605). Now Bacon has laid it down in this work that by *imagination* he means *poetry*.*

One of the most remarkable features of the "De Augmentis" of 1623 are the prætermitted parts, or "*Deficients*," which are fifty in number. Now it is very curious to find some of these "*Deficients*," *are works already completed by Bacon*. For example, the Sixth Deficient is "*Sapientia Veterum*," or Bacon's "Wisdom of the Ancients." Although it does not openly say so, the title is sufficient. And here is a still more pertinent hint for the 1623 Folio, that it is in context with "*Parabolical Poesy*," for he introduces this Deficient upon page 108, following the discussion of the drama and stage plays. The thirty-first Deficient is the "Organum Novum," or true directions for the Interpretation of Nature. And the reader is begged to mark a strange thing, worthy profound reflection,—that in the 1640 translation of the "De Augmentis," by Gilbert Wats, we find most of these Deficients marked by an asterisk in the margin. But these particular subjects are not so marked, but passed over. The twenty-fifth Deficient is entitled "*Prolongando Curriculo Vitæ*," and is evidently a finger-post for Bacon's "History of Life and Death."

* "That is the truest partition of humane learning, which hath reference to the three faculties of Man's soul, which is the seat of learning. *History* is referred to *Memory*, *Poesy* to the *Imagination*, *Philosophy* to *Reason*" (Lib. II., "Advancement of Learning").

In the Catalogue of these "Deficients" (at the end of both the 1623 "De Augmentis" and 1640 translation), we find one entitled "*Satyra, Seria,*" which we re-find in the Seventh Book (p. 351), and called "*De Interioribus Rerum.*" This Deficient is also omitted from the margin of the paging. Now there is a very strong parallel (we are about to endeavour to maintain), this Deficient alludes to the Essays, because Bacon calls them "*The Interior of Things,*" and to the final edition (published in "*Operum Moralium et Civilium,*" by Rawley, 1638) we find this actual title heading them, "*Interiorum Rerum.*" The Essays are undoubtedly ethical, and this Seventh Book deals also with the Will of Man, which Bacon calls *Moral Knowledge.* The Essays are, moreover, *satirical,* inasmuch as they censure and lay bare the vices, follies, impostures, and subtle reaches of human character, passions, and appetites. Such of the Essays as "Revenge," "Simulation and Dissimulation," "Envy," "Boldness," "Superstition," "Atheism," "Cunning," "Of Seeming Wise," "Suspicion," "Ambition," "Usury," "Deformity," "Vain Glory," "Anger," "Riches," "Fortune," "Of Nature in Men," "Of Wisdom for a man's self," &c., are really a keen analysis of the impostures, frauds, vices, and passions in human nature. And we must be careful not to rely too much on the bare titles of these Essays, which are mingled and obscured with others (Prophecies, Plantations, Expense, Judicature, Faction, &c.), purposely to veil by art their close approximation to the characters of the Drama, inasmuch as we find their "*Antitheta*" (which are connected with them) in the Sixth Book of the "De Augmentis," as *Appendices* (see Platform) to Rhetoric (or illustration of Speech), giving us further the titles "Pride," "Ingratitude," "Cruelty," "Loquacity," "Flattery," "Silence," "Violent Counsels," "Incontinence," with other subjects already existing as Essays ("Beauty," "Youth," "Health," "Riches," "Fortune," "Empire," "Nature," "Superstition," &c.). We find these "Antitheta" have each a particular Essay to which they belong. This has been already pointed out by Whately (Essays) and by Dr Abbott (Essays). What we really are striving to draw attention to, is first, that the "De Augmentis," is a "*preparative or key for the better opening of the Instauration,*" and that these introductions or sketches and titles in connection with other works of Bacon's, are so placed as to show us the use they are intended to serve. Thus all these "*Antitheta*" (following the "Colours of Good and Evil") are part of Bacon's system of Delivery, and come under the great heading of *Tradition or Elocution, which latter Bacon terms Poetry* (See Platform of Book VI., "Advancement of Learning," 1640).

Archbishop Whately, in the Preface to the Essays (1860), remarks:—"He is throughout, and especially in his Essays, one of the most suggestive authors that ever wrote. And it is remarkable that, compressed and pithy as the Essays are, and consisting chiefly of brief hints, he has elsewhere condensed into a still smaller compass the matter of most of them. In his *Rhetoric* (Sixth Book '*De Augmentis*') he has drawn up what he calls '*Antitheta*,' or common-places, 'locos,' *i.e., pros and cons,* opposite sentiments and reasons on various points, *most of them the same that are discussed in the Essays.* It is a compendious and clear mode of bringing before the mind the most important points in any question, to place in parallel columns, as Bacon has done, whatever can be plausibly urged, fairly or unfairly, on opposite sides; and then *you are in the condition of a judge who has to decide some cause after having heard all the pleadings.* I have accordingly appended to most of the Essays some of Bacon's '*Antitheta*' on the same subjects" (page v.).

The important point is, Bacon introduces these "*Antitheta*" as "*Promptuary part of Rhetoric*" (following the "Colours of Good and Evil"), or as "a second collection or preparatory store"; and in "The Two Books of the Advancement" (1605) we find the early sketch of this now more developed germ entitled, "*Preparation and Suggestion,*" coming under "*Literate Experience and Interpretation of Nature*" (pages 51, 52). "And we see the ancient writers of *Rhetoric* do give it in precept:

That Pleaders should have the places whereof they have most continual use, ready handled in all the varieties that may be, as that to speak for the literal interpretation of the law against equity and contrary ; and to speak for presumptions and inferences against testimony and contrary."

Archbishop Whately remarks :—" Several of these ' Antitheta ' were either adopted by Bacon from proverbial use, or have (through him) become proverbs." This is perfectly true, for a vast number of them do come from the proverbs of Solomon, a collection of which is one of the curious features of the " Advancement of Learning." Whately continues : " Proverbs accordingly are somewhat analogous to those medical formulas which being in frequent use, are kept ready made up in the chemists' shops, and which often save the framing of a distinct proposition " (page vi., Preface, " Essays "). Now this is exactly what Bacon says of his " Antitheta," though in other words. He calls them " *seeds*," " *store*," " *skeins, or bottoms of thread to be drawn out and unwinded into larger discourse as occasion should be presented.*" And he concludes : " Seeing they are *seeds and not flowers.*" Our conviction is *they are the seeds of the Shakespeare (so called) Theatre ; being the pithy abstract of certain virtues and vices, passions and affections, or attributes of human characters portrayed in action in the plays.* And we are to unwind these "*skeins of thread,*" develop these seeds by analysing the plots and the motives of each particular play. They seem to us *texts for and against.* The headings alone of these " Antitheta " do a tale unfold, inasmuch as they constitute not only a supplement to the subjects of the Essays, but speak loudly enough for themselves, *as the colours of the dramatic artist, viz. :* " *Pride,*" " *Envy,*" " *Revenge,*" " *Boldness,*" " *Ingratitude,*" " *Incontinence,*" " *Vain-Glory,*" " *Cruelty,*" which we may term vices. Then we also find these headings : " *Praise,*" " *Fortitude,*" " *Temperance,*" " *Constancy,*" " *Magnanimity,*" " *Learning,*" " *Love,*" " *Friendship,*" " *Beauty,*" " *Youth,*" " *Nobility,*" " *Riches,*" " *Honours,*" " *Fortune,*" " *Empire.*" These are connected with the Essays—at least most of them. And there seems to be a probability Bacon disguised the titles of some of the Essays, and mixed them up with subjects not connected with the Theatre at first sight. For example, Bacon writes in a letter to Bishop Andrews: "And again for that my Book of Advancement of Learning, may be some *preparative or key for the better* opening of the Instauration; because it exhibits a mixture of new conceits and old" (Prefixed to the Advertisement of the "Holy War"). Again, evidently alluding to this particular work, which he considered his favourite writing: "Therefore, having not long since set forth a part of my Instauration, which is the work that in mine own judgment (*Si nunquam fallit imago*) I do most esteem. . . . . Yet, nevertheless, I have just cause to doubt *that it flies too high over men's heads*" (*Ibid.*). In a letter to Dr Playfer on this same work: "And therefore the *privateness of the language* considered, wherein it is written, *excluding so many readers*, as on the other side the *obscurity of the argument, in many parts of it*, excludeth many others, &c." (Part I., "Resus.," p. 28). It appears as if Bacon associated himself personally with this particular work. For in a letter to Sir Thomas Bodley, upon sending his book of "Advancement of Learning," we read: "And the second *copy* I have sent unto you, not only in good affection, *but in a kind of congruity*, in regard of your great and rare desert of learning. For *Books* are the shrines where the *Saint* is or believed to be. And you having built an *Ark* to save learning from *deluge*, deserve propriety in any new instrument or engine whereby learning should be improved or advanced." It is very difficult to comprehend in what sense Bacon signifies the "Advancement" to be a "*preparative or key for the better opening of the Instauration*"?

Dr Abbott, in his scholarly introduction to Bacon's "Essays," writes that the latter "*embody the Antitheta*" (page xvii.). Now this is well worthy attention, because it shows these Essays were written without any particular bias, but embrace both sides of their subjects in *pro* and *contra*. And therefore the attempt to extract any opinion as to Bacon's particular subjectivity out of them is as absurd as the laying of weight upon selections out of the plays, to illustrate their author. Why were these "Antitheta" not published with the Essays? Why are they to be found in the "De Augmentis," and particularly in the Sixth Book handling *Traditive Art*, that is the "*Delivery of Secret Knowledge*" to Posterity? The "Colours of Good and Evil" were published with the Essays in 1597 (first edition). And we refind them in this Sixth Book of the "De Augmentis" entitled "*Promptuary part of Rhetoric*," and appendices of the "*Wisdom of Private Speech*," so that they are evidently introduced here as helps, aids, or *cues to something else that is "private" (or obscure) and traditive!* I take the entire Sixth Book of the "De Augmentis," to consist of nothing but the different methods and ways, by which Bacon has determined to hand on to us, the problem of the authorship of the plays.

Upon page 209, Book IV., of the "Advancement of Learning," 1640, we find Bacon writing of "Divination" and of the "Faculties of the Soul." Very strangely the paging proceeds correctly to page 280, when it suddenly *becomes* 209, falsely mispaged, and continues for eight pages, when once more it takes up the correct paging, 289, as if there had been no lapses. Now it is very remarkable this false page, 209 (*bis*), Book VI., introduces us to the relationship of Logic to Ethic, and upon page 210 * to the "*Wisdom of Private Speech*," embracing the "*Colours of Good and Evil.*" There can be, no doubt, the last point to the Essays, for they were published together in 1597. And this is corroborated by the "*Antitheta*" (which follow upon the "*Colours of Good and Evil*"), being the kernels or pith of the Essays placed *pro* and *con*. This needs no apology as a statement, for it has not only been recognised by Whately and Dr Abbott, but the "*Antitheta*" speak loudly enough for themselves as to their origins. The "*Colours of Good and Evil*" are examples of the working of these "*Antitheta*," that is, with the sophisms, re-argued by Bacon.

* This page 210 is exactly the double of page 105, *upon which latter Poetry is first discussed. It is striking to find that* 105 *is the sum of the two first false pagings* 52 *and* 53, *Shakespeare's age* 1616, *full years and year he had just entered.*

CHAPTER VIII.

HISTORY, POETRY, AND PHILOSOPHY.

IN the relationship of History to Poetry may be refound some profound study by Bacon of Aristotle ("De Augmentis"). Aristotle writes:—"The difference between the *historian and the poet* is not that one speaks in *verse* and the other in *prose*. The real distinction is, that the one relates what has been, the other what might have been. On this account *Poetry is more philosophical* and a more excellent thing than history, for poetry is conversant with the universal, history with the particular." How frequently Bacon implies the same thing may be seen in the following passages:—"By Poesy in this place, we understand nothing but *feigned History or fables*." "*History is properly of individuals circumscribed within time and place*." "Poesy in that sense we have expounded it, is *likewise of individuals*, fancied to the similitude of those things which in true history are recorded, yet so as often it exceeds measure; and those things which in nature would never meet, nor come to pass, *Poesy* composeth and introduceth at pleasure, even as *Painting* doth" (p. 77, Book II., "Advancement," 1640). There is a relationship implied here between History and Poetry, the one being circumscribed to time and place, the other not so. Again, "for a *true narration* may be composed in *verse*, and *a feigned in prose*. In the latter sense we have already determined it a principal member of learning, and have placed it next unto history, seeing it is nothing else than *imitation of history at pleasure*" (Poetry, Book II. p. 105, "Advancement," 1640). Again, "*Dramatical or Representative* (Poetry) is, as it were, a *visible history*" (p. 106). We may perceive how determined Bacon is to class History and Poetry together, as particular and universal aspects of past and present history.

Let us consider that out of the thirty-six plays of the 1623 Folio, no less than ten are entitled "*Histories*," and are nothing but "*feigned histories*," or "*imitation of history at pleasure*," in exactly the sense Bacon inculcates in the passage quoted. If we add to the Chronicle plays, the historical plays of "Coriolanus," "Julius Cæsar," "Timon of Athens," "Titus Andronicus," "Antony and Cleopatra," "Macbeth," how great is the number of these "*feigned histories*," treated poetically, and "*fancied to the similitude of those things which in true history are recorded*"! Indeed, almost the entire Folio consists of plays of this character. For "Hamlet," "Lear," "Othello," "Cymbeline," though not so strictly in accord with history as the chronicles and classical plays, are nevertheless each founded upon, and woven round certain historical figures, traditions, or myths the dramatist borrowed from. "Hamlet," taken from Saxo-Grammaticus, has an historical basis for facts. Cymbeline really lived; his uncle, Cassibulan, holding for chief town *Verolanium* (or Verulam), the site of St Albans, Bacon's home. "Othello" (borrowed from Cinthio's novel) has probably some origin in fact. In short, the only plays not of this character of "*feigned history*" are the Comedies, if even certain pieces like the "Comedy of Errors" borrowed from Plautus, do not belong to "Dramatic history" redressed? Only thirteen plays out of thirty-six do not belong to what, strictly speaking, is only "*feigned history*," as Bacon calls poetry. Therefore, in classing History and Poetry together, in an interchangeable sense of past made present, and calling dramatical poetry "*visible history*," Bacon is perfectly logical, and at the same time presents us with a hint for the greater part of the character of the 1623 Folio.

We are bound to allow the possible truth of the theory we postulate in connection with this cipher problem, that the plays may contain a great deal more "*true narration*" though written "*in verse*," than we imagine. So likewise this actual book of "De Augmentis" we quote from, may contain a great deal "*feigned in prose*," seeing it is "*obscurely*" *written* and the "*privateness of the language excludeth so many readers*" as Bacon writes.

HISTORY, POETRY, AND PHILOSOPHY.

Much of Bacon's poetry or "*feigned history*," may contain real history of "*lives*," and "*relations*," and "*times*," as yet hidden in undiscovered cipher. But be this true or no, Poetry is nothing but Memory or feigned History, and it seems to us almost evident, Bacon introduces History with regard to Poetry and with regard to *Memory* or *Custody* (chap. v. Book V.), which we find immediately followed by the great book of Delivery or Ciphers. Indeed it is not going too far to suggest, it is impossible to imagine three more perfect foundations than Memory, Imagination, and Reason, emanating into History, Poetry, and Philosophy, as three great principles (implying faculties of the mind), underlying a philosophical Drama, intended for revelation or discovery. In the light of a great Cipher Key work, pointing to the plays, this book of "De Augmentis," is sufficiently pregnant in these tripartite divisions (bracketed together in the table or platform of the design) to suggest all we claim for the character of this work. If Bacon had been no poet, we suggest he would not have thus brought poetry into prominence and classed it amongst the sciences. The work is the basement, door, and access to a *structure of literature*, and nobody we maintain knew this better than the writer. "*Poetry is not a knowledge*," he writes, "*but a play of wit*,"* and the scientific air with which he disguises all this was only part of his design. What we ask has the Instauration, of which this is the *first part* (called a preparative or key for the better opening of it) to do with Poetry and History? Let those who would reply "the work is only an enumeration and review of the chief divisions of learning" study the prefaces. They will see the Great Instauration is an *entire whole*, and, moreover, a *creative whole* (compared to the six days), one part to be applied to another part, and embracing types of invention as examples of illustration to the Baconian logic or inductive system.

In the "Advancement and Proficience of Learning," 1605

---

* In spite of this statement, Bacon *makes Poetry one of the Foundations of his "Advancement of Learning"*! The fact that his third faculty, "*Reason*," should consist of "Ciphers" and "Delivery of Secret Knowledge" is suspicious.

(which may be considered the *first birth* of the 1623 "De Augmentis") we read:—"It (Poetry) is taken in two senses in respect of *words or matter*." "In the first sense it is but a character of style and belongeth to arts of speech, and is not pertinent for the present. *In the latter it is (as hath been said) one of the principal portions of learning, and is nothing else but feigned history, which may be styled as well in prose as verse*" (Book II., iii. 4). It is most important to note the distinction Bacon makes between *words and matter* with regard to poetry. For he evidently must have had some reason for so doing. And we get a hint in the words, "So as theology consisteth also of history of the Church, *of parables, which is divine poesy*." This thoroughly is in keeping with his statement that Poetry is "*feigned history*," which may be styled as well in prose as in verse. In the "Advancement of Learning," 1640, he writes:—"As for *Narrative Poesy*, or, if you please, *Heroical (so you understand it of the matter, not of the verse)*, it seems to be raised altogether from a noble foundation" (p. 106). Again, "Representative (*Poetry Dramatical*) is as a *visible history*, and is an image of actions as if they were present, as history is of actions in nature as they are (that is) past" (1605, Book II., iv. 3). Bacon's two great divisions (or emanations of memory and imagination), History and Poetry, become really two aspects of History, viz., "*Real History*" and "*Feigned History*," the former past, the latter present in the Chronicle historical plays, and perhaps more real in the sense of immortality, than the dead personages of the past they are copied from.

If we now turn to Bacon's third faculty of the mind—Reason—we find it interpreted as Philosophy. When we come to study it in the "De Augmentis" critically, we are surprised to find what prominence Bacon has given, in part of an entire book, to "*Ciphers*," "*Handing on the lamp for posterity*," and "*The Wisdom of Private Speech*." For these subjects are not concerned with philosophy or science in the accepted sense, or in the spirit of Bacon's inductive inquiries into "Cold and Heat," "Motion," "Heavy and Light," and kindred subjects. These subjects do not stand singly in the Sixth Book, but are affiliated to the art of *judging or logic*, and are really part of Bacon's first faculty, Memory or History as Custody. To the profound thinker (who studies these things in the work) there is palpable method and sequence throughout all this. The glaring point is that all this applies to *Literature, and not to Nature at all*. For example, how are we to explain what Bacon calls "*Experientia Literata sive Venatis Panis*"? (Lib. v., p. 226). He calls this "*Literate Experience*," and an "*Art of Discovery*" at the same time. He distinctly separates this from "*Interpretatio Naturæ or Novum Organum*." But why it should have this name, "*Literate Experience*," is a mystery, unless it refers, as we believe, to some other of Bacon's writings? In the "Platform of the Design" (Table of divisions of the work) we find

III. CUSTODY or MEMORY into CHAPTER V.	*Helps to memory.*	*Writing.*
	Memory itself by	*Prenotion. Emblem.*

The reader who turns to page 255 and reads what is discussed under these last sub-divisions, will find all this is applied to "*Invention*," and not to nature or science. He will find the next page introducing the Sixth Book a great system of *Mnemonics* in the words commencing the subject (p. 258). "Now let us come unto the Art of Delivery, or of expressing, and *transferring those things which are invented, judged and laid up in the* MEMORY, *which, by a general name, we will call Tradition*." This establishes the connection or affiliation we postulate, between this Cipher system, and *Custody, Memory, or History*. We must remember that Bacon has called Poetry "*feigned History*," and declared a "*true history*" may be written in Poetry, and a "*feigned in prose*." Truly considered, the plays of the Shakespeare so-called Theatre are nearly all Histories, and are just as entitled to the title as Holinshed's Chronicles, from which in great measure some are borrowed. They are living, speaking histories of action, and are "true histories," in the sense they are not circumscribed to any time, and are representative of the past made present. But waiving even this claim for the title we beg for them, they may contain cipher records that are of amazing interest and truth for humanity, in the sense of history of quite another sort. And it is in this belief we point to these *Mnemonics* as an art of Delivery from Custody or Memory, to wit, *recollection or remembrance !* * The student will find all this deals with *writing, literate experience*, and not with Science or Nature at all. Bacon has given us outlines, hints, sketches of a great method of Ciphers of signs and emblems *for Something outside the work itself, yet affiliated to things invented, which are connected with History and Poetry.* Is it nothing that we have these *outside things invented*, described as "types and platforms of Invention," upon pages 35, 36 of the Distribution Preface, and re-find the great system of "*Delivery,*" giving us under the Thirty-fifth and Thirty-sixth Stars, "*gestures by congruity,*" "*characters real*" or "*dead figures,*" "*Ciphers,*" and that the plays are thirty-five in the Catalogue and thirty-six in the (body of the work) 1623 Folio? Side by side these two works (the plays and the "De Augmentis") are published the same year! The proof that Bacon's "*Literate Experience*" or "*Hunting of Pan,*" is purely connected with the plays, may be seen in the fable of Pan, which is introduced on the heels of the Drama and Poetry, and is embraced in the Theatre (page 109)!

In studying this problem, it is highly indispensable to collate the 1605 "Two Books of the Advancement of Learning" with the 1623 "De Augmentis" and its translation, 1640, by Gilbert Wats. If the student will study the two last as a development out of the second book of the first, he will arrive at the conclusion Bacon was maturing some plan, repeating the same thing in 1623, viz., reproducing the first book or "*Dignity of Learning*" entirely, which is curious, seeing it already existed. In 1605 Bacon

* Upon page 53, "Merry Wives of Windsor" (Shakespeare's monumental age, 1616), we find the 107th, 106th words *counted up from the bottom of the column* (106) *to be* "*Your Remembrance.*" *Upon pages* 107, 106 *of the* 1640 "*Advancement,*" *Stage Plays and the Drama are discussed.*

HISTORY, POETRY, AND PHILOSOPHY.

published "The Two Books of the Advancement and Proficiency of Learning," dedicated to the King. This work contains the three fundamental faculties of the mind, Memory, Imagination, Reason, corresponding to History, Poetry, Philosophy, as in the "De Augmentis," 1623. In 1612 Bacon writes a treatise entitled, "A Description of the Intellectual Globe," which commences with (in substance) the same subject Parts of human learning as the Second Book of the 1605 "Advancement." So that, as Spedding truly tells us, this tract was an attempt to rewrite or recast the Second Book of the 1605 "Advancement." It shows very plainly Bacon held the plan before him as he grew older (and perhaps wrote more plays), of *altering and developing the scheme and subdivisions of his subject based upon History, Poetry, and Philosophy*. Let it ever be borne in mind the first book of the "Dignity of Learning" is only preparative, and cannot be esteemed more than a proem. Bacon left that as it was, and it is only in the emanations of History, Poetry, and Philosophy we find development and progress. In the 1623 "De Augmentis" we find nine Books. Eight of these Books are developed or amplifications of the sketches of most of the subjects embraced in the Second Book of the 1605 "Advancement." So the reader must remember, that we are in possession of three works (if not four) which are only continual repetitions, enlargements, upon fundamentally the same theme. Inasmuch as the translation of the "De Augmentis" (1640) differs largely in details from the Latin version from which it was supposed to be translated, it requires to be introduced into the series for comparison. Thus we have all these as a trunk or tree with its branches and growth :—

1605.	"Two Books of the Advancement of Learning."
1612.	"Description of Intellectual Globe," and "Thema Cœli."
1623.	"De Augmentis," Ninth Book.
1640.	Translation of "De Augmentis."

Bacon was ever altering, and he writes, "Nothing is finished till all is finished."

Sir Philip Sidney, in his "Defence of Poesie," maintains that the "Ancient Philosophers, disguised or embodied their philosophies and cosmogonies in their poetry, as Thales, Empedocles, Parmenides, Pythagoras, and Phocyclides, who were poets and philosophers at once." We have only to recall the fragments of sacred verse preserved to us in the hymns of Orpheus, Hesiod, Sancumathon, &c. (*vide* Cory's "Ancient Fragments"), to endorse this assertion. Bacon very frequently quotes almost every one of these philosophers, and if the student will read what Bacon writes upon the Drama, Stage Plays, and Parabolical or Allusive Poetry (pages 106, 107, 108, "Advancement," 1640), he will find all this repeated in substance and at length, showing how much it had hold of Bacon's mind. "But Poetry Parabolical *excels all the rest*, and seemeth to be a sacred and venerable thing; especially seeing Religion itself hath allowed it in a work of that nature, and by it traffics divine commodities with man. For it serves for *obscuration and it serves for illustration*" (p. 107, "Advancement"). Nor does he here drop the subject, but returns to it again upon page 108. "There is another use of Parabolical Poetry, opposite to the former, which tendeth *to the folding up* of those things, the dignity whereof deserves to be retired, and distinguish't *as with a drawn curtain*." All this follows directly, and is indeed part of his discussion upon the Drama and Stage Plays. In studying these passages, we must reflect upon Bacon's deeply religious side, illustrated in this work by 150 quotations from the Bible. We must further note his extraordinary profundity of mind and extreme resemblance to those ancient Philosopher Poets he so often quotes in this work, as Thales, Democritus, Heraclitus, Orpheus, Anaxagoras, Leucippus, Plato, Lucretius, Parmenides, all of whose philosophies he had exhaustively studied and contemplated. The extraordinary resemblance of Bacon in depth of philosophical research to this class of poet philosophers of

HISTORY, POETRY, AND PHILOSOPHY. 161

antiquity is very striking, and is united at the same time to an inspired and religious style, half obscure and half prophetic. We have already alluded to this classical and curious combination of philosophy, poetry, and religion in this work, which is most remarkable. It is just in these points, Bacon seems to unite all that was best in antiquity, to all that is best in the modern world, illustrated by his inductive method. We seem to refind every one of these classical sages reincarnate in him, yet a mind "o'erpeering" them, and entirely original. It is the most wonderful combination, without subjection to any one of them, of spirit and essence it is possible to explain, and yet withal there is the presence felt of the prophet of the Old Testament joined to all this. I do not write this under the influence of enthusiasm, but in calmly critical spirit. And it jumps exactly with what Bacon writes upon antiquity and novelty, inclining to neither unduly, but uniting both as God-Man.* This may invoke ridicule or excite laughter, but is very short indeed of what all the best pens of posterity will record upon this marvellous man, when the truth is more plainly recognised.

There is hardly an author quoted, illustrated, or borrowed from in Shakespeare, which we do not find also quoted or alluded to by Bacon in his prose writings. For example, the classical historical plays like "Julius Cæsar," "Antony and Cleopatra," "Timon," "Coriolanus," are exclusively drawn from Plutarch's "Lives," and Lucian. All the trifling details entered into by Plutarch are reproduced in the play of "Antony and Cleopatra," even to the incident of the salt fish placed upon the hook of Antony by a diver. Open the "De Augmentis" of 1623 (or its translation of 1640 by Wats), and see how often Plutarch is quoted—pages 16, 20, 21, 24, 52, 53 (twice), 54 (three times), 56, 57, 99, 121, 211, 351, 352, 356, 366, 375, 399, 400, 413 (twice), 421, 425, 426, 427, 469, and we are not at all sure this exhausts all Bacon's quota-

---

* "For we are carried in some degree, with an equal temper of desire, both to improve the labours of the Ancients, and to make farther progress" (Distribution Preface, p. 22, "Advancement," 1640).

tions. How fond he must have been of this author may be judged. The "Comedy of Errors" was borrowed from the "Menæchmi" of Plautus. In "Troilus and Cressida," the personages are reproduced from Homer's "Iliad." In the "De Augmentis" Plautus is quoted pages 24, 34, 53, 54, 56, 99, 283, 296, 338, 351, 365, 366, 375, 389, 400, 413, 421, 425, 426, 427, 469, showing Bacon had him by heart, and was as deeply read in this classical dramatist as in Plutarch's "Lives." Seneca (quoted in "Hamlet") also was one of Bacon's favourite authors, and is quoted pages 15, 23, 36, 53, 113, 178, 219, 247, 300, 334, 336, 343, 351. And it is certainly worthy note Bacon quotes Plutarch twice upon page 53, three times upon page 54 ; Plautus also pages 53, 54, 56 ; Seneca, page 53 ; * for these figures represent Shakespeare's and Bacon's ages, 1616 (fifty-three and fifty-six, and it is upon pages 53, 54 of both Comedies and Histories Bacon's name, and the Christian names Francis and William, are introduced). If the reader will turn to the Index of "Humane Authors," cited by Bacon in the "Advancement" ("De Augmentis") of 1640, at the end of the work, he will in a moment find himself in the position of forming a judgment, of Bacon's favourite studies or authors. At a glance he will see an enormous preponderance of quotations from Plautus, Seneca, Virgil (26 quotations), Ovid (13), Horace (7), Plato (16), Tacitus (15), and Cicero (31), showing the inclinations of Bacon's mind.

Very curiously Plutarch is omitted from the Index. There is scarcely a rare author cited, or imitated in the plays, we do not find Bacon familiar with. For example, Pythagoras is alluded to in the "Merchant of Venice" (act iv. sc. 1), "Twelfth Night" (act iv. sc. 2), "As You Like It" (act iii. sc. 2) ; Heraclitus is indirectly introduced act i. sc. 2, "Merchant of Venice ;" Epicurus is presented as the pleasure-seeking materialist of history in "Antony and Cleopatra" (act ii. sc. 1) ; "King Lear" (act i. sc. 4), "Macbeth" (act v. sc. 3), "Merry Wives of Windsor"

* Attention is called to this, because in the 1640 "Advancement of Learning," page 55 *is mis-paged* 53, *Shakespeare's age*, 1616.

(act ii. sc. 2). Heraclitus was evidently a favourite study of Bacon's. He quotes him in his "Union of Kingdoms," in his "Apophthegms," and in this "De Augmentis." Pythagoras, p. 108, and frequently elsewhere (not in the Index). Essay on "Friendship" (Epicurus, p. 118, "Advancement," 1640).

Gervinus writes:—"If Shakespeare had had occasion at any time to name his ideal, and to denote the highest examples of dramatic art which lay before him, he would have named none but Plautus and Seneca." Now here we find Bacon quoting or alluding, in one work only, twenty-four times to Plautus. Cicero, Aristotle, Virgil, and Plautus stand first in the Catalogue of the 1640 "Advancement" in point of quotations or allusions thus: Cicero (quoted 31 times), Aristotle (28), Virgil (26), Plautus (24). Persius was evidently known to the author of the plays (act i. sc. 1, "Hamlet,") and upon p. 222 "Advancement," Bacon alludes to him. Aristotle is quoted in "Troilus and Cressida" with the same mistake as we refind Bacon repeating. Paul Stapfer writes:—"If we take the word 'learning' in its large and liberal sense, *then of all men that ever lived, Shakespeare is one of the most learned*" (p. 105). * How this accords with Bacon's assertion, " have taken all learning for my province." The most obstinate and prejudiced opponent of the Baconian theory must grant Bacon was as deeply read in the classical dramatical models and poets as the author of the plays, and it is surprising to find the bent of Bacon's mind as much inclined to poetry as philosophy.

Rabelais is alluded to in "As You Like It" (act iii. sc. 2):—

Celia. You must borrow me *Gargantuas'* mouth.

Compare Holofernes in "Love's Labour's Lost." In the opening of the Sixth Book of the "De Augmentis" Bacon writes:— "Who then knows if this work of ours be not perchance a transcript *out* of an ancient book found of that famous library of *St Victor*, a catalogue whereof *M. Fra Rabelais* hath collected. For there a book is found entitled, *Fornicarium Artium.*" This

* "Shakespeare and Classical Antiquity."

is actually a title given in Rabelais' works. Another author read by Shakespeare was Du Bartas' "Week," quoted by Bacon in the "De Augmentis." Montaigne's Essays had evidently an enormous influence upon both Shakespeare and Bacon. For the Essay upon "Death" is almost a reproduction of some passages in the Essay upon the same subject by the Frenchman. There cannot be a doubt the author of the plays knew Montaigne's Essays, as there are to be refound passages in the play of the "Tempest," particularly a reproduction of the chapter on "Cannibals." M. Chasles looks upon the year 1603, in which (from the date 1603 written in Shakespeare's own hand (?) in the British Museum copy of the Essays translated by Florio) he imagines Montaigne exercised a powerful influence upon the author of the plays, as a turning-point in his literary career. Now, Bacon in his Essays openly alludes to Montaigne, and if he was not the author himself of these Essays, as some people believe, borrowed in a reckless manner from them. Montaigne's admiration for Plutarch finds a strange parallel in Bacon's fondness for this author. But we cannot enter into that at present. There is no doubt Sir Thomas North's translation of Plutarch's "Lives" was the source studied by Shakespeare, and possibly this accounts for the omission of Plutarch from the Index of authors quoted in the "Advancement."

The fondness of Bacon for Plato must be duly weighed side by side with the Platonic character of the so-called Shakespeare Sonnets and some of the plays. Mr Simpson in his work ("The Sonnets of Shakespeare") writes of the Platonism of the Italian Sonneteers as follows:—"From Italy it radiated through Europe, and was taken up by Surrey and Spenser. But it was treated by none with such depth and variety *as by Shakespeare, who has devoted all his sonnets and poems, and perhaps half his plays to the subject.*" Nathaniel Holmes ("Authorship of Shakespeare"): —"A thorough student may discover in the plays not only traces of Plato, but a wonderful approximation to the depth and breadth of the Platonic philosophy" (p. 58). Plato's Philosophy in its full creative sense or poetic aspect, has always been known as the *Love Philosophy*, and is best summed up in the ideal doctrines (connected with the mysteries) discussed in the Banquet, and illustrated by Socrates. The philosophy of Plato is the philosophy of the poet *par excellence*. We find it at the Rennaisance inspiring Dante, Petrarch, and passing to Spenser, Daniel, and Drayton. Sir Philip Sidney wrote:—"And truly even Plato, whosoever well considereth, shall find, that in the body of his work, though the inside and strength were philosophy, *the skin, as it were, and beauty depended most of Poetry.*" Now, Bacon, in his Philosophical works, " On Principles and Origins according to the Fables of Cupid and Cœlum," gives us nothing short of Plato's doctrine of Love (discussed in the Banquet), seriously considered and worked out at extraordinary length, as Principles and Origins, to be refound in the *Creative Doctrines* of the hymns attributed to Orpheus (see Cory's "Ancient Fragments"), which are most intimately connected with the Greek Mysteries and origins of the Classic Drama. The solid and lengthy treatment of such a subject by Bacon, is most suspicious in itself, without counting the parallels betrayed by his style with passages in "Romeo and Juliet." The influence of Plato and Cicero in the plays is very conspicuous. The idea of the music of the Spheres expressed in the "Merchant of Venice" (act. v. sc. 1), in "Antony and Cleopatra" (act v. sc. 2), and in "Twelfth Night," or "Pericles" (when upon the discovery of his daughter Marina he hears sounds of music, which he calls the "music of the Spheres"), may be undoubtedly traced to the philosophy of Plato. Knight points out an idea in "Henry V.," (act i. sc. 2), which he refers to Cicero's "De Republica," reproduced from a fragment by St Augustine of Cicero's lost treatise. This is the comparison of a well-governed state to the "work of honey-bees."

> For so work the honey-bees,
> Creatures that by a rule in nature teach
> The act of order to a peopled kingdom.
>
> (Act i. sc. 2.)

The frequent introduction of Latinisms in the plays (ably pointed out by Hallam), dwelt upon by Gervinus and others, with the introduction of quotations in Latin from Ovid and Terence in "The Taming of the Shrew," proves the scholarship of the author of the plays, and that the absurd theory, that translations of Greek and Latin authors were studied only, has no leg of proof to stand upon.

In the "Advancement of Learning" (Book II., ch. iv. § 2) upon Poetry, we find this passage:—

"The use of this *feigned History* (as he calls poetry) hath been to give some shadow of satisfaction to the mind of man, in those points, wherein the nature of things doth deny it, the world being in proportion inferior to the soul; by reason whereof there is, agreeable to the spirit of man, a more ample greatness, a more exact goodness, and a more absolute variety, than can be found in the nature of things. Therefore, because the acts or events of true history have not that magnitude which satisfieth the mind of man, poesy feigneth acts and events greater and more heroical. Because true history propoundeth the successes and issues of actions, not so agreeable to the merits of virtue and vice, therefore poesy feigns them more just in retribution and more according to revealed providence. . . . And therefore poesy was ever thought to have some participation of divineness, because it doth raise and erect the mind, by submitting the shows of things to the desires of the mind; whereas reason doth buckle and bow the mind into the nature of things."

We can see by this passage in what high estimation Bacon held poetry, in the sense of the ideal, real or true. "The more poetical the more real," writes Novalis. Sir Philip Sidney writes:—"Of all writers under the sun, the poet is the least liar" ("Defence of Poesie"). And do we not see all that Bacon claims for poetry—"*a more ample greatness, a more exact goodness, and a more absolute variety*," exemplified to an extraordinary degree in the Theatre attributed to Skakespeare? Have we not in such characters as Prospero, Theseus, Cæsar, Hamlet, Isabella,

Cordelia, Ophelia, just this "ample greatness" and "exact goodness" in endless variety? Bulwer remarks (in the Introduction to "Zanoni") "Shakespeare never created a real personage," and in a sense it is true. Hamlet is a creation, so is Prospero, and the originals of these characters had no living prototypes outside the poet's brain. Falstaffe is, on the other hand, the copy of a man who lived and was possibly noted by the author. For Bacon was a keen observer, and Osborn relates how he could "*outcant* a London Chirurgeon in his own professional slang," or "be equally at home with a Lord upon Hawks or Horses." But in the ethical bearing of the plays, in such characters as Lear, Timon, Othello, Macbeth, all the good and bad qualities of soul are idealised, and carried to a tragic point. Bacon shows that in the realm of poetry he was by conviction Idealist. And does this not at once suggest Plato, and account for the Platonic character of the Sonnets, and some plays like the "Midsummer Night's Dream"? Plato's entire Love Philosophy is that of the soul, *remembering its divine origin*.

Resort to translations, instead of to originals, by the author of the plays, has been made a point in favour of Shakespeare's authorship, inasmuch it seems improbable a scholar of such classical attainments (as Bacon undoubtedly reveals) should betake himself to English versions and not to the source itself. YET IT IS CERTAIN BACON BORROWS IN HIS ESSAYS FROM NORTH'S TRANSLATION OF PLUTARCH'S "LIVES," AS WELL AS THE PHANTOM CAPTAIN SHAKESPEARE! Here is proof in point. In Bacon's Essay upon "Fortune" he writes:—"It is written that Timotheus the Athenian, after he had, in the account he gave to the state of his government, often interlaced this speech, '*and in this fortune had no part*,' never prospered in anything he undertook afterwards" ("Fortune," 1612, 1625). Compare with this "Timotheus" (North's "Plutarch," page 388): "Timotheus . . . . said, 'My Lords of Athens, *Fortune hath had no part in all this which I have told unto you.*' Hereupon the Gods, it would seem, were so angry with this foolish ambition of

Timotheus, that he never afterwards did any worthy thing; but all went utterly against the hair with him, until at length he came to be so hated of the people that in the end they banished him from Athens." Bacon writes in the same Essay upon "Fortune":—"Certainly there be whose fortunes are like Homer's verses, that have a slide *and an easiness* more than the verses of other poets; as Plutarch saith of Timoleon's fortune, in respect of that of Agesilaus or Epaminondas" (1625, not in 1612 Essays).

Compare North's "Plutarch," page 235 :—" And like as . . . . in Homer's verses, besides the passing workmanship and singular grace in them, a man findeth at the first sight, that *they were easily made*, and without great pain, even so in like manner, whosoever will compare the painful bloody wars and battles of Epaminondas and Agesilaus with the wars of Timoleon, in the which besides equity and justice, there is also great ease and quietness, &c." I think nobody will question Bacon borrowed from North's "Plutarch,"—the words Bacon uses are the same,—" *Fortune had no part*,"—(" *Fortune (hath) had no part*"),—" *an easiness*,"—(" *were easily made* "). These complete plagiarisms of language prove our case. And here let us acknowledge we first discovered this in Dr Abbott's valuable notes to the Essays (1876). In the Essay on "Prophecies," Bacon again quotes from Plutarch, the evil spirit which appeared to Brutus before the battle of Philippi, *which episode is introduced in the play of Julius Cæsar*. Dr Abbott writes as follows :—

"Bacon's moral teaching is greatly influenced by two teachers, *Plutarch* (taken as the type of the historians of Greece and Rome) and Machiavelli " (Abbot, Introduction, p. 134, Essays).

> Am I a Machiavel ?
> ("Merry Wives of Windsor," act iii. sc. 1.)
>
> Alençon ! That notorious Machiavel !
> (" 1 King Henry VI.," act iii. sc. 2.)
>
> The murderous Machiavel to school.
> ("3 King Henry VI., act iii. sc. 2.)

Shakespeare (save the mark!) borrows from North's "Plutarch," Timon's speech, as follows:—

> I have a tree which grows here in my garden
> That mine own use invites me to cut down,
> And shortly must I fell it.
>
> (Act v. sc. 2.)

Bacon evidently in his Essay upon "Goodness of Nature," or what we should call *Good nature*—"*Misanthropi*, that make it their practice to bring men to the bough and yet never have *a tree for the purpose in their gardens as Timon had.*" The title of Bacon's Essay carries conviction of its application to the play of "Timon of Athens," inasmuch as Timon is portrayed as a man of *good nature, carried to excess,* giving away right and left, and becoming a *misanthrope* because his friends are not as foolish as himself.

NORTH'S "PLUTARCH."

Paul Stapfer (in his "Shakespeare and Classical Antiquity") writes:—"One thing, however, is certain, and that is, that it was only through Amyot, or rather *through his English translator, Sir Thomas North, that Shakespeare became acquainted with Plutarch.* The proof of this is easy and amusing. In comparing the texts, we find the poet following the translator so closely, as to borrow from him not only whole passages, and various little peculiarities —an indulgence in epithets, and a certain redundancy of expression characteristic of good old Amyot,—*but also even his errors and mistranslations*" (Introductory, p. 7).

Every Shakespearian scholar is acquainted with this unquestionable *fact, or certainty*, that the plays of "Julius Cæsar," "Antony and Cleopatra," and "Coriolanus," were taken not only entirely from Plutarch's "Lives," *but from North's translation* of the French Plutarch of Amyot, who first rendered the "Lives" from the original Greek into the French tongue.

"Certainly destiny may easier be foreseen than avoided, considering the strange and wonderful signs that were said to be seen before Cæsar's death. For, touching the fires in the element, and spirits running up and down in the night, *and also the solitary birds to be seen at noondays sitting in the great market-place;* are not all these signs perhaps worth the noting in such a wonderful chance as happened? But Strabo the philosopher writeth, that divers men were seen going up and down in fire: and furthermore *that there was a slave of the soldiers that did cast a marvellous burning flame out of his hand, insomuch that they who saw it thought he had been burnt; but when the fire was out, it was found he had no hurt*" (North's "Plutarch").

>*Cicero.* Why are you breathless? and why stare you so?
>*Casca.* Are not you moved, when all the sway of earth
>Shakes like a thing infirm? O Cicero,
>I have seen tempests, when the scolding winds
>Have rived the knotty oaks; and I have seen
>The ambitious ocean swell, and rage, and foam,
>To be exalted with the threat'ning clouds:
>But never till to-night, never till now,
>Did I go through a tempest dropping fire.
>Either there is a civil strife in heaven;
>Or else the world, too saucy with the gods,
>Incenses them to send destruction.
>   *Cic.* Why, saw you anything more wonderful?
>   *Casca. A common slave (you know him well by sight),
>Held up his left hand, which did flame and burn
>Like twenty torches join'd; and yet his hand,
>Not sensible of fire, remain'd unscorch'd.*
>Besides (I have not since put up my sword),
>Against the Capitol I met a lion,
>Who glared upon me, and went surly by
>Without annoying me: and there were drawn
>Upon a heap a hundred ghastly women,
>Transformed with their fear; who swore they saw
>*Men all in fire walk up and down the streets.
>And yesterday the bird of night did sit,
>Even at noon-day, upon the market-place,
>Hooting and shrieking.* When these prodigies
>Do so conjointly meet, let not men say
>"These are their reasons,—They are natural,"
>For I believe they are portentous things
>Unto the climate that they point upon.
>
>   ("Julius Cæsar.")

Compare Bacon on these portents:—"Talia enim evenerunt anno DCCXC., per septendecim dies, et temporibus Justiniani per annum dimidium, *et post mortem Julii Cæsaris per complures dies, Atque Julianæ illius obtenebrationis manet testimonium illud insigne Virgilii*:—

> Ille etiam extincto miseratus Cæsare Romam
> Cum caput obscura nitidum ferrugine texit,
> Impiaque æternam timuerunt secula noctem."

(P. 752, vol. iii., Phil. Wks. E. and Spedding.)

CHAPTER IX.

CYMBELINE.*

VERULAM AND CYMBELINE.

IT is a curious thing to find the last play in the Folio 1623, viz., "Cymbeline," *closely connected with the old town of Verulam*, from whence Bacon took his final title, and which is identical with the site of St Albans and Gorhambury Park.

Old Verulam was the ancient seat of Cassibulan (or Casibelane), who was *uncle to Cymbeline*:—

> *Cymb.* Now say, what would *Augustus Cæsar* with us?
> *Luc.* When *Julius Cæsar* (whose remembrance yet
> Lives in men's eyes, and will to ears and tongues
> Be theme and hearing ever) was in this Britain,
> And conquer'd it, Cassibulan thine Uncle
> (Famous in *Cæsar's* praises, no whit less
> Then in his feat deserving it) for him,
> And his succession, granted Rome a tribute,
> Yearly three thousand pounds.

Cassibulan lost his seat, the town of Verolanium (Verulamium), together with his own liberty, to Caius Julius Cæsar. Verulam

---

* Cymbeline was an early British King of the name *Cuno-Belinus Rex*, whose coins are common enough in the country. Nimrod writes:—"These are talismanic medals (such as, I think, the Chevalier Hammer has proved to have been frequently struck off the preceptories of the Temple *and other secret fraternities*), and they signify (as I understand them) the symbol of the *Magna Mater* and the name of *Belenus*, the Druidical Apollo; or, in the Romance language, Termagant or Tervagana and Apolin. If not, how happens it, I ask, that King Cuneboline is sometimes a gentleman, sometimes a lady, and sometimes a Janus-like figure, with the two heads upon one neck? But there is a name on the reverse of these coins, which has baffled all investigation of British antiquarians, *Tacis, Tascio,* or *Tascia*.

"It is a matter of serious doubt whether the British kings of Cunobelinus' time coined any money at all, and it is rather the better opinion that they did not. See Pegge on the coins of Cunobeline, London, 1765. As the ques-

was some time a city of great renown, and held in great regard by the Romans. Tacitus terms it a free town, and one of the richest in the land, wherein have been found both pillars and pavements, and Roman coins. Is there not some evidence suggested by this connection of Cymbeline's uncle with Verulam to point to Bacon? If not mistaken (as we only quote from memory), Cymbeline lived in the thirty-third year of our *Saviour*, or at the time of His birth. This is possibly in connection with the prediction of the Soothsayer, "When as a Lion's Whelp," &c., pointing to Christ as the "Lion of the Tribe of Judah." This play is the last in the Folio, and that should be well borne in mind in connection with its mysterious prediction at the end.

Imogen is sister to Guiderius and Arviragus, the exact relationship of Helen (Imorgen or Morgana) to Castor and Pollux. And Bacon, in his "History of the Winds," interprets them both,

tion proposed is, whether the numismatic Cunobeline belongs to the age of Caligula, or to the Romance age, it is no light circumstance, that we find him figuring away as a hero of romance and father of *Imorgen* or *Imogen* the *Princess of the Morning*, whose wild adventure *Shakespeare has preserved to us*. *Imorgen* is the witch *Morgana*, by whom Arthur's grievous wound was healed in Avalon" (Vol. I., p. 466, "Nimrod").

Nimrod connects the name of Morgan, Imogen, or Imorgen with the *Morwening*, or the break of day, with the city of *Aurora*, or the city of Medea and of Circe. Adonis the hunter was the son of the Morning. He identifies Imogen with Morgana, whose history seems to imply that she was Helen" (pp. 70, 71, Vol. III.).

All this is very important when examined by the light of the play of "Cymbeline." Because Helen or Imorgen was the sister of Castor and Polydeuces, and there is a striking parallel between Imogen and the two lost or banished brothers in the play. It is to be questioned whether the author was not quite conscious of all this? Imogen is very pointedly connected with the morning in the following verse sung by Cloten under her window:—

> Harke, Harke, the Larke at Heaven's gate sings,
> And Phœbus 'gin arise,
> His steeds to water at those springs
> On chaliced flower that lies:
> And winking Mary-buds begin to ope their golden eyes,
> With everything that pretty is, My Lady sweet arise,
> Arise, Arise!

with their sister Helen, as prognostics of a severe storm at sea, in short, as winds. He writes:—

"The ball of fire, called *Castor* by the ancients, that appears at sea, if it be single, prognosticates a severe storm (seeing it is Castor the dead brother), which will be much more severe if the ball does not adhere to the mast, but rolls or dances about. But if there are two of them (that is, if Pollux the living brother be present), and that too when the storm has increased, it is reckoned a good sign. But if there are three of them (that is, if Helen, the general scourge, arrive), the storm will become more fearful. The fact seems to be, that one by itself seems to indicate that the tempestuous matter is crude; two, that it is prepared and ripened; three or more, that so great a quantity is collected as can hardly be dispersed."

The reader will see that Helen is the emblem of the gale that brings the Tempest. Now we have seen that Helen is another name for Imogen according to the learned Nimrod. Compare this in "Cymbeline." Arviragus says of Imogen:—

>Nobly he yokes,
>A smiling, with a sigh; as if the sigh
>Was that it was, for not being such a smile:
>The smile, mocking the sigh, that it would fly
>From so divine a Temple, to commix
>*With winds that sailors rail at.* (Act iv. sc. 2.)

The last line is a hint for a gale or tempest. The critic smiles. But wait a bit. Both Castor and Pollux are also connected with winds, as harbingers, as we find Bacon stating. Compare *Guiderius* and *Arviragus*:—

>*Bel.* O thou goddess,
>Thou divine Nature, how thyself thou blazon'st
>In these two princely boys! They are as gentle
>*As zephyrs, blowing below the violet,*
>Not wagging his sweet head: and yet as rough
>Their royal blood enchaf'd, as the rud'st wind,
>That by the top doth take the mountain pine
>And make him stoop to the vale.
>(Act iv. sc. 2.)

Here again we have gentle breezes or "zephyrs," which can

become gales or tempests and make the mountain pine "stoop to the vale." But we have yet the most striking and forcible proof to adduce with regard to Imogen or Helen. In the last scene of the last act we have the soothsayer's prediction, in which he identifies Imogen with a piece of "*tender air*." Now we are going to show that Bacon, in his Latin "De Augmentis," 1623, uses the same Latin words for "*tender air*" as we find in the play, and that in the 1640 "Advancement" (which is one of Bacon's true works) it is translated a "*gentle gale of wind*." The soothsayer says:—

> Thou *Leonatus* art the Lion's whelp,
> The fit and apt construction of thy name
> Being *Leonatus*, doth import so much:
> The piece of tender air, thy vertuous daughter,
> Which we call *Mollis Aer*, and *Mollis aer*
> We term it *Mulier;* which Mulier I divine
> Is this most constant wife.
>
> ("Cymbeline," act v. sc. 5.)

Now in the Fourth Book of the 1623 "De Augmentis," we find Bacon writing of the *Soul*, which he identifies with *Spirit*, as follows:—

"Quid enim ad *Doctrinam de substantia* Animæ faciunt, ACTUS ULTIMUS, et Forma Corporis, et hujusmodi Nugæ Logicæ? Anima siquidem, Sensibilis sive Brutorum plané substantia Corporea censenda est, à calore attenuata, et facta Invisibilis; aura (inquam) ex Naturâ Flammeâ et Aërea conflata, AËRIS MOLLITIE ad impressionem recipiendam," &c. (p. 606, vol. i., Phil. Wks.).

We find this passage rendered in the 1640 translation of the "De Augmentis":—"For what makes these terms of *Actus Ultimus*, and *Forma Corporis*, and such-like wild logical universalities, to the knowledge of the soul's substance? For the sensible soul, or the soul of beasts, must needs be granted to be a corporal substance attenuated by heat and made invisible. I say a thin, *gentle gale of wind*, swell'd and blown up from some flamy and airy nature, indeed, with the softness of air to receive impression" (p. 208, Lib. IV., 1640, "Advancement of Learning"). Now we cannot believe that any translator would take it upon himself to render "*Aeris Mollitie*" as "*a gentle gale of wind*" unless instructed to do so. But the reader will see how thoroughly this is in harmony with what we have already quoted from "Cymbeline" in both passages, for what is the line—

> With winds that sailors rail at,

or,

> Zephyrs blowing below the violet,

but a *gentle gale, or a tempest of wind?*

"Cymbeline" is the *last play* in the 1623 Folio, and upon the *last page, final scene, last act*, we find the soothsayer's prediction already quoted with the *same Latin words* "*aeris mollicie*," or "*mollis aer*," as in the 1623 "De Augmentis." Our conviction is that the twenty-sixth star, under which this section about Soul or Spirit occurs, is connected with the twenty-sixth star of the MSS. in Bacon's hand attached to the title page, or a loose leaf, of Hermes Stella. We find Guiderius connected with a star.

> Guiderius had
> Upon *his neck* a mole, *a sanguine star*.
> It was a mark of *wonder*.
>
> ("Cymbeline," act v. sc. 5.)

In the second decan of Cassiopeia there is a star called *Mira*, or the changeable star *in the Neck, meaning Wonder*.* Bacon mentions in his "Cogitationes Rerum," a star which appeared in 1572 in Cassiopeia. He writes :—"Mutationes in regionibus cælestibus fieri, ex cometis quibusdam satis liquet ; iis dico qni certam et constantem configurationem cum stellis fixis servarunt ; qualis fuit illa quæ in Cassiopeâ nostrâ ætate apparuit." † "This star" (writes Spedding) "in Cassiopeia appeared in 1572." *Mazzaroth considers the star of 1572 to have been the star of Bethlehem,*

* See page 9, "Mazzaroth, or the Constellations."

† P. 33, vol. iii., Phil. Wks., Spedding. "Id enim perspicitur in cometis sublimioribus, iis nimirum qui et figuram stellæ induerunt absque coma, neque solum ex doctrina parallaxium supra lunam collocati esse probantur, sed configurationem etiam certam et constantem cum stellis fixis habuerunt, et stationes suas servarunt, neque errones fuerunt ; quales ætas nostra non semel vidit, primo in Cassiopea, iterum non ita pridem in Ophiucho " (p. 752, vol. iii., Phil. Wks., E. and S.)

which he says returns every 300 years.* He writes:—"The bright star which appeared between Cepheus and Cassiopeia in the years 945, 1264, and 1572, the last time being observed by Tycho, the great Danish Astronomer, is considered to have probably been the same star at its periodical return of about 300 years" (p. 604).

But to return from this speculation. We find in "Cymbeline" this passage:—

In a great pool, a swan's nest.

(Act iii. sc. 4.)

Out of the egg of Leda or the swan, were born Castor and Polydeuces, and the third to come out was Helen.

We cannot of course produce any evidence of the opinions we now are going to adduce. But our own conviction is that this last play of "Cymbeline," if not probably the last written, certainly the last in the Folio, is an astronomical play in connection with the Cipher, and the entire revelation of the cycle of this enchanted art. Leonatus, the "*Lion's whelp*" *of the tribe of Judah, is an unmistakable hint for a Messiah.* Leo and Virgo are two signs that are most important in their connection. Virgo, is but a form of Persephone or Proserpine, in the heavens, the summer child of Ceres, crowned at Midsummer with the sun in Leo. Bacon interprets Proserpine as Spirit, exactly what we have found Imogen, as "*tender air*," or "*mollis aer*," or wind. Spirit and air or wind are interchangeable. Bacon constantly uses the word air for Spirit as we have already seen. Virgo was the seed bearer in the zodiac. She is intimately connected with the

* This same star is expected to reappear in 1890 or 1891. Spedding writes:—"The new star in Cassiopeia shone with full lustre on Bacon's freshmanship." Mazzaroth writes:—"The new star seen by Tycho Brahe, in Cassiopeia, which blazed for a short time (1572-1574) and then disappeared, sufficiently authorises us to regard this star as no meteor of our earth or sky, but as one of the heavenly bodies pre-ordained to the glorious office of heralding, by an increase of its own brightness, the coming in splendour of Him, the true Light, by whom and for whom all things were created" ("Constellations," i. 16). "Some have thought that Virgil (Ecl. ix. 47) speaks of this star as 'Cæsaris astrum.' There is a star so-called often an antique gem of Julius Cæsar" (*Ib.*, p. 106).

"Lion's Whelp" or the Messiah. "The two signs of Leo and Virgo are often found together on the breasts of mummies" ("Rosicrucians," Jennings, 65). "The attributes of Demêter (Ceres, Isis) and Persephone *are ears of corn, poppy, and a torch*" ("Preller," i. 492). "Her representation is very nearly identical with the figure of the VIRGO in Albumazar (pp. 78, 79, Eschenburg Plate, xi. p. 428, § 64). Her *dragons* which draw her chariot seem to indicate the return from Hades (Hell)." Now the scene in "Cymbeline," in which Imogen's bed-chamber is introduced, and Iachimo comes out of his chest, parallels the winter sleep of Persephone in Hades or Hell. Dionysus Chthonios, a divinity of the underworld for a season, "*sleeps in the sacred abode of Persephone.*" Iachimo exclaims in the chamber of Imogen:—

> Swift, swift you *dragons* of the night! that dawning
> May bare the raven's eye: I lodge in fear;
> Though this a *heavenly angel*, *hell* is here.
>
> (Act ii. sc. 2.)

Imogen, indeed, throughout the play presents the picture of a Spirit or Angel. Not only is this apparent everywhere, but the text supports it repeatedly. When Imogen enters the cave (the sixth scene of the third act), Belarius exclaims:—

> *Bel.*   Stay! come not in:
> But that it eats our victuals, I should think
> Here were *a fairy*.
> *Guid.*   What's the matter, sir?
> *Bel.* By Jupiter, *an angel:* or if not,
> An earthly paragon! Behold *diviness*
> No elder than a boy.
>
> (Act iii. sc. 6.)

No pains have been spared to associate Imogen with Spirit, Air, as an Angel or Fairy. We find her in context with a monument, and thus with Death. Iachimo exclaims of Imogen whilst he gazes on her asleep:—

> O sleep thou *Ape of death*, lie dull upon her,
> And be her sense but as a monument,
> Thus in a Chapel lying.
>
> (Act ii. sc. 2.)

He compares her to the Phœnix:—

> All of her, that is out of door, most rich:
> If she be furnish'd with a mind so rare,
> She is alone th' Arabian bird.
>
> (Act i. sc. 7.)

The "Arabian bird" was the Phœnix, the bird of resurrection or revelation. We are immediately in context with that prophetic and mysterious Threne, which ends the poems known as Shakespeare's,—the "Phœnix and Turtle:"—

> Let the bird of loudest lay,
> On the *sole Arabian tree*
> Herald sad and trumpet be,
> To whose sound chaste wings obey.

All these points we bring forward are in startling harmony with each other. Prosperine or Spirit (as Bacon interprets her in his "Wisdom of the Ancients") typified the *resurrectionary power of nature asleep during Winter*, rearising with Spring and Summer. In fact, Prosperine's awakening is the Phœnix of Nature arising out of its ashes. Cannot the student see a profound parallel in all this, particularly in the connection *with Death* of Imogen? And also the parallel of her bedchamber, with its comparison to Hell or the Underworld? For Prosperine was supposed to pass the six winter months with Pluto in the Underworld.

THE LION OF THE TRIBE OF JUDAH.

"1. And I saw in the right hand of Him that sat on the throne a book *written within* and on the back side, sealed with seven seals.

"2. And I saw a strong angel proclaiming with a loud voice, Who is worthy to open the book, and to loose the seals thereof?

"3. And no man in heaven, nor in earth, neither under the earth, was able to open the book, neither to look thereon.

"4. And I wept much, because no man was found worthy to open and to read the book, neither to look thereon.

"5. And one of the elders saith unto me, Weep not: *behold*, *the Lion of the Tribe of Judah*, the root of David, hath prevailed to open the book, and to loose the seven seals thereof" (Revelation, ch. v.).

Compare Lord Bacon's motto in chief (attached to "Novum Organum," and "De Augmentis," 1623): "But thou, O Daniel, shut up the words, *and seal the book, even* to the time of the end: many shall run to and fro, and knowledge shall be increased" * (ch. xii. 4). We find this also attached to one of the works of Thomas Vaughan, the celebrated Rosicrucian ("Theosophica Magica"). In "Cymbeline" we refind the "*Lion's Whelp*" identified with Leonatus Posthumus, by the soothsayer. "Whenas a Lion's Whelp shall to himself unknown, without seeking, find and be embraced by a piece of tender air," &c. Now it is very curious to find Bacon, under the twenty-sixth star, describing the nature of the soul, in Latin, in the same words as the soothsayer here employs, viz., "*mollis aer*," and as a *gentle " gale of wind."* Spirit is, of course, implied in air. It may be disputed whether Bacon attached any belief to the prophecies of Scripture, so we give his own words, showing clearly he had faith in the Scriptural succession of ages.

"As to the interpretation of the Scripture solute and at large, there have been divers kinds introduced and devised, some of them rather curious and unsafe, then sober and warranted. Notwithstanding, this much must be confessed, that the Scriptures being given by inspiration, and not by humane reason, do differ from all other books in the Author, which by consequence doth draw on some difference to be used by the Expositor. For the inditer of them did know four things which no man attains to know, which are the mysteries of the Kingdom of Glory, the perfection of the Laws of Nature, the secrets of the heart of Man,

* Bacon writes:—"And this excellent felicity in nautical art, and environing the world, may plant also an expectation of farther PROFICIENCIES AND AUGMENTATIONS OF SCIENCES; specially seeing it seems to be decreed by the Divine Council, that these two should be coevals, for so the Prophet Daniel speaking of the latter times foretells *Plurimi pertransibunt et augebitur scientia*" ("Advancement of Learning").

and the future succession of all ages" "Advancement of Learning," Book II.).

The learned authoress of the "Perfect Way" writes:—

"That the time of the rising of this Celestial Virgin, and of the rehabilitation of truth by the Woman-Messias of the Interpretation is near at hand, they who watch the 'times' and the 'heavens' may know by more than one token. To name but one: the sign Leo, which upon the celestial chart precedes the ascension of the Woman, going before her as her herald, is the sign of the present head of the Catholic Church (Pope Leo). When assuming that title, he declared his office to be that of the '*Lion of the tribe of Judah*,' the domicile of the Sun, the tribe appointed to produce the Christ. To the ascension of this constellation, preparing, as it were, the way of the Divine Virgin, the prophecy of Israel in Genesis refers:—

"'Judah is a strong Lion; my son thou art gone up. The sceptre shall not be taken away from Judah till the coming of the messenger—or Shiloh—the expectation of the nations.'

"And not only does the chief bishop of the Church bear the significant name of the 'Lion,' but he is also the Thirteenth of that name, and Thirteen is the number of the Woman, and of the Lunar cycle, the number of Isis and of the Microcosm. It is the number which indicates the fulness of all things, and the consummation of the Divine Marriage, 'the at-one-ment of Man and God.' Moreover, the Arms of Leo XIII. represent a Tree on a mount between two triune lilies, and in the dexter chief point a blazing star, with the motto '*Lumen in cœlo*.' What is this tree but the Tree of Life; these Lilies but the Lilies of the new annunciation—of the *Ave* which is to reverse the curse of *Eva?* What star is this, if not the star of the second advent? For the signs of the Zodiac, or of the 'Wheel of Life,' as the name signifies, are not arbitrary, they are the words of God traced on the planisphere by the finger of God, and first expressed in intelligible hieroglyphics by men of the Age of *Saturn*, who knew the truth and held the Key of the Mysteries. The wheel of the Zodiac thus constituted the earliest Bible; for on it is traced the universal history of the whole humanity" ("The Perfect Way," pp. 174, 175, Kingsford).

"Only when the Naros, or Cycle of the Six Days shall again reach their seventh day, will 'the Lord of the Seventh,' whom the Latins adored with unveiled heads under the name of *Septimanius*, return, and the veil of illusion of Maya be taken away. The anticipation of the seventh day of the renewed Arcadia, the Seven Days' Festival of Liberty and Peace was held by the Greeks under the name of the *Kronia*, and by the Latins under that of the *Saturnalia*. This redemptive Sabbath is spoken of in the Gospel as the 'harvest of the end of the world,' when Saturn, or Sator (the Sower), as Lord of the Harvest, 'shall return again with joy, bringing his sheaves with him'" (p. 172, "Perfect Way").

> Iam redit et Virgo, redeunt *Saturnia* regna,
> Iam nova progenies cœlo dimittitur alto.
> (Virgil, "Eelog.," iv.)

"At the opening of the year the constellation of the Celestial Virgil, Astræa, Isis, or Ceres, is in ascension. She has beneath her feet in the lower horizon the sign Python or Typhon, of the Dragon of the Tree of the Hesperides, who rises after her, aiming his fangs at her heel."

Sir Tobie Matthew seems undoubtedly to have enjoyed the entire and unbounded confidence of Bacon. Indeed he is the only writer whose letters give us a clue to the real authorship of Shakespeare, if we may so put it. It is Sir Tobie Matthew who writes: "The most prodigious wit that ever I knew, of my nation and of this side of the sea, is of your Lordship's name, though he be known by another." It is to Sir Tobie Matthew that Bacon writes: he has put the works of the alphabet into frame. This word "*frame*" immediately recalls page 36 of the Distribution Preface, where Bacon, writing of the types and platforms of the uncompleted Fourth Part of his "Instauration," says: "For it came into our mind, that in MATHEMATICS the *frame* standing, the Demonstration inferred is facile and perspicuous." It appears from the following that Bacon consulted Sir Tobie Matthew on his works:—

"My *Instauration* I reserve for our conference; it sleeps not. Those works of the *Alphabet* are in my opinion of less use to you where you are now, than at Paris; and therefore I conceived that you had sent me a kind of tacit countermand of your former request."

The following curious manuscript[*] has been found, pointing to the date 1640 (the date of the "Advancement of Learning," translated by Wats). It is worthy note we find a "*Posthumus*" in the last play of the Folio "Cymbeline," in context with a book—"*a rare one*"—which is a mystery as to meaning.

A BRIEF DESCRIPTION
OF A CURIOUS MANUSCRIPT

In the Collection of the Rev. Dr NELIGAN, with Extracts.

THE MANUSCRIPT IS ENTITLED

A TRUE HISTORICALL RELATION

OF THE CONVERSION OF

SIR TOBIE MATTHEWS

TO THE HOLIE CATHOLIC FAYTH,

With the Antecedents and Consequents thereof,

To a deare Friend.

This highly curious Manuscript consists of three separate treatises, and is dated 8th 7ber, 1640. It is signed by Sir Tobie Matthew himself in two places, viz., at the end of the history of his conversion, where it also bears the name of several witnesses in their own autographs; and again after the treatise called "*Posthumus, or the Survivour*," to which Sir T. Matthew has likewise affixed his seal in red wax.

[*] Published by Mr Smith in his little work upon the authorship of the plays.

We are then presented with "*Posthumus, or the Survivour*," a treatise which occupies twenty-one pages; and from page 22 to the end, page 59, we have the "Five-and-twenty Considerations" alluded to, dated 1641, and apparently "signed, James Louth." At the end of "*Posthumus, or the Survivour*," is the following, in the autograph of Sir Tobie Matthew, and an impression of his seal in red wax :—

"Signed by me in London, as in
ye presence of Almighty God, for
most certainly and intirely
true ; upon ye 8th day of 7ber.
1640.

"TOBIE MATTHEW."

The seal bears a Lion Rampant in the first and fourth quarters, and *three* Chevrons in the second and third.

Then follows the attestation by witnesses, in a different writing, and their autograph signatures.

The name of Posthumus suggests something born or published *Posthumously, that is, after the death of the Father or Author*. Sir Tobie Matthews was Bacon's most bosom friend, indeed *the only friend* to whom he seems to have unclasped the secret book of his very soul. Sir Tobie Matthews seems to have been one of Bacon's literary executors. At any rate, in the play of "Cymbeline," we find Posthumus Leonatus presented to us in the following scene in connection with *some book,—a rare one*, suggested as some terminal revelation :—

> A book ?   O rare one !
> Be not, as is our fangled world, a garment
> Nobler than that it covers : let thy effects
> So follow, to be most unlike our courtiers,
> As good as promise.

CYMBELINE.

[*Reads.*] "*When as a lion's whelp shall, to himself unknown, without seeking find, and be embraced by a piece of tender air; and when from a stately cedar shall be lopped branches, which, being dead many years, shall after revive, be jointed to the old stock, and freshly grow; then shall Posthumus end his miseries, Britain be fortunate, and flourish in peace and plenty.*"

Of course the Lion's Whelp is a reference to the "Lion's Whelp" of the House of Judah, and is evidently connected with the sign Leo—the Lion, or Separating. In "Cymbeline" the Father of Leonatus is introduced as *Sicilius Leonatus*, a name which takes us at once to Sicily and to *Leontes*, King of Sicily, in the "Winter's Tale." "The Lion of the Tribe of Judah" (Rev. v. 5) "is known to have always been borne on the standard of Judah, whether in the wilderness (Num. ii.) or in after times."

CHAPTER X.

BACON'S HOME.   TEMPLE AND VERULAM HOUSE, GORHAMBURY.

> When Verulam stood
> St Albans was a wood;
> But now Verulam's down,
> St Albans is become a town.

THE chief parts that are now standing of the remains of Temple House, Gorhambury, are the ruins of the hall, which constituted the inner side of the court, and a lofty octagonal tower. The inside, which is now quite open, appears from the Aubrey manuscripts to have been highly ornamented in the splendid style of the age. "In the hall," writes Aubrey, "is a large storie, very well painted, of the feast of the Gods, where Mars is caught in a net by Vulcan. On the wall over the chimney is painted an oak, with acorns falling from it, with the words *Nisi quid potius;* and on the wall over the table is painted *Ceres teaching the sowing of corn*, the words *Moniti Meliora*." *

This was Lord Bacon's motto, and finds particular reflection in connection with his concluding words to the "De Augmentis" of 1623—that he had "*sown unto posterity.*" May we not venture to suppose that this picture had some association with the introduction of Ceres in the play of "The Tempest"?

---

* Prima Ceres ferro mortales vertere terram
Instituit, cum jam glandes atque arbuta sacræ
Deficerent silvæ, et victum Dodona negaret.
(Virgil, "Georgics," i. 147.)

There is an allusion to these lines in the third Sophism of Bacon's "Colours of Good and Evil." "Propter comparationem; si bonum fuerit generi humano privari esu glandium, non sequitur quod malus ille erat; sed Dodona bona, Ceres melior." (Spedding, i. 676.)

> Ceres, most bounteous Lady, thy rich leas
> Of Wheat, Rye, Barley, Vetches, Oats, and Peas.
>
> (Act iii. sc. 3.)

It was Ceres, as represented in the painting, who first taught men agriculture and a civil life. And it was round her worship that the Greek Drama took its origin. "The religion which produced the Drama, is essentially connected with the worship of the elements, and that the Greek Drama in particular manifests itself in the cognate worship of Apollo, Demeter (*Ceres*), and Dionysus" (Donaldson's "Greek Theatre," p. 10). "It was as a Phallic God, and as the giver of wine, that Dionysus retained his place in the worship of ancient Greece. And in this capacity his worship connects itself indissolubly with the mysteries of Demeter and her daughter, the goddesses of the earth and under-world. Generally the productiveness of the earth is regarded as the result of a marriage between the God of the sky—whether he appears as the genial sun or as the refreshing rain—and the goddess who represents the teeming earth and weds her daughter to Plutus, the owner of the treasure hidden below the surface of the ground, either actually as metallic riches, or potentially as the germs of vegetable growth" (*Ibid.* 19).

So it seems Bacon, as a boy, must have early been made acquainted with this subject, seeing in his "Wisdom of the Ancients," he so thoroughly apprehends the meaning of Proserpine who was the daughter of Ceres. Bacon's father, Sir Nicholas Bacon, is described by Naunton in his "Fragmenta Regalia" as "an arch-piece of wit and wisdom." Again, "Those that lived in his age, and from whence I have taken this little model of him, give him a lively character, and they decipher him to be another Solon, and the Simon of those times, such an one as Œdipus was in dissolving riddles." In the garden close to the house was a statue of Orpheus, another supposed founder of the mysteries, and in a niche in a broken wall, a full length statue of Henry VIII. in gilt armour, but greatly defaced and mutilated. So that Bacon had enough around him to stimulate his poetical, classical, and historical genius into thought. This wall, in which the fragment of Henry VIII. stands, formed part of a noble piazza or porticus, which, according to Aubrey, was built by the Lord Chancellor Bacon, and is described by Pennant as having a range of pillars of the Tuscan order in front. "Opposite to every arch of this portico," writes Aubrey, "and as big as the arch, are drawn by an excellent hand (but the mischief of it is, in water-colours) curious pictures, all emblematical, with mottoes under each : for example, one, I remember, is a ship tossed in a storm, the motto, *Alter eritum Typhys*. (This is an allusion to the Pilot of the Argonautic expedition). Over this portico is a stately gallery, whose glass windows are all painted ; and every pane with several figures of beast, bird, or flower : perhaps his Lordship might use them as topics of local use. The windows look into the garden : the side opposite them has no windows, but is hung all with pictures at length, as of King James, his Lordship, and several illustrious persons of his time. At the end you enter is no window, but there is a very large picture thus : in the middle, on a rock in the sea, stands King James in armour, with his regal ornaments ; on his right hand stands (but whether or no on a rock, I have forgot) Henry IV. of France, in armour ; and on his left hand, the King of Spain in like armour. These figures are, at least, as big as life ; they are done only with umbre and shell gold ; all the heightening and illuminated part being burnished gold, and the shadow umbre. The roof of this gallery is semicylindrique, and painted by the same hand, and same manner, with heads and busts of Greek and Roman emperors and heroes." In an orchard connected with the old mansion was a small banquetting or summer-house, the walls of which were curiously painted *al fresco*, with representations of the liberal arts, having appropriate mottoes under them, and above them, the heads of the most illustrious of those who had excelled in each art, whether ancient or modern. The mottoes are preserved in Weever (p. 584), and also in the "Biographica Britannica," vol. i. p. 446, where they are given with translations. This mansion was reduced to its present ruinous state when the house of the Lords Grimston was built in the years 1778-1785.

Bacon also erected a house within the walls of ancient Verulam, which, according to Aubrey, "he had a great mind to have made a city again; and he had designed it to be built with great uniformity." Verulam House, continues the writer, "was the most ingeniously contrived little pile that I ever saw. No question but his Lordship was the chiefest architect; but he had for his assistant a favourite of his, a St Albans man, Mr Dobson (father of Dobson, the celebrated portrait painter), who was his Lordship's right hand.

"This house did cost nine or ten thousand (pounds) the building, and was sold about 1665 or 6, by Sir Harbottle Grimston, Bart. (now Master of the Rolls), to two carpenters, for four hundred pounds, of which they made eight hundred pounds; there were good chimney-pieces; the rooms very lofty, and very well wainscotted; there were two bathing rooms, or stuffes, whither his Lordship retired afternoons as he saw cause: all the tunnels of the chimneys were carried into the middle of the house, and round about them were seats. From the leads was a lovely prospect to the ponds, which were opposite to the east side of the house, and were on the other side of a stately walk of trees that leads to Gorhambury House, and also over that long walk of trees, whose tops afford a most pleasant variegated verdure, resembling the works in Irish stiches. In the middle of the house was a delicate staircase of wood, which was curiously carved; and on the post of every interstice was some pretty figure, as of a grave divine with his book and spectacles, a mendicant friar, &c., not one thing twice: on the doors of the upper storey on the outside, which were painted dark umbre, were figures of the Gods of the Gentiles; viz., on the South door, second storey, was Apollo; on another *Jupiter, with his thunderbolt, bigger than the life, and done by an excellent hand; the lightnings were of hatchings of gold, which when the sun shone on them, made a most glorious show.* This was his Lordship's summer house; for he said one should have seats for summer and winter, as well as clothes. The kitchen, larder, cellars, &c., are under ground."

In these trifles we see reflected Bacon's classical tastes and predilections. This pictorial Jupiter seems to find reflection in the play of "Cymbeline," where in the last act *Jupiter is introduced throwing a thunderbolt.*

Jupiter descends in thunder and lightning, sitting upon an eagle: he throws a thunder-bolt. (Act. v.)

When this play was written Verulam House had been built, and these decorations existed. "The Tempest"—another of the final plays—also presents us with Jupiter. We consider these points show strong parallel evidence that Bacon was surrounding himself with paintings of subjects we refind in the last plays. Apollo, the God of poetry and song, Jupiter, the protagonist of classical mythology, how often do we refind all this in the book of books?

> And the fire-rob'd God
> Golden Apollo, a poor humble swain
> As I seem now.
>
> ("Winter's Tale," act iv. sc. 4.)

> To the dread rattling thunder
> Have I given fire, and rifted Jove's stout oak
> With his own bolt.
>
> ("Tempest.")

"From hence to Gorhambury is about 2 little miles; the way ascending hardly so acclive as a desk: three parallel walkes leade to Gorhambury in a straight line; in the middlemost, three coaches may pass abreast; in the wing walkes, two: they consist of severall stately trees of the like growth and height, elme, chesnut, beach, horn-beam, Spanish ash, Cervice-tree, &c. whose tops, as aforesaid, doe afford from the walke on the howse, the finest shew that I have seen. The figures of the ponds were thus: they were pitched at the bottomes with pebbles of severall colours, which were workt into severall figures, as of fishes, &c. which in his Lordship's time were plainly to be seen through the clere water, (though) now overgrown with flagges and rushes. If a poor bodie had brought his lordship halfe a dozen pebbles of curious colour, he would give them a shilling, so curious was he in perfecting his fish ponds, which I guess doe containe four acres. In the middle of the middlemost pond in the island is a curious banquetting house of Roman architecture, paved with black and white marble, covered with Cornish slate, and neatly wainscotted" ("History of Verulam and St Albans." F. L. Williams, p. 140, 1822).

CHAPTER XI.

PARALLELS.

"For it is a rule of *Traditive Art*,* that whatsoever science is not consonant to anticipations or presuppositions *must pray in aid of similitudes and comparisons*" (Book VI., page 276, "Advancement of Learning").

"For many forms of speaking *are equal in signification which are different in impression*" (Book VI., page 211, "Advancement of Learning").

> "Pro Verbis legis
> Non est interpretatio, *sed divinatio*, quæ recedit a litera :
> Cum receditur a litera, judex transit in legislatorem.
> Pro sententia legis.
> Ex omnibus verbis est eliciendus sensus qui interpretatur singula."
> ("Advancement," Book II.)

"For, as the fable goeth of the *basilisk*, that if he see you first you die for it; but if you see him first, he dieth" ("Advancement," Book II., xxxi. 9).

> It is a *basilisk* unto mine eye,
> Kills me to look on't.
>
> ("Cymbeline," act ii. sc. 4, 107.)

"There is an ancient received tradition of the *Salamander*, *that it liveth in the fire*, and hath force also to extinguish the fire" (Exp. 860, "Natural History").

> I have maintained that Salamander of yours with fire
> Any time this two and thirty years.
>
> ("1 King Henry IV.," act iii. sc. 3.)

"Affliction only level those *mole-hills* of pride" ("Letter LXX. to Lord Chief Justice Coke," 1702).

* The fact Bacon makes these remarks in connection with *Tradition*, which he calls "*The Art of Delivery, or of expressing, and transferring those things which are invented*," is a significant hint of itself.

> The blind *mole* casts
> Copp'd *hills* towards heaven, to tell the earth is throng'd
> By man's oppression.
>
> ("Pericles," act i. sc. 1.)

"But as for *imitation*, it is certain that there is in men and other creatures a predisposition to *imitate*. We see how ready *apes* and monkeys are to imitate all motions of man. And besides you shall have *parrots that will not only imitate voices but laughing*" ("Sylva Sylvarum," Cent. III., Exp. 236, 237).

> Now by two-headed *Janus*,
> Nature hath framed strange fellows in her time:
> Some that will evermore peep through their eyes,
> And *laugh like Parrots* at a bagpiper.
>
> ("Merchant of Venice," act i. sc. 1.)

Imitari is nothing : so doth the hound his master, the *Ape* his Keeper.
("Love's Labour's Lost," act iv. sc. 2.)

> *Cleopatra.* Hast thou the pretty worm of Nilus there,
> *That kills and pains not?*
>
> ("Antony and Cleopatra," act v. sc. 2.)

"*The death that is most without pain*, hath been noted to be upon the taking of the potion of hemlock, which, in humanity, was the form of execution of capital offenders in Athens. *The poison of the asp that Cleopatra used hath some affinity with it*" ("Natural History," Exp. 643, Cent. VII.).

"That the note of a thing chosen for *Opinion, and not for truth*, is this, that if a man thought that what he doth should never come to light, he would never have done it" ("Colours of Good and Evil," 10).

A plague of *Opinion*, a man may wear it on both sides like a leather jerkin.
("Troilus and Cressida.")

> This fool's gudgeon, this *opinion*.
> ("Merchant of Venice," act i. sc. 1.)
>
> Be cured of this diseased *opinion*.
> ("Winter's Tale," act i. sc. 2.)

"So in like manner, although our persons live in the view of heaven, yet our spirits are included in the caves of our own complexions and customs, which minister unto us infinite errors and vain opinions, if they be not recalled to examination" ("Advancement of Learning," Book II., p. 56).

"And *the opinion of Epicurus*, answerable to the same in Heathenism who supposed the gods to be of human shape" ("Advancement of Learning," Book II., p. 56).

> *Cassius.* You know that I held *Epicurus strong*,
> And his *opinion*.
>
> ("Julius Cæsar," act v. sc. 1.)

"The deformity of flattery is comical, but the damage tragical" (Flattery, XXXVIII., "Antitheta").

How exactly this is reflected in "Timon of Athens," where the flattery of his friends is comically transparent, the end being so tragical!

"The first precept may be that whereof we have admonished already; let the greater revolutions be retain'd; the lesser horoscopes and houses *casheer'd*" ("Advancement of Learning," 1640, p. 149).

> For naught but provender, and when he's old *casheer'd*.
> ("Othello," act i. sc. 1.)

"For it was both pleasantly and wisely said by a nuncio of the Pope, returning from a certain nation where he served as *leiger*" ("Advancement of Learning," Book II., xxiii. 19).

> Lord Angelo, having affairs to heaven,
> Intends you for his swift ambassador,
> Where you shall be an everlasting *leiger*.
> ("Measure for Measure," act iii. sc. 1, 59.)

"The blessing of *Judah* and *Issachar* will never meet: That the same people or nation should be both the *Lion's Whelp* and the ass between burdens" ("Greatness of Kingdoms").

Compare soothsayer's prediction ("Cymbeline," act v.):—

> When as a Lion's Whelp, &c.

PARALLELS.

> Good friend, for Jesus' sake, forbeare
> To dig the dust enclosed here:
> Blest be the man that spares these stones,
> And curst be he that moves my bones.
>
> (Shakespeare's Epitaph.)
>
> Blest be the hearts that wish my soveraign well!
> Curst be the soul that thinks her any wrong!
>
> (Bacon's "Retired Courtier.")

One of Bacon's similes for nature is that of a *volume* or *book*. In the "De Augmentis" he writes of Aristotle's "Book of Nature": "The world is a volume of God, a kind of *Second Scriptures*, and as the words or terms of all languages in an immense variety, are composed of a few simple letters, so all the actions and powers of things, are formed by a few natures and original elements of simple motions" ("Works," vol. v., p. 426). Again: "Heraclitus gave a just censure, saying men sought wisdom in their own little worlds, and not in the great and common world: for they disdain to spell, and so by degrees to read *in the volume of God's works.*" The thoughtful student may perhaps be inclined to think Bacon is hinting at the "volume of Nature" of the so-called Shakespeare plays. It is worthy notice, we find in "As You Like It," Nature identified with a book—

> Find tongues in trees, *books* * in the running brooks,
> Sermons in stones, and good in everything.
>
> ("As You Like It.")
>
> In nature's *infinite book of secrecy*,
> A little I can read.
>
> ("Antony and Cleopatra," act i. sc. 2.)

The sympathies of the author of the plays for the Trojans rather than the Greeks, is very marked in "Troilus and Cressida."

* This idea is entirely Rosicrucian. "All herbs, flowers, trees, and all the fruits of the earth," says the author in his treatise on Signatures, "are books and magic signs given us by the mercy of God" ("Signaturis Rerum Internis," Oswald Crollius, 1609). "If thou hast but leisure, *run over the Alphabet of Nature, examine every letter, I mean every particular creature in her book*—what becomes of her grass, her corn, her herbs, her flowers?" ("Cœlum Terræ; or the Magician's Heavenly Chaos," p. 128, Thomas Vaughan Waite).

Hector is the real hero, modest, and a great contrast to the proud insulting Achilles, by whom he is killed when defenceless and unarmed. Bacon shows a similar sympathy for Æneas, and quotes the lines of Virgil—

> At domus Æneæ cunctis dominabitur oris
> Et nati natorum, et qui nascentur ab illis.
>
> ("Prophecies.")

This sympathy very likely is borrowed from Virgil.

"A man may destroy the force of his words with his countenance" ("Advancement of Learning," Book II., p. 78).

> Fie treacherous hue, that will betray with blushing
> The close enacts and counsels of the heart.
>
> ("Titus Andronicus," act iv. sc. 2.)

"For I know *Fame* hath swift *wings;* specially that *which hath black feathers*" (Letter to Sir George Villiers, 19th Feb. 1615).

> That thou are blam'd shall not be thy defect,
> For slander's mark was ever yet the fair;
> The ornament of beauty is suspect,
> *A crow that flies in heaven's sweetest air.* (Sonnets.)

"And there has insinuated into men's minds *a still subtler error*—namely this, that art is conceiv'd *to be a sort of addition to nature*" ("Advancement of Learning").

> So over that art
> Which you say *adds to nature,* is an art
> That nature makes. You see, sweet maid, we marry
> A gentle scion to the wildest stock,
> And make conceive a bark of baser kind
> By bud of nobler race: this is an art
> Which does mend nature, change it rather; *but
> The art itself is nature.*
>
> ("Winter's Tale.")

"For high Treason is not written in *ice, that when the body relenteth, the impression should go away*" (Charge of Owen indicted of High Treason in the King's Bench, by Sir Francis Bacon, p. 55, Part I., "Resuscitatio," 1671).

Compare—

> *Duke.* This weak impress of Love is a figure
> *Trenched in ice*, which with an hour's heat
> Dissolves in water, and doth lose his form :
> A little time will melt her frozen thoughts.
> ("Two Gentlemen of Verona," act iii. sc. 1.)

> Half won is match well made ; match and well make it.
> ("All's Well that Ends Well," act iv. sc. 3.)

"Dimidium facti qui bene cæpit habet" ("Colours of Good and Evil," 9).

Seneca saith well ; "*That anger is like ruin, which breaks itself upon what it falls*" ("Anger").

> *Cardinal Wolsey.* What should this mean ?
> What sudden anger this ? How have I reap'd it ?
> He parted *frowning from me, as if ruin*
> *Leap'd from his eyes.*
> ("Henry VIII.," act iii. sc. 2.)

> They say, my Lords, *Ira furor brevis est*,
> But yond man is very angry.
> ("Timon of Athens," act i. sc. 1.)

"The third is, where a man is killed upon a sudden heat or affray, whereunto the Law gives some little favour, because a man in fury is not himself. *Ira furor brevis*, wrath is a short madness" (Sir Francis Bacon's Charge, "At a Session of the Verge").

"Sure I am, it was like a *Tartar's* or *Parthian's bow*, which shooteth backward" (Speech upon Subsidy, p. 4, "Resuscitatio," 1671).

> Arm me audacity from head to foot !
> Or, like the *Parthian*, I shall *flying fight*.
> ("Cymbeline," act i. sc. 7.)

> Now am I like that proud insulting ship,
> *Which Cæsar and his fortune bare at once.*
> ("1 King Henry VI.," act i. sc. 2.)

"So Cæsar said to the Pilot in the Tempest, *Cæsarem portas et fortunam ejus*" ("Of Fortune").

"So when the four *pillars* of government are mainly shaken or weakened (which are Religion, Justice, Counsell, and Treasure) men had need to pray for fair weather" ("Seditions and Troubles").

> Brave peers of England, *pillars* of the State.
> ("2 Henry VI.," act i. sc. 1.)

"There be that can *pack the cards*, and yet cannot play well" ("Cunning").

> She Eros has
> *Pack'd cards* with Cæsar, and false play'd my glory
> Unto an enemy's triumph.
> ("Antony and Cleopatra," act iv. sc. 14.)

> *Where like Arion on the Dolphin's back*,
> I saw him hold acquaintance with the waves
> So long as I could see.
> ("Twelfth Night," act i. sc. 2.)

> Orpheus in sylvis, inter delphinas Arion.
> (Virgil, "Eclogue VIII.," 56.)

("Two Books Advancement of Learning," Book II., p. 179.)

"The tongue speaks to the ear, but the gesture speaks to the eye" ("Advancement of Learning," 1640, p. 182, Book III.).

> A jest's propriety lies in the ear.
> ("Love's Labour's Lost," act v. sc. 2.)

"It was a sparing speech of the ancients to say *That a Friend is another himself: for that a friend is far more than himself*" ("Friendship").

> Make thee *another self*, for Love of me.
> ("Sonnets.")

> 'Tis thee (*myself*) *that for myself I praise*,
> Painting my age with beauty of thy days.
> ("Sonnets.")

> But here's the joy—*my friend and I are one*;
> ("Sonnets.")

The parallel is all the more striking, inasmuch as these Sonnets are addressed *to a friend*. And Bacon continues in this Essay:—"If a man have a true Friend he may rest almost secure that the care of those things will continue after him. So that a man hath, as it were, *two lives in his desire*" ("Friendship"). This idea of *a second life through friendship* is repeated in the Sonnets:—

> You should *live twice;* in it and in my rhyme.
> ("Sonnets.")

"They *perfect Nature*, and are *perfected* by *Experience*" (Essay on "Studies").

> *Experience* is by industry achieved,
> And *perfected* by the swift course of time.
> ("Two Gentlemen of Verona," act i. sc. 3.)

"And yet that is the case of bad officers, treasurers, ambassadors, generals, and other false and corrupt servants, which set *a bias upon their bowl*, of their own petty ends and envies, to the overthrow of their master's great and important affairs" ("Of Wisdom for a Man's Self," 1625).

> *Pet.* Well, forward, forward! thus *the bowl should run,*
> *And not unluckily against the bias.**
> ("Taming of the Shrew," act iv. sc. 5.)

"Wisdom for a man's self is, in many branches thereof, a depraved thing. It is the *Wisdom of Rats, that will be sure to leave a house before it fall*" ("Of Wisdom for a Man's Self").

> A rotten carcass of a boat, not rigg'd,
> Nor tackle, sail, or mast; *the very rats*
> *Instinctively have quit it.*
> ("Tempest," act i. sc. 2.)

---

* You bowl well, if you do not horse the bowl an hand too much. You know the fine bowler is knee almost to ground in the delivery of the cast. (Conf. 13th June 1623, p. 353, Birch's Letters.)

"It is the wisdom of crocodiles that shed tears when they would devour" ("Wisdom for a Man's Self").

> If that the earth could teem with woman's tears,
> Each drop she falls would prove a Crocodile.
>
> ("Othello," act iv. sc. 1.)

Of all the myriad minded characters of the plays, Cardinal Wolsey represents and embodies best the dangers and the glories of *ambition*. In Bacon's Essay upon "Nature in Men," he writes:—

"And at the first, let him practise with helps, *as swimmers do with bladders.*"

> I have ventured,
> Like little wanton boys *that swim on bladders*,
> This many summers in a sea of glory.
>
> ("Henry VIII.," act iii. sc. 2.)

"What a man hath contracted through his own default, is a greater evil; what is imposed from without, is a less evil. Where the evil is derived from a man's own fault, there the grief strikes inward, and does more deeply wound and pierce the heart" (8, "Colours of Good and Evil," p. 289, "Advancement of Learning").

> Those wounds heal ill that men do give themselves.
>
> ("Troilus and Cressida," act iii. sc. 3.)

"The stairs to honours are steep, *the standing slippery*, the regresse a downfall" (Antitheta Rerum, Honour, vii. p. 303, "Advancement of Learning").

> The art o' the court,
> As hard to leave as keep; whose top to climb
> Is certain falling, or so *slippery* that
> The fear's as bad as falling.
>
> ("Cymbeline," act iii. sc. 3.)

> *Cæsar.* But I am *constant* as the Northern *star*,
> Of whose true fixt and resting quality
> There is no fellow in the firmament.
>
> ("Julius Cæsar," act iii. sc. 1.)

"If it were not for two things, that are *constant;* the one is that the *fixed stars* ever stand at like distance one from another" (Essay 58, "Vicissitude of Things").

"To conclude *the irregularities of Mars*, the expiations of *Venus*, the wondrous labours or passions, which are often found in the sun or in *Venus*" (Book III., "De Augmentis," p. 152, 1640).

> *Mars* his true moving, even as in the heavens
> So in the earth to this day is not known.
> ("1 King Henry VI.," act i. sc. 2.)

> Fair Diomed, you do as Chapmen do,
> *Dispraise the thing that you desire to buy.*
> ("Troilus and Cressida," act iv. sc. 1.)

"Out of fraud, and circumventive cunning, for *Praisers and Dispraisers* many times *do but aim at their own ends*, and do not think all they say:—

> Laudat venaleis qui vult extrudere merces.

So '*It is naught, it is naught,' saith the buyer*, and when he is gone he vaunteth" ("Colours of Good and Evil," 1). (Bacon borrows the quotation from *Horace* (lib. 2) and Proverbs xx.)

"He *conquers* twice who upon victory overcomes himself" (Bacon).

> Brave *conquerors!* for so you are,
> That war against your own affections,
> And the huge army of the world's desires.
> ("Love's Labour's Lost," act i. sc. 1.)

"To praise a man's self cannot be decent, except it be in rare cases" (Bacon).

We wound our modesty, and make foul the clearings of our deservings, when of ourselves we publish them. ("All's Well that Ends Well," act i. sc. 3.)

> The southern *wind*
> Doth play the trumpet to his purposes,
> And by his *hollow whistling* in the leaves,
> *Foretells a tempest*, and a blustering day.
> ("1 King Henry IV.," act v. sc. 1.)

"And as there are certain *hollow blasts of wind, and secret swellings of seas before a tempest*, so are there in states" ("Seditions and Troubles").

> Before the times of change, still is it so:
> By a divine instinct men's minds mistrust
> Ensuing dangers: as by proof we see
> *The waters swell before a boisterous storm.*
> ("Richard the Third," act ii. sc. 2.)

"Yet beware of being too *material* when there is any impediment or obstruction in men's wits" ("Dispatch").

> A material fool.
> ("As You Like It," act iii. sc. 3.)

"And therefore, whether your Majesty will any more rest, and build this *great Wheel of your Kingdom* upon these broken and brittle pins, and try experiments further upon the health and body of your state, I leave to your princely judgment" (Letter LX. to King James).

> *Ros.* The single and peculiar life is bound,
> With all the strength and armour of the mind,
> To keep itself from noyance; but much more
> That spirit upon whose weal depend and rest
> The lives of many. The cease of majesty
> Dies not alone; but, like a gulf, doth draw
> What's near it with it: *it is a massy wheel*
> Fix'd on the summit of the highest mount,
> To whose huge spokes ten thousand lesser things
> Are mortised and adjoin'd; which, when it falls,
> Each small annexment, petty consequence,
> Attends the boisterous ruin. Never alone
> Did the king sigh, but with a general groan.
> ("Hamlet," act iii. sc. 3.)

One of Bacon's metaphors is the "*wheel*," which he employs in various ways to illustrate movement, connection, and carriage:—

"The commodity as Nature yieldeth it, the manufacture ; and the vecture or carriage, so that if these *wheels* go wealth will flow as in a spring-tide" (Essay on "Seditions and Troubles").

" As if they were dead images and engines moved only by the *wheels* of custom" ("Custom and Education").

"But that the *wheels* of his mind keep way with the *wheels* of his Fortune" ("Of Fortune").

> Fortune's furious, fickle wheel.
> ("Henry V.," act iii. sc. 6.)

> Fortune from her wheel.
> ("As You Like It," act i. sc. 2.)

> Fortune break her wheel provoked.
> ("Antony and Cleopatra," act iv. sc. 13.)

> Though *Fortune's* malice overthrow my state,
> My mind exceeds the compass of her *wheel*.
> ("3 King Henry VI.," act iv. sc. 3.)

"Corrupt statesman, you that think by your engines and motions to govern the wheel of fortune" ("Reply of the Squire").

"Attend, you *beadsman* of the muses, you take your pleasure in a wilderness of variety ; but it is best of shadows" ("Reply of the Squire").

> For I will be thy *beadsman*, Valentine.
> ("Two Gentlemen of Verona," act i. sc. 1.)

"I have been the keeper of your seal, and now am your *beadsman*" (Letter to the King, 5th Sept. 1621, pub. 1763, Birch, p. 278). Bacon signs this letter "Your Majesty's faithful, poor servant and *beadsman*."

> Thy very *beadsmen* learn to bend their bows
> Of double-fatal yew against thy state.
> ("Richard II.," act iii. sc. 2.)

"This is the quality of things, in their nature excellent and predominant, that though they do not extenuate and impoverish the substance of things adjoining them, *yet they darken and shadow them*"

("Colours of Good and Evil," p. 214, "Advancement of Learning," 1640).

> *Por.* That light we see is burning in my hall,
> How far that little candle throws his beams!
> So shines a good deed in a naughty world.
> *Ner.* When the moon shone, we did not see the candle.
> *Por.* So doth the greater glory dim the less:
> A substitute shines brightly as a king
> Until a king be by, and then his state
> Empties itself, as doth an inland brook
> Into the main of waters. Music! hark!
> *Ner.* It is your music, madam, of the house.
> *Por.* Nothing is good, I see, without respect:
> Methinks it sounds much sweeter than by day.
> *Ner. Silence bestows that virtue on it, madam.*
>
> ("Merchant of Venice," act v. sc. 1.)

"Many times a suspension of a small decision engageth and implicates us in more necessities than if we had determined of somewhat" (Essays).

> Our indiscretion sometimes serves us well,
> When our deep plots do pall.
>
> ("Hamlet," act v. sc. 2.)
>
> Omission to do what is *necessary*
> Seals a commission to a blank of danger.
>
> ("Troilus and Cressida," act iii. sc. 2.)

> Suspicion always haunts the guilty mind,
> The thief doth fear each bush an officer.
>
> ("3 Henry VI.," act v. sc. 6.)

"Suspicions amongst thoughts *are like bats amongst birds, they ever fly by Twilight*" ("Suspicion").

> *Macb.* O, full of scorpions is my mind, dear wife!
> Thou know'st that Banquo, and his Fleance, lives.
> *Lady M.* But in them nature's copy's not eterne.
> *Macb.* There's comfort yet; they are assailable;
> Then be thou jocund: *ere the bat hath flown*
> His cloistered flight, ere to black Hecate's summons
> The shard-borne beetle with his drowsy hums
> Hath rung night's yawning peal, there shall be done
> A deed of dreadful note.
>
> ("Macbeth," act iii. sc. 2.)

"An ill man is always ill; but he is then worst of all when he pretends to be a saint" (Bacon).

> 'Tis too much proved, that with devotion's visage,
> And pious action, we do sugar o'er
> The devil himself.
>
> ("Hamlet," act iii. sc. 1.)

"Good things never appear in their full beauty, *till they turn their back and be going away*" ("Colours of Good and Evil, 6).

This is repeated in the plays in many forms. For example, Antony, on hearing of his wife Fulvia's death, exclaims:—

> Forbeare me
> There's a great Spirit gone, *thus did I desire it:*
> What our contempts doth often hurl from us,
> *We wish it ours again.* The present pleasure,
> By resolution lowering, does become
> The opposite of itself: *She's good being gone,*
> The hand could pluck her back, that shoved her on.
>
> ("Antony and Cleopatra," act i. sc. 1.)

> And the ebb'd man,
> Ne'er loved, till ne'er worth love,
> *Comes fear'd by being lack'd.*
>
> ("Antony and Cleopatra," act i. sc. 1.)

> It so falls out,
> That what we have, we prize not to the worth,
> Whiles we enjoy it; *but being lacked and lost,*
> Why then we rack the value.
>
> ("Much Ado about Nothing," act iv. sc. 1.)

Bacon writes: "That a man do not dismantle himself, and expose his person to scorn and injury by his *too much goodness and facility of nature*" ("De Augmentis," Book VIII., p. 413).

"That there are times when a man's virtues may be his undoing" (*Ib.*).

"Errors indeed in this virtue of goodness or charity may be committed. The Italians have an ungracious proverb, *Tanto buon che val niente: So good that he is good for nothing*" ("Goodness of Nature").

> Poor honest Lord, brought low by his own heart,
> *Undone by goodness.*
>
> ("Timon of Athens," act iv. sc. 2.)

"Guicciardine maketh the same judgment (not of a particular person, but of the wisest state of Europe, the Senate of Venice, when he *sayeth their prosperity had made them secure, and under weighers of perils*" (Bacon to King James I., July 31, 1617, Cabala, Birch, 1654).

> All know *security*
> *Is mortal's chiefest enemy.*
>
> ("Macbeth," act iii. sc. 5.)

> The wound of peace is surety
> Surety secure.
>
> ("Troilus and Cressida," act ii. sc. 2.)

In a letter to King James I., Bacon writes of England:—"The fields growing every day by the improvement of grounds, from the desert to *the garden;* the city grown from wood to brick, your *sea-walls or Pomerium of your island* surveyed, &c." (Letter, 2nd Jan. 1618, Cabala, Birch, 1654).

Compare:—

> *Serv.* Why should we in the compass of a pale
> Keep law and form and due proportion,
> Showing, as in a model, our firm estate,
> When our *sea-walled garden*, the whole land,
> Is full of weeds, her fairest flowers choked up,
> Her fruit-trees all unpruned, her hedges ruin'd,
> Her knots disorder'd and her wholesome herbs
> Swarming with caterpillars?
>
> ("Richard II.," act iii. sc. 4.)

Note the expressions "sea-walled," "sea-walls."

> Like one
> Who having unto truth, by telling of it,
> Made such a sinner of his memory
> *To credit his own lie.*
>
> ("Tempest," act i. sc. 2.)

This idea is repeated (page 32, Book I., "Advancement of Learning," 1640) thus:—"An inquisitive man is a prattler; so upon the like reason, *a credulous man is a deceiver*. As we see it in Fame and Rumours, that he that will easily believe Rumours, *will as easily augment rumours;* which Tacitus wisely notes in these words, *Fingunt simul creduntque* ("They invent and at the same time *believe their own inventions*"); such affinity there is between a propensity to *deceive* and a facility to *believe*."

> But curst the gentle gusts,
> And he that *loos'd them forth their brazen caves*,
> And bid them blow towards England's blessed shore,
> Or turn our stern upon a dreadful rock :
> Yet *Æolus* would not be a murderer.
> ("2 King Henry VI.," act iii. sc. 2.)

"The Poets feigned *Æolus* his kingdom to be placed under ground *in dens and caves*, where the wind's prison was, *out of which they were at times let forth*" ("Natural History of Winds," p. 17, "Resuscitatio").

"And all this while I have been a little imperfect in my foot. But I have taken pains more like the beast *with four legs* than like a man with scarce two legs" (Letter to Buckingham, 8th June 1617, Birch, 1654).

> This is some monster of the island *with four legs*.
> ("Tempest," act ii. sc. 2.)

> 1*st Gent.* Well: there went but a pair of *sheares* between us.
> *Luc.* I grant: as there may between the lists and the velvet,
> Thou art the list.
> 1*st Gent.* And thou the velvet.
>
> ("Measure for Measure.")

"All which authorities and presidents may overweigh Aristotle's opinion that would have us change *a rich wardrobe for a pair of sheares*" ("Advancement of Learning," Book II., p. 52, 1605).

"He had gotten for his purpose, or beyond his purpose, two instruments, Empson and Dudley (whom the people esteemed as his *horse-leeches* and *shearers*" ("History of King Henry VIII.," p. 209).

> Let us to France; like *horse-leeches*, my boys,
> To suck, to suck, the very blood to suck.
> ("King Henry V.," act ii. sc. 3.)

> In memory of her when she is dead,
> Her ashes in an urn more precious
> *Than the rich jewell'd coffer of Darius*,
> Transported shall be at high festivals.
> ("1 King Henry VI.," act i. sc. 6.)

"Secondly, in the judgment or solution he gave touching *that precious cabinet of Darius*, which was found amongst his jewels" ("Two Books of Advancement of Learning," Book I., p. 59, Wright).

This is an allusion to the finding amongst the spoils taken by Alexander the Great from Darius, of a richly jewelled cabinet. Pliny describes it in these words (L. vii. c. 29):—"*Itaque Alexander magnus inter spolia Darii Persarum Regis unguentorum scrinio capto, &c.*" Strabo also mentions this coffer (L. xiii.). Alexander *placed Homer's works in it, as alone worthy of such a chest.* It was covered with precious stones and pearls. (Quintus Curtius, Freinshemii, Supplem., 1, 4, 3, 1724.) This coffer had been used as a receptacle for unguents and incense by the Persian king, and on this account the rare edition of Homer's works preserved in it by Alexander was called "*è narthecio.*" Bacon introduces this story upon page 52 of the "Advancement of Learning," 1640, with, we are convinced, allusion to Shakespeare by analogy.

"The ripeness or unripeness of the occasion (as we said) must ever be well weighed" ("Delays").

> That we would do,
> We should do when we would; for this "would" changes,
> And hath abatements and *delays* as many
> As there are tongues, are hands, are accidents.
> ("Hamlet," act iv. sc. 7.)

"Affected *dispatch* is one of the most dangerous things to business that can be. It is like that which the Physicians call *Predigestion*, or *hasty digestion;* which is sure to fill the body full of crudities and secret seeds of disease. Therefore, measure no *dispatch* by the times of sitting, but by the advancement of the business. And *as in races, it is not the large stride, or high lift, that makes the speed*, so in business, the keeping close to the matter, and not taking too much of it at once, procureth *Dispatch*. I knew a wise man that had it for a by-word, when he saw men hasten to a conclusion: *Stay a little, that we may make an end the sooner*" ("Dispatch").

> We may outrun,
> By violent swiftness, that which we run at,
> And lose by over-running. Know you not,
> The fire, that mounts the liquor till it run o'er,
> In seeming to augment it, wastes it?
> ("Henry VIII.," act i. sc. 1.)

> Too swift arrives as tardy as too slow.
> ("Romeo and Juliet," act ii. sc. 6.)

"Perfectly wicked and desperately impious persons do not corrupt public manners so much as they do who seem to have *some soundness and goodness in them, and are diseas'd but in part*" ("Advancement of Learning," Book III., p. 134, 1640).

> An evil soul producing holy witness
> Is like a villain with a smiling cheek,
> *A goodly apple rotten at the core.*
> ("Merchant of Venice," act i. sc. 3.)

> But here upon this *bank* and school of *time*
> We'd jump the life to come.
> ("Macbeth," act i. sc. 7.)

This expression *bank*, as applied to time, is peculiar, and only to be refound in Bacon's works:—

Compare:—"These examples confirmed me much in a resolution to spend my time wholly in writing; and to put forth that poor talent, or half talent, or what it is, that God hath given me, not as heretofore to particular exchanges, but to *banks and mounts of perpetuity*" ("Epistle to Bishop Andrews").

"*Adversity* is not without comforts and hopes. Adversity is the blessings of the New (Testament). It was an high speech of *Seneca* (after the manner of the Stoics), *That the good things which belong to Prosperity are to be wished; but the good things that belong to Adversity are to be admired*" ("Of Adversity").

Where are we going to refind this profound philosophy outside the Bible, or outside Shakespeare's supposed plays?

> Sweet are the uses of adversity,
> Which like the toad, ugly and venomous,
> *Wears yet a precious jewel in his head.*
>
> ("As You Like It.")

"Certainly, *Vertue is like precious odours, most fragrant when they are incens'd or crush'd*" (Essay on "Adversity"). The imagery between the play and the Essay differs, but the philosophy is identical, and Bacon shows the same metaphor, loving mind, as the poetical passage betrays.

"Vertue is like a *rich stone*, best plain set" ("Beauty").

"The most *precious things* have the most *pernicious keepers*" ("Advancement of Learning," II., Book XVII., p. 12, 1605).

"Whereunto they say the *Toad-stone* * likewise helpeth" ("Syl. Syl.," Cent. x., 968).

"If you be wise you are a fool, if you be a fool you are wise" ("Loquacity," Antitheta Rerum, xxxi., "Advancement of Learning," 1640).

The fool doth think he is wise, but the wise man knows himself to be a fool. ("As You Like It," act v. sc. 1.)

"*Silence* is a candidate for *Truth*" ("Loquacity," xxxi., Antitheta Rerum, "Advancement of Learning," 1640).

* "*Quære*, if the stone taken out of the toad's head be not of the like vertue" ("Sylv.," Exp. 967).

> *Ant.* Thou art a soldier only; speak no more.
> *Eno.* That truth should be silent I had almost forgot.
> ("Antony and Cleopatra," act ii. sc. 2.)

"Better, saith he, *Qui finem vitæ extremum inter Munera ponat Naturæ.* It is as natural to die as to be born; and to a little infant, perhaps the one is as painful as the other" ("Death").

> Seeing that *Death, a necessary end,*
> Will come, when it will come.
> ("Julius Cæsar," act ii.)

"And as in the *tides of people* once up, there want not commonly *stirring winds to make them more rough*" (p. 164, "History of King Henry VII.").

> Ay, now begins a second storm to rise;
> For this is he that moves both wind and tide.
> ("3 King Henry VI.," act iii. sc. 3.)
>
> O then began the Tempest of my soul.
> ("King Richard III.," act i. sc. 4.)

"The conscience of good intentions, however succeeding, is a more continual joy to nature, than all the provision which can be made for security and repose" (Bacon).

> I feel within me
> A peace above all earthly dignities,
> A still and quiet conscience.
> ("King Henry VIII.," act iii. sc. 2.)
>
> A good conscience will make any possible satisfaction.
> ("King Henry IV.," second part, act v. sc. 5.)

"The winds gave *wings* to men; for by their assistance men are carried up through the air and fly; not through the air indeed, *but upon the sea*, and a wide door is laid open to commerce" (Entry into the "History of the Winds").

Bacon is of course here alluding to the sails of ships as wings.

Compare:—

> *Sal.* Your mind is tossing on the Ocean
> There where your argosies with portly sail,
> Like Signiors and rich Burghers on the flood,
> Or as it were the pageants of the sea,
> Do over-peere the petty trafficquers
> That curtsy to them, do them reverence
> As they fly by them with their *Woven Wings.*
> ("Merchant of Venice," act i. sc. 1.)

"And it is worth the noting that however *Pedants* have been the derision and scorn of *Theatres*, as the apes of *Tyranny*," &c. (Book I., "De Augmentis").

In the plays we find Pedants always ridiculed. Of Malvolio:—

Sir To. And Cross-gartered?
Maria. Most villainously ; *like a pedant that keeps a school i' the church.*
("Twelfth Night," act iii. sc. 2.)

Here is the idea of *tyranny* in context with criticism and a Pedant:—

> *Biron.* A *critic*, nay, a night-watch constable ;
> A *domineering pedant* o'er the boy.
> ("Love's Labour's Lost," act iii. sc. 1.)

> I tell thee what, Antonio—
> I love thee, and it is my love that speaks—
> There are a sort of men whose visages
> Do cream and mantle like a standing pond,
> And do a wilful stillness entertain,
> With purpose to be dress'd in an opinion
> Of wisdom, gravity, profound conceit,
> As who should say, " I am Sir Oracle,
> And when I ope my lips let no dog bark !"
> O my Antonio, I do know of these
> That therefore only are reputed wise
> For saying nothing, when, I am very sure,
> If they should speak, would almost damn those ears
> Which, hearing them, would call their brothers fools.
> ("Merchant of Venice," act i. sc. 1.)

The whole of Bacon's Essay upon "*Seeming Wise*" is but a prose paraphrase or sermon upon this text. "So certainly there

PARALLELS.

are in point of wisdom and sufficiency, *that do nothing or little very solemnly; Magno conatu nugas.* Some are so close and reserved as they will not show their wares but by a dark light, and seem always to keep back somewhat. Some help themselves with countenance and gesture, and are wise by signs" ("Seeming Wise").

"It is more pleasing to have *a lively work upon a sad and solemn ground*, than to have a dark and melancholy work upon a lightsome ground; judge therefore of the pleasure of the heart by the pleasure of the eye" ("Adversity").

> *And like bright metal on a sullen ground:*
> My reformation glittering o'er my fault,
> Shall show more goodly, and attract more eyes,
> *Than that which hath no foil to set it off.*
> ("Henry IV.," act i. sc. 2.)

"In third place I set down reputation, because of the peremptory *tides* and *currents* it hath, which if *they be not taken in their due time are seldom recovered*, it being extreme hard to play an after-game of reputation" (Book II., page 304, "Proficience and Advancement").

> There is a tide in the affairs of men,
> Which taken at the Flood, leads on to Fortune.
>
> . . . . . .
> And we must take the *current* when it serves.
> ("Julius Cæsar," act iv. sc. 3.)

"Fortune began to take place in the king (as with a strong *tide*), his affections and thoughts unto the gathering and heaping up of treasure" ("King Henry VII.," p. 209).

> *Timon.* My Lord in heart; and let the health go round.
> *Sec. Lord.* Let it flow this way, my good Lord.
> *Apem.* Flow this way! A brave fellow! *He keeps his tides well.*
> ("Timon of Athens," act i. sc. 2.)

"And therefore, as secretaries and spials of princes and states bring in bills for intelligence, so you must allow the *spials and intelligencers* of nature to bring in their bills ; or else you shall be ill advertised" ("Advancement of Learning," Book II., p. 10).

This word "*intelligencers*" is very rare, used in the sense of an *informer* or *spial* (that is a spy) :—

> Richard yet lives, hell's black *intelligencer*.
> ("Richard III.," act iv. sc. 4, 71.)

"But yet their trust towards them, had rather been as to good *spials*, and good whisperers ; than good magistrates and officers" (Essay, "Of Deformity").

> But will the King
> *Digest* this letter of the Cardinals ?
> ("Henry VIII.," act iii. sc. 2.)

"Some books are to be tasted, others to be swallowed, and some few to be *chewed and digested*" ("Studies").

> Heaven in my mouth,
> As if I did but only *chew* his name.
> ("Measure for Measure," act ii. sc. 4.)

"*Suspicions* that the mind of itself gathers are but *buzzes ;* but *suspicions that are artificially nourished, and put into men's heads by the tales and whisperings of others have stings*" ("Suspicion").

> There be moe wasps that *buzz* about his nose
> Will make this *sting* the sooner.
> ("Henry VIII.," act iii. sc. 2.)

"For he that turneth the *humours back, and maketh the wound bleed inwards*, endangereth malign ulcers and pernicious *Imposthumations*" ("Seditions and Troubles").

> This is the *imposthume* of much wealth and peace,
> That *inward breaks*, and shows no cause without
> Why the man dies.
> ("Hamlet," act iv. sc. 3.)

"*Titus Manlius took his son's life* for giving battle against the prohibition of his General" (Letters to the Lords, Cabala, 1617).

In the play of "Titus Andronicus," *Titus* takes his son's life (act i. sc. 1).

> *Mutius.* My Lord, you pass not here.
> *Titus.*   What villain boy !
> Barr'st me my way in Rome ?   [*Stabbing Mutius.*]
> *Mutius.*   Help, Lucius, help !   [*Dies.*]
> *Lucius.* My Lord, you are unjust, and more than so
> In wrongful quarrel *you have slain your son.*

"Secondly, that you beware of delaying and putting off a business" (Lib. VIII., p. 373, "De Augmentis," translation 1640).

> The flighty purpose never is o'ertook
> Unless the deed go with it.
>
> ("Macbeth," act iv. sc. 1.)

In Bacon's translation of the 104th Psalm we find these two lines :—

> But who can blaze thy beauties, Lord, aright ?
> They turn the brittle beams of mortal sight.

The alliteration here is remarkable, and shows the author was no novice in the art of poetry. This "affecting of the letter" is most conspicuous in the versification of the plays :—

> The praiseful Princess pierc'd and prick'd
> A pretty pleasing Pricket ;
> Some say a sore, but not a sore,
> Till now made sore with shooting.
>
> ("Love's Labour's Lost.")

> The blind cow-boy's butt-shaft.
> ("Romeo and Juliet," act ii. sc. 4.)

"But even, without that, a man learneth of himself, and bringeth his own thoughts to light, and *whetteth his wits as against a stone*" (Essay on "Friendship").

Compare—

Peradventure this is not Fortune's work neither, but Nature's, who perceiveth our natural *wits* too dull to reason of such a Goddess, hath sent this Natural for our *whetstone*, for always the dulness of the fool is the *whetstone of the wits*. ("As You Like It," act i. sc. 1.)

"The Muses are seen in the company of Passion : and there is almost no affection so depraved and vile which is not soothed by some kind of learning" ("De Augmentis," II. xiii.; "Wisdom," A 24).

> In Law what plea so tainted and corrupt,
> But being seasoned with a gracious voice,
> Obscures the show of evil ? In Religion,
> What damned error, but some sober brow
> Will bless it, and approve it with a text ?
> ("Merchant of Venice," act iii. sc. 2, 75.)

The two lines from the Psalm reveal the hand that wrote Macbeth. The "*walking woods*" remind us of "Great Birnam wood that moves to Dunsinane." In the plays we repeatedly find use of the word "*floods*" in context with "*ships*":—

> There do the stately ships plough up the *floods*,
> The *Greater Navies* look like *walking woods*.
>
> (Psalm civ.)
>
> Our *great navy's* rigged.
> ("Antony and Cleopatra," act iii. sc. 5, 20.)
>
> Rich burghers of the flood.
> ("Merchant of Venice," act i. sc. 1, 10.)
>
> The embarked traders on the flood.
> ("Midsummer Night's Dream," act ii. sc. 1, 127.)

"And whereas Pan is reported to have called the *Moon* aside into *a high shadowed wood*, seems to appertain to the convention *between sense and heavenly or divine things*. For the case of Endymion and Pan are different; *the moon of her own accord came to Endymion as he was asleep*" ("De Augmentis," II. xiii.).

> Peace, ho ! the *moon sleeps with Endymion*,
> *And would not be awakened*.
> ("Merchant of Venice," act v. sc. 1, 109.)

> The moon sleeps with Endymion every day.
> (Marlowe's "Ovid," act i. sc. 13, 43.)

"There is no man of judgment that looketh into the nature of these times, but will easily descry that the wits of these days are too much refined for any man *to walk invisible*" ("Obs. on a Libel").

> We steal as in a castle, cocksure: we have the receipt of fernseed: *we walk invisible*. ("1 Henry IV.," act ii. sc. 1, 95.)

"And knowing for the other point that *envy ever accompanieth greatness*, though never so well deserved" ("Envy").

> As full of *envy at his greatness*.
> ("Troilus and Cressida," act ii. sc. 1.)

"The *moon* so constant *in inconstancy*" (Trans. 104th Psalm).

"I will preserve, therefore, even as the heavenly bodies themselves do, *a variable constancy*" ("Thema Cæli").

> Oh, swear not by the *moon*, the *inconstant moon*,
> That monthly changes in her circled orb,
> Lest that thy love prove likewise variable.
> ("Romeo and Juliet," act ii. sc. 2, 109.)

"Now for the evidence against this Lady, I am sorry I must rip up. I shall first show you the purveyance or provision of the poisons; that they were seven in number, brought to this Lady and by her billetted and laid up till they might be used; and this done with an oath or vow of secrecy which is like the Egyptian darkness, a gross and palpable darkness that may be felt" ("Speech against Somerset," 1616).

> There is no darkness but ignorance, in which thou art more puzzled than the Egyptians in their fog. ("Twelfth Night," act iv. sc. 2, 46.) *

---

* The preceding seven parallels have already appeared in the Bacon Journal under the author's name.

"Amongst which that of all others is the most frequent, where the question is, of *a great deal of good to ensue of a small injustice*" ("Advancement of Learning," Book II., xxi. 2).

> To do a great right, do a little wrong.
> ("Merchant of Venice," act iv. sc. 1, 216.)

"Nevertheless, since I perceive *that this cloud still hangs over the house*" ("Resuscitatio," 1671, Part I., p. 40. "Speech delivered by Sir Francis Bacon in the Lower House about the Undertakers. Parliament," 12th Tac.).

> Now is the winter of our discontent
> Made glorious summer by this son of York:
> And all the *clouds that loured upon our house*
> In the deep bosom of the ocean buried.
>
> ("Richard III.")

"It is certain that the best governments, yea, and the best of men, are like the best precious stones, wherein every flaw or icicle or grain, are seen and noted more than in those that are generally foul and corrupted" ("Resuscitatio," 1671, Part I., p. 79. His Lordship's Speech in the Parliament, being Lord Chancellor, to the Speaker's excuse).

> Thou art a traitor and a miscreant;
> Too good to be so, and too bad to live,
> *Since the more fair and christal is the sky,*
> *The uglier seem the clouds that in it fly.*
>
> ("Richard II.," sc. 1.)

"Sir Fulke Grevill had much private access to Queen Elizabeth, which he used honourably, and did many men good; yet he would say merrily of himself, *That he was like* ROBIN GOODFELLOW, *for when maids spilt the milk-can, or kept any racket, they would lay it upon* ROBIN, so what tales the ladies about the Queen told her, or other bad offices that they did, they would put it upon him" (235, p. 172, Blackbourne's Works, vol. i.).

> *Fai.* Either I mistake your shape and making quite,
> Or else you are that shrewd and knavish sprite

> *Call'd Robin Goodfellow: are not you he*
> *That frights the maidens of the villagery;*
> *Skim milk, and sometimes labour in the quern*
> And bootless make the breathless housewife churn
> And sometime make the drink to bear no barm;
> Mislead night-wanderers, laughing at their harm?
> Those that Hobgoblin call you and sweet Puck,
> You do their work, and they shall have good luck:
> Are not you he?
> *Puck.* Thou speak'st aright;
> I am that merry wanderer of the night.
> I jest to Oberon and make him smile
> When I a fat and bean-fed horse beguile,
> Neighing in likeness of a filly foal:
> And sometime lurk I in a gossip's bowl,
> In very likeness of a roasted crab,
> *And when she drinks, against her lips I bob*
> *And on her wither'd dewlap pour the ale.*
> The wisest aunt, telling the saddest tale,
> Sometime for three-foot stool mistaketh me;
> Then slip I from her bum, down topples she,
> And "tailor" cries, and falls into a cough;
> And then the whole quire hold their hips and laugh,
> And waxen in their mirth and neeze and swear,
> A merrier hour was never wasted there.
> But, room, fairy! here comes Oberon.
>
> ("Midsummer Night's Dream," act ii. sc. 1.)

The entire characters of the Fairy mythology introduced into the "Midsummer Night's Dream," are borrowed from Hugh de Bordeaux (*Huon de Bourdeaux*), and are given by Hazlitt under the title, "Fairy Mythology of Shakespeare." Oberon, Titania, and Puck deal in a species of magic closely allied to Nature, for the former two call themselves "*parents and original*" of Nature. Indeed, it is hardly asking too much to assume that there is something suspiciously near the subject, to find Bacon introducing this book of *Huon de Bourdeaux*, in context with "Natural Magic."

"As for the Natural Magic (which flies abroad in many men's books) containing certain credulous and superstitious traditions and observations of *sympathies* and *antipathies*, and of hidden and specific properties, with some experiments commonly frivolous,—strange, rather, for *the art of conveyance and disprisement* than the thing itself; surely he shall not much err who shall say that this sort of magic is as far differing in truth of nature from such a knowledge as we require, as the Books of the Jests of *Arthur of Britain* or of *Huon of Bourdeaux differ from* Cæsar's Commentaries, in truth of story" ("De Augmentis," III. v.).

Here then we have proof positive that Bacon was acquainted with the source from which Oberon and Puck are drawn. It is another link in the interminable chain of evidence to find him familiar with this poetical and magical class of literature, belonging to the Arthurian romance cycle. It is just in the character of "*Natural Magic*" that Puck, Oberon, and Titania are introduced. Bacon goes on to say "the operation of this superficial and degenerate *Natural Magic* upon men is like some soporiferous drugs, which procure *sleep*, and withal exhale into the fancy, merry, and *pleasant dreams in sleep.*" Observe that the title of the play in which Oberon and Puck are introduced is "A Midsummer Night's Dream," which concludes with these words—

> *Puck.* If we shadows have offended,
> Think but this and all is mended,
> That you have but slumber'd here,
> While these visions did appear.
> And this weak and idle theme,
> No more yielding but a *dream*.

So that we have the reprehension of the play as *merely a dream* insisted upon in the same way by Shakespeare.

"So as a vertuous man will be vertuous in *solitudine* and not only in *theatre*, though percase it will be more strong by glory and fame, *as an heat which is doubled by reflexion*" ("Colours of Good and Evil," 3).

> *Ulyss.* A strange fellow here
> Writes me: "That man, how dearly ever parted,
> How much in having, or without or in,
> Cannot make boast to have that which he hath,
> Nor feels not what he owes, but by reflection;
> As when his virtues shining upon others

> Heat them and they retort that heat again
> To the first giver."
>   *Achil.*   This is not strange, Ulysses.
> The beauty that is borne here in the face
> The bearer knows not, but commends itself
> To others' eyes ; nor doth the eye itself,
> That most pure spirit of sense, beheld itself,
> Not going from itself ; but eye to eye opposed
> Salutes each other with each other's form ;
> For speculation turns not to itself,
> Till it hath travell'd and is mirror'd there
> Where it may see itself. This is not strange at all.
>   *Ulyss.* I do not strain at the position,—
> It is familiar,—but at the author's drift ;
> Who, in his circumstance, expressly proves
> That no man is the lord of any thing,
> Though in and of him there be much consisting,
> Till he communicate his parts to others ;
> Nor doth he of himself know them for aught
> Till he beheld them form'd in the applause
> Where they're extended ; who, like an arch, reverberates
> The voice again, or, like a gate of steel
> Fronting the sun, receives and renders back
> His figure and his heat.
>
>   ("Troilus and Cressida.")

Note the complete parallel of the word "heat," twice used, and the metaphor of the sun, as producing "light," "glory," "fame." We may refind in this passage Bacon's study of "Echoes and their Reflections," in the "Sylva Sylvarum,"

> Who like an arch reverberates,
> The voice again.

Bacon, in one of the subtlest analogies between "Visibles and Audibles" (sight and sound) ever made, describes the cause of a repeated echo, and its gradual extinction, by the splendid simile of two opposite mirrors in a room, reflecting the apartment and each other over and over again, each image becoming in perspective fainter and fainter. Thus an "echo," he writes, "in a chapel or vaulted place, is tossed like a ball, backwards and forwards, from wall to wall, *getting weaker and weaker at each reflection.*" The mind capable of this striking and beautiful illustration of two senses (so unlike as sight and hearing) by each other, must indeed have been a very marvellous one, and we may see in the above passage the influence of these studies of "*Reflection*," introduced to bear upon Fame and Glory.

"For the motions of the greatest persons in a government ought to be *as the motions of the Planets, under Primum Mobile*, according to the old opinion, which is that everyone of them is carried swiftly by the highest motion, and softly in their own motion. And therefore, when great ones in their own particular motion, move violently, and as Tacitus expresseth it well, '*Liberius, quam ut Imperantium meminissent*,' *it is a sign the orbs are out of frame*" ("Seditions and Troubles").

This comparison of well-ordered government *to the motions of the planets*, is to be refound in "Troilus and Cressida." The "*hollow factions*," reigning in the "Græcian tents," Ulysses declares are owing to want of subordination, or of a head to govern :—

>   Degree being vizarded
> The unworthiest shows as fairly in the mask.
> The heavens themselves, the planets and this centre
> Observe degree, priority and place,
> Insisture, course, proportion, season, form,
> Office and custom, in all line of order;
> And therefore is the glorious planet Sol
> In noble eminence enthroned and sphered
> Amidst the other ; whose medicinable eye
> Corrects the ill aspects of planets evil,
> And posts, like the commandment of a king,
> Sans check to good and bad : but when the planets
> In evil mixture to disorder wander,
> What plagues and what portents ! what mutiny !
> What raging of the sea ! shaking of earth !
> Commotion in the winds ! frights, changes, horrors,
> Divert and crack, rend and deracinate
> The unity and married calm of states
> Quite from their fixure !
>
>   ("Troilus and Cressida," act i. sc. 3.)

"So when any of the four pillars of government are *shaken* or weakened (which are Religion, Justice, Counsel, and Treasure) men had need to pray for *fair weather*" ("Seditions and Troubles").

> O when degree is *shaked*,
> Which is the ladder to all high designs
> Then enterprise is sick.
>
> (Act i. sc. 3.)

"Also when discords, and quarrels, *and factions* are carried openly and audaciously, it is a sign the reverence of government is lost" ("Seditions and Troubles").

> *Nest.* Most wisely hath Ulysses here discover'd
> The fever whereof all our power is sick.
>
> . . . . . .
>
> *Ulysses.* And look, how many Græcian tents do stand
> Hollow upon this plain, *so many hollow factions*.

Bacon's Essays upon "Faction" and "Seditions and Troubles," are full of direct applications to passages in such plays, as "Coriolanus," "Troilus and Cressida," "Julius Cæsar" (where we have the *factions* of Brutus and Cassius), "Antony and Cleopatra" (factions of Pompey, and finally of Cæsar against Antony, &c.). In his Essay upon "Faction," he again repeats: "The motions of *Factions* under kings ought to be like the motions (as the astronomers speak) of the inferior orbs; *which may have their proper motions, but yet still are quietly carried by the higher motion of Primum Mobile*" ("Faction").

This is a magnificent and striking application, of the particular dependence and independence of the several degrees of well-ordered government, to the laws of the solar system.

Bacon's comprehension of the balance of power in Kingcraft may be illustrated from his Essay on "Empire":—"The answer of Apollonius to Vespasian is full of excellent instruction; Vespasian asked him, '*What was Nero's overthrow?*' He answered, 'Nero could touch and tune the harp well; but in government sometimes he *used to wind the pins too high, sometimes to let them down too low.*' And certain it is, that nothing destroyeth authority so much as the unequal and untimely *enterchange* of power pressed too far, and relaxed too much" ("Empire").

By "*enterchange*" Bacon seems to mean "*intermission*," that is "pressing too far," and "relaxing too much," from one extreme to the other. "To speak now of the true temper of empire; it is a thing rare and hard to keep: for both temper and distemper consist of contraries. *But it is one thing to mingle contraries, another to enterchange them*" ("Empire").

"*To mingle contraries*" signifies balance, temperance, and evidently Bacon had applied this law of opposites to almost everything, to appetites, passions, affections, as we refind in the plays. He had evidently worked this idea out as a great moral law, far deeper than it is possible as yet to apprehend in its full force, and is applied as a law to the play of passion against passion, affection against affection in the plays. "For who knows not that the doctrine of contraries are the same, though they be opposite in use?" (Book VI., p. 209, "Advancement of Learning").

> *Ulysses.* Fie, fie upon her!
> There's language in her eye, her cheek, her lip,
> Nay, her foot speaks; her *wanton spirits* look out
> At every joint and motive of her body.
>
> ("Troilus and Cressida.")

One of Bacon's studies, which he introduces in the Fourth Book of the "Advancement of Learning," is "*The relationship of the mind to the body.*" "*How these two, namely, the mind and the body, disclose one the other, and how one worketh upon the other, by discovery or indication, and by impression*" (Lib. IV., p. 181, "Advancement of Learning," 1640).

Again, "The first is Physiognomy, which discovers the dispositions of the mind by the lineaments of the body." "Aristotle hath very ingeniously and diligently handled the postures of the body, *while it is at rest, but not the gestures of the body when it is in motion;* which are no less comprehensible by art, and of greater use" (PHYSIOGNOMIA CORPORIS IN MOTU, *Cap.* I., Sec. 3, § 1, "Advancement of Learning," 1640).

The passage from "Troilus and Cressida" leaves the impression Ulysses reflects upon Cressida's *motions or movements*.

At every joint and *motive* of her body.

That Bacon should have proposed to make a study of such a subject is excessively curious, and speaks for his extraordinary observing powers, showing he was a keen student of human nature externally, as well as internally.

"So in all physiognomy the lineaments of the body will discover those natural indications of the mind which dissimulation will conceal or discipline will suppress" ("Natural History," Book IX., Ex. 800).

"For it is a rule that whatsoever science is not consonant to presuppositions, must *pray in aid* of similitudes" ("Advancement of Learning," Book II., p. 174).

> A conqueror that will *pray in aid* for kindness,
> Where he for grace is kneel'd to.
> ("Antony and Cleopatra," act v. sc. 2, 27.)

Mr Aldis Wright remarks:—

Sir T. Hanmer in his note on this passages says: "*Praying in aid* is a term used for a petition, made in a court of justice, for the calling in of help from another, that hath an interest in the cause in question" (Glossary, "Advancement of Learning").

Bacon always uses the archaic form "*statua*" for statue:—
"Encompassed also with fine rails of low *statuas*" ("Gardens").

> Even at the base of Pompey's *statua*.
> ("Julius Cæsar," act iii. sc. 2.)

"Let the songs be loud and cheerful, and not chirpings or *pulings*" ("Masques and Triumphs").

> To speak *puling* like a beggar at *Hallowmass*.
> ("Two Gentlemen of Verona," act ii. sc. 1.)

P

"A servant or a favourite, if he be *inward*, and no other apparent cause of esteem, is commonly thought but a by-way to close corruption" ("Great Place").

> Who is most *inward* with the noble duke.
> ("Richard III.," act iii. sc. 4.)

"I knew two that were competitors for the secretary's place in Queen Elizabeth's time, and yet kept good *quarter* between themselves" ("Cunning").

> Friend all but now
> In *quarter*.

"Some build rather upon the *abusing* of others" ("Cunning").

> The Moors *abused* by some most villianous knave.
> ("Othello," act iv. sc. 2.)

"Yet the more subtile sort of them doth not only put a man besides his answer, but doth many times *abuse* his judgment" ("Advancement of Learning," Book II., ch. xiv. 3).

> Whether thou bee'st he or no,
> Or some enchanted trifle to *abuse* me.
> ("Tempest," act v. sc. 1, 112.)

"So in most things men are ready to *abuse* themselves in thinking the greatest means to be best, when it should be the fittest."

The employment of this word "*abuse*" by Bacon is in the sense of *deception or falsity*.

"Here is observed that in all causes the first tale possesseth much; in short, that the prejudice thereby wrought will be hardly removed, except some *abuse or falsity* in the information be detected" ("Advancement of Learning," Book II., ch. xxiii. p. 6).

"But you are much *abused* if you think your virtue can withstand the King's power" ("Advancement of Learning," Book I., ch. vii. p. 30).

"In which error it seemeth Pompey was, of whom Cicero saith, that he was wont often to say, *Sylla potuit, ego non potero?* Wherein he was much *abused*," &c. ("Advancement of Learning," Book II., ch. xxiii. p. 26).

It is perfectly plain Bacon uses this word just in the place where we should employ the word "*deceived*," and if the reader now will turn to the citations from "Othello" and "The Tempest," he will find how truly this applies to the sense of the context.

> I am *abused*, and my relief
> Must be to loath her.
> ("Othello," act iii. sc. 3.)

"Know you not of many which have made provision of laurel for the victory, and have been fain to exchange it *with cypress* for the funeral?" ("Squire's Speech").

> Come away, come away, death,
> And in sad *Cypress* let me be laid.
> (Song, "Twelfth Night," act ii. sc. 4.)

"Some men are praised maliciously to their hurt, thereby to stir envy and jealousy towards them; *Pessimum Genus inimicorum laudantium;* insomuch as it was a proverb, amongst the Græcians, that *He that was praised to his hurt* should have a push rise upon his nose: as we say: *That a blister will rise upon one's tongue that tells a lie*" ("Praise").

> *Paulina.* I'll take't upon me;
> If I prove honey mouth'd, *let my tongue blister.*
> ("Winter's Tale," act ii. sc. 2.)

"Concerning the *materials of seditions*, the *matter of seditions* is of two kinds; *much poverty and much discontentment.* It is certain so many *overthrown estates*, so many votes for troubles. Lucan noteth well the state of Rome before the civil war. . . . And if this *poverty* and broken estate in the better sort, be joined with *a want and necessity in the mean people*, the danger is imminent and great. *For the rebellions of the Belly are the worst*" ("Of Seditions and Troubles").

The tragedy of "Coriolanus" opens with a *sedition of the people caused by poverty and want.*

> *1st Citizen.* You are all resolv'd rather to die than to famish?
> *1st Citizen.* For the Gods know I speak this *in hunger for bread*, not in thirst for revenge.
> *1st Citizen.* First, you know *Caius Martius* is chief enemy to the people.
> *All.* We know't, we know't.
> *1st Citizen.* Let us kill him, and we'll have corn at our own price. Is't a verdict?
> *All.* No more talking on't; let it be done: away, away.
> ("Coriolanus," act i. sc. 1.)

Upon this enters *Menenius Agrippa*, who endeavours to assuage the people by the fable of the Belly and the Members.

> *Men.* There was a time *when all the body's members*
> *Rebell'd against the belly.*

Let the reader note the *sedition caused by poverty and want* (in the play) and this fable, all occur upon the first page of the tragedy (Folio 1623), and see how the prose *portrait or analysis of all this*, even to the fable of the Rebellion of the Belly, is given by Bacon in the Essay quoted.

"For the wit and mind of man, if it work upon matter, which is the contemplation of the creatures of God, worketh according to the stuff, and is limited thereby; but if it work upon itself, as the spider worketh his web, then it is endless" ("Advancement of Learning," Book I. p. 20).

> But spider-like,
> Out of his *self-drawing web* he gives us note.
> ("Henry VIII.," act i. sc. 1.)

"*Iterations* are commonly loss of time" ("Of Dispatch").

> What means this *iteration*, woman?
> ("Othello," act v. sc. 2.)

"In a word, a man were better relate himself to a statue or picture, than to suffer his thoughts to pass *in smother*" ("Of Friendship").

> Then must I from the smoke into the *smother*,
> From tyrant duke unto a tyrant brother.
> ("As You Like It," act i. sc. 2.)

"For it is a dull thing to tire, and, as we say now, to *jade* anything too far" ("Of Discourse").

> I do not now fool myself to let imagination *jade* me.
> ("Twelfth Night," act ii. sc. 5.)

"Tell truly, was there never a *flout or dry blow given?*" ("Discourse").

> Full of comparisons and wounding *flouts*.
> ("Love's Labour's Lost," act v. sc. 2.)

> But what's your jest?
> A *dry jest*, sir.
> ("Twelfth Night," act i. sc. 3.)

The use of the word "*augmented*" is so peculiarly Baconian, and refound under the expressions "*augmentation* of sciences" (see preface to "Instauration"), that to find it in Shakespeare is not astonishing:—

> And since the quarrel
> Will bear no colour, for the thing he is,
> Fashion it thus: that what he is *augmented*.
> ("Julius Cæsar," act ii. sc. 2.)

"For it is reported that at the celebration of his orgies, two famous worthies, *Pentheus* and *Orpheus*, were torn in pieces by certain mad-enraged women" ("Fable of Dionysus").

Compare—

> The riot of the tipsy Bachanals
> Tearing the Thracian singer in their rage?
> ("Midsummer Night's Dream," act v. sc. 1.)

Mark the perfect parallelism of language and subject matter, inasmuch as the "*Thracian singer*" was Orpheus; and Bacon introduces this in context with the history of Bacchus. Only three lines before the passage quoted we read:—"He took to wife Ariadne, forsaken and left by Theseus." Considering Theseus is the leading or chief character in the "Midsummer Night's Dream," how convincing is this context, which finds a further parallel in the lines:—

> And make him with fair Ægle break his faith,
> With Ariadne and Antiopa?
> ("Midsummer Night's Dream," act ii. sc. 1.)

> For I did play a lamentable part,
> (Madam) 'twas *Ariadne* passioning
> For *Theseus*' perjury, and unjust flight.
> ("Two Gentlemen of Verona," act iv. sc. 4.)

"An ill man is always ill; but he is then worst of all when he pretends to be a saint" (Bacon).

> Oh what may man within him hide,
> Though angel on the outward side.
> ("Measure for Measure," act iii. sc. 2.)

> What is't I dream on?
> O cunning enemy, that to catch a saint,
> With saints doth bait thy hook!
> ("Measure for Measure," act ii. sc. 2.)

"Of this, however, I shall speak presently upon the question *whether the stars are real fires*" ("Description of the Intellectual Globe," p. 533).

"Another question is, *are the stars true fires?*" (*Ibid.*, p. 538).

> Doubt thou the *stars are fire*,
> Doubt that the sun doth move,
> Doubt truth to be a liar,
> But never doubt I love.
> ("Hamlet," act ii. sc. 2.)

> The skies are painted with unnumbered sparks,
> *They are all fire*, and every one doth shine.
> ("Julius Cæsar," act iii. sc. 1.)

"*For the fire of the stars* is pure, perfect, and native, whereas our fire is degenerate, like Vulcan thrown from heaven and halting with the fall" ("Description of the Intellectual Globe," p. 538).

Bacon's view of young and old men, repeats itself in phantom Captain Shakespeare's supposed works. Essay 43, upon "Youth and Age," Dr Abbott sums up thus: "Youth is frank and sincere, old age cautious and reserved. Youth is inclined to religion and devotion by reason of its fervency, in old age piety cools."

> Youth is full of pleasance, age is full of care;
> Youth like summer morn, age like winter weather;
> Youth like summer brave, age like winter bare.
> Youth is full of sport, age's breath is short;
>   Youth is nimble, age is lame;
> Youth is hot and bold, age is weak and cold;
>   Youth is wild, and age is tame.
> Age, I do abhor thee; youth, I do adore thee;
> ("Passionate Pilgrim.")

"There is no greater impedient of action than an over-curious observance of decency, which is time and season. For as Solomon says, 'He that observeth the wind shall not sow, and he that regardeth the clouds shall not reap.' A man must make his opportunity as oft as find it" (Bacon).

> Let's take the instant by the forward top;
> For we are old, and on our quick'st decrees
> The inaudible and noiseless foot of time
> Steals ere we can effect them.
> ("All's Well that Ends Well," act v. sc. 2.)

HAMLET.

Sil. What, angry, Sir Thurio! do you *change colour?*
Val. Give him leave, madam, he is a kind of Chameleon.
("Two Gentlemen of Verona," act ii. sc. 3.)

I can add colours to the Chameleon,
Change shapes with Proteus for advantages.
("3 King Henry VI.," act iii. sc. 2.)

In Bacon's "Wisdom of the Ancients" he describes Proteus as one who could, "turn himself into all manner of forms and wonders of Nature; sometimes into fire, sometimes into water, sometimes into the shape of beasts and the like."

In the "Sylva Sylvarum" (16, 360) we find *Bacon* writing: "A *Chameleon* is a creature about the bigness of an ordinary lizard, his head unproportionately big, his eyes great. He moveth his head without the writhing of his neck (which is inflexible), as a *Hog* doth." Bacon continues to tell us the Chameleon "*changes its colours:*" "If he laid upon green, the green predominateth; if upon yellow, the yellow; laid upon black, he looketh all black." Is it not possible in thus introducing the parallel of a *Hog*, in context with the changes of colours in the Chameleon, Bacon is slyly alluding to his own *disguise and change of colours* under the name of Hog? It is evident the *Chameleon* is thus pictured by Bacon, as an animal that can disguise its true character.

"*He feedeth not only upon air*, though that be his principal sustenance, for sometimes he taketh flies, as was said; yet some that have kept Chameleons a whole year together, could never perceive that ever they fed *upon anything else but air*" ("Natural History," Ex. 360).

King. How fares our cousin Hamlet?
Ham. Excellent, i'faith, of the Chameleon's dish: I eat the air promis'd cramm'd, you cannot feed capons so.

("Hamlet," act ii. sc. 2.)

"Lucretius the Poet, when he beheld the act of Agamemnon, that could endure the sacrificing of his own daughter, exclaimed—

Tantum Religio potuit suadere malorum.

What would he have said if he had known of the *Massacre in France, or the Powder Treason of England ?* He would have been seven times more epicure and atheist than he was" ("Of Unity in Religion").

This Essay is an example of Bacon's cautiousness in discussing religious questions. There are certain historical events which happened during Bacon's childhood, which must have had an extraordinary effect upon his young mind. We allude to the Revolt of the Netherlands (1566-7), the defeat of the Turks off Lepanto (1571), the Massacre of St Bartholomew, 1572. Just at an age when precocious children are beginning to imbibe knowledge, that is, at the ages of six, seven, eleven, and twelve years, Bacon was hearing of these stirring events, at the bottom of which were questions of religion. Well indeed must the reflection have been drawn from him, "Alas! Religion how powerfully couldst thou prompt to evil!" And in the same Essay, 1612, we read:—
" The quarrels and divisions for religion were evils unknown to the Heathen : and no marvel ; for it is the true God that is the zealous God, *and the Gods of the Heathen were good fellows.*" Bacon seems to us here, to forget for a moment his caution, and to show us the "nakedness of his mind." It is plain he contrasts Antiquity with his own times, to the evident disadvantage of the latter. And it is well to notice the large classic element entering into the plays, particularly the first and last of the Folio, viz., "The Tempest" and "Cymbeline," in each of which *Jupiter* is introduced as some *Deus ex machinâ*. In the Essay of 1612 Bacon continues : " Neither is there such a sin against the Holy Ghost (if one should take it literally), as instead of the likeness of a dove, to bring him down in the likeness of a *Vulture or Raven ;* nor such a scandal to their Church as out of the bark of St Peter to set forth the *flag of a barge of Pirates and Assassins.*"* In pass-

* Compare how Hamlet falls into the hands of *Pirates* (act iv. sc. 6): " Ere we were two days old at sea, a *pirate* of very warlike appointment gave us chase," &c.

ing, let us notice we repeatedly find this "*Raven,*" introduced in Rosicrucian literature, in some symbolical sense connected apparently with *persecution or danger*. In the "Chymical Nuptials of Christian Rosy Cross" (published in Mr E. Waite's "Real History of the Rosicrucians"), this Raven is prominently introduced.

We should like here to point out a parallel (in the play of "Hamlet") to the line quoted by Bacon from "Lucretius" ("De Rerum Natura," I. 95) as to the sacrificing of Agamemnon's daughter:—

Ham. O Jephthah, judge of Israel, what a treasure hadst thou!
Pol. What a treasure had he, my lord?
Ham. Why,

" One fair daughter, and no more,
The which he loved passing well."

Pol. [*Aside*] Still on my daughter.
Ham. Am I not i' the right, old Jephthah?
Pol. If you call me Jephthah, my lord, I have a daughter that I love passing well.
Ham. Nay, that follows not.
Pol. What follows, then, my lord?
Ham. Why,

" As by lot, God wot,"

and then, you know,

" It came to pass, as most like it was,"—

the first row of the pious chanson will show you more; for look, where my abridgement comes.

("Hamlet," act ii. sc. 2.)

There is a *dogmatic element of certainty* about Polonius' character which must have struck all students of "Hamlet." Are we sure the references to Wittenberg (thrice) in this play do not refer to the Reformation and Luther? Polonius answers to what is summed up by Hamlet, as "Words, Words, Words." He thus presents a parallel to the infallibility and endless verbal dogmas of the Papacy, as it existed about this time. Bacon writes upon authority:—

"Now, of all the enemies that have contributed to the divorce between the intellect and the world, *authority* is the most formidable. *Authority* has substituted the little world of this or that philosopher for the great and common world; it has encouraged indolence and suppressed inquiry. Authority must therefore be first pulled down from her throne before truth can reign supreme in the realm of philosophy" ("Introd. Essays," LXX., Abbott).

"*Martin Luther*, conducted (no doubt) by an higher providence, but in *discourse of reason*, &c." ("Advancement of Learning," Book I., iv. 2).

> A beast that wants *discourse of reason*
> Would have mourn'd longer.
>
> ("Hamlet," act i. sc. 2.)

> Or is your blood
> So madly hot, that no *discourse of reason*
> Nor fear of bad success, in a bad cause,
> Can qualify the same?
>
> ("Troilus and Cressida," act ii. sc. 2.)

Upon the same column and page, the quotation from the tragedy of "Hamlet" appears, we find Wittenberg introduced *three times*:—

> For your intent
> In going back to school in *Wittenberg*,
> It is most retrograde to our desire.
>
> (Act i. sc. 2.)

> And what make you from *Wittenberg*, Horatio?
> (Act i. sc. 2.)

Considering Wittenberg was where Martin Luther burnt the Pope's Bull, it may, indeed, be taken as an emblem of the Reformation movement. Therefore, to find Bacon coupling Martin Luther with a parallel expression which we refind in the play of "Hamlet" ("discourse of reason") upon the same column, and only a few lines separated from Wittenberg, is a curious connection of mind which, I do not doubt, will be perceived. An association of ideas, and a connotation of thought, may almost be traced here, viz., "*Martin Luther*," "*discourse of reason*," "*Wittenberg*." The first two we find Bacon connoting, the last two Shakespeare. The *middle term* is common to both Bacon and the author of the plays.

Of divination of the soul, Bacon writes: . . . . "Which therefore appeareth most in sleep, in *ecstasies*, and near death" ("Advancement of Learning," Book V., xi. 2).

> This is the very coinage of your brain,
> This bodiless creation *ecstasy* is very cunning in.
> ("Hamlet," act ii. sc. 2.)

Othello (act v. sc. 1) falls in a *trance*, produced by Iago working upon his jealousy. Iago says to Othello:—

> I shifted him away,
> And laid good excuses upon your *ecstasy*.
> (Act iv. sc. 1.)

"The *passions of the mind* work upon the body, the impressions following. Fear causeth paleness; trembling; *the standing of the hair upright; starting*" ("Sylva Sylvarum," Exp. 713).

> Thy knotted and combined locks to part,
> *And each particular hair to stand on end,*
> Like quills upon the fretful porpentine.
> ("Hamlet," act i. sc. 4.)

> *Your bedded hair* like life in excrements
> *Start up and stand on end.*
> ("Hamlet," act iii. sc. 4.)

"*Grief and pain* cause sighing, sobbing, groaning, screaming, and *roaring*" ("Sylva Sylvarum," Exp. 714).

> He cried almost to *roaring*.
> ("Antony and Cleopatra," act iii. sc. 2.)

"*Laughing* causeth . . . shaking of the breast *and sides*" ("Sylva Sylvarum," 721).

> Your Lord, I mean—*laughs* from free lungs, cries Oh,
> *Can my sides hold.*
> ("Cymbeline," act i. sc. 5.)

Bacon was evidently a deep student of the PASSIONS OF THE MIND, and this is just what we should expect of a *Dramatic Artist*, observing closely human nature, in order to create truthfully.

"It is manifest that flies, spiders, ants, or the like small creatures falling by chance into *amber* or the *gum of trees*" ("Life and Death," 21).

> Their eyes purging thick *amber and plum-tree gum*.
> ("Hamlet," act ii. sc. 2.)

"It is an observation amongst country people, that years of store of *Haws and Hips* do commonly portend cold winters, and they ascribe it to *God's Providence, that* (as the Scripture saith) *reacheth even to the falling of a sparrow*" ("Sylva Sylvarum," Exp. 737).

Hamlet. Not a whit, we defy augury : *there's a special providence in the fall of a sparrow.* ("Hamlet," act v. sc. 2.)

"But I find in Plutarch and others, that when *Augustus Cæsar* visited the sepulchre of *Alexander the Great*, in Alexandria, he found the body to keep his dimension" ("Sylva Sylvarum," Ex. 771).

Ham. Dost thou think Alexander looked o' this fashion i' the earth ?
Hor. E'en so.
Ham. And smelt so ? pah !   [*Puts down the skull.*
Hor. E'en so, my lord.
Ham. To what base uses we may return, Horatio ? Why may not imagination trace the noble dust of Alexander, till he find it stopping a bung-hole ?
Hor. 'Twere to consider too curiously, to consider so.
Ham. No, faith, not a jot ; but to follow him thither with modesty enough, and likelihood to lead it : as thus : Alexander died, Alexander was buried, Alexander returneth into dust ; the dust is earth ; of earth we make loam ; and why of that loam, whereto he was converted, might they not stop a beer-barrel ?

> Imperial Cæsar, dead and turn'd to clay,
> Might stop a hole to keep the wind away :
> O, that that earth, which kept the world in awe,
> Should patch a wall to expel the winter's flaw !
> ("Hamlet," act v. sc. 1.)

Note the subject is identical, viz., *Alexander's dead body and Augustus Cæsar* (that is, *Imperial Cæsar*) in both quotations. Hamlet puts the question to the gravedigger :—

Ham. How long will a man lie i' the earth ere he rot?

First Clo. I' faith, if he be not rotten before he die—as we have many pocky corses now-a-days, that will scarce hold the laying in—he will last you some eight year or nine year: a tanner will last you nine year.

Ham. Why he more than another?

First Clo. Why, sir, his hide is so tanned with his trade, that he will keep out water a great while; and *your water is a sore decayer of your whoreson dead body.* (Act v. sc. 1.)

"The means to induce and accelerate putrefaction are first by *adding some crude or watery moisture*" (Ex. 329, "Natural History").

"That a *Satyr may be a truer table* of a man's life than many such histories" (Lib. II., p. 93, "Advancement of Learning," 1640).

> So excellent a king; that was, to this,
> Hyperion to a Satyr.
> ("Hamlet," act i. sc. 2.)

"The two last acts, which you did for me, in procuring the releasement of my *fine* and my *Quietus est*" (Letter CXXXIX., 1702).

> When he himself might his *quietus* make
> With a bare bodkin.
> ("Hamlet," act iii. sc. 1.)

"It is the life of an *ox or beast always to eat*, and never to exercise; but men are born (especially Christian men) not to cram in their fortunes, *but to exercise their virtues*" (Letter LXXXI., 1702).

> What is a man,
> If his chief good and market of his time
> Be but to sleep *and feed? A beast, no more.*
> Sure, he that made us with such large discourse,
> Looking before and after, gave us not
> That capability and God-like reason
> *To fust in us unused.*
> ("Hamlet," act iv. sc. 4.)

"We see the *Switzers* last well notwithstanding their diversity of religion" ("Nobility").

> Where are my *Switzers?*
> ("Hamlet," act iv. sc. 5.)

"And let a man *beware* how he keepeth company with *choleric and quarrelsome persons; for they will engage him into their own quarrels*" ("Travel").

> *Beware of entrance to a quarrel.*
> ("Hamlet," act i. sc. 3.)

"And in his discourse *let him be rather advised in his answers than forward to tell stories*" ("Advice on Travel").

> Give every man thine ear; but few thy voice.
> ("Hamlet," *Ib.*)

"*For the common people understand not many excellent virtues;* the lowest virtues draw praise from them, the middle virtues work in them astonishment or admiration; but of the highest virtues they have no sense or perceiving at all. *But Shows and Species virtutibus similes serve best with them*" ("Praise").

To split the ears of the *groundlings;* who for the most part *are capable of nothing but inexplicable dumb shows and noise.* ("Hamlet," act ii. sc. 2.)

"Certainly he that hath a *Satirical vein*, as he maketh others afraid of his wit, so he had need be afraid of other's memory" ("Of Discourse").

Slanders, sir, for the *satirical* rogue says here that old men have grey beards, that their faces are wrinkled. ("Hamlet," act ii. sc. 2.)

"The expectation [of death] brings terror, and that exceeds the evil" ("Death").

> But that the dread of something after death,
> The undiscover'd country from whose bourne
> No traveller returns, puzzles the will.
> ("Hamlet," act iii. sc. 1.)

"He had such *Moles* perpetually working and casting to undermine him" ("History King Henry VII.," p. 240, 1641).

> Well said old *Mole*, can'st work in the ground so fast?
> A worthy *Pioneer*.
> ("Hamlet," act i. sc. 5.)

"Why then may we not divide philosophy into two parts, the *mine* and the furnace, and make two professions or occupations of Natural Philosophers, *pioneers or workers in the mine* and smiths or refiners?" (Book III., "De Augmentis," chap. iii., p. 140).

It is very well worthy note the above quotation is from Bacon upon "*Spirits*," because the Ghost of Hamlet's Father is a *Spirit*, and is introduced as working secretly in the ground as a *pioneer or mole in the mine of the earth*.

"But these three be the true *Stages of Sciences*, and are to men swelled up with their own knowledge, and a daring insolence, to invade Heaven, like the three hills of the giants.

> Ter sunt conati imponere Pelio Ossam,
> Scilicet atque Ossæ frondosum involvere Olympum."

("Two Books Advancement of Learning," II., p. 7).

Compare:—

> *Lærtes.* Now pile your dust upon the quicke and dead,
> Till of this flat a mountain you have made,
> To o'ertop old *Pelion*, or the skyish head
> Of blue *Olympus*.
> *Hamlet.* Let them throw
> Millions of acres on us; till our ground,
> Singeing his pate against the burning zone,
> Make *Ossa* like a wart.
>
> ("Hamlet," act v. sc. 1.)

It is well worthy noting that *Pelion*, *Ossa*, and *Olympus* are brought in together in context, and it can hardly be doubtful that the author of the passage from "Hamlet" had the quotation from the 1st Georgic of Virgil in his mind which Bacon gives.

"And, therefore, it is good *a little to be familiar*" ("Ceremonies and Respects").

> Be thou familiar but by no means vulgar.
>
> ("Hamlet," act i. sc. 3.)

This is qualified by what precedes it:—

"And, therefore, it is good a little to keep state" (*Ib.*).

"'Reprime te paululum, et dignitatem tuem,' keep state—repress yourself a little and keep your dignity (The Latin edition 1638, "Operum Moralium et Civilium").

(This 1638 Latin edition differs from all the preceding editions of Bacon's Essays, and proves he was emendating works *which were to be posthumously published*.)

"And, it may be, you shall do posterity good, if out of the carcase of dead and rotten greatness (as out of Samson's lion) there may be honey gathered for the use of future times" (Bacon).

> 'Tis seldom when the *bee* doth leave her *comb*
> *In the dead carrion.*
> ("2 Henry IV.," act iv. sc. 4.)

For if the sun breed maggots in a dead dog, being a God-kissing *carrion*.*
("Hamlet.")

"DEMONAX, the philosopher, when he died, was asked touching his burial. He answered, *Never take care for burying me, for stink will bury me*" (Blackbourne's Works, V. i. p. 170).

But indeed, if you find him not within this month, you shall *nose him* as you go up the stairs into the lobby. ("Hamlet," act iv. sc. 3.)

"And as wholesome meat corrupteth to little worms; so good forms and orders corrupt into a number of petty observances" ("Superstition").

King. Now, Hamlet, where's Polonius?
Ham. At supper.
King. At supper? Where?
Ham. Not where he eats, but where he is eaten, a certain convocation of worms are e'en at him. Your worm is your only Emperor for diet.
("Hamlet," act iv. sc. 3.)

"The history of providence containeth that excellent correspondence which is between God's revealed will and His secret will, which though it be so obscure as, for the most part, it is not

* "For corruption is a reciprocal to generation. And they two are as nature's two terms, or boundaries; and the guides to life and death" ("Natural History").

legible to the natural man,—no nor many times to those who behold it from the tabernacle,—yet at some times it pleaseth God, for our better establishment, and the confuting of those which are as without God in the world, to write it in such text and capital letters that as the prophet says, 'He that runneth may read it'" ("Advancement of Learning," Book II., iii. 2).

> There's a divinity that shapes our ends,
> Rough hew them how we will.
>
> ("Hamlet," act v. sc. 2.)
>
> We are in God's hands.
>
> ("King Henry V.," act iii. sc. 6.)

"I might say much of the commodities that death can sell a man, but briefly death is a friend of ours, *and he that is not ready to entertain him is not at home*" ("Death").

If it be now, 'tis not to come: if it be not to come, it will be now; if it be not now, yet it will come: *the readiness is all*. ("Hamlet," act v. sc. 2.)

> Men must endure
> Their going hence, even as their coming hither;
> *Ripeness is all*.
>
> ("King Lear," act v. sc. 2.)

In a letter to King James (concerning Peacham's trial) Bacon writes:—"I hold it fit that myself and my fellows go to the Tower, and so I purpose to examine him upon these points and some others. I think also, it were not amiss to make a *false fire*, as if all things were ready for his going down to his trial," &c. ("Works," v. 354).

> *Ophelia.* The King rises.
> *Hamlet.* What, frighted with *false fire!*
>
> ("Hamlet," act ii. sc. 2.)

"And therefore we see that voluptuous men turn friars, *and ambitious Princes turn melancholy*" (Book I., p. 71, "Advancement of Learning," Wright).

King. There's something in his soul,
O'er which *his melancholy* sits on brood.

. . . .

Hamlet. Sir, I lack advancement.

("Hamlet," act iii. sc. 2.)

"My letters out of the Tower were *De Profundis ; and the world is a prison*" (Letter to Buckingham, 22nd June 1621).

Guil. Prison, my Lord?
Ham. Denmark's a prison.
Rosin. Then is the world one.
Ham. A goodly one, in which there are many confines, wards, and dungeons. ("Hamlet," act ii. sc. 2.)

"This kind of oppression was wont also to be resembled to *sponges*, which being *dry suck in strongly;* not so being moist" (Parable xxiv., Book VIII., p. 390, "Advancement of Learning," 1640).

Hamlet. Besides to be demanded of a *sponge*, what replication should be made by the son of a king?

Rosencrantz. Take you me for a *sponge*, my Lord?

Hamlet. I, sir, that *soaks up the King's countenance, his rewards, his authorities* (but such officers do the King best service in the end). When he needs what you have gleaned, it is but *squeezing you and sponge you shall be dry again.* (Act ii. sc. 2.)

"The modern languages give unto such persons, the name of *Favourites* or *Privadoes*" ("Friendship").

In "Hamlet" we have the Courtiers *Rosencrantz* and *Guildenstern*, who are undoubtedly the King's "*favourites.*"

Ham. Guildenstern? Ah, Rosencrantz! Good lads, how do ye both?
Ros. As the indifferent children of the earth.
Guil. Happy, in that we are not over happy;
On fortune's cap we are not the very button.
Ham. Nor the soles of her shoe?
Ros. Neither, my lord.
Ham. Then you live about her waist, or in the middle of her favour.
Guil. Faith her *privates* we.

(Act ii. sc. 2.)

In the Latin version of the Essays, the word "*Privadoes*" is rendered "*Amicorum Regis*" (friends of the King), just what the courtiers Rosencrantz and Guildenstern really are. And we want to know why Bacon was continually altering the successive editions of the Essays, putting in just these fine touches which seem to corroborate contact with the plays? Was this one of his designs?*

Spur, Spurred, &c.

An expression common and peculiar to both Bacon and the plays is the simile of the word "*spur, spurs,*" *as pricks* and incentives to action.

"It is an offence (my Lords) that hath the two *spurs* of offending: *spes perficiendi* and *spes celandi*" (p. 59, Part I., "Resuscitatio").

Each man to his stool, with that *spur* as he would to the lip of his mistress. ("Timon of Athens.")

> But love will not be *spurr'd* to what it loathes.
> ("Two Gentlemen of Verona," act v. sc. 2.)
>
> What need we any *spur*, but our own cause,
> To prick us to redress?
> ("Julius Cæsar," act ii. sc. 1.)
>
> The venom'd vengeance ride upon our swords,
> *Spur* them to ruthful work, rein them from ruth.
> ("Troilus and Cressida," act v. sc. 3.)

"As if there were two horses, and the one would do better without the *spur* than the other; but again, the other with the *spur* would far exceed the doing of the former, giving him the *spur* also; yet the latter will be judged to be the better horse,

* "The composition, correction, and augmentation of these Essays stretched over a period of thirty years. Mr Martin has noted and translated all the important variations in the fifty-six Essays common to the two editions; these amount to over 1900 in number" (Introd., Arber's "Harmony of the Essays").

and the form as to say, *Tush, the life of this horse is but in the spur*" ("Colours of Good and Evil," 3).

"Glory and honour are the *goads and spurs* to virtue" ("Colours of Good and Evil," 10).

> She is a theme of honour and renown
> A *spur* to valiant and magnanimous deeds.
> ("Troilus and Cressida," act ii. sc. 2.)
>
> Finds brotherhood in thee no sharper *spur?*
> ("Richard II.," act i. sc. 2.)
>
> He tires betimes, that *spurs* too fast betimes.
> ("Richard II.," act ii. sc. 1.)
>
> From giving reins and *spurs* to my free speech.
> ("Richard II.," act i. sc. 1.)

"Whosoever hath anything fixed in his person that doth induce contempt, hath also a perpetual *spur* in himself to rescue and deliver himself from scorn" ("Deformity").

> I have no *spur*
> *To prick the sides of my intent*, but only
> Vaulting ambition, which o'er-leaps itself,
> And falls on th' other.
> ("Macbeth," act i. sc. 7.)

"But yet, nevertheless, it did take off from his party, that great tie and *spur of necessity* to fight, and go victors out of the field" ("History of King Henry VII.," page 145, ed. 1641.)

"But yet, nevertheless, these positions *Faber quisque fortunæ suæ, sapiens dominabitur astris; invia virtuti nulla est via*, and the like being taken and used as *spurs to industry*" ("Advancement of Learning," Book II., p. 93, 1605).

"Secondly, it deceives because necessity, and this same *jacta est alea*, awakens the powers of the Mind, *and puts the spurs to any enterprise*" ("Colours of Good and Evil," Lib. VI., p. 289, "Advancement of Learning").

"As for the times succeeding (I mean after the thirtieth year of her reign), though indeed our fear of Spain, which had been the *spur* to this rigour" (Elizabeth, p. 150, "Resuscitatio," 1671).

> She's tickled now, her fume needs no *spurs*,
> She'll gallop far enough to her destruction.
> ("2 King Henry VI.," act i. sc. 3.)

"Besides, such excesses do excite and *spur* nature, which thereupon riseth more forcibly against the disease" ("Sylva Sylvarum," Ex. 62).

> How all occasions do inform against me,
> And *spur* my dull revenge?
> ("Hamlet," act iv. sc. 4.)

BACON'S "WISDOM OF THE ANCIENTS."

Cassandra.

The first piece in Bacon's "Wisdom of the Ancients" is Cassandra:—"The Poet's Fable that Apollo, being enamoured of Cassandra, was by her many shifts and cunning sleights still deluded in his desire, but yet fed on with hope, until such time as she had drawn from him the *Gift of Prophesying*, and having by such her dissimulation in the end, attained to that which from the beginning she sought after, at last flatly rejected his suit. Who finding himself so far engaged in his promise as that he could not by any means revoke again his rash gift, and yet inflamed with an earnest desire of revenge, highly disdaining to be made the scorn of a crafty wench, annexed a penalty to his promise, *viz.*, that she should ever foretell the Truth, but never be believed. *So were her divinations always faithful, but at no time regarded, whereof she still found the experience, yea even in the ruin of her own country, which she had often forewarned them of; but they neither gave credit nor ear to her words.*" The following splendid piece from "Troilus and Cressida" repeats all this in action:—

PARALLELS.

Cas. [*Within*] Cry, Trojans, cry!
Pri. What noise? what shriek is this?
Tro. 'Tis our mad sister, I do know her voice.
Cas. [*Within*] Cry, Trojans!
Hect. It is Cassandra.

Enter CASSANDRA, *raving*.

Cas. Cry, Trojans, cry! lend me ten thousand eyes,
And I will fill them with prophetic tears.
Hect. Peace, sister, peace!
Cas. Virgins and boys, mid-age and wrinkled eld,
Soft infancy, that nothing canst but cry,
Add to my clamours! let us pay betimes
A moiety of that mass of moan to come.
Cry, Trojans, cry! practise your eyes with tears!
Troy must not be, nor goodly Ilion stand;
Our fire-brand brother, Paris, burns us all.
Cry, Trojans, cry! a Helen and a woe:
Cry, cry! Troy burns, or else let Helen go. [*Exit.*]
Hect. Now, youthful Troilus, *do not these high strains
Of divination* in our sister work
Some touches of remorse? or is your blood
So madly hot that no discourse of reason,
Nor fear of bad success in a bad cause,
Can qualify the same?
Tro. Why, brother Hector,
We may not think the justness of each act
Such and no other than event doth form it,
Nor once deject the courage of our minds,
Because Cassandra's mad: her brain-sick raptures
Cannot distaste the goodness of a quarrel
Which hath our several honours all engaged
To make it gracious.

(Act ii. sc. 2.)

Mark that Bacon terms Cassandra's gift "*Divination*," and Hector in the above passage.

Do not these high strains
Of *divination* in our sister work
Some touches of remorse?

Enter CASSANDRA.

Cas. Where is my brother Hector
And. Here, sister; arm'd and bloody in intent.
Consort with me in loud and dear petition,

> Pursue we him on knees ; *for I have dream'd*
> *Of bloody turbulence,* and this whole night
> Hath nothing been but shapes and forms of slaughter.
>
> (Act v. sc. 3.)

Directly we turn to Bacon's Fourth Book of the "Advancement of Learning" ("De Augmentis," 1623), we find under *Divination,* this:—"But the *Divination natural,* which springeth from the internal power of the soul, is that which we now speak of. This is of two sorts, the one native, the other by influxion. Native is grounded upon this supposition, that the mind when it is withdrawn and collected into itself, and not diffus'd into organs of the body, hath from the natural power of its own essence, *some prenotion of things future. And this appears most in sleep;* ecstacies, propinquity of death ; more rare in waking, or when the body is healthful and strong" (p. 210, "Advancement of Learning," 1640). It may be seen that Andromache is presented as having *dreamt* of the disasters awaiting Troy.

Prometheus.

"Prometheus, by Jupiter's command, was brought to the mountain *Caucasus, and there bound fast to a pillar* that he could not stir" (Prometheus).

> Fetter'd in amorous chains
> And faster bound to Aaron's charming eyes
> *Than is Prometheus tied to Caucasus.*
>
> ("Titus Andronicus" act ii. sc. 1.)

Actæon.

"In his fable of Actæon Bacon writes: "Actæon having unawares, and as it were by chance, *beheld Diana naked, was turned into a stag, and devoured by his own dogs*" (X. Actæon, "Wisdom the Ancients").

> Oh when mine eyes did see Olivia first,
> Methought she purg'd the air of pestilence ;
> That instant was *I turned into a hart,*

And my desires like fell and cruel hounds
Ere since pursue me.
("Twelfth Night," act i. sc. 1.)

Had I the power that some say Dian had,
Thy temples should be planted presently
With horns, as was Actæon's; and the hounds
Should drive upon thy new-transformed limbs.
("Titus Andronicus," act ii. sc. 3.)

Juno's Suitor.

"The Poets say that *Jupiter*, to enjoy his lustful delights, took upon him the shape of sundry creatures, *as of a bull, of an eagle, of a swan*, and of a golden shower" ("Wisdom of the Ancients," Juno's Suitor).

> The gods themselves,
> Humbling their deities to love, have taken
> The shapes of beasts upon them: Jupiter
> Became a bull, and bellow'd.
> ("Winter's Tale," act iv. sc. 3.)

Remember, Jove, thou wast a bull for thy Europa; love set on thy horns. You were also *Jupiter, a swan*, for the love of Leda. ("Merry Wives of Windsor," act v. sc. 5.)

> Great Jupiter upon his eagle backed.
> ("Cymbeline," act v. sc. 5.)

Dædalus.

"This *Dædalus* was persecuted by *Minos* with great severity, diligence, and inquiry, but he always found the means to avoid and escape his tyranny. Lastly, he taught his son *Icarus* to fly, but the office, in ostentation of this art, soaring too high, fell into the sea and was drowned" (Dædalus or Mechanic, "Wisdom of the Ancients," XIX.).

> *Glou.* Why, what a peevish fool was that of Crete,
> That taught his son the office of a fowl!
> And yet, for all his wings, the fool was drown'd.
> *K. Hen.* I, *Dædalus*; my poor boy *Icarus*;
> Thy father *Minos*, that denied our course;
> The sun that sear'd the wings of my sweet boy, &c.
> ("3 King Henry VI.," act v. sc. 6.)

Orpheus.

"And this kind of merit was lively set forth in that feigned relation of *Orpheus Theatre, where all beasts and birds assembled, which, forgetting their proper natural appetites of prey, of game, of quarrels, stood all sociably and lovingly together, listening unto the airs and the accords of the harp*" ("Advancement of Learning," Book I., p. 49).

> *Orpheus* with his lute made trees
> And the mountain tops that freeze
> Bow themselves when he did sing
> To his music, plants and flowers
> Even spraug, at sun and showers
> These had made a lasting spring.
> Everything that heard him play,
> Even the billows of the sea
> Hung their heads and then lay by.
> In sweet music is such art,
> Killing care and grief of heart,
> Fall asleep, or hearing die.
> ("King Henry VIII.," act iii. sc. 1.)

"For the poets feigned that Orpheus, by the vertue and sweetness of his harp, did call and assemble the *beasts and birds* of their nature wild and savage, to stand about him *as in a Theatre*" ("Considerations touching the Plantation in Ireland," 1606. "Resuscitatio," Part I., p. 191, 1671).*

> For *Orpheus'* lute was strung with poets' sinews,
> Whose golden touch could soften steel and stones;
> Make tigers tame, and huge leviathans
> Forsake unsounded deeps to dance on sands.
> ("Two Gentlemen of Verona," act iii. sc. 2.)

---

* Compare Robert Fludd:—"Qualis denique erat philosophica illa Orphei musica admirabilis, cujus melodiâ Poëtæ saxa etiam saltavisse finxerunt? Aut illa Arionis cujus vigore et efficacia compassio et admiratio etiam piscibus impressa erat: credo equidem hoc a viventibus in occulto latere, aut saltem perpaucissimis notum esse" ("Tractatus Apol.," Pars. ii., p. 112, 1617).

Horticultural Parallels.

"For we see a *scion* or young *slip* grafted upon the trunk of a tree, to shoot forth more prosperously, than if it had been set in earth" (Book V., "Advancement of Learning," 1640, p. 227).

> *Perdita.* I care not
> To get *slips* of them.
> *Polix.* We marry
> A gentle *scion* to the wildest stock.
> ("Winter's Tale," act iii. sc. 4.)

It may be seen that the words, "*scion*" and "*slips*," are found in close context in both quotations.

"For though we principally pursue operation and the active part of sciences; *yet we attend the due season of harvest; nor go about to reap the green herb of the blade*" (Distribution Preface, p. 32, "Advancement of Learning," 1640).

Compare:—

> *Biron.* Well, say I am, why should proud summer boast,
> Before the birds have any cause to sing?
> Why should I joy in any abortive birth?
> At Christmas I no more desire a rose,
> Than wish a snow in May's new-fangled shows.
> ("Love's Labour's Lost," act i. sc. 1.)

"Nay, it were better *to meet some dangers half way*, though they come nothing near, than to keep too long a watch upon their approaches" ("Delays").

> Out of this nettle danger, we pluck this flower safety.
> ("1 Henry IV.," act ii. sc. 3.)

"The caterpillar is one of the most general of worms, and breedeth of dew and leaves; for we see infinite number of caterpillars which breed upon trees and hedges, by which the leaves of the trees or hedges *are in great part consumed;* as well by their breeding out of the leaf, *as by their feeding upon the leaf*" ("Sylv. Sylv.," Ex. 728).

> Thus are my blossoms blasted in the bud,
> And caterpillars eat my leaves away.
> (2 "King Henry VI.," act iii. sc. 1.)

> Which the hot tyrant stains and soon bereaves,
> As caterpillars do the tender leaves.
> ("Venus and Adonis.")

In Bacon's "Natural History" (Ex. 464, Century V.) he writes:—"As Terebration doth meliorate fruit, so upon the like reason *doth letting of plants blood; as pricking vines or other trees after they be of some growth; and thereby letting forth gums or tears*."

This is curious horticultural lore, yet it is repeated in the following passage from (act iii. sc. 4) "Richard the Second":—

> *Gardener. And wound the bark the skin of our fruit-trees,*
> Lest being overproud *with sap and blood,*
> With too much riches it confound itself?

"There are many ancient and received traditions and observations touching the sympathy and antipathy of plants: for that some will *thrive best* growing near others" ("Sylva Sylvarum," Century V., 479-480, pp. 121, 122). Bacon gives examples, and almost always (as in the quotation), of a *baser* plant in contact with a higher class. "Take common-brier, and set it amongst violets or wall-flowers, and see whether it will not make the violets or wall-flowers sweeter" (488, "Experiment"). So also he cites examples of the corn-flower, poppy, and fumitory growing in corn.

> The strawberry grows underneath the nettle,
> And wholesome berries *thrive* and ripen *best*,
> *Neighbour'd by fruit of baser quality.*
> ("King Henry V.," act i. sc. 1.)

"After these two noble fruits of friendship (peace in the affections and support of the judgment) followeth the last fruit; which is like *the pomegranate full of many kernels*" ("Friendship").

> *Lafen.* Go to, sir, you were beaten in Italy for picking
> *A kernel out of a pomegranate.*
> ("All's Well that Ends Well," act ii. sc. 3.)

"Periander, being consulted with how to preserve a tyranny, bid the messenger stand still, and he walking in a garden topp'd all the highest flowers, signifying the cutting off and the keeping low of the nobility" ("De Augmentis," VI. i.).

> Go thou, and like an executioner,
> Cut off the heads of too fast-growing sprays,
> That look too lofty in our commonwealth;
> All must be even in our government.
> ("Richard II.," act iii. sc. 4, 33.)

"There is use also of ambitious men in *pulling down* the greatness of any subject that *overtops*" ("Ambition").

> *Prospero.* Being once perfected how to grant suits,
> How to deny them: who t'advance, and who
> To trash for *over-topping;* new created
> The creatures that were mine, I say, or chang'd 'em,
> Or else new found them; having both the key,
> Of officer and office, set all hearts i' th' state,
> To what tune pleas'd his ear, that now he was
> The ivy which had hid my princely trunk
> And suck't my verdure out on't.
> ("Tempest," act i. sc. 1.)

"But it was ordained that this *winding ivy of a Plantagenet should kill the tree itself*"* (Bacon's "History of King Henry VII.").

Dr Abbott writes:—"The cautious, jealous Cecils, *in whose time able men were suppressed of purpose*" (Introduction, "What Bacon was Himself," p. xxviii., Bacon's Essays).

---

* Ut hedéra serpens vires arboreás necat,
Ita mé vetustas amplexu annorum enecat.
("Frag. Laberius.")

"A man that is *young in years may be old in hours*, if he have lost no time" ("Youth and Age").

"For the *experience of age* in things that fall within the compass of it directeth it."

> Yet hath Sir Proteus, for that's his name,
> Made use and fair advantage of his days :
> *His years but young, but his experience old.*
> ("Two Gentlemen of Verona," act ii. sc. 4.)

"Neither can justice yield her fruit with sweetness amongst the *briars and brambles* of catching and polling" ("Indicature," 1625).

> Oh, how full of *briers* is this working-day world.
> ("As You Like It," act i. sc. 3.)

"And if any man should do wrong out of ill-nature, why, yet it is but like the *thorn or brier*, which prick and scratch because they can do no other" ("Revenge").

> *Gloucester.* And I—like one lost in a thorny wood,
> That rends the thorns, and is rent with the thorns,
> Seeking a way, and straying from the way.
> ("3 King Henry VI.," act iii. sc. 2.)

CUSTOM, HABIT, USE.

In Bacon's Seventh Book of the "Advancement of Learning," we find him discussing morality, touching the "*power and energy of custom, exercise, habit,*" &c., exactly as we find so often inculcated in the plays. "We will therefore insinuate a few points *touching custom and habit.* That opinion of Aristotle seemeth to me to favour of negligence and a narrow contemplation where he asserts, *that those Actions which are natural cannot be changed by custom.*" Again: "But howsoever this case be determined, by how much the more true it is, that both *Virtues and Vices consist in habit*" (pp. 356, 357 ; 1640).

> That monster custom who all sense doth eat
> Of habits devil is angel yet in this,
> That to the use of actions fair and good
> He likewise gives a frock or livery
> That aptly is put on.
>
> ("Hamlet," act iii. sc. 4.)

Compare again: "For custom, if it be wisely and skilfully induced, proves (as it is commonly said) *another nature*" ("Advancement of Learning," p. 358, Book VII.).

> If damned custom have not biass'd it so.
> ("Hamlet," act iii. sc. 4.)

"But *custom* only doth alter and subdue Nature" ("Of Nature in Man").

"We see also the reign or tyranny of custom" ("Of Custom and Education").

> How *use doth breed a habit* in a man.
> ("Two Gentlemen of Verona," act v. sc. 4.)

In Bacon's Essay upon "Custom and Education," he writes:—"Many examples may be put of the force of custom, both upon mind and body: therefore, since custom is the principal magistrate of man's life, let men by all means endeavour to obtain good customs. Certainly custom is most perfect when it beginneth in young years: this we call education, which is in effect but an early custom." Again: "There is no trusting to the force of nature, nor to the bravery of words, except it be *corroborate by custom*."

> *For use almost can change the stamp of nature,*
> And either (master?) the devil, or throw him out
> With wondrous potency.
>
> ("Hamlet," act iii. sc. 4.)

> The *tyrant custom*
> Hath made the flinty and steel couch of war
> My thrice driven bed of down.
>
> ("Othello," act i. sc. 3.)

> Naught so vile that on the earth doth live,
> But to the earth some special good doth give;

Nor naught so good, but strained from that fair use,
Revolts from true birth, stumbling on abuse:
Virtue itself turns vice, being misapplied;
And vice sometimes by action dignified.
("Romeo and Juliet," act ii. sc. 3.)

LOVE.

"Both which times kindle *Love*, and make it more fervent, and therefore show it to be the child of folly" ("Of Love").

> *Valentine.* To be in love where scorn is bought with coy looks,
> With heart-sore sighs: one fading moment's mirth
> If hap'ly won, perhaps a hapless gain;
> If lost, why then a grievous labour won;
> However: but a *folly* bought with wit,
> Or else a wit by *folly* vanquished.
> ("Two Gentlemen of Verona," act i. sc. 1.)

"One of the *Fathers*, in great severity, called Poesie *Vinum Dæmonum*, because it filleth the imagination, and yet it is but with the shadow of a lie" ("Truth").

"Did not one of the *Fathers*, in great indignation, call *Poesy Vinum Dæmonum*, because it increaseth temptation, perturbations, and vain opinions" ("Advancement of Learning," ii. 22, § 13).

The *Father* Bacon probably alludes to is St Augustine, and the quotation occurs in the "Confession," i. 16, "*Vinum erroris ab ebriis doctoribus propinatum.*" This is referred to in Burton's "Anatomy of Melancholy" ("Democritus to the Reader," p. 103, 1813), and is introduced in these words:—"Frascatorius, a famous poet, freely grants *all poets to be mad;* so doth Scaliger; and who doth not? (*Aut insanit homo, aut versus facit,* Hor., 'Sat.' 7, l. 2.) *Insanire lubet,* i.e., *versus componere,* Virg., 'Ecl.' 3. So Servius interprets *all poets are mad,* a company of bitter *satyrists,* detractors, or else parasitical applauders; and what is poetry itself, but (*as Austin holds*) *vinum erroris ab ebriis doctoribus propinatum?*"

Rosalind. Love is merely a madness, and I tell you deserves as well a dark house and a whip *as madmen do;* and the reason why they are not so punished and cured is, that the lunacy is so ordinary, that the whippers are in love too. ("As You Like It," act iii. sc. 2.)

> The lunatic, the lover, and the poet
> Are of imagination all compact.
> One sees more devils than vast hell can hold;
> That is the madman. The lover, all as frantic,
> Sees Helen's beauty in a brow of Egypt;
> The poet's eye in a fine frenzy rolling doth glance
> From heaven to earth, from earth to heaven,
> And as imagination bodies forth the form of things
> Unknown; the poet's pen turns them to shapes
> And gives to airy nothing a local habitation
> And a name.—Such tricks hath strong imagination.
> ("Midsummer Night's Dream.")

We find Bacon attributing Poetry in similar way to Imagination. He writes: "For *Poesy* which hath ever been attributed to the *imagination*, is to be esteemed rather a play of the wit than a knowledge" (Book V., p. 219, "Advancement of Learning," 1640). In his Essay upon "Love," he writes: "You may observe, that amongst all the great and worthy persons whereof the memory remaineth, either ancient or recent, there is not one that hath been transported to the *mad degree of love*, and which shows that great spirits and great business do keep out of this weak passion." Here we find Bacon identifying *Love with madness*, as in the above passage from the "Dream."

"It is the speech of a lover, not of a wise man, *Satis magnum Alter alteri Theatrum sumus*" (p. 23, Book I., "Advancement of Learning," 1640).

"I may obtain the excuse of affection, for that *it is not granted to man to love and to be wise*" (p. 76, Book II., "Advancement of Learning," 1640).

The Latin quotation is from *Epicurus*, quoted by Seneca, and this Latin author is to be traced in the plays. In "Troilus and Cressida" we read:—

> *For to be wise and love,*
> Exceeds man's might, that dwells with Gods above.
> (Act iii. sc. 2.)

"And therefore it was well said, *That it is impossible to love and to be wise*" (Essay on "Love"). This is possibly taken from "Publius Syrus":—

> Ἐρᾶν ἅμα φρονεῖν τε κοὐ θεῷ πάρα.
> Amare et Sapere vix Deo conceditur.
>
> (Sententiæ.)

"That he that preferred *Helena* quitted the gifts of Juno and Pallas. For whosoever esteemeth too much of amorous affection, quitteth both riches and wisdom" ("Love").

"Non est ejusdem amare et sanæ mentis esse" (Erasmus).

"I know not how, *but martial men are given to love; I think it is but as they are given to wine*" ("Love").

> But we are soldiers,
> And may that soldier a mere recreant prove
> That means not, hath not, or is not in love.
> ("Troilus and Cressida," act i. sc. 3.)

"For it is a true rule that Love is ever rewarded either with the reciproque or with an inward and secret *contempt*" ("Of Love," 1625).

> For in revenge of my *contempt of love*,
> Love hath chased sleep from my enthralled eyes.
> ("Two Gentlemen of Verona," act ii. sc. 4.)

"There be none of the *affections* which have been noted to fascinate *or bewitch* but Love and Envy" ("Envy").

> Now Romeo is beloved, and loves again,
> Alike *bewitch'd* by the charm of looks.
> ("Romeo and Juliet," act i. sc. 5.)

FALCONRY, SWANS, &c.

Bacon's knowledge of *hawks and hawking* is not only revealed in his writings, but Francis Osborne, a contemporary writer, testifies to Bacon's ability to discuss upon hawks with a Lord in these words: "So as I have heard him entertain a country *Lord* in the proper terms, relating to *Hawks and Dogs;* and at another time out-cant a London chyrurgeon" (Second Part of his "Advice to his Son").

"For no man will take that part except he be like *a seeled dove, that mounts and mounts, because he cannot see about him*" ("Ambition").

This word "*seeled*" is a term of falconry, and means covered up, hoodwinked; we refind it in the plays:—

> To *seel* her father's eyes up, close as oak.
> ("Othello," act iii. sc. 3.)

Compare the following scene from the Second Part of "King Henry the Sixth," and very curiously *laid at Saint Alban's*,* *Bacon's home* :—

ACT II.

SCENE I. *Saint Alban's.*

Enter the KING, QUEEN, GLOUCESTER, CARDINAL, *and* SUFFOLK, *with* Falconers *halloing.*

> *Queen.* Believe me, lords, for flying at the brook,
> I saw not better sport these seven years' day:
> Yet, by your leave, the wind was very high:
> And, ten to one, old Joan had not gone out.
> *King.* But what a point, my lord, your falcon made,
> And what a pitch she flew above the rest!
> To see how God in all his creatures works!
> Yea, man and birds are fain of climbing high.
> *Suf.* No marvel, an it like your majesty,
> My lord protector's hawks do tower so well;
> *They know their master loves to be aloft*
> And bears his thoughts above his falcon's pitch.
> *Glou. My lord, 'tis but a base ignoble mind*
> *That mounts no higher than a bird can soar.*
> *Car.* I thought as much; he would be above the clouds.
> *Glou.* Ay, my lord cardinal? how think you by that?
> Were it not good your grace could fly to heaven?

Both Bacon and the author of the plays borrow from the soaring of birds (or "*mounting*"), in order to illustrate *ambition in*

* The first treatise on hunting and hawking which issued from the press was printed at St Albans, by Dame Juliana Berners.

rising men. Perfect knowledge of hawking is conspicuous in the plays :—

> And like the Haggard check * at every feather
> That comes before his eye.
>
> ("Twelfth Night," act iii. sc. 1.)

> If I do prove her Haggard,
> Though that her Jesse's were my dear heartstrings,
> I'd whistle her off, and let her down the wind
> To prey at Fortune.
>
> ("Othello," act iii. sc. 3.)

"The Heron when she soareth high (so as sometimes she is seen to pass over a cloud) showeth winds; but kites flying aloft show fair and dry weather."

Ham. I am but mad north-north-west: when the wind is southerly I know a hawk from a handsaw. (Act ii. sc. 2.)

> Who finds the partridge in the puttock's nest,
> But may imagine how the bird was dead,
> Although the kite soar with unbloodied beak?
>
> ("2 King Henry VI.," act iii. sc. 2.)

"And for the other I could never show it hitherto to the full; being as a hawk tied to another's fist that might sometimes bait and proffer, but could never fly" (Letter written after Earl of Salisbury's death, May 29, 1612, p. 27, Birch, Letters, 1763).

> Dost thou love hawking? *Thou hast hawks will soar*
> *Above the morning lark.*
>
> (Introduction, "Taming of the Shrew.")

"Learning is not like a lark which can mount and sing, and please itself and nothing else; *but it partakes of the nature of a hawk which can soar aloft, and can also descend and strike upon its prey at leisure*" (Works, vol. vi. p. 58).

Mr Spedding says of Bacon: "He had breeding swans and

---

* "For if it *check* once with business, it troubleth men's fortunes, and maketh men that they can no ways be true to their own ends" ("Love"). This word "*check*" is a term in falconry used as "stopping suddenly in flight," when diverted from the quarry (Dr Abbott, "Notes and Essays").

"Kites flying aloft show fair and dry weather, . . . for that they mount most into the air of that temper wherein they delight" ("Natural History," 824).

feeding swans" (Works, i. 14). "I have somewhat of the French; I love birds as the French king doth" (Life, vii. 444).

"The last words of those that suffer death for religion, like the songs of *dying swans*, do wonderfully work upon the minds of men" ("Wisdom of the Ancients," Diomedes).

"Amongst these birds there were a *few swans*,* which if they got a medal with a name, they used to carry it to a certain temple consecrate to immortality. But such swans are rare in our age" ("De Augmentis," 1640, p. 96).

> 'Tis strange that *death* should sing
> I am the cygnet to this pale-faced *swan* †
> Who chants a doleful hymn to his own death.
>
> ("King John," v. 7.)

> *Enter a* Townsman *of Saint Alban's, crying,* "A miracle!"
> *Glou.* What means this noise?
> Fellow, what miracle dost thou proclaim?
> *Towns.* A miracle! a miracle!
> *Suf.* Come to the king and tell him what miracle.
> *Towns.* Forsooth, a blind man at Saint Alban's shrine,
> Within this half-hour, hath received his sight;
> A man that ne'er saw in his life before.
> *King.* Now, God be praised, that to believing souls
> Gives light in darkness, comfort in despair!
>
> *Enter the* Mayor *of Saint Alban's and his brethren, bearing* SIMPCOX, *between two in a chair*, SIMPCOX's Wife *following.*
>
> *Car.* Here comes the townsmen on procession,
> To present your highness with the man.
> *King.* Great is his comfort in this earthly vale,
> Although by his sight his sin be multiplied.

---

* *Swans were sacred to Apollo* (see Cicero's "Tuscul," i. 30.)

† It is well worthy note that Orpheus, whom Bacon quotes so frequently, was, according to Plato, following the Pythagorean system of the transmigration of souls, turned into a swan. "Putabant autem Pythagoræ, corpora cuique aptari pro vitæ genere quod ante egisset. Quo modo et secundum Platonem in X de legibus Orpheus a morte esset CYGNUS; Thamyras PHILOMELA," &c. ("De Palingenesia Veterum," Guil. Irhovii. Amstelodami, 1733). Pythagoras declared the soul of the swan to be immortal, because it sang as death approached. Ben Jonson wrote of Shakespeare:—

> Sweet Swan of Avon! what a sight it were
> To see thee in our waters yet appear.

Glou. Stand by, my masters: bring him near the king;
His highness' pleasure is to talk with him.

King. Good fellow, tell us here the circumstance,
That we may for thee glorify the Lord.
What, hast thou been long blind and now restored?

Simp. Born blind, an't please your grace.

Wife. Ay, indeed, was he.

Suf. What woman is this?

Wife. His wife, an't like your worship.

Glou. Hadst thou been his mother, thou couldst have better told.

King. Where wert thou born?

Simp. At Berwick in the north, an't like your grace.

King. Poor soul, God's goodness hath been great to thee:
Let never day nor night unhallow'd pass,
But still remember what the Lord hath done.

Queen. Tell me, good fellow, camest thou here by chance,
Or of devotion, to this holy shrine?

Simp. God knows, of pure devotion; being call'd
A hundred times and oftener, in my sleep,
By good Saint Alban; who said, "Simpcox, come,
Come, offer at my shrine, and I will help thee."

Wife. Most true, forsooth; and many time and oft
Myself have heard a voice to call him so.

Car. What, art thou lame?

Simp.   Ay, God Almighty help me!

Suf. How camest thou so?

Simp.   A fall off a tree.

Wife. A plum-tree, master.

Glou.   How long hast thou been blind?

Simp. O, born so, master.

Glou.   What, and wouldst climb a tree?

Simp. But that in all my life, when I was a youth.

Wife. Too true; and bought his climbing very dear.

Glou. Mass, thou lovedst plums well, that wouldst venture so.

Simp. Alas, good master, my wife desired some damsons,
And made me climb, with danger of my life.

Glou. A subtle knave! but yet it shall not serve.
Let me see thine eyes: wink now: now open them:
In my opinion yet thou see'st not well.

Simp. Yes, master, clear as day, I thank God and Saint Alban.

Glou. Say'st thou me so? What colour is this cloak of?

Simp. Red, master; red as blood.

Glou. Why, that's well said. What colour is my gown of?

Simp. Black, forsooth; coal-black as jet.

King. Why, then, thou know'st what colour jet is of?

Suf. And yet, I think, jet did he never see.

Glou. But cloaks and gowns, before this day, a many.

Wife. Never, before this day, in all his life.

PARALLELS.

Glou. Tell me, sirrah, what's my name?
Simp. Alas, master, I know not.
Glou. What's his name?
Simp. I know not.
Glou. Nor his?
Simp. No, indeed, master.
Glou. What's thine of a name?
Simp. Saunder Simpcox, an if it please you, master.

Glou. Then, Saunder, sit there, the lyingest knave in Christendom. If thou hadst been born blind, thou mightst as well have known all our names as thus to name the several colours we do wear. Sight may distinguish of colours, but suddenly to nominate them all, it is impossible. My lords, Saint Alban here hath done a miracle; and would ye not think his cunning to be great, that could restore this cripple to his legs again?

("2 King Henry VI.," act ii. sc. 2.)

It is a remarkable thing this scene cited is laid at *Saint Alban's*.

Humphrey, Duke of Richmond, who plays so large a part in this play (uncle to King Henry VI.), was buried in St Alban's Abbey, and to this day his tomb is pointed out to the visitor. It is indeed remarkable how prominently he is brought forward in the second part of "King Henry the Sixth" (entitled in the Folio, "The second part of King Henry the Sixth, with the death of the Good Duke Humfrey"), in context with St Alban's, his burial place. "There was a Latin inscription to the memory of the Good Duke Humphrey, on the east wall (now removed) of the aisle (of the abbey), written by a master of the Grammar School in the seventeenth century. It contained an allusion to a religious fraud, practised by a man who pretended he had been miraculously restored to sight at the shrine of St Alban's, and said to have been exposed by Duke Humphrey. Shakespeare describes the legend in the second part of 'Henry the Sixth,' act the second, the scene being laid at St Alban's" (Mason's "Guide to St Albans").

In 1703 the body of the Duke was discovered, from the following accidental occasion. In this year a flight of stone steps were discovered in the chapel by a man who was digging a grave there, for the family of Gape, leading to an arched stone vault, where the remains of this prince were found deposited in a fluid and in a lead coffin covered with wood, which lead coffin time had not entirely decayed. Against the wall of the east end of the south aisle, close to the monument, was the following inscription painted upon the wall in black :—

Piæ Memoriæ V. Opt.
Sacrum
Serotinum.

Hic jacet HUMPHREDUS, Dux ille GLOCESTRIUS olim
HENRICI Sexti Protector, fraudis inceptæ
Detector, dum ficta nolat miracula cœci :
Lumen erat patriæ, columen venerabili Regni,
Pacis amans, Muisq. favens melioribus, unde
Gratum opus OXONIO, quæ nunc Scola sacra refulget
Invidia sed mulier Regno, Regi, sibi nequam
Abstulit nunc humili, vix hoc dignata sepulchro ;
Invidia rumpente tamen, post funera vivat.
Deo Gloria.

Sacred to the pious memory of an excellent man,

Interred within this consecrated ground
Lies he, whom HENRY his protector found ;
Good HUMPHREY, *Gloucester's* Duke, who well could spy
Fraud couch'd within the blind impostor's eye.
His country's delight,—the State's rever'd support,
Who peace and rising learning deign'd to court.
Whence his rich library at Oxford plac'd,
Her ample schools with sacred influence grac'd.
Yet fell beneath an envious woman's wile,
Both to herself, her king, and kingdom vile ;
Who scarce allow'd his bones this spot of land,
Yet spite of envy shall his glory stand.

The fact that this scene of the detection of the miracle-working impostor, is laid at Saint Alban's, goes a long way to prove the author was acquainted with the minute details of the occurrence.

That Shakespeare should have been impressed with this incident is extremely doubtful, but that Bacon should, from his earliest years, have been acquainted with this history, stands to reason, seeing Gorhambury is about twenty minutes' walk from the Abbey. Hatfield, the ancient seat of his uncle, Lord Burleigh, is only five miles from St Alban's, and is now the residence of Lord Salisbury. Bacon shows in one line in this play how well acquainted he was with the family history of this princely place. For he makes *Salisbury* say:

> But William of Hatfield died without an heir.

Such a detail is not likely to have come from the pen of Shakespeare. And the putting this line in the mouth of the Earl of Salisbury is proof positive the author was Bacon. Cecil, Bacon's cousin, was Earl of Salisbury, this being the title of the family living at Hatfield, as it is to this day. William of Hatfield was second son to King Edward the Third.

Music.

"As musicians used to do with those that dance too long *galliards*" ("Of Discourse").

Sir Toby Belch. Why dost thou not go to church in a *galliard*?
. . . .
I did think by the excellent constitution of thy leg, it was form'd under the star of a *galliard.* (Twelfth Night," act i. sc. 3.)

Notice how *Music and Moonlight* are introduced together in the "Merchant of Venice":—

> Music, hark.
> *Ner.* It is your music, madam, of the house.
> . . . . . .
> Peace, now, the Moon sleeps with Endymion,
> And would not be awak'd.
>
> (Act v. sc. 1.)
>
> How sweet the moonlight sleeps upon this bank,
> Here will we sit, and let the sounds of music
> Creep in our ears, soft stillness, and the night,
> Become the touches of sweet harmony.
>
> (*Ib.*)

Compare: "There be in music certain figures, or tropes;

almost agreeing with the figures of Rhetoric; and with the affections of the mind, and other senses. First, the division and quavering, which please so much in music, have an agreement with the glittering of light, *as the moonbeams playing on a wave*" ("Sylva Sylvarum," Exp. 113).

> The setting sun, and *music at the close,*
> As the last taste of sweets, is sweetest last.
> ("Richard II.," act ii. sc. 1.)

How exactly this re-echoes Bacon:—"The sliding from the close or cadence, hath an agreement in Rhetoric, which they call *Præter expectatum*" (*Ib.*).

"It is first to be considered, what *Great Motions* these are in Nature, which pass *without sound or noise*. The *Heavens* turn about in a most rapid motion, *without noise to us perceived;* though *in some dreams* they have been said to make an excellent music" ("Sylva Sylvarum," Cent. II., Exp. 115).

> The moon shines bright:—in such a night as this,
> When the sweet wind did gently kiss the trees,
> *And they did make no noise.*
> ("Merchant of Venice," act i. sc. 1.)

> Soft stillness, and the night,
> Become the touches of sweet harmony.
> Sit, Jessica. Look, how the floor of heaven
> Is thick inlaid with patines of bright gold:
> There's not the smallest orb which thou behold'st,
> But in his motion like an angel sings,
> Still quiring to the young-eyed cherubims:
> Such harmony is in immortal souls;
> But whilst this muddy vesture of decay
> Doth grossly close it in, *we cannot hear it.*
> ("Merchant of Venice," act i. 56.)

Bacon also writes: "The winds in the upper regions, which move the clouds above, which we call the rack, and are not perceived below, *pass without noise*. The lower winds in a plain, except they be strong, *make no noise*" ("Sylva Sylvarum," 115).

The student may perceive both Bacon and the author of the

plays allude *to the music of the Spheres*, which belongs to Plato, although we are of opinion Bacon is thinking of the fragment by Cicero, called "*The Dream of Scipio*," inasmuch as he writes, "though *in some dreams* they have been said to make an excellent music." The parallels in these passages touch not only language but subject matter, for Cicero expresses the same idea about this "music of the Spheres" as Plato. But it is possible Bacon alludes to the plays, for he writes at the commencement of the Third Book, "Poesy is as it were a *dream of knowledge ;* a sweet pleasing thing, full of variations : and would be thought to be somewhat inspired with divine rapture ; *which dreams likewise pretend.*"

"It is true, nevertheless, that a *great light* drowneth a smaller, *that it cannot be seen ;* as the sun that of a glow-worm ; as well as a great sound drowneth the lesser" ("Sylva Sylvarum," 224).

> *Portia.* That light we see is burning in my hall,
> How far that little *candle* throws his beams ;
> So shines a good deed in a naughty world.
> *Nerissa.* When the moon shone we did not see the candle.
> *Portia. So doth the greater glory dim the less.*
> ("Merchant of Venice," act v. sc. 1, 89.)

A few lines further on, Bacon introduces *candles*, showing the identity of thought in both passages :—

"And *two candles* of like light will not make things seem twice as far off as one" ("Sylva Sylvarum," 224).

Bacon writes (Book III., "Advancement," p. 134) :—"To fall suddenly from a *Discord upon a Concord* commends the air, is a rule in music, *the like effect it worketh in morality and the affections.*"

Compare :—

Theseus. Merry and tragical ? Tedious and brief ? This is hot ice and wondrous strange snow. How shall we find *the concord of this discord ?*

A philosophy of opposition or contrast, as light and shadow, indispensable to the perfection of all art, is apparent in both these passages. Mark to what profound extent Bacon had applied this law to ethics ("*morality and the affections*"), and let us reflect that the art of the Dramatist depends largely upon this turning of discord into concord or their opposites. It is evident Bacon had rightly apprehended and studied the effect of light and shade in the realms of passion, morality, and affections, which constitute the playwright's stock-in-trade and their right, or ethical use.

"I understand it that the song be in Quire placed aloft, and accompanied with some *broken music*" ("Masques and Triumphs").

> Here is good *broken music*.
> ("Troilus and Cressida," act iii. sc. 1.)
>
> But is there any else longs to see this *broken music* in his sides?
> ("As You Like It," act i. sc. 2.)

BACON, SHAKESPEARE, AND THE ROSICRUCIANS.

"Multos absolvemus, si cœperimus antè judicare quàm irasci" ("Seneca. de Ira," lib. iii. c. 29).

"Disbelieve after inquiry, if you see cause to; but never begin with disbelief. Premature condemnation is the fool's function. It goes for nothing to say that the evidence of the truth of a proposition does not appear. Do you see the evidence of its falsity? Before you reject a proposition or series of propositions, for what you suppose to be their error, take care that you apprehend all their truth; or as Carlyle shrewdly advises, 'Be sure that you see, before you assume to oversee'" ("Life," p. 167, Grindon).

"Facile est ut quis Augustinum vincat, videant utrum veritate an clamore" (Bacon's "Promus.," 263, Mrs Pott, p. 161).

CHAPTER I.

BACON AND THE ROSICRUCIANS.

"I should here except some cynics, Menippus Diogenes, that Theban Crates, or to descend to these times, THAT OMNISCIOUS ONLY WISE FRATERNITY OF THE ROSIE CROSS, those great theologues, politicians, philosophers, physicians, philologers, artists, &c., of whom, St Bridget, Albas Joachimus, Leicenbergius, and such divine spirits, have prophesied, and made promise to the world, if at least there be any such (Hen. Neuhnsius makes a doubt of it, Valentinus Andreas, and others), or an Elias Artifex, their Theophrastian master; whom, though Libavius and many deride and carp at, *yet some will have to be the* RENEWER OF ALL ARTS AND SCIENCES, REFORMER OF THE WORLD AND NOW LIVING" (Burton's "Anatomy of Melancholy." "Democritus to the Reader," p. 72, 1621).

"Utopian parity is a kind of government, to be wished for rather than effected, RESPUR. CHRISTIANOPOLITANA, Campanella's CITY OF THE SUN, and that NEW ATLANTIS, witty fictions but mere chimeras." Footnote—"JOHN VALENT ANDREAS, LORD VERULAM" (p. 60, "Democritus to the Reader," *Ib.*).

"Our age doth produce many such, one of the greatest (impostors) being a STAGE PLAYER, a man with sufficient ingenuity for imposition" ("Rosicrucian Confession," 1615).

DE QUINCEY'S celebrated "Inquiry into the Origin of the Rosicrucians and Free-masons" is full of false statements, undigested evidence, and superficial assumptions. For example, De Quincey writes: "Certain follies and chimeras of the Rosicrucians (as gold making)." This is an error almost every writer on this subject falls into. But the Rosicrucians *did not pretend, or aim at gold making,** which was a dream of the Alchymists, with whom they are often confounded, because many of their doctrines and tenets are drawn from Alchymical sources, and are couched in

* The celebrated Rosicrucian, Thomas Vaughan, writes in the "Secrets Revealed; or, an open way to the shut palace of the King":—"I disdain, I loathe, I detest, this idolising of gold and silver, by the price whereof the pomps and vanities of the world are celebrated. We travel through many nations, just like vagabonds."

Alchymical terms. Nor is it to be denied there were Rosicrucians who were Alchymists at the same time, and who might have carried on the work of seeking for gold. But the internal evidence afforded by the Rosicrucian Manifestoes must be our judge. In the celebrated Rosicrucian Manifesto of 1614 (on the title page of the third Frankfort edition we read, "First printed at Cassel, 1616," the year Shakespeare died), entitled "Fama Fraternitatis; or a Discovery of the Fraternity of the most laudable Order of the Rosy Cross":—" But now concerning, and chiefly in this our age, *the ungodly and accursed gold making*,[*] which hath gotten so much the upper hand, whereby under colour of it, many runagates and roguish people do use great villainies, and cozen and abuse the credit which is given them," &c. (p. 82, Waites' "Real History of the Rosicrucians").

Throughout the Rosicrucian Confessions and Manifestoes we find observation and study of Nature inculcated and recommended in thoroughly Baconian language, and placed before gold making. This indeed is the striking and strange parallel running between Bacon's great system of Induction by experimental research into Nature, that *the Rosicrucians joined hands with him*. The whole of the Baconian philosophy may be summed up in the end to discover "*how far man's knowledge extendeth in nature?*" To this was joined the overthrow of the authority of Aristotle, which was the earliest notice we have of Bacon's precocity when a freshman at Cambridge. The discovery of the New World by Columbus so fired his mind, that he applied the simile of *plus ultra*,[†] not only to his daring method,

---

[*] "But thus you see, we maintain a trade, not for gold, silver, or jewels; nor for silks; nor for spices; nor any other commodity of matter; but only for God's first creature, which was Light: to have Light (I say) of the growth of all parts of the world" ("New Atlantis"). Compare Robert Fludd:— "Light is the cause of all energies—*nihil in hoc mundo peractum fuerit, sine lucis meditatione aut actu divino*" ("History of the Rosicrucians," p. 292. Waite, quoted from Fludd's "Tract. Apol.," 1617. De Luce).

[†] "Wherefore, sciences also have, as it were, *their fatal columns;* being men are not excited, either out of Desire, or Hope, to penetrate farther" (Preface, "Great Instauration").

but takes the emblem of a ship sailing beyond the pillars of Hercules,* for the title-page engraving, and emblem of the "Novum Organum," and "Advancement of Learning," 1640. He says: "For how long shall we let *a few received authors* stand up like Hercules' columns, beyond which there shall be no sailing or discovery in science, when we have so bright and benignant a star as your Majesty to conduct and prosper us?" These "*few received authors*" were Aristotle, Galen, Porphyry, and others. A *Book of Nature* was one of Bacon's cherished dreams, of which the "Sylva Sylvarum" is an exemplar or sketch. Now if the reader will carefully read and analyse the opening of the "Fama Fraternitatis; or a Discovery of the Fraternity of the most laudable Order of the Rosy Cross" (1614, Cassel), he will find all these points closely packed together.

"Seeing the only wise and merciful God in these latter days hath poured out so richly His mercy and goodness to mankind, whereby we do attain more and more to the perfect knowledge of His Son Jesus Christ and of Nature, that justly we may boast of the happy time wherein there is not only *discovered unto us the half part of the world*, which was heretofore unknown and hidden, but He hath also made manifest unto us many wonderful and never heretofore seen works and creatures of Nature, and, moreover, hath raised men, indued with great wisdom, which might partly renew † and reduce all arts (in this our spotted and imperfect age) to perfection, so that finally man might thereby under-

* "It is in Nature as it is in Religion; we are still hammering of old elements, *but seek not the America that lies beyond them*" ("The Author to the Reader," Thomas Vaughan, "Anthroposophia Theomagica"). Here is Bacon's influence visible (*i.e., plus ultra*), exemplified by a Rosicrucian.

† Fludd uses the same words: "Unde fit quod Fratres renovationem et restaurationem mundi ethicam seu moralem, hoc est morum, *scientiarum, et artium instaurationem*, correctionem et exaltationem, et hominum in obscuritate, &c." ("Tractatus Apol.," 1617). Compare Bacon's title in chief, "*Magna Instauratio.*"

"*Restabat illud unum ut res de integro tentetur melioribus præsidiis, utque fiat scientiarum et artium atque omnis humanæ doctrinæ in universum Instauratio, a debitis excitata fundamentis*" ("Franciscus de Verulamio sic cogitavit," vol. i., Phil. Wks., Spedding).

stand his own nobleness and worth, and why he is called *Microcosmus, and how far his knowledge extendeth in Nature.*

"Although the rude world herewith will be but little pleased, but rather smile and scoff thereat; also the pride and covetousness of the learned is so great, it will not suffer them to agree together; *but were they united,* they might out of all those things which in this our age God doth so richly bestow upon us, collect *Librum Naturæ,* or, a Perfect Method of all Arts. But such is their opposition that they still keep, and are loth to leave, the old course, esteeming *Porphyry, Aristotle, and Galen,* yea, and that which hath but a mere show of learning, more than the clear and manifest Light and Truth" (Waite's "Real History of the Rosicrucians").

If this was not written or inspired by Bacon himself, all we can say is, Bacon's claim as the protagonist or representative of the revolt against Aristotle is seriously threatened, and we must consider the author of this "Fama Fraternitatis" (supposed to have existed in manuscript as early as 1610, as appears in a passage in the Cassel edition of 1614) in the light of a serious rival or plagiarist of Bacon. But nobody will believe this. The details of this passage are so wonderfully reflected by some of Bacon's peculiar and cherished ends, that the parallel is too striking to be either accidental, or imitation. For example, we find the idea of scientific collaboration in physical research inculcated, just as we find it in Bacon's writings, which resulted in the formation of the Royal Society. A Book of Nature, "*Librum Naturæ,*"* or a collection of "Natural History," was a peculiar idea of Bacon's, upon which Spedding comments: "He might still indeed have hoped to arrive ultimately at an *Alphabet of Nature* (his principles being probably few and simple, though his phenomena be enormously complex); but he would have found that a *dictionary or index of Nature* (and such was to be the office of the 'Natural History') to be complete enough for the purposes of

* "For I want this primary history to be compiled with a most religious care, as if every particular were stated upon oath; seeing that is the *book of God's works,* and (so far as the majesty of heavenly may be compared with the humbleness of earthly things) *a kind of second Scripture.*"

the 'Novum Organum,' must be nearly as voluminous as Nature herself" (Phil. Wks., vol. i. p. 385).

We read in the "Fama Fraternitatis": "After this manner began the Fraternity of the Rosie Cross—first by four persons only, and by them was made the magical language and writing with a *large dictionary*." Bacon claims the exclusive copyright to this idea of a *Librum Naturæ*. He writes: "*Atque posterius hoc nunc agitur; nunc inquam, neque unquam antehac. Neque enim Aristoteles, aut Theophrastus, aut Dioscorides, aut Caius Plinius, multo minus moderni, hunc finem (de quo loquimur) historiæ naturalis unquam sibi proposuerunt.*" Bacon was wrong, for the passage cited from the "Fama" proves there was a contemporary, who was insisting upon the collaboration of wits with the end of collecting facts into a *Librum Naturæ*, or Natural History. In the discussion between Spedding and Ellis (Preface to Parasceve), we find Spedding saying: "You think that the difference between what Galileo did and what Bacon wanted to be done, lay in this, that Bacon's plan presupposed a *History* (or *Dictionary*, as you call it) of *Universal Nature, as a store-house of facts to work on?*" *

Mr Ellis replies: "Bacon wanted *a collection large enough to give him the command of all the avenues to the secrets of Nature.*" The importance Bacon assigned to this work cannot be over-estimated.† He placed it in the very front and entrance to his design. And the reader should not only study the "Descriptio Historiæ Naturalis et Experimentalis Qualis sufficiat et sit in ordine ad basin et fundamenta Philosophiæ Veræ," but Spedding's and

* "To close in a word, let no man upon a weak conceit of sobriety or ill applied moderation, think or maintain that a man can search too far, or be too well studied in the *Book of God's word*, or in the *Book of God's works*" (Lib. I., "De Augmentis," ch. i. p. 9).

† "That if all the wits of all ages, which hitherto have been, or hereafter ever shall be, were clubb'd together; if all mankind had given, or should hereafter give their minds wholly to Philosophy; and if the whole earth were, or should be composed of nothing else but Academies, Colleges, and Schools of learned men; yet without such a *Natural and Experimental History* as we shall now prescribe, we deny that there could be, or can be any progress in philosophy and other sciences worthy of mankind." (The description of such a Natural and Experimental History as may be sufficient in order to the basis and foundation of true philosophy.)

Ellis' "Preface to the Parasceve." We cannot afford space to illustrate the subject as we would like. But certainly the most distinctive peculiarity of the Baconian philosophy was just this Collection of Natural History, which we find inculcated as a "*Librum Naturæ*" in the Rosicrucian manifesto already cited, and which exists in the collection by Bacon, known as the "Sylva Sylvarum." The "Novum Organum" is indeed an attempt to furnish just what the "Fama" terms (in connection with this "*Librum Naturæ*," or collection based upon observation of natural phenomena), "*a perfect method of all arts*" ! And is it not striking we find Bacon declaring, "As for the third part, namely the 'Natural History,' that is plainly a work for a king or pope, *or some College or order* "? (Letter to Father Fulgentio). The Rosicrucians called themselves *a College*,* and here again we find a parallel in the fact Bacon terms his "New Atlantis," "the *College* of the six days' work." Again, "For this I find done, not only by Plato, who ever anchors upon that shore, but also by *Aristotle, Galen*, and others " (vol. vii.).

Note how Bacon couples "*Aristotle*" *and* "*Galen*" together, just as in the passage cited from the "Fama," "esteeming Porphyry, Aristotle, and Galen," &c. ! This Father Fulgentio, according to Tenison ("Baconiana," p. 101), was "a divine of the republic of Venice," and the same who wrote the life of his colleague, the excellent Father Paul. (Spedding, vol. vii., p. 531). Bacon's correspondence with this man illustrates the fact he was acting in collaboration with men in Italy. And it is noteworthy Boccalini's "Ragguagli di Parnasso" (from which the "Universal Reformation of the whole Wide World" is borrowed almost line for line) was first published at Venice. In the same letter Bacon writes, "*I work for posterity; these things requiring ages for their accomplishment*" † ("Life and Letters," vii.

---

* "That their college, which they name the *College of the Holy Ghost*, can suffer no injury; even should a hundred thousand persons behold and remark it " (Gabriel Naudé).

† "As for my labours, if any man shall please himself or others in the reprehension of them, certainly they shall cause me put up that ancient request, but of great patience, *verbera sed audi ;* let men reprehend as they please, so

532). Are we certain that the Baconian philosophy was not writen for posterity to discover, and has yet to be divulged in practice? This may excite a smile, yet surely we cannot laugh at Mr Ellis: "If I may trust my own eyes and power of construing Latin I must think that the *Baconian philosophy has yet to come*" (vol. i., p. 374, Ellis and Spedding). Upon page 52 (*bis*) of the 1640 "Advancement of Learning," we find Bacon using this same term "*Book of Nature*": "His reprehensory letter to Aristotle, after he had set forth his '*Book of Nature*.'" *
Again: "For I want this primary history to be compiled with a most religious care, as if every particular were stated upon oath, seeing that it is *the book of God's works*, and (so far as the majesty of heavenly may be compared with the humbleness of earthly things) a kind of second Scripture."

The first Rosicrucian manifesto or pamphlet published, and which made the society known openly, was entitled "A Universal Reformation of the whole Wide World by order of the God Apollo" (1614). George Withers furnishes us a list of "The Great Assizes holden by Apollo and his assessours at Parnassus."

Apollo.

THE LORD VERULAM, Chancellor of Parnassus.
SIR PHILIP SIDNEY, High Constable of Parnassus.
WILLIAM BUDÆUS, High Treasurer.
JOHN PICUS, EARL OF MIRANDULA, High Chamberlain.

Julius Cæsar, Scaliger.	Isaac Casaubon.
Erasmus Roteroclam.	John Selden.
Justus Lipsius.	Hugo Grotius.
John Barklay.	Daniel Heinsius.
John Bodine.	Conradus Vorstius.

&c., &c.

they observe and weigh what is spoken. Verily the appeal is lawful, if it be *made from the first cogitations of men unto the second; and from the nearer times to the times farther off*" (Book VIII., "Advancement," 1640).

* This is a favourite and constant simile of the Rosicrucians. Robert Fludd devotes a chapter, entitled, "*De Libris Dei tam invisibilus quam visibilus*," taken from the text of the "Confession of the Rosicrucian Fraternity," 1615, "*Licet magnus Liber Naturæ omnibus pateat, tamen pauci sunt qui eum possunt legere*" ("Tractatus Apol.," 1617).

Shakespeare's name is placed last but one. The reader will see the parallel, in which Bacon figures as the head of some poetic society of literati, and that the Rosicrucians *also regarded Apollo as their ideal representative*. Does this not imply poetry—Apollo—Parnassus? And does not Bacon stand at the top of the list *as Apollo himself?* *

But we have now to adduce an important piece of evidence. Michael Maier was, according to De Quincey, the first who transplanted Rosicrucianism into England. He wrote his first work, *Jocus Severus*, Francof., 1617. It is addressed (in a dedication written *on his road from England* to Bohemia), "Omnibus veræ chymiæ amantibus per Germaniam." This work, De Quincey states, "*had been written in England*" (p. 398, "Rosicrucians"). And we are going to show that Maier apparently (following De Quincey's statement) did not bring Rosicrucianism from Germany *to England*, but after his return from England established by his efforts such an order. This is important, because it shows Maier had been influenced by his visit to this country. De Quincey writes:—

"On his return to Germany he became acquainted with the fierce controversy on the Rosicrucian sect; and as he firmly believed in the existence of such a sect, *he sought to introduce himself to its notice; but finding this impossible, he set himself to establish such an order by his own efforts; and in his future writings he spoke of it as already existing*—going so far even as to publish its laws (which indeed had previously been done by the author of the *Echo*). From the principal work which he wrote on this subject, entitled *silentium post clamores*,† I shall make an extract,

* Thomas Vaughan, describing the *Locus Sancti Spiritus* of the Rosicrucians:—"Vidi aliquando Olympicas domos, non procul a Fluviolo et Civitate notâ, quas S. Spiritus vocari imaginamur Helicon est de quo loquor, aut biceps Parnassus, in quo Equus Pegasus fontem aperuit perennis aquæ adhuc stillantem, in quo Diana se lavat, cui Venus et Pedissequa et Saturnus ut Anteambulo conjunguntur." These allusions to Olympus, Helicon, Pegasus, show an undoubted connection with Poetry.

† "Silentium post clamores, h. e. Tractatus Apologeticus, quo causæ non solum *Clamorum* (seu revelationum) Fraternitatis Germanicæ de R. C., sed et

because in this work it is that we meet with the first traces of Masonry. '*Nature is yet but half unveiled. What we want is chiefly experiment and tentative inquiry.* Great, therefore, are our obligations to the Rosicrucians for labouring to supply this want'" (p. 398, "Critico Inquiry into the Origin of Freemasons and Rosicrucians," De Quincey).

The Rosicrucians declared that, "all science *is based upon the observation of facts*, and facts must be perceived before they can be observed, but the spiritual *powers of perception are not yet sufficiently among mankind as a whole to enable them to perceive spiritual things*" (Introduction to "The Secret Symbols of the Rosicrucians," by Franz Hartmann). Note how thoroughly this agrees with the Baconian Philosophy by Induction, viz., "*observation of facts.*" In the "De Augmentis" we find Bacon, under the twenty-eighth deficient or star, discussing this very subject of *the difference between Perception and Sense* under the title "*De Differentia Perceptionis et Sensus,*" in which he declares that, "*there is a manifest power of perception in natural bodies very much more subtle than the senses of man.*"

Bacon was acquainted with all the Rosicrucian authors of note, and quotes Fludd, Oswald Crollius, Campanella, Du Bartas, Severinus, in his "Advancement of Learning," 1640. Spedding points out that the same doctrine concerning the difference between perception and sense taught by Campanella, had been followed by Telesius, one of Bacon's favourite authors (Liber IV., "De Augmentis," p. 612). Spedding writes: "In the 'Novum Organum' Bacon perhaps intended particularly to refer to the Mosaical philosophy of Fludd (the great English Rosicrucian), who is one of the most learned of the Cabalistic writers" (p. 92, vol. i., "Phil. Works"). One of Bacon's titles and subjects is "Magnalia Naturæ," in which he sets forth the titles of a number of extraordinary and seemingly miraculous ends to be attained

Silentii (seu non redditæ, ad singulorum vota responsionis) traduntur et demonstrantur" (Autore Michaele Maiero, Imp. Consist. Comite, et Med. Doct. Francof. 1617).

or hoped for by the human race. Spedding points out this is a favourite phrase with Paracelsus.

Do we not seem to hear Bacon speaking in the words, "*Nature is half unveiled. What we want is chiefly experiment and tentative inquiry*"? The reader must remember that Bacon stands alone, the protagonist of this philosophy by Induction, and *unless there were two Bacons in the field at the same time,* how are we to explain the fact that the Rosicrucians were preaching the same principles? Somebody with a philosophic mind, and scientific bias for inquiry and experiment into Nature, was evidently inspiring and acting behind these Rosicrucian writings. The entire Baconian philosophy or system is "*experiment and tentative inquiry*" writ large. Bacon was actively engaged in enlisting disciples and recruits for his ends. For we read amongst his memoranda of the 26th July 1608: "*Query, of learned men beyond the seas to be made, and hearkening who they be that may be so inclined.*"* This is curious, and furnishes evidence Bacon was a propagandist upon the continent, either for philosophic or other ends. And it is noteworthy, six years after this note the first great Rosicrucian pamphlet, entitled "Die Reformation der Ganzen Weiten Welt," appeared, which De Quincey states contained a distinct proposition to inaugurate a secret society, *having for its object the general welfare of mankind.* This was about 1614. It is evident the promoter of this scheme was a man endowed with extraordinary philanthropy. Now one of the most remarkable features in Lord Bacon's character, from his earliest years, was his evident love for his fellow-creatures, which, except to those acquainted with his writings, must appear almost incredible from its consistency and strength. For example, in a letter written to Lord Burghley, in his thirty-second year, he writes: "Lastly, I confess that I have as vast contemplative ends as I have moderate

* Among Bacon's foreign correspondents was Father Redemptns Baranzano (see "Life and Letters," vol. vii., p. 375, Ellis and Spedding). Upon page 79, "Instruction a La France sur La Roze-Croix," 1623, by Naudé, may be found proof Baranzano was in correspondence with Tobias Adami, the Rosicrucian.

civil ends: for I have taken all knowledge to be my province, and if I could purge it of two sorts of rovers, whereof the one with frivolous disputations, confutations, and verbosities, the other with blind experiments and auricular traditions and impostures, hath committed so many spoils, I hope I should bring in industrious observations, grounded conclusions, and profitable inventions and discoveries ; the best state of that province. This, whether it be curiosity, or vain glory, or nature, *or philanthropia, is so fixed in my mind as it cannot be removed. And I do easily see that place of any reasonable countenance doth bring commandment of more wits than of a man's own ; which is the thing I greatly affect*" ("Letters," Vol. I., 109, Ellis and Spedding). Here we find Bacon, at an age when most men are most ambitious for private or personal ends, seeking place in order only to *command wits*, and this passage is an earlier proof of the one already cited, dated 1608, or sixteen years later. It may be replied that the Royal Society was the result of all this. But it is very curious how the origin of the Royal Society is mixed up with the history of Masonry and of the Rosicrucians. The reader will, in Disraeli's "Calamities and Quarrels of Authors" (p. 351), find how Stubbe accused the Royal Society of "*having adopted the monstrous projects of Campanella*," in a work entitled "Campanella Revived, or an Enquiry into the History of the Royal Society." The learned author of "Nimrod" ("Discourse on certain Passages of History and Fable") in his article "Monarchy of the Sol Ipse," distinctly declares Campanella and his collaborateur Tobias Adami * to have been members of the Rosicrucian fraternity.

* "Sieur Adami gentilhomme Allemand, auquel nous serons perpetuellement obligez pour les œuvres de ce Phœnix de tous les philosophes et politiques Thomas Campanella" ("Instruction sur Les Freres de La Roze-Croix," Naudé, 1623).

"Tob. Adami, in his Preface to the 'Realis Philosophia,' of that excellent Philosopher Campanella (who lives to enjoy that Fame, which many eminent for their learning rarely possesse after death), speaks his opinion thus :—*We erect no sect, establish no Placits of Eresie, but endeavour to transcribe universale and ever-veritable Philosophy out of the Ancient Originall Copy of the world: not according to variable and disputable speculations, but according to*

"Now it so happens that Tobias Adami was one of the reputed founders of the association or gang called the *Illuminated Brothers of Rosy Cross*," p. 515 (see "Struv. Not. Liter.," p. 467. Compare "Andreæ Myth. Christ.," p. 14). "Campanella had an assistant by name Tobias Adami, who acted as his amanuensis and editor to prepare his works for publication, and who has acquired a certain degree of celebrity by no merit of his own, but merely by his obstetrical services to the infernal muse of Campanella" (p. 515). Professor Fowler writes: "*Campanella, whose name is frequently coupled with that of Bacon by the German writers of the seventeenth century*, and who was celebrated in his time as the disciple of Telesius" (Introduction "Novum Organum," p. 95).

De Quincey writes of Maier: "In the same year with this book he published a work of Robert Fludd's (with whom he had lived on friendly terms in England), *De Vitá, morte, et resurrectione.*" Note that Bacon in 1623 writes a work on parallel lines, "*The History of Life and Death*,"* in which the Rosicrucian dream of *prolonging life and restoring youth in some degree*, is treated not only seriously, but with extraordinary care and curious style. It is also to be remarked how all these Rosicrucian works, manifestoes, and confessions are published about the time of Shakespeare's death, viz., 1614, 1616, 1617.† That Germany was not the source or origin of the Rosicrucians is proved by De Quincey's statement, "that in Germany, as there is the best reason to believe, no regular lodge of Rosicrucians was ever established. *Des Cartes,*

the Conducture of sense and irrefragable depositions of the Architect himselfe, whose hand in works, dissents not from his word in writing. And if the 'Great Instauration' *of the deep-minding Philosopher*, Fra. Bacon Lo. Verulam, Chancellor of England, *a work of high expectation, and most worthy, as of Consideration, so of assistance, be brought to perfection, it will perchance appeare, that we pursue the same ends, seeing we tread the same foot-steps in traceing, and as it were, hounding nature, by* Sence *and* Experience, *&c.*" (Judgments upon Bacon, "Advancement of Learning," 1640).

* "Historia Vitæ et Mortis," 1623.

† "Nach dem Jahr 1620 die Rosenkreuzerische gährung, allmählig zur Ruhe kam und sich am ende ganz verlor" ("Johann. Val Andreas und sein Zeitalter," Berlin, 1819). Almost all the Rosicrucian writings bear date 1616, 1617, 1618, 1619, just on and after Shakespeare's death!

who had heard a great deal of talk about them in 1619, during his residence at Frankfort-on-the-Maine, sought to connect himself with some lodge (for which he was afterwards exposed to the ridicule of his enemies); *but the impossibility of finding any body of them formally connected together, and a perusal of the Rosicrucian writings, satisfied him in the end that no such order was in existence"* (p. 402).

This is sufficient proof Germany was not the head-quarters of the society. "Many years after Leibnitz came to the same conclusion. 'Il me paroit,' says he in a letter to a friend, published by Feller in the 'Otium Hannoveranum' (p. 222), 'que tout ce, que l'on a dit des freres de la Croix de la Rose, est une pure invention de quelque personne ingenieuse' (p. 402, De Quincey). Again, 'Fratres Rosæ Crucis fictitios fuisse suspicor; quod et Helmontius confirmavit'" (*Ib.*). Leibnitz was, we think, a German, and it goes far to show that Germany could not have held the originators of the society, else they would have made themselves known, or at least felt.

De Quincey writes: "The *exoterici*, at whose head Bacon stood, and who afterwards composed the Royal Society of London, were the antagonist party of the Theosophists, Cabbalists, and Alchemists, at the head of whom stood Fludd, and from whom Freemasonry took its rise." We undertake to prove this statement of De Quincey false and misleading. Anybody acquainted with Bacon's "Two Books of the Advancement of Learning," and the "De Augmentis" of 1623, must confess to the Theosophical side of Bacon's writings, to say nothing of the "Holy War," his "Confessions of Faith," translation of the Psalms, and endless allusion to Scripture. There are *seventy citations* or allusions to the Bible in the Essays alone (Preface, "Bible Truths and Shakespeare Parallels"), and *one hundred and fifty* in the "De Augmentis." And the way he quotes is often, if not always, in the last work obscured by Cabbalistical doctrine. Space forbids our illustrating this assertion. But Bacon's description of Natural Theology, of the knowledge of

Angels and Spirits, in the Third Book "De Augmentis," is entirely Theosophical and Cabbalistic. What are we to say to his collection of Parables from Solomon; in the eighth book—*thirty-four in number, and covering twenty-four pages of letterpress?* What has the Royal Society to do with this quotation repeated twice in the "De Augmentis":—"I am verily of opinion, that if those commentaries of the same Solomon were now extant concerning nature (wherein he hath written of all vegetables, from the moss upon the wall, to the Cedar of Lebanus; and of living creatures), it were not unlawful to expound them according to a natural sense" (Book VIII., p. 372, "Advancement of Learning," 1640). The whole of the Sixth Book of this same work is purely esoteric or Cabbalistical, in the same sense as the works of Raymond Lully, or Baptista Porta, *upon the secret delivery of knowledge.* The system of Ciphers,* of "Notes of Things," of the "Prudence of Private Speech," &c., prove this. And if we turn to Bacon's curious "History of Life and Death," we find numbers of citations taken, as Spedding states, from the writings of Cardanus, Paracelsus, Porta, Roger Bacon, and other Alchymical or Cabbalistical writers. But the proof lies patent in what Bacon calls "*Magnalia Naturæ,*" a list of extraordinary pretensions or things he deems attainable, viz., "The Prolongation of Life," "The Restitution of Youth in some Degree," "The Raising of Tempests," &c. The word "*Magnalia*" is borrowed from Paracelsus. The "Natural History" or "Sylva Sylvarum" is anything but a scientific work, being full of extraordinary things. Paracelsus was the herald of the Rosicrucians.

Bacon, as Professor Fowler in his "Novum Organum" points out, believed in Astrology (Introduction, p. 26). "After beginning with the remark, 'At Astrologia multa superstitione referta est, ut vix aliquid sanum in ea reperiatur,' and rejecting various

---

* The general belief has obtained, that Bacon introduced his system of Ciphers in the "De Augmentis" of 1623, as part of the knowledge of his age only. But close study will reveal the fact, *they are affiliated to the entire work as a great system of Mnemonies to restore from custody Poetry and History!*

branches of the pretended science, he, nevertheless, allows that the study of the stars may enable us to predict not only natural events, like floods, frosts, droughts, earthquakes, &c., but wars, seditions, transmigrations of peoples, and in short all commotions or great revolutions of things, natural as well as civil." Professor Fowler writes: "The curious and absurd speculations *on Spirit which abound in the 'Novum Organum' and elsewhere—many of which seem to have been derived from Paracelsus*—I shall frequently have occasion to call attention to in the notes. A typical passage may be found in the 'Novum Organum,' ii. 40." Professor Fowler may consider these speculations absurd, but it is certain they form an integral and leading feature in the character of the Baconian Philosophy, as may be refound in the fable of Proserpine ("Wisdom of the Ancients"), endlessly in the "Sylva Sylvarum," and "History of Life and Death." Are we certain that there is not something more in this doctrine than absurdity, seeing how potent are *the invisible power of electricity in matter?* It may be remarked here, that Bacon's style is often obscure, and that his works (as Kuno Fisher has observed) are full of antinomies, contradicting or modifying in one place, an assertion in another. Like the works of Shakespeare his universality is so circular, that except upon certain subjects like his Inductive System, it is impossible to clearly apprehend how much he intends to withhold or convey. He tells us that "*the privateness of the language must exclude many readers*" of the "De Augmentis" (Letter to Dr Plafer). And this proves not only he had some secret to veil and obscure, but is a caution against accepting any of his statements unreservedly or as full disclosures.

It is very curious and striking to find Bacon purging the word Magia (Magic),* exactly as we find Robert Fludd doing in

---

* Gabriel Naudé, in his "History of Magic," writes: "We may therefore conclude with the learned Verulam, that this fourth kind of Magic, *Naturalem Philosophiam à veritate speculationum ad magnitudinem operum revocare nititur*, it being nothing else than a practical physic, as physic is a con-

his reply to the attacks of Libavius upon the pretensions of the Rosicrucians. In this point Bacon joins hands with the latter, declaring Natural Magic to be not supernatural but only supra-sensible. This is a most important point to consider, because Fludd disclaims for the fraternity any superhuman pretensions. Like Bacon he bases a great part of his writings upon Scripture, and claims for science and mechanical skill power to accomplish things deemed impossible or superhuman. He frequently cites the works of Roger Bacon in proof, and writes: "Quare sapientis est, quid res sit diligenter inquirere priusquam eam temerè condemnet. Communis est igitur opinio nomem hoc (Magia) esse vocabulum Persicum, idem lingua sonans Persica, quod sapientia apud Latinos. Hujus varias esse species ab invicem exertissime differentes, ex philosophorum veterum et recentiorum authoritate colliguimus, cum alia sit naturalis, alia mathematica, alia venefica, et necromantica et alia præstigiatrix." Again: "Magi in specie mathematica experti absque, occulto rerum naturalium auxilio, vel saltem exiguo virtute mathematica, et precipue Geometrica res admirabiles, et planè stupendas struunt atque ædificant, cujusmodi fuerunt columba Architæ lignea quæ volabat et capita illa ænea Rogeri Baconis, et Alberti Magni, que locuta fuisse perhibentur. In hac etiam parte excelluisse fertur Boetius, vir maximi ingenii. Sic etiam et egomet, hujus artis industria, taurum ligneum composui, gemitum et mugitum more tauri naturalis per vices edentem; draconem alas moventem et sibilantem, ignemque et flammas in taurum ab ore suo evomentem : lyram per se absque : viventis auxilio, cantum symphoniarum modulantem : et multa alia quæ merâ arte

templative magic; and consequently, since what is sub-alternate to the one is the same to the other, it will not be hard to disentangle it out of an infinite web of superstitions," &c. (p. 22, 1657).

De Quincey writes: "Undoubtedly amongst the Rosicrucian titles of honour we find that of *Magus*" (p. 372, "Inquiry into the Origin of the Freemasons and Rosicrucians"). This is undoubtedly of Persian origin, giving in its plural form *Magi*. It is striking to find Bacon discussing the "Persian Magic."

mathematicâ, sine magie, naturalis supplemento, præstare non potuisse, fateor" ("Tractatus Apol.," 1617, pp. 23, 24). Again: "Ex his igitur manifestum est non omnem magiæ speciem esse repudiandam, cum prima ejus differentia et secunda sint laudabiles et admirabiles; ultimas vero pro turpissimis Diaboli soidibus esse habendas, et in ultimas oblivionis oras ab hominibus relegandas, cum D. Libavio putamus. Et procul dubio Fratres de R. C. has Magiæ species, et præcipuè primam, cum de naturæ facultatibus arcanis loquantur, intelligere eo loco videntur, ubi de Magica scriptura, et nova lingua mentionem fecerunt; quoniam scripturam illam characteribus magni libri Naturæ factam esse alibi agnoverunt" (*Ib.*). In short, Fludd claims the word magic for natural philosophy, or science after the Baconian system. Now compare Bacon, and note he alludes to the *Persian Magic* like Fludd. "But it seems requisite in this place that the word *Magia*, accepted for a long time in the worst part (sense), be restored to the ancient and honourable place. *Magia amongst the Persians* was taken for a sublime sapience, and a science of the harmony, and consents of universal in nature; so those three eastern kings, which came to adore Christ, are styled by the name of Magi; and we understand it in that sense as to be a science which deduceth the knowledge of hidden forms to strange and wonderful effects and operations, and as it is commonly said by joining Actives with Passives, which discloseth the great wonders of nature" (Book III., p. 169, "Advancement of Learning"). Now, here is the wonderful parallel, for continuing the quotation from Fludd first given (and which we expressly abridged for the sake of clearer exposition) from "*Præstigiatrix*," he continues— "Occultissimam et arcanissimam illam physices partem, qua mysticæ creaturarum naturalium proprietates eliciuntur Naturalem appellamus. *Sic Sapientes regii qui Christum natum (stellâ novâ ab Oriente duce) quæsiverunt, Magi sunt dicti, quoniam ad summam rerum naturalium cognitionem tam cœlestium quam sublunarium, attigerunt. Sub hac ipsa etiam Magorum Specie comprehensus est, Salomon, quatenus arcanas rerum omnium creatarum facultates, et proprietates novit, dicitur enim omnium plantarum naturas à cedro montis Libani usque ad Hyssopum intellexisse,*" &c. ("Tractatus Apolog.," Pars. I., p. 24, 1617). I hope the reader perceives the three extraordinary parallels running between Bacon and Fludd in these passages, viz., the subject matter—purging or examination of the term Magia or Magic—the same allusion to Persian Magic—the same reference to the nativity of Christ and the star in the East, and the final identical allusion to Solomon! But the striking part is that the famous star which appeared in 1572 is supposed by astronomers (see Mazzaroth) to have been the star of Bethlehem. And it was this star, in connection with the prophecy of Paracelsus, that gave rise to the Rosicrucians.* All this receives further suspicious evidence when we reflect that the "New Atlantis" is termed "*Solomon's House.*" Bacon again repeats there the passage cited upon Solomon: "Ye shall understand (my dear friends) that amongst the excellent acts of that king, one above all hath the pre-eminence. It was the erection and institution of *an order or society, which we call Solomon's House.* The noblest foundation (as we think) that ever was upon the earth, and the lanthorn of this kingdom. *It is dedicated to the study of the works and creatures of God.* Some think it beareth the founder's name a little corrupted, as if it should be Solamona's House. But the records write it as it is spoken. So as I take it to be denominate of the King† of the Hebrews, which is famous with you, and no stranger to us. For we have some parts of his works, which with you are lost. *Namely, that Natural History, which he wrote of all plants, from the Cedar of Libanus, to the moss that groweth out of the wall*" (p. 18). Now, mark the parallel, Bacon like, Solomon writes a " Natural His-

---

* "The Comet of 1572 was declared by Paracelsus to be '*the sign and harbinger of the approaching revolution,*' and it will readily be believed that his innumerable disciples would welcome a secret society whose vast claims were founded on the philosophy of the master, whom they venerated" Waite's "Real History of the Rosicrucians").

† Bacon, in speaking of this king who symbolises with Solomon, seems to allude to James I. R. L. Ellis (vol. iii. "Works").

tory" in ten centuries, and again introduces this passage (Century VI., p. 113, Exp. 536), "The Scripture saith that Solomon wrote a 'Natural History,' *from the cedar of Libanus to the moss growing upon the wall;* for so the best traditions have it." The reader must see how curious it is to find Bacon telling us the founder of the order or society of the "College of the Six Days" *bears Solomon's name a little corrupted*, and how strange to find Bacon imitating Solomon's "Natural History" in the plan of his "Sylva Sylvarum," which largely deals in plants and vegetable life! Are we sure Bacon himself was not a representative Solomon, and the founder of the order or society of the Rosicrucians, whom John Heydon declares to be the people of Bacon's "New Atlantis"? But at any rate the reader must see the absurdity of De Quincey's statements, for he does not explain how it is Solomon plays such a great part in Free-masonry, and in the "New Atlantis."* If Fludd quotes Solomon, so does Bacon in the same words, and in a marked and extraordinary manner, over and over again. The weight of all this evidence can only come home with full force and appreciation to Masons or students of these subjects. I have the opinion of a gentleman who not only was a member of the modern society of Rosicrucians (to which the late Lord Lytton belonged), but is a voluminous author on masonic subjects, that I have, "*primâ facie*, made out my case." This gentleman, to whom I was recommended as one of the highest authorities in England upon this subject, declares that the "'New Atlantis' is probably the key to the ritual of Free-

* Fludd repeats in the second part ("De Scientiarum Impedimentis"). "Nonne etiam commemoratum est in sacris Hebræorum historiis, Solomonem regem ad hujus Sapientiæ Naturalis apicem et culmen attigisse? Cui à Deo concessum erat a Cedro Libani usque ad Hysopum disputasse" (p. 94). In one of the Rosicrucian manifestoes we read: "Our philosophy also is not a new invention, but as Adam after his fall hath received it and as *Moses and Solomon* used it."

Here we have proof of Bacon's connection with the society from his frequent quotations and proverbs from Solomon ("Advancement of Learning"), and chiefly in the "New Atlantis," which he calls, "*Solomon's* House." The striking point is the identity of the quotation, repeated thrice by Bacon.

masonry," and I consider the evidence of such an expert outweighs in value the scoffing incredulity or hostile criticism of a multitude of outside unbelievers. Mr Hughan, to whom I refer, is the author of "Masonic Sketches and Reprints," inaugurated by him in 1869, and which have been heartily appreciated in Great Britain and America.

De Quincey ascribes to Fludd the origin of Masonry in England—that is of modern Masonry—confessing thus the Rosicrucian source. The parallels shown between Fludd's works and Bacon's endorse De Quincey's last assumption, and show Bacon's claim to be founder stands upon a far stronger chain of evidence than Fludd's. Bacon, we can understand, had every object in the world for concealing his Rosicrucian foundership. He seems to hint at this when he so frequently quotes Solomon, to the effect that, "*The glory of God is to conceal a thing, but the glory of the King is to find it out.*" This he repeats frequently. It seems almost a text illustrating the divine secrecy and reserve of his mind, which is as subtle as Nature itself. Any confession openly made to the effect that he was the founder of the order, could hardly be expected, seeing they called themselves *invisibles*, and covered themselves with a cloud. Mystery was part of their power, a great way if not entirely, their first moving principle. *Self-sacrifice*, borrowed from the example of Christ, I am certain was the foundation or corner-stone of their *Spiritual Temple*, the rebuilding of which could only be effected by ages unborn. Intense religious faith, belief in the ultimate regeneration of man, and the scriptural succession of times, they laboured *to sow the good seed in silence, in darkness, in self-renunciation*. The sacrifice all this implies finds its re-echo in Bacon's appeal to future ages, in his hints of self-sacrifice, in his love for humanity, in his endless citations from the Bible. Judging from the Rosicrucian writings only, we should expect to find in the founder and promoter of this society, a man bent upon reforming philosophy by direct appeal to Nature, yet subordinating all this to Scripture.

It is very certain Bacon believed in the *Succession of Times*, in a scriptural sense. Not only is this shadowed forth in his motto from Daniel, "Many shall go to and fro, and knowledge shall be increased," which is attached to both the title pages of the "Novum Organum" and "Advancement of Learning" (1640), but this as is well known is in contact with the *Book of Seven Seals* mentioned in Revelation. Did Bacon take this motto from Daniel with the thought of the context in his mind? "But thou, O Daniel, *shut up the words, and seal the Book, even to the time of the end:* many shall run to and fro, and knowledge shall be increased" (Daniel xii. 4). This has been accepted by a number of divines as a prophecy of the present age, and has been wonderfully fulfilled in its latter sense. It is curious to find this motto attached to the "Advancement of Learning," 1640, with its mispaging, its endless enigmas, its esoteric style, its Secret Delivery of Knowledge by means of Ciphers, and the "Wisdom of Private Speech"! The concluding book of this work — the ninth—deals with "Emanations from Scripture," which Bacon calls "Utres Cœlestes," where he deals with the "*manner of interpreting,*" which he divides into *Methodical* and *Solute*, or at large. It is easy to see that he hints at a *profound system of interpretation*, esoteric in distinction to an exoteric system for general use. "For this divine water, which infinitely excells that of Jacob's Well, is drawn forth and delivered much after the same manner as Natural Waters use to be out of wells; for these at the first draught are either receiv'd into cisterns, and so may be convey'd and deriv'd by many pipes for public and private use, or is poured forth in buckets and vessels, to be us'd out of hand, as occasion requires" (p. 474). This seems a clear hint for an underground interpretation—Truth being at the bottom of a well and hidden from sight. "For it must be remembered, that there are two points known to God; the author of Scripture, which man's nature cannot comprehend, that is the secrets of the heart *and the succession of times*" (p. 475).

Fludd writes: "Nos docet Apostolus ad mysterii perfectionem vel sub *Agricolæ, vel Architecti, typo* pertingere;" either under the *image of a husbandman who cultivates a field, or of an architect who builds a house:* and had the former type been adopted we should have had *Free-husbandmen* instead of Free-masons." Again in another place Robert Fludd writes: "Atque sub istiusmodi *Architecti typo* nos monet propheta ut ædificemus *domum Sapientiæ*" (see "Inquiry into the Origin of the Rosicrucians and Free-masons, 410, De Quincey). Now here is an extraordinary parallel. Bacon's Ethics are entitled "*Georgics of the Mind*" (Georgica Animi), and of course this title applies to the culture of the character in an agricultural sense. Elsewhere we point out how Bacon closes the "De Augmentis" with an agricultural simile, "*I have sowen unto Posterity and the immortal God.*" The title page of Bacon's "Advancement of Learning," translated by Gilbert Wats, is as follows,

Francisci De Verulamio,

Architectura Scientiarum.

Here indeed is Fludd's typical emblem of *architecture and architect*, applied by Bacon to himself, with regard to the "General Idea and Project of the Instauration." And this is no casual simile, but frequently to be refound affecting the imagery and style of the text. For example, in the Sixth Book, writing of the scheme, method, parts of the "Instauration": "But these are the kinds of Method; the parts are two; the one of the disposition of a whole work, or of the argument of some book; the other of the limitations of propositions. For there belongs to *Architecture* not only the frame of the whole *building*, but likewise the form and figure of the *columns, beams, and the like; and Method is, as it were, the architecture of sciences.*" Upon the title page prefixed to the "Platform of the Design," we find the motto, "Deus omnia in mensura, et numero et ordine disposuit." This thoroughly agrees with the last passage, that "method is, as it were, the Architecture of the Sciences." With regard to Fludd's statement as to the "building of the *House of Wisdom*" (domum sapientiæ), we very strangely find Tenison, in "Baconiana," twice calling Bacon's "Instauration" by this title. "The work, therefore, of the 'Instauration' was an original, and a work so vast and comprehensive in its design, that though others in that age might *hew out this or the other pillar, yet of him alone* [Bacon] *it seemeth true that he framed the whole model of the House of Wisdom*" (p. 9). The reader perceives the *architectural language* Tenison employs.* And it is still more striking to find amongst the initials of the members or founders of the Rosicrucians, the initials F. B., with the words "*Pictor et Architectus*" following them. "After this manner began the fraternity of the Rosie Cross,—first by four persons only, and by them was made the magical language and writing, with a large dictionary, which we yet daily use to God's praise and glory, and do find great wisdom therein. They made also the first part of the book M, but in respect that that labour was too heavy, and the unspeakable concourse of the sick hindered them, and also whilst his new building (called *Sancti Spiritus*) was now finished, they concluded to draw and receive yet others into their fraternity. To this end was chosen Brother R. C., his deceased father's brother's son ; *Brother B., a skilful painter*" ("Fama Fraternitatis." Waite's "Real History of the Rosicrucians," pp. 71, 72). Who was this "*Brother B., a skilful painter*"? It is excessively curious to refind these initials and titles amongst the members' names, inscribed under the altar in the vault, where the body of Christian Rosencreutz lay buried. That the whole story was a splendid fiction to conceal the names of persons living at the time, is not only proved by Burton's testimony, 1621, who writes of the founder "*now living*," but by the evidence of Leibnitz and Van Helmont. Amongst modern critics, De Quincey and Mr Waite (the latest writer on this subject) both arrive at the same conclusion. De Quincey says, quoting Professor J. G. Buhle's work on this subject: "To *a hoax* played off by a young man of extra-

---

* Tenison writes: "And those who have true skill in the works of the Lord Verulam, like great masters in painting, can tell by the *design*, the *strength, the way of coloring*, whether he was the author of this or the other piece, *though his name be not to it*" (p. 79, "Baconiana").

ordinary talents in the beginning of the seventeenth century (*i.e.*, about 1610-14), but for a more elevated purpose than most hoaxes involve, the reader will find that the whole mysteries of Free-masonry, as now existing all over the civilized world, after a lapse of more than two centuries, are here distinctly traced" (p. 357, "Inquiry into the Origin of the Rosicrucians and Free-masons"). De Quincey, who only acts in the sense of an expounder of Buhle's work, agrees in the main with this hypothesis. He conclusively proves the fictitious character of the entire narrative concerning the discovery of Father Rosy Cross's Grave and Vault, by showing that the statement that the *Vocabularium* of Paracelsus was found in the vault *before it existed*, manifestly is absurd! "Finally, to say nothing of the Vocabularium of Paracelsus, which must have been put into the grave before it existed, the Rosicrucians are said to be Protestants, though founded upwards of a century before the Reformation. In short, the fiction is monstrous, and betrays itself in every circumstance. Whosoever was its author must be looked upon as the founder, in effect, of the Rosicrucian order, inasmuch as *this fiction was the accidental occasion of such an order being really founded.*"

It seems to us highly probable that *Brother B., pictor et Architectus*, was the Architect and *Poet Painter* of this society —its originator. The reader will be surprised to find Sir Philip Sidney, Ben Jonson, and Bacon each describing *Poetry as a kind of painting.**

"The most notable illustration we have of the close connection

---

* "*Poesis, et pictura—Plutarch.*—Poetry and Picture are arts of a like nature, and both are busy about imitation. It was excellently said of Plutarch, poetry was a speaking picture, and picture a mute poesy. For they both invent, feign, and devise many things, and accommodate all they invent to the use and service of nature" ("Discoveries," Ben Jonson).

"*De Pictura.*—Whosoever loves not picture is imperious to truth, and all the wisdom of poetry" (*Ibid.*).

"*De Progres. Picturæ.*—Picture took her feigning from poetry" (*Ibid.*).

"Poesy composeth and introduceth at pleasure, *even as painting doth:* which indeed is the work of the imagination" (ch. i. Lib. II., "Advancement of Learning," 1640).

of Free-masonry and Rosicrucianism is in the case of Elias Ashmole, who was initiated at Warrington, Lancashire, on the 16th October 1646, along with Colonel Henry Mainwaring, the descendant of an ancient Cheshire family. At this meeting were present, Mr Rich. Penket, *Warden*, Mr James Collier, Mr Richard Sankey, Henry Littler, John Ellam, Richard Ellam, and Hugh Brewer. These chemical adepts met at Mason's Hall, Basinghall Street, London; and Ashmole frequently records that he attended the 'Feast of the Astrologers.' The association is said to have been formed on the model of the German society, *and of the literary association allegorically described in Lord Bacon's 'New Atlantis' as the 'House of Solomon.' De Quincey asserts that this is the true origin of the Society of Free-masons . . . . there is evidence that genuine operative Free-masonry adopted Customs from the Rosicrucians and Templars"* ("Mysteries of Antiquity," p. 106, Yarker).

It is most important to note that we find Nicolai, Murr, Buhle, and De Quincey all agreeing that Freemasonry grew out of Rosicrucianism. De Quincey writes: "I shall now sum up the results of my inquiry into the origin and nature of Free-masonry. I. The original Free-masons were a society that arose out of the Rosicrucian mania, certainly within the thirteen years from 1633 to 1646, and probably between 1633 and 1640" (p. 413). Lord Bacon died in 1626. Again: "There is nothing in the imagery, myths, ritual, or purposes of the elder Free-masonry, which may not be traced to the romances of Father Rosycross, as given in the 'Fama Fraternitatis'" (p. 416). This is a great point gained, because Nicolai and Murr maintain that the object of the elder Free-masons was *to build Lord Bacon's imaginary Temple of Solomon.** This De Quincey will not allow. Simply because his

---

* In the Preface to the "Fama Fraternitatis," we find the opening words quoting Solomon:—

"Wisdom (sayeth Solomon) is a treasure unto men that never faileth, for she is bred of the power of God and an inheritance flowing from the glory of the Almighty; . . . .

"The wise King Solomon doth testify of himself that he upon his earnest

mind is prejudiced with the idea there could be nothing in common between the scientific or philosophic ends proposed by Bacon and Rosicrucianism. He seems entirely ignorant of the great point we have adduced, that *the ends of the Rosicrucians were Baconian*—experimental research, tentative inquiry into nature as we have seen in the writings of Maier, the declarations of the Rosicrucian manifestoes, and as the works of Robert Fludd abundantly testify. He was not aware Bacon writes in "Valerius Terminus" of an *oral method* of transmission, which he publishes as one of his *intentions*, joined to a reserved or posthumous system of publishing. De Quincey writes quite ignorantly of the religious side of Bacon's writings, his endless allusions to Solomon, and does not see any affiliating evidence in the fact *Solomon was the biblical Father, or protagonist of the Rosicrucians, and that Bacon's College of the Six Days is called by him Solomon's House.* De Quincey did not know John Heydon reproduces Bacon's "New Atlantis" word for word, with the title, "Land of the Rosicrucians." He does not suggest an explanation why the elder Freemason in 1646 at a lodge meeting at Warrington adopted Bacon's two pillars, which may be re-seen upon the title-page of the "Librum Naturæ," or "Sylva Sylvarum," with which the "New Atlantis" is bound up! The truth is, De Quincey knew next to nothing of Bacon's works, and occupied himself exclusively upon the problem of the

prayer and desire obtained such wisdom of God, that thereby he knew how the world was made, understood the operation of the elements, the beginning, ending, and middle of the times, the alterations, the days of the turning of the sun, the change of seasons, the circuit of years and the positions of stars, the natures of living creatures and the furies of wild beasts, the violence of winds, the reasonings of men, the diversities of plants, the virtues of roots, and all such things as are either secret or manifest, them he knew."

This is proof that Solomon was the authority or inspirer of the Fraternity. With this must be compared the repeated quotations Bacon makes in his works to Solomon. Over and over again he quotes him calling him the Holy Philosopher. "That the glory of God is to conceal a thing, but the glory of the King is to find it out: as if the Divine Nature, according to the innocent and sweet play of children, which hide themselves to the end they may be found, took delight to hide his works, to the end they might be found out" (Preface to the "Great Instauration").

connection of the Rosicrucians with Freemasonry only. Bacon's part in the mystery he only superficially glances at, and sets aside the really far profounder researches of Nicolai and Murr, both of whom living in Germany, had so many more sources of literature upon this question at hand. De Quincey writes: "The Temple of Solomon which they professed to build, together with all the Masonic attributes, pointed collectively to the grand purpose of the society—*the restoration of the Templar order."* De Quincey had probably not read Bacon's "Holy War," in which Bacon writes like a Knight Templar, introducing the Templar and Rosicrucian motto or emblem of the Red Cross founded by Constantine *in hoc signo vinces*. If he had studied Bacon's "New Atlantis" carefully, he would have found that the *Tirson* is described as having a small *red Cross* on his turban. John Val Andreas states: "The Rosicrucians were formed out of the ruins of the Knight Templars by one faithful brother." Their great authority was Saint Augustine, and Bacon's fondness for this author may be discovered by anyone who studies the last book of the "De Augmentis." Bacon writes: "Notwithstanding we thought good to set down amongst Deficients as a wholesome and profitable work a treatise touching the degrees of Unity *in the City of God*" (p. 472, Book IX., "Advancement").

CHAPTER II.

NOTES ON ROSICRUCIAN LITERATURE.

I WISH to point out how remarkable a thing it is to find the Rosicrucians and their literature appearing on the stage of Europe, and making themselves first known *on and about the date of Shakespeare's death*, 1616. "The whole Rosicrucian controversy," writes Mr Waite (in his fifth chapter of the "Real History of the Rosicrucians"), "centres in a publication entitled 'The Chymical Marriage of Christian Rosencreutz.' It was first published at Strasbourg in the year 1616. Two editions of the German original are to be found in the British Museum,* both bearing the date 1616—'Chymische Hochzeit: Christiani Rosencreutz. Anno 1459.' 'Erstlick Gedructzor Strasbourg. Anno MDCXVI.'" It appears from Mr Waite that this romance "is supposed to have existed in manuscript as early as 1601-2, thus ante-dating by a long period the other Rosicrucian books" (p. 99). If this is a fact, which we see no reason to doubt, it seems to us very curious it was not published before, and it is possible its publication depended upon some event. We are bound to consider our evidence altogether, and we must call attention again to the suspicious hint given in the "Confessio Fraternitatis" of 1615, where we read of impostors, "One of the greatest being a STAGE PLAYER, *a man with sufficient ingenuity for imposition.*" †

* In the Harleian MSS., from 6481 to 6486, are several Rosicrucian writings, some translated from the Latin by one Peter Smart, and others by a Dr Rudd, who appears to have been a profound adept.

† We take the following from the "Confession of the Rosicrucian Fraternity," published 1615 :—

"For conclusion of our Confession we must earnestly admonish you, that

Shakespeare, as we know by the list of actors given in the 1623 Folio, was an actor, his name figuring first out of twenty-six. And though we are quite alive to the fact that at this date—1615—Shakespeare had retired, some years back, to Stratford, all these Rosicrucian manifestoes seem to have been existing in manuscript some years before they were published. This is no ingenious theory of ours, as Mr Waite's pages will testify. For example, he writes: "The original edition of the 'Universal Reformation' contains the manifesto bearing the above title ('Fama Fraternitatis'), but which the notary Haselmeyer declares to have existed in manuscript as early as the year 1610, as would also appear from a passage in the Cassel edition of 1614, the earliest which I have been able to trace" (p. 64, "Real History of the Rosicrucians"). It is a remarkable fact that the three publications which made, as it were, the mysterious fraternity known to the world, follow the dates 1614, 1615, 1616—that is the two years preceding and the year Shakespeare died. The uproar resulting from these publications amongst the learned and even unlearned of Europe, reaches its climax in 1617, when Robert Fludd, the apologist for the order, replies to the attacks of Libavius. This is the year following Shakespeare's death. In 1623, the date of the publication of the first Folio edition of the plays, we read of a meeting in Paris of thirty-six Rosicrucians, and the uproar recommences, and Gabriel Naudé writes, like Mersenne and Gassendi, to expose the pretensions of the society. Fludd's "Tractatus Apologetici integritatem societatis de Rosea Cruce defendens Leiden," 1617, proves that the year following Shakespeare's death the battle of the critics was at its height. I cannot believe this coincidence accidental. Nothing is heard of the Rosicrucians before 1614, when their manifestoes

you cast away, if not all, yet most of the worthless books of pseudo chymists, to whom it is a jest to apply the Most Holy Trinity to vain things, or to deceive men with monstrous symbols and enigmas, or to profit by the curiosity of the credulous; our age doth produce many such, *one of the greatest being a* STAGE-PLAYER, *a man with sufficient ingenuity for imposition*" (chapter xii., "History of the Rosicrucians").

and confessions appear yearly for three years, up to Shakespeare's death, 1616. We hear no more (directly) of them till 1623. Bacon dies 1626, and De Quincey points out that with the "Summum Bonum," 1629, they vanish from literature. The dates are as follows of the three great manifestoes:—

> "Fama Fraternitatis," 1614.
> "Confessio Fraternitatis," 1615.
> "Chemical Marriage of C. R. C.," 1616.

Now it is worthy of note that in 1614 Bacon was fifty-three years of age, and in his fifty-fourth year; Shakespeare, fifty years old, and in his fifty-first year. Because Shakespeare died in 1616 in his fifty-third year, and thus 1614 and 1616 give Bacon and Shakespeare the same age—fifty-three. We mention this because every sort of suggestion is valuable, seeing the word "*Bacon*" and the Christian name "*Francis*" (the latter twenty-two times) are to be refound on pages 53 of the Comedies, and 53 and 54 of the Histories. Shakespeare never attained the age of fifty-four. But in 1614, as already observed, the first Rosicrucian publication appears—Bacon being fifty-three, and in his fifty-fourth year. It is highly probable, if the Rosicrucian mystery is at the bottom of the plays and their authorship, the first publication of the society would constitute an initial starting-point. Thus the three great dates would be 1614, 1615, 1616. It is curious to find the first mispaging in the Folio upon page 50, this being Shakespeare's age, 1614. And in the Histories we find Bacon's Christian name, "*Francis*," twenty-two times on pages 53, 54, which are mispaged (evidently intentionally), 55, 56. Now taking Bacon's age as a basis for dates, these ages give us 1614, 1616, the date of the first Rosicrucian publication and fame, and the date of Shakespeare's death—1616. It is noteworthy, though perhaps merely a speculation, that Christian Rosy Cross, the founder of the society, dies at the age of 106. It is upon page 106 of the 1640 "Advancement of Learning" that the drama is first introduced, and this number is exactly the double of fifty-three, Bacon's age in 1614, and Shakespeare's—1616—when he died.

It is indeed striking to find almost all the Rosicrucian literature appearing at and about the date Shakespeare died—1616. For example:

"Rosa Florescens contra F. G. Menapii calumnias," &c., was published at Frankfort, 1617.

"*Echo* der von Gott hocherleuchteten fraternität des löblichen ordens R. C." (Danzig, 1616).

"Judicium Theologicum, oder : Christliches und Kurzes bedenken von der fama und Confession der brüderschaft des löblichen ordens der Rosenkreuzers " (David Maier, 1616).

"Turris Babel, sive Judicior de fraternitat Rosaceae Crucis Chaos," Argent., 1619 (John Val Andreas).

"Analysi Confessionis Fraternitatis De Rosea Cruce" (And. Libavius, 1616).

"Reipublicæ Christianopolitanæ descripto," Agentor., 1619 (Andreæ, J. V.).

"Silentium post clamores, h. e. Tractatus Apologeticus, quo causæ non solum *Clamorum* (seu Revelationum) Fraternitatis Germanicæ de R. C., sed et Silentii traduntur et demonstrantur " (Michaeli Maiero, Francof., 1617).*

It is well worthy reflection the Rosicrucian manifestoes of 1615, were published *at Frankfort, where Fludd was publishing his works*. Gabriel Naudé writes: "L'an 1615 Jean Bringern imprima a Francfort un liure en Allemand contenant deux opuscules, intitulees Manifeste et Confession de foy des Freres de la R. C. lesquels pour estre les deux premures qui ont annoncé les nouvelles de cette congregation, nous apprennent que le premier fondaten d'icelle fut in Allemand, lequel estant né l'an 1378," &c. ("Instruction à la France sur la verité de l'histoire des Freres de la Roze-Croix," 1623). Another point is that the Rosicrucians used the expression *Instauration* for their promised reformation of arts and sciences. Gabriel Naudé in

---

* A slight study of the Kloss Catalogue of Rosicrucian works will convince the student of the enormous quantity of R. C. works which appeared in 1617, the year following Shakespeare's death.

the work just quoted from, entitles one of his chapters "Response à la principale raison de *l'instauration* promise," &c. Postel, who evidently was a precursor of the society, wrote: "De ultima nativitate mediatoris: De *instauratione rerum omnium* * per magnus Heliæ prophetæ," &c. The reader will see how suspicious it is to find Bacon joining hands with the Rosicrucians in this title *Instauration*. Bacon writes: "This one way therefore remaineth, that the whole business be attempted anew, with better preparations or defences against error; and that there be a universal *Instauration or reconstruction of the arts and sciences, and of all human learning upon a due basis.*" That is the meaning of the word *Instauratio*: it was used by the Romans for the repetition of anything, and generally with a special view to correctness or completeness of performance, as for instance, of games *or sacrifices*, of which the first performance had been unsatisfactory. "It is properly a *building up, and is nearly the same thing with a restoration*" (Craik's "Bacon," p. ii. 2).

The connection between the works of Roger Bacon and the Rosicrucians is most apparent, and points to England as the origin of the Society. Naudé says: "Et certain Anonyme qui a mis en lumiere l'epistre de Roger Bacon *De potestate artis et naturæ*, passe bien plus outre et se donne carriere en ses imaginations: car en la Preface au Lecteur il dit que cette renovation et instauration future se fera principalement remarquer en trois poincts: le premier en *l'unitie de Religion* † par la conversion des Juifs, Idolatres et Ismaelites: le second

---

* Fludd writes: "Unde sit (ut mihi videtur) quod Fratres renovationem et restaurationem mundi Ethicam seu moralem, hoc est morum, *scientiarum et artium instaurationem*, correctionem et exaltationem, et hominum in obscuritate et tenebris vitas degentium libertatem et illuminationem, et perspicuam veritatis olim tabescentes lumen et splendorem, cum falsitatas detrimento, exilio, ac runia, et repetitionem atque mutuo quasi nixu renovationem ætatis aureæ, non ineptè præsagiverint: dicentes in uno confessionis loco: *Quod, Mundus debeat renovari*," &c. ("Tract. Apol.," p. 81, 1617).

† Note Bacon wrote an Essay upon "Unity in Religion."

en l'abondance et richesse de toutes sortes de biens : et le dernier fera reluire les vertus, esclater les sciences et obligera un chacun a vivre comme eust faict notre premier pere s'il fut demeuré en l'estat de la justice originelle : laquelle distribution il confirme par une infinité de passage de la saincte Escriture, le tout pour piloter et establir le premier principe et fondement de cette congregation de la Roze-Croix" (pp. 43, 44, " Instr. Sur les Frères de la Roze-Croix," 1623).

It is most remarkable that we always hear of the Rosicrucians and their founder in connection with Roger Bacon. For Burton writes in his "Anatomy of Melancholy," p. 72 (Democritus to the Reader): "That omniscious, only wise fraternity of the Rosie Cross . . . . their Theophrastian master, whom though Libavius and many deride and carp at, yet some will have to be the *Renewer of all arts and sciences* (Footnote—*Omnium artium et scientiarum instaurator*), reformer of the world, and now living ; for so Johannes Montanus Strigoniensis (that great patron of Paracelsus) contends and certainly avers, *a most divine man* (Footnote—*Divinus ille vir. auctor notarum in ep. Rog. Bacon, ed Hamburg*, 1608), and the quintessence of wisdom, wheresoever he is." The reader perceives that this supposed founder of the fraternity is the author of notes upon Roger Bacon ! Let it be here remarked Francis Bacon is supposed to have borrowed his doctrine of Idols from the four-fold classification of Roger Bacon's " Offendicula, quæ omnem quemcunque sapientem impediunt " (Opus Magus, first part, and Opus Tertium, cap. 22). In the " New Atlantis " may be refound a number of marvels, which are borrowed from this Book of Roger Bacon, mentioned by Naudé, i.e., "*De potestate artis et naturæ*," and "*De secretis artis et Naturæ*," viz., to make chariots move without animals, diving boats, flying, telescopes, magnifying glasses, &c.* The invention of Spectacles,

---

* The whole of Bacon's prophecies in his " New Atlantis " regarding the march of science are being realised. Will the world not recognise that "*Looking Forward*" belongs to Bacon and not to only modern writers, like Bellamy and Thuisen ?

like that of the Microscope and Telescope, has been ascribed to Roger Bacon. (Compare "Novum Organum," Book II. xxxix.) In the "Temporis Partus Masculus," Bacon writes praisingly of his great namesake, "Siquidem utile genus eorum est, qui de theoriis non admodum solliciti, mechanica quadam subtilitate rerum inventarum extensiones prehendunt, *qualis est Bacon.*"

Another convincing proof that the origin of the Rosicrucians really was *connected with England*, and was transmitted abroad, is the fact that it never took any hold in the countries where it made most noise, but took lasting root *only in England*. De Quincey writes: "In France it never had even a momentary success." Again: "Rosicrucianism received a shock from the writings of its accidental father, Andreä and others, such as in Germany it never recovered. And hence it has happened that, whatever numbers there may have been of individual mystics calling themselves Rosicrucians, no collective body of Rosicrucians acting in conjunction was ever matured or actually established in Germany. *In England the case was otherwise, for there, as I shall show, the order still subsists under a different name*" (De Quincey, 404).

The striking point that Andreas disclaimed the society in the words, "*Planissime nihil cum hac Fraternitate* (sc., *Ros Crucis*) *commune habeo*" (*die Alethia*, or Truth speaking), is to be placed alongside with the fact that the cudgels of the society are taken up by Robert Fludd, *an Englishman*, who may be regarded as their champion. It is also noteworthy that all the great writers upon this subject are Englishmen, viz., Thomas Vaughan, John Heydon. Michael Maier, the most important of the foreign writers, having visited England in 1616 and staying with Fludd, who publishes first 1616. The great fact the society was antipapal and in secret harmony with the work of the Reformation, points to England or Germany as the countries most likely to produce such a society. If the reader will only weigh the evidence, that in 1614, 1615 these pamphlets are published in Germany, that in 1616 Fludd is perfect master of their secrets, and writes *Ex*

Cathedrâ, he will, considering how cut off by the sea England was from the Continent (and taking into consideration the nature of communication in those days), see that everything points to this country.

A very convincing, or at least strong presumptive piece of evidence pointing to England as the headquarters of the Rosicrucians and their fountain head, is afforded by the fact that Robert Fludd, the great English Rosicrucian, took up the cudgels for the society against the attacks of the foreigners, Gassendi and Mersenne. De Quincey writes: "*Fludd it was, or whosoever was the author of the 'Summum Bonum,' 1629, that must be considered as the immediate father of Freemasonry, as Andreä was its remote father.* What was the particular occasion of his own first acquaintance with Rosicrucianism is not recorded: all the books of Alchemy or other occult knowledge, published in Germany, were at that time immediately carried over to England—provided they were written in Latin; and, if written in German, were soon translated for the benefit of English students. He may therefore have gained his knowledge immediately from the three Rosicrucian books. But it is more probable that he acquired his knowledge on this head from his friend Maier (mentioned in the preceding chapter), who was intimate with Fludd during his stay in England" (p. 406, "Inquiry," &c.). The profound student will notice how curious it is to find that it is English Rosicrucianism that gives birth to Masonry. De Quincey's suggestion, Fludd gained his knowledge from Maier, is a mere haphazard statement, and of no value. On the contrary, what little we can gather points the opposite way, for it is quite impossible Fludd could have gathered from Maier (who was in England, 1617) the information which led to such works as "Utriusque Cosmi, majoris et minoris Technica Historia," published 1617, in two volumes; "Tractatus apologeticus—integritatem Societatis de Roseâ Cruce defendens" (Authore Roberto De Fluctibus, Anglo, M.D.L. Lugd. Bat. 1617). Fludd wrote two works in reply to Father Mersenne and Gassendi.

That Robert Fludd's philosophy *did not come from abroad but rather went abroad*, we are about to prove. It is, indeed, a singular thing *that none of his works were published in England*, and this goes a long way towards showing that the source and fountainhead of the fraternity *was in this country*. If the reader will attentively study the following extract from Disraeli's "Amenities of Literature," he will at once perceive Fludd *was receiving letters, praise, money from the Continent*, and he himself lets the "cat out of the bag" when he declares (disgusted with the indifference of his own countrymen to his speculations), "*no man is a prophet in his own country.*"

"'I tell this to my countrymen's shame,' exclaims Fludd, 'who, instead of encouraging me in my labours, *as by letters from Polonia, Suevia, Prussia, Germany, Transylvania, France, and Italy, I have had*, do pursue me with malice, which when a learned German heard of, it reminded him of the speech of Christ, that '*no man is a prophet in his own country.*' Without any bragging of my knowledge, be it spoken, I speak this feelingly; but a guiltless conscience bids me be patient.'

"The writings of Fludd are all composed in Latin; it is remarkable that the works of an English author, residing in England, should be printed at Frankfort, Oppenheim, and Gouda. This singularity is accounted for by the author himself. Fludd, in one respect, resembled Dee; he could find no English printers who would venture on their publication. When Foster insinuated that his character as a magician was so notorious, that he dared not print at home, Fludd tells his curious story: 'I sent my writings beyond the seas, because our home-born printers demanded of me five hundred pounds to print the first volume, and to find the cuts in copper; but beyond the seas it was printed at no cost of mine, and as I could wish; *and I had sixteen copies sent me over, with forty pounds in gold, as an unexpected gratuity for it.*' It is evident that, throughout Europe, they were infinitely more inquisitive in their occult speculations than we in England" (p. 648, "Amenities of Literature," The Rosacrucian Fludd. D'Israeli).

Is it likely Fludd would be receiving money, letters, praise from abroad, and getting his works paid for on the Continent, if the source, origin, and headquarters of the society were on the other side of the channel? It would be like "sending coals to Newcastle." A plagiarist would never lay claim, as he does, to the title of prophet! Why does Fludd receive all these letters from abroad? Have we not at once an explanation of the connection of Germany with the origin of the society in the fact Fludd published at Frankfort, Oppenheim, and Gouda, and not in England?

Bacon writes: "For there are, as we see, many orders and societies, which, though they be divided under several sovereignties and spacious territories, yet they do contract and maintain a society and a kind of *Fraternity* one with another, in so much that they have their *Provincials* and *Generals*, to whom all the rest yield obedience. And surely as nature creates *Brotherhoods* in *Families;* and arts mechanical contract *Brotherhoods* in communalities; the anointment of God super-induceth a *brotherhood in king and bishops;* vows and canonical rules unite a *brotherhood in Orders;* in like manner there cannot but intervene a *Noble and generous Fraternity between men by Learning and Illuminations;* reflecting upon that relation which is attributed to God, who himself is called *The Father of Illuminations or Lights*" (Lib. II. pp. 74, 75, "Advancement of Learning," 1640).

This is an excessively curious and suspicious passage. The italics and capitals are not ours, but as in the original text. The Rosicrucians called themselves *Brothers* (*Fratres*), and all their addresses, as well as the writings of Fludd, are full of this term. For example, at the end of Fludd's "Tractatus Apologetici" of 1615 (p. 195), we see this title, "Epilogus Authoris ad *Fratres de Rosea Cruce.*" But what is far more important, they coupled to this title of *Brotherhood* the description,

Illuminate * (or Illuminates), by which they have ever since been known. This title they derived from their deep researches into the nature of *Light*, which is one of their principal doctrines. Mosheim tells us that the *Rosicrucians* derived their name from the three letters Lux (Light). "Lux is the menstruum of the red dragon (*i.e.*, corporeal light)." Fludd deduces everything from *Light*, and compares it (if he does not even identify it) with *Spirit*: "Lucem actionum omnium causam esse, ut et spiritum humidum passionis, subjectum ex præcedentibus satis declaratum est" (p. 155, "Tract. Apol.," 1617).

Again: "In hominibus est lucidus rationis discursus. In cæteris animalibus est ignis occultus, actiones vitæ, et sensus manifestè gubernans. In vegetabilibus est anima quædam lucida, circa eorum centra delitescens, vegetationem, et multiplicationem causans in infinitum. In mineralibus etiam est splendoris scintilla versus perfectionis metam illa promovens. Atque ita quælibet creatura actiones et proprietates suas à luce recipit, unde patet quod omnia Naturæ arcana, ab hujus creaturæ proprietate derivata fuerint, et originem suæ virtutis sumpserint, et quod nihil in hoc mundo peractum fuerit, sine lucis mediatione aut actu divino" (p. 157, "Tractatus Apol.," 1617). Those acquainted with Bacon's writings will recognise the parallels endlessly spread throughout his works. Indeed, his "Novum Organum" is constantly alluded to in the sense of Light.† Bacon writes: "And

---

* Fludd writes: "Prophetas autem illos vocamus, qui Spiritu Sancto permissione divina *illuminati* sunt; atque hujusmodi etiam erant Patriarchæ, et Apostoli, et omnes, quibus Deus effudit, Spiritum suum" (Ch. vii., "Tractatus Apologetici," Pars. II., p. 146).

† The enormous weight the Rosicrucians placed upon *Light* as a first principle in creation may be seen by Fludd's words, "*nihil in hoc mundo peractum fuerit, sine lucis mediatione aut actu divino,*" already quoted by Mr Waite. The motto upon Bacon's "Sylva Sylvarum" or "Natural History" (title-page engraving), placed underneath a fiery semi-circle of creative Light, is—

Et vidit Deus lucem quod esset bona.

Fludd:—"Ex his igitur colligendum est, quod Deus diligenter observaverit effigies, figuras, lineas, et characteres cujuslibet sui operis, quoniam post cujuslibet eorum creationem commendare solebat perfectionem ejus Genes. I. *Et vidit Deus lucem quod esset bona,*" &c. ("Tractatus Apol.," ch. iv. pars. i., 1617).

men ought to submit their contemplations awhile, and to inquire what is common to all *Lucid Bodies* as of the *Form of Light*. For what an immense difference of body is there betwixt the sun and rotten wood, or the putrid scales of fish? They should likewise make inquiry what should be the cause why some things take fire, and once thoroughly heated cast forth a light; others not? Iron, metal, *stones*, glass, wood, oil, &c." . . . (Book IV., p. 215, "Advancement of Learning," 1640). Compare Fludd: "Similiter ignem ex lignis et lapidibus expressum dicunt, quem narrant per multos annos vitro inclusum, etiam in maris vel putei profunditate arcisse" (p. 158, "Tractatus Apol.").

If space permitted I could adduce endless parallels between Bacon and Fludd on this point. Bacon's theory is that there exists *an invisible internal light* producing no flame. "How comes it to pass Owls and Cats and many other creatures see in the night? Nay, many have understood so little on this point, as many have thought *the sparks from a flint* to be attrited air" (Book IV., "De Augmentis").

Light (with Bacon) did not exist before *darkness*, but was extracted or evolved *out of it*. "Whereas Holy writ sets down plainly *the mass of Heaven and Earth to be a dark chaos before the creation of Light*" (p. 215, "Advancement," 1640). Now compare Fludd, which I take for the reader's impartial judgment from Mr Waite's interpretation.

"The third part is entitled 'De Naturæ Arcanis,' and treats of the mysteries of Light, &c., developing in a small space a curious and profound philosophy. It describes God as the *ens entium*, eternal form, inviolable, purely igneous, without any intermixture of material, *unmanifested before the creation of the universe*, according to the maxim of Mercurius Trismegistus, '*Monas generat monadem, et in seipsum reflectit ardorem suum.*' Earth is defined to be a gross water, water a gross air, air a gross fire, fire a gross ether, while the ether itself is the grosser part of the empyrean, which is distinguished from the ethereal realm, and is described as a water of extreme tenuity, constituted of three parts of luminous substance to one aqueous part; it is the purest essence of all substances, *and is identical with the luminiferous ether of the latest scientific hypothesis.* Its place is the *medium mundi*, wherein is the *sphæra æqualitatis*, in which the sun performs its revolution. The sun itself is composed of equal parts of light and water. Light is the cause of all energies—*nihil in hoc mundo peractum fuerit, sine lucis mediatione aut actu divino.* 'It is impossible for man to desire more complete felicity than the admirable knowledge of light and its virtues,' by which the ancient magi constructed their ever-burning lamps, *forced fire out of stones and wood*, kindled tapers from the rays of stars, and naturally, by means of its reflections, produced many wonders in the air, such as phantom writing, and more than all by the true use of the *lux invisibilis*, made men themselves invisible" (Waite's "Real History of the Rosicrucians," p. 292).

Here is Fludd repeating Bacon's doctrine of the priority of darkness before Light. "Et posuit tenebras latibulum suum in circuitu ejus, tabernaculum ejus tenebrosa aqua in nubibus densis, &c. At vero cum ejus voluntas esset macrocosmum condere in gremio seu ventre hyles adhuc informis (*nam tenebræ fuerunt supra faciem Abyssi infinitæ*) ut cum Trismegisto loquar, *mutavit formam et universa subito revelavit, et omnia in lumen conversa sunt, suave nimium. Et paulo post Umbra quædam horrenda obliquâ revolutione subterlabebatur vel, Psal. xviii.* 12, *præ fulgore in conspectu ejus nubes tenebrosæ et densæ transierunt*" ("Tractatus Apol.," p. 152).

Bacon writes in the "New Atlantis": "We maintain a trade, not for gold, silver, or jewels; nor for silks; nor for spices; nor any other commodity of matter; but only for God's first creature, which was Light: *to have Light (I say) of the growth of all parts of the world.*"

It is curious to find this doctrine of *internal light* repeated in "Love's Labour's Lost".—

> Light seeking light doth light of light beguile:
> So ere you find *where light in darkness lies*,
> Your light grows dark by losing of your eyes.
>
> (Act i. sc. 1.)

Compare Fludd on this *Invisible Interior Light* :—" Hinc hominem internum ab homine externo distinguimus. Hinc facultates in hoc sive illo animali, et minerali, vegetabili, et minerali ad corporis humani morbo languescentis curationes, Magiæ naturalis operationes et infinitalia, derivantur. Ex quibus constat, quod licet manifestæ rerum proprietates, et corporum effectus oculis nostris et sensibus offerantur, *non tamen ea condemnare oporteat, quæ sensui nostro non succedunt*, videlicet quæ occultè in corporibus delitescunt, et obsconduntur; quoniam, ut præstantior pars totius creationis est invisibilis, videlicet spiritus ille Empyreus, *lucesque invisibiles* ejusdem, nempe Angeli, et totus Cœlestis exercitus invisibilis ad cujus esse, *Lux invisibilis et spiritus similis concurrebant ;* sic præstantiora Dei atque naturæ arcana sunt invisibilia et non nisi ab oculis intellectualibus percipienda " (pp. 160, 161, " Apol."). *Spirit and Light* Fludd almost, if not indeed, identifies.

"We read that the first of created forms *was light ;* which hath a relation and correspondence in nature and corporal things, to knowledge in spirits and incorporal things" ("Advancement of Learning," Lib. I.). This doctrine, which is especially Baconian, and belongs also to the "Novum Organum," is to be refound in Fludd's "Apology of the Rosicrucians," in answer to Libavius (1617). One of his chapters is entitled "*De Luce.*"

Compare Bacon's "*Radix Perspectivæ sive de Forma Lucis*" (Book IV., "De Augmentis). Bacon writes :—" Some of Plato's school have introduced *Light* as a thing more ancient than *matter* itself ; for when empty space was spread they affirmed it was, in a vain imagination, that it was first filled with light, and afterwards with a body, whereas Holy Writ set down plainly the mass of heavens and earth to be a dark chaos before the creation of Light." Just as Bacon fetches all his authority from the Bible, so Fludd, one of his leading doctrines being this first existence of darkness and chaos.

CHAPTER III.

ROSICRUCIAN PARALLELS TO BACON'S WRITINGS.

"Shakespeare, in the person of Prospero, has exhibited the prevalent notions of the judicial astrologer combined with the adept, whose white magic, as distinguished from the black or demon magic, holds an intercourse with purer spirits. Such a sage was

——— transported,
And rapt in secret studies;

that is, in the occult sciences; and he had

Volumes that he prized more than his dukedom.

These were alchemical, astrological, and cabalistical treatises. The magical part of 'The Tempest,' Warton has observed, 'is founded on that sort of philosophy which was peculiar to John Dee and his associates, and has been called "the Rosicrucian."'" (D'Israeli's "Amenities of Literature," p. 617.)

AIR, SOUL, SPIRIT.

"THE wind is an angelical Spirit clothed with air, which moveth occultly and invisibly this way and that way, according unto the secret will of Him that created it, *whose voice, although it be heard, yet is the place from whence it came, or the mark whither it tendeth, unknown of mortal men*" (p. 92, "Mosaical Philosophy," Rob. Fludd, 1659). Ariel, in the play of "The Tempest," closely follows this description even in name, being described as "*an airy spirit*" in the list of *Dramatis Personæ*. In the second scene of the third act, Ariel is introduced *invisibly playing on a tabor and pipe*, giving Caliban, Stephano, and Trinculo the lie,—the voice being heard, but the place whence it came from unknown.

Stephano. What is this same?
Trin. This is the tune of our catch played by the picture of nobody.

Fludd writes: "Nay, verily we will prove that the internal mover in the winds is the essential inspiration or breath proceeding immediately from God" (p. 88, "Mosaical Philosophy," 1659). Fludd everywhere identifies *spirit with wind or air, as the soul*. It is well worthy attention that Prospero, in the play of "The Tempest," is introduced as a representative God, for he has power over the elements, and his wrath is portrayed to us in the storm he raises. In the Fourth Book of Bacon's "De Augmentis," he identifies the soul with air, as "*a gentle gale of wind*,"* suspiciously allied to a Tempest. "For the *sensible soul* must needs be granted, to be a corporal substance attenuated by heat and made invisible: I say *a thin gentle gale of wind* swell'd and blown up from some flamy and airy nature, indeed, with the softness of air to receive impression, and with the vigor of fire to embrace action" (p. 208, Book IV., "Advancement of Learning," 1640).

BEES AND ROSES.

There can be very little doubt that the emblem of the *Bee* was an important Rosicrucian symbol, because we find a great number of Rosicrucian writers alluding to it in almost if not identical words. Upon the title-page of Fludd's "Summum Bonum," 1629, there is a large *Rose drawn, on which two bees have alighted*, with the motto:—

"*Dat Rosa mel apibus.*"

Now, as the Rose was the especial symbol of the Society (as

---

* Twenty-sixth Star. De Substantia Animæ Sensibilis. "Anima siquidem sensibilis sive brutorum, plane substantia corporea censenda est, a calore attenuata, et facta invisibilis ; aura (inquam) ex naturâ flammeâ et aëreâ conflata, *aëris mollitie* ad impressionem recipiendam, ignis vigore ad actionem vibrandam dotata ; partim ex oleosis, partim ex aqueis nutrita ; corpore obducta, atque in animalibus perfectis in capite præcipuè locata ; in nervis percurrens, et sanguine spirituoso arteriarum refecta et reparata ; *quemadmodum Bernardinus Telesius et discipulus ejus Augustinus Domus aliquâ ex parte, non omnino inutiliter asseruerunt.*" ("De Augmentis," ch. iii., Lib. IV.)

Telesius revived the philosophy of Parmenides. He wrote "De Rerum Natura" (in nine books, Napoli, 1586), "De Colorum Generatione" (1570), "De Mari" (1570); see Maurice, "Mod. Phil.," 162. Donius was a physician of Cosenza. He wrote "De Natura Hominis" (1581).

we know from their jewel), it is highly probable the Bee was also included, or part of the emblem. In an address to the brotherhood which prefaces Thomas Vaughan's "Anthroposophia Theomagica," we read: "To the most illustrious and truly regenerated brethren R. C.; to the peace-loving apostles of the Church in this contentious age. Salutation from the centre of Peace." Upon the first page we read: "I have wandered *like the bees* (not those of Quintillian in poisoned gardens), *touching lightly the Cœlestial flowers*, which derive their scents from the Aromatic mountains. If here there be aught of *honey, I offer unto you this honeycomb and bee-hive. Roses, however, are wont to be soiled upon the breasts of most persons; peradventure also this handful is sullied, for it is of my gathering*" (Dedication, "The Magical Writings of Thomas Vaughan," by A. E. Waite). It may be perceived that *Bees and Roses* are brought into context in this dedicatory address to the Fraternity, in an evidently symbolical or esoteric sense. Bacon, in describing the seats of Learning, *foundations of Colleges* (the Rosicrucians called themselves a College), writes: "The works which concern *the seats of the Muses* (Musarum Sedes) are four, *foundations of Houses*, endowments, franchises, and privileges . . . much like the stations which Virgil prescribeth for the *hiving of Bees.*"

> Principio sedes apibus statioque petenda
> Quo neque sit ventis aditus, &c.
>
> (First for thy bees a quiet station find,
> And lodge them under covert of the wind.)
>
> (Virgil, "Georg.," iv. 8.)
>
> (P. 69, "Advancement," 1640.)

"For he that shall attentively observe how the mind doth gather this excellent *dew of knowledge*, like unto that which the poet speaketh of, *Aerei mellis cœlestia dona*, distilling and contriving *it out of particulars, natural and artificial, as the flowers of the field and garden*, shall find that the mind of herself by nature doth manage and act an induction much better than they describe it" ("Advancement of Learning," Book II., p. 152). It is easy to perceive by the Latin quotation, Bacon is alluding to the *industry* of *Bees*, in order to illustrate the collection of honey, *or dew of knowledge*, from out of infinite particulars. In Michael Maier's "Septimana Philosophica" (1620, Francof.) we read: "At quid de Apibus dicendum? (Hyramus). Illarum *cœlestis seu aëria videtur origo*, cum domunculæ earum, id est, cellæ cereæ, nutrimentum seu ambrosia et Manna mellis, nec non tota prosapia ex floribus ortum ducant; flores autem à *cœlo et aëra rorem* et fragrantium mutuo accipiant. Cæli virtus melli in favis existenti, dum adsunt tamen examina in illis, infunditur, unde Apiculæ novæ generantur" (p. 195). Here we find a connotation of bees, honey, dew, and flowers. Canto xxxi. of Dante's "Paradiso" opens with the connotation of "*a snow-white rose*" *and bees*:—

> In fashion then as if *a snow-white rose*
> Displayed itself to me the saintly host,
> Whom Christ in his own blood had made his bride,
> But the other host, that flying sees and sings
> The glory of him who doth enamour it,
> And the goodness that created it so noble,
> Even as a swarm of bees that sink in flowers
> One moment, and the next returns again
> To where its labour is to sweetness turned,
> Sunk into the great flower, that is adorned
> With leaves so many, and thence reascended
> To where its love abideth evermore.*
>
> LONGFELLOW.

Bacon almost always compares knowledge *to Water or a Foun-*

---

* G. Rossetti maintains in his "Antipapal Spirit which produced the Reformation," that Dante's Divine Comedy is nothing but an exposition of the secret mysteries and symbolism of the Knight Templars, to which order he belonged, and that Dante was active in preparing by his writings the way for the Reformation. Mr Waite, quoting "Eliphas Lévi," writes (p. 16, "History of the Roscrucians"): "Not without astonishment will it be discovered," continues Lévi, "that the *Roman de la Rose* and the Divine Comedy are two opposite forms of the same work—initiation into intellectual independence, satire on all contemporary institutions *and allegorical formulations of the great secrets of the Rosicrucian Society*. These important manifestations of occultism coincide with the epoch of the downfall of the Templars, since Jean de Meung or Clopinel, contemporary of Dante's old age, flourished during his most brilliant years at the Court of Philippe le Bel. The 'Romance of the Rose' is the epic of ancient France. It is a profound work in a trivial guise, as learned an exposition of the mysteries of occultism as that of Apuleius.

tain. "For as water will not ascend higher than the level of the first *Springhead* from whence it descendeth, so knowledge derived from Aristotle, and exempted from liberty of examination, will not rise again higher than the knowledge of Aristotle" ("Advancement of Learning," Book I. 37). Again: "Was not the *Persian Magic* a reduction of correspondence of the principles *and architectures of nature to the rule and policy of government?* Is not the precept of a musician, to fall from a discord or harsh accord upon a concord or sweet accord, alike true in affection?" (page 107, Book II., "Advancement of Learning," Wright). This Persian magic Bacon calls "*Philosophia prima, sive de fontibus scientiarum.*" "This science, therefore (*as I understand it*), I may justly report as deficient, for I see sometimes the profounder sort of wits, in handling some particular argument, will now and then draw a *bucket of water out of this well for their present use, but the springhead thereof* seemeth to me not to have been visited ; being of so excellent use for the disclosing of nature and the abridgement of art" (*Ibid.*, p. 108). How is it we find the Rosicrucians studying especially *this Persian or Chaldæan Magic* exactly as Bacon does, and even upon the same subject—music as applied to the affections? In describing *foundation of Colleges*, Bacon writes: "For as water, whether it be the *Dew of Heaven* or the *Springs of the Earth*, doth scatter and leese itself in the ground, unless it be collected into some receptacle where it may by union comfort and sustain itself; and for that cause the industry of man hath made and framed *Springheads, Conduits, Cisterns, and Pools*, &c. ("Advancement," II., i. 3). ("Quemadmodum enim Aqua, sive ex *Cœlesti Rore descendens*, sive *ex fontibus scaturiens,*" &c., 1638.) The Rosicrucians, according to Mosheim, drew their title or name from *ros crux* or *dew Cross*. And it is certain the Rosicrucians termed their headquarters or source

The Rose of Flamel, of Jean de Meung, and of Dante, blossomed on the same rose-tree." This indeed may well be believed, for there is a large amount of evidence pointing to the origin of the Rosicrucian revival of the seventeenth century in the Knight Templars.

a fountain or well. "Quod sit Castellum in quo Fratres degunt?" (Gassendus, 1630). Castellum means not only a town or village, but a *conduit or pipe to convey water* (Ainsworth's "Latin Dictionary").

ROSE AND LILY.

The Rose and the Lily were the two flowers especially representative and emblematic of the Rosicrucian fraternity. Their jewel was a crucified rose mounted on a Calvary, and for the connection of the Lily or Fleur-de-Lis with the society, I must refer the reader to Hargreave Jennings' "Rosicrucians, their Rites and Mysteries" (chapter viii., vol. i.) where he will find a strange history of the *Fleur-de-Lis, Lucifera Lisses*, &c. Now it is very curious to find the author of the plays frequently introducing the *Rose in context with the Lily* :—

> Of Nature's gifts, thou may'st with Lilies boast,
> And with the half-blown Rose.
> ("King John," act iii. sc. 1.)

> 'Nor did I wonder at the Lily's white,
> Nor praise the deep vermilion of the Rose.
> (Sonnets, 98.)

> Their silent war of Lilies and of Roses.
> ("Lucrece," 71.)

> That even for anger makes the Lily pale,
> And the red Rose blush at her own disgrace.
> ("Lucrece," 477.)

> The air hath starv'd the Roses in her cheeks,
> And pinch'd the Lily tincture of her face.
> ("Two Gentlemen of Verona," act iv. sc. 4.)

The religious character of the Lily is evidently connected with Solomon, "Consider the Lilies of the field," &c. We find Bacon, in a letter to King James I., writing:—"It is observed upon a place in the Canticles by some ; *Ego sum flos Campi et Lillium Convallium*, that *à dispari*, it is not said, *Ego sum flos Horti et Lillium Montium ;* because the *Majesty* of that *Person* is not enclosed for a few nor appropriate for the great" (*i.e.*, "I am the Flower of the Field, and the Lily of the Valleys, that it is not said,

I am the flower of the garden, and the Lily of the mountains
James I. was, we believe, a Mason.*

It seems to us Bacon is addressing the king in *masonic language*, with a side hint for Solomon. In this letter Bacon says, "Now the *corner-stone* is laid of the mightiest monarchy in Europe." Is Bacon implying, by a compliment to the king, that he (Bacon) is the flower of the *fields* and the *Lily of the Valley*—the king (seated on a higher place) the flower of *the garden* and Lily of the *mountains?* The next letter is to Sir John Davies (upon the king's coming in), and concludes, "*So desiring you to be good to concealed poets.*" How could Sir John Davies favour Bacon's advancement through this allusion? My opinion is that this was meant as a possible recommendation to the king, and suggests some *secret society or brotherhood, and the claims arising out of it.* This quotation proves not only that Bacon was "*a concealed poet,*" but that there were *other concealed poets, bound by brotherhood to do each other service.* Sir John Davies wrote a poem upon the "Immortality of the Soul," a highly metaphysical and, we might almost say, masonic poem. The thoughtful reader must see that Bacon could have no claim upon Sir John Davies' favour with the king, from the fact that he (Bacon) alone was a "*concealed poet,*" unless Sir John Davies understood this in some reciprocal sense, as a secret sign between members of a fraternity. And it is curious this letter bears date 1603,† the year Robert Fludd adduces as heralding, by the new stars in the breast of the Swan

> * "Why doth my face so much enamour thee,
> That to the garden fair thou turnest not,
> Which under the rays of Christ is blossoming?
> There is the *Rose* in which the *Word Divine*
> Became incarnate; *there the Lilies are*
> By whose perfume the good way was discovered."
> (Canto XXIII., "Paradiso," Dante.)

James I. was a Grand Master of Masonry, 1603 (see "Royal Masonic Cyclopædia," p. 285, M'Kenzie). So was also William Herbert, Earl of Pembroke.

† This is also the date (1603) of those strange Astrological Notes in Bacon's hand, which Spedding discovered written upon the title-page of "Hermes Stella."

and in Serpentarius,* the augmentation, if not the formation upon a new basis, of the society of Rosy Cross. Bacon does not say a "*concealed poet*," but uses the plural, "*concealed poets*," showing there was a bond of brotherhood between Davies and himself, if not others. It is difficult to imagine or ascribe a reason for this concealment, unless it had some religious or some reforming and advanced views connected with it. The Freemasons, as far as we know, did not exist at this period. But we can easily imagine the Rosicrucians, who called themselves *Literati*, being connected with Poetry. The reasons for this belief are obvious, for they called themselves the *Literati of Apollo*, who was the God of Music and Song; and we find references in their writings to Parnassus, Helicon, the Muses, so often as to produce the conviction that, joined to their ends of reforming philosophy and arts, they indulged in poetical literature.

Amongst Bacon's fragments is an Essay upon *Fame*. We find it in the first part of the 1671 "Resuscitatio," and it is curiously not included in the Essays. It stands alone, and the title is printed in extraordinary large capitals, quite one inch in height. The style is exceedingly unlike Bacon's Essays, being obscure, half allegorical, and entirely inapplicable to *Fame* in its usually accepted sense. The title of the celebrated Rosicrucian first Manifesto of 1614 was "*Fama Fraternitatis; or a discovery of the Fraternity of the most Laudable Order of the Rosy Cross.*" It was reprinted with the "Confessio Fraternitatis" and the

* "There appeared also of late a new star *in the breast of Cygnus*, which has now lasted for twelve whole years" ("Description of the Intellectual Globe").

"God, indeed, hath already sent messengers which should testify His will, to wit, some new stars which have appeared in *Serpentarius and Cygnus*" (Confession of Rosicrucian Fraternity, p. 93, Waite's "Real Hist. Rosicrucians").

"Cum igitur stellas in longitudine signi istius Iovis, in Serpentario repertas, et illas similiter Cygni ruminaverimus; Iovis conjunctionem cum Saturno, circa tempus apparitionis earum, et non multum ante revelationem Fraternitatis istius de Rosea Cruce, speculari nobiscum proposuimus" (De Characteribus Mysticis, "Tract. Apol.," p. 75. 1617, Fludd). This date was 1603.

"Allgemeine Reformation der Ganzen Welt" at Frankfort-on-the Maine in 1615. It is the *first genuine Rosicrucian manifesto* of which there is proof indubitable, for the "Reformation of the whole Wide World," though anonymously printed the same year, was borrowed entirely from the 77th advertisement of Boccalini's "Ragguagli di Parnasso," and was disclaimed by writers like Fludd. I therefore venture to suggest Bacon's fragment upon "*Fame*," may possibly allude in guarded language to the celebrated "Fama." "The *Poets* make *Fame* a *monster*. They describe her in part, finely and elegantly; and in part, gravely and sententiously. They say, look how many feathers she hath, so many eyes she hath underneath: so many tongues, so many voices; she pricks up so many ears. This is a flourish: there follow excellent *parables ;* as that she gathereth strength in going; that she goeth upon the ground, and *yet hideth her head in the clouds.*" In chapter v. of the "Confessio Fraternitatis R. C., 1615," we read: "A thousand times the unworthy may clamour, a thousand times may present themselves, yet God hath commanded our ears that they should hear none of them, and *hath so compassed us about with His clouds,** that unto us His servants no violence can be done; wherefore now no longer are we beheld by human eyes, *unless they have received strength borrowed from the eagle*" (Waite, p. 90, "History of Rosicrucians").

The Rosicrucian pamphlets mentioned were published in five languages, and may not Bacon be hinting at this in the words "*so many tongues*," "*so many voices*"? And in making *Fame* a monster, there is the suggestion implied of a shapeless, headless, or formless creation, which was exactly the character of this Brotherhood—its origin, founder, pretensions, being always in-

---

* "As to the heathen antiquities of the world, it is in vain to note them for deficient; deficient they are, no doubt, consisting mostly of fables and fragments, but the deficience cannot be holpen, *for antiquity is like* FAME, *Caput inter nubila condit*, her head is muffled from our sight" ("Two Books of the Advancement," p. 92, Wright).

defined and without outline. Bacon continues: "That in the day time she sitteth in a watch-tower, *and flyeth most by night.*" This implies an active armed defence and look-out, joined to secrecy and mystery. The Rosicrucian publications were all issued anonymously, and left the public *in the dark* as to their real author, or the real source from whence they came. Bacon continues: "*And that she is a terror to great cities.*" In 1623, the date of the plays (first Folio), there was a meeting of thirty-six members of the Rosicrucians in Paris, and the reader will find in "De Quincey's" Essay, how the city was thrown into uproar and consternation, by certain placards attached to the walls.

THE RAVEN.

Bacon writes: "Neither is there such a sin against the Person of the Holy Ghost (if one should take it literally) as instead of *the likeness of a Dove*, to bring him down in the likeness of a *Vulture or Raven;* nor such a scandal to the Church, as out of the bark of Saint Peter to set forth the flag of a barge of Pirates and Assassins" ("Of Unity in Religion").

Compare the *Dove* and *Raven* in this passage from the "Chymical Marriage of Christian Rosencreutz" ("The Second Day," p. 109, Waite's "Real History of the Rosicrucians"). "I was so perplexed that, for great weariness, hunger and thirst seized me, whereupon I drew out my bread, cut a slice of it, which *a snow-white dove*, of whom I was not aware, sitting upon the tree espied, and therewith came down, betaking herself very familiarly with me, to whom I willingly imparted my food, which she received, and with her prettiness did again a little refresh me. But as soon as her enemy, *a most black Raven, perceived* it, he straight darted down upon the dove, and taking no notice of me, would needs force away her meat, who could not otherwise guard herself but by flight. Whereupon, both together flew toward the South, at which I was so hugely incensed and grieved, that without thinking, I made haste after the filthy Raven, and so, against my will, ran into one of the fore-mentioned ways a whole field's length. The Raven being thus chased away, and the Dove delivered, I first observed what I had inconsiderately done, and that I was already entered into a way, from which, under peril of punishment, I durst not retire, and though I had still wherewith to comfort myself, yet that which was worst of all was, that I had left my bag and bread at the Tree, and could never retrieve them, for as soon as I turned myself about, a contrary wind was so strong against me that it was ready to fell me, but if I went forward, I perceived no hindrance, wherefore I patiently took up my cross, got upon my feet, and resolved I would use my utmost endeavour to get to my journey's end before night. Now, although many apparent bye-ways showed themselves, I still proceeded with my compass, and would not budge one step from the meridian line. Howbeit, the way was oftentimes so rugged that I was in no little doubt of it. I constantly thought upon the Dove and Raven, and yet could not search out the meaning, until upon a high hill afar off I espyed a stately Portal, to which, not regarding that it was distant from the way I was in, I hasted, because the sun had already hid himself under the hills, and I could elsewhere see no abiding place, which I verily ascribe only to God, Who might have permitted me to go forward, and withheld my eyes that so I might have gazed beside this gate, to which I now made mighty haste, and reached it by so much daylight as to take a competent view of it. It was an exceeding Royal, beautiful Portal, whereon were carved a multitude of most noble figures and devices, every one of which (as I afterwards learned) had its peculiar signification. Above was fixed a pretty large Tablet, with these words, '*Procul hinc procul ite profani*,' and more that I was forbidden to relate."

This allegory is so transparent that it needs little apology for interpretation. The words in Latin, "*Procul hinc procul ite profani*," are but a transcript of Virgil's

> Procul, O ! procul este, profani,
> Conclamat vates, totoque absistite loco.
> (Book VI., 258, 259, "Æneid.")

In the notes to "Anthon's Virgil" by Metcalfe we read, "*Procul, O ! procul*, &c. This was the solemn preamble with which the celebration of the *Sacred Mysteries* used to be ushered in, the form of expression in Greek being ἑκάς, ἑκὰς, ἐστὲ βέβηλοι" (p. 476). Warburton says: "The *procul, O procul este profani!* of the Sybil is a literal transition of the formula used by the mystagogue at the opening of the *Mysteries*" ("Diving Legation," p. 270). I have in my possession a copy of Khunrath's "Amphitheatrum Sapientiæ Æternæ." It contains a curious number of symbolical Rosicrucian charts. A remarkable one depicts the portals of a gigantic subterranean passage, and upon a stone over the gateway are the words, "*Procul hinc Abeste Profani!*" *i.e.*, "From hence depart ye profane (uninitiated) ones!" This proves to anyone conversant with this subject, the Mysteries—and probably the Eleusinian Mysteries (Virgil's Sixth Book)—were implied behind these words. It is not difficult to see in the secrecy and brotherhood of societies, like the Rosicrucians, the only safety from the persecution of the *Raven*, or Papal power, existed.

WEAPON-SALVE.

Bacon writes : "It is constantly received and avouched *that the anointing of the weapon that maketh the wound* will heal the wound itself " * (Century x., 998, " Natural History ").

* "We smile at the *sympathy* of 'the weapon-salve ;' but we must not forget that this occult power was the received philosophy of the days of our Rosicrusian. Who has not heard of 'the sympathetic powder' of Sir Kenelm Digby, by which the bloody garter of James Howell was cured, and consequently its pleasant owner, without his own knowledge? or of the 'sympa-

A curious tract was written by Fludd in reply to one Foster, who had declared, in a book attacking Fludd, that to "*cure by applying the salve to the weapon is magical and unlawful.*" The title of this book was, "A Sponge to wipe away the Weapon-salve." Fludd replied by, "The Squeezing of Parson Foster's Sponge," 1631, 4to. (It is also found bound up with the "Philosophia Moysaica," published 1638, Goudæ.) Fludd undertakes in this reply to answer in the affirmative this question, "An curatio vulnerum præstita per unguentum armarium veneficium sit et illicita?" Bacon continues: "In this experiment, upon the relation of men of credit (though myself as yet am not fully inclined to believe it), you shall note the points following. First, the ointment, wherewith this is done, is made of divers ingredients, whereof the strangest and hardest to come by, are *the moss upon the skull of a dead man unburied;* and the fats of a boar and a bear, killed in the act of generation. These two last I could easily suspect to be prescribed as a starting hole; that if the experiment proved not, it might be pretended, that the beasts were not killed in the due time; for as for the moss, *it is certain there is a great quantity of it in Ireland, upon slain bodies laid on heaps unburied.* The other ingredients are, the bloodstone in powder and some other things, which seem to have a virtue to stanch blood; as also the moss hath. And the description of the whole ointment is to be found in the chemical dispensatory of Crollius. Secondly, the same kind of ointment applied to the hurt itself worketh not the effect, but only applied to the weapon. Thirdly, (which I like well), they do not observe the confecting of the ointment under any certain constellation, which commonly is the excuse of magical medicines, when they fail that they were not

thetic needles' of the great author of 'Vulgar Errors,' by which, though somewhat perplexed, he concluded that two lovers might correspond invisibly ? and, above all *others, the warts of the illustrious Verulam, by sympathy* with the lard which had rubbed them, wasting away as the lard rotted when nailed on the chamber window? Lord Bacon acquaints us that 'It is constantly received and avouched, that *the anointing of the weapon that maketh the wound* will heal the wound itself'" (D'Israeli's "Amenities of Literature").

made under a fit figure of heaven. Fourthly, it may be applied to the weapon, though the party hurt be at a great distance," &c. Is Bacon laughing at us? It hardly seems so. He concludes: "Lastly, it will cure a beast as well as a man; which I like well, because it subjecteth the matter to an easy trial."

The fact Bacon condescends to record or discuss such a subject at all is astonishing in the face of his denunciations elsewhere of impostures and quackery. He evidently was studying the Rosicrucians, for Crollius, as well as Fludd, was a member of the fraternity. Rawley concludes his preface thus: "I will conclude with an usual speech of his Lordship's, that this work of his *Natural History* is the world as God made it, and not as men have made it,—*for that it hath nothing of imagination.*" This is an astounding assertion, seeing it is full of extraordinary marvels— more or less of a Rosicrucian or Alchemical nature. It is my sincere conviction that Bacon's "Natural History," is an imitation of Solomon's work upon trees and plants, he mentions in the "New Atlantis." It is therefore a Rosicrucian "*Book of Nature*" *par excellence*, and the fact it is always to be found bound up with and was published with the "New Atlantis," or "Land of the Rosicrucians," goes a long way towards endorsing this theory. The title-page engraving is thoroughly Masonic, and in touch with the Creation of Light (Genesis), with the two pillars of the Lodge—Jachiz and Boaz.

In one of Robert Fludd's works ("De Macrocosmi Historia") he gives a chart of Nature evidently taken from Antiquity. It is circular, consisting of concentric circles representing the nine spheres, the animal, vegetable, and mineral kingdoms, with the globe of the world for centre, with an *ape* seated upon it. The *ape* is held by a chain attached to the wrist, the other end being held by an immense female figure representing Nature. The woman's right wrist is also bound by a chain to the throne of the Almighty. This, of course, is an emblem of the *chain of natural causes, or of natural law* descending from God to Nature, and from Nature to Man. About the figure of the monkey are the words—

> L'homme est le singe de la nature.

This is indeed the Darwin theory with a vengeance!

> But man, proud man,
> Drest in a little brief authority,
> Most ignorant of what's he most assured,
> *His glassy essence like an angry ape*
> Plays such fantastic tricks before high heaven
> As make the angels weep; who with our spleen
> Would all themselves laugh mortal.
>
> ("Measure for Measure," act ii. sc. 2.)

"*It is true* that the *Ape* is a merry and bold beast. *And that* the same *heart* likewise of an *Ape*, applied to the neck or head, helpeth the wit, and is good for the *Falling sickness* ("Sylva Sylvarum," Cent. x. 978).

This is very curious, because we might feel inclined to believe Bacon is not serious when he makes these assertions, and only alluding to them in a spirit of irony.

D'Israeli writes:—"This Rosacrusian philosopher seeks for man in nature herself, and watches that creative power in her little mortal miniatures. In his Mosaic philosophy, founded on the first chapter of Genesis, our seer, standing in the midst of Chaos, separates the three principles of the creation: the palpable darkness—the movement of the waters—*at length the divine light!* The corporeity of angels and devils is distinguished on the principle of *rarum et densum*, thin or thick. Angelic beings, through their transparency, reflect the luminous Creator; but, externally formed of the most spiritual part of water or air, by contracting their vaporous subtilty, may "visibly and organically talk with man." The devils are of a heavy gross air; so Satan, the apostle called "the prince of air;" but in touch they are excessive cold, because the spirit by which they live—as this philosopher proceeds to demonstrate—drawn and contracted into the centre, the circumference of dilated air remains icy cold. From angels and demons, the Rosacrusian would approach even to the Divinity; calculating the infinity by his geometry, he reveals the nature of the Divine

Being, as '*a pure monad, including in itself all numbers.*' A paradoxical expression, lying more in the words than the idea, which called down an anathema on the impiety of our Theosophist, for ascribing 'composition unto God.' The occult philosopher warded off this perilous stroke. 'If I have said that God is in composition, I mean it not as a part compounding, but as the sole compounder, in the apostolic style, "He is over all, and in all."' *He detects the origin of evil* * *in the union of the sexes; the sensual organs of the mother of mankind were first opened by the fruit which blasted the future human race.* He broods over the mystery of life —production and corruption—regeneration and resurrection! On the lighter topics of mortal studies he displays ingenious conceptions. The title of one of his treatises is 'De Naturæ Simia,' or '*The Ape of Nature,*'—*that is,* ART *! a single image, but a fertile principle*" (D'Israeli's "Amenities of Literature," Fludd).

THE CHAIN OF NATURE.

"The *chain of Nature* hath its highest and *last link* fastened unto the foot of *Jupiter's* chair in heaven, as the lower is fixed on the earth" (To the Judicious and Discreet Reader. "Mosaicall Philosophy," Robert Fludd, 1659).

Compare Bacon: "Nor need we wonder if the horns of Pan

---

* The same view taken in the Sonnets:—

> The expense of spirit in a waste of shame
> Is lust in action; and till action, lust
> Is perjured, murderous, bloody, full of blame,
> Savage, extreme, rude, cruel, not to trust,
> Enjoy'd no sooner but despised straight,
> Past reason hunted, and no sooner had
> Past reason hated, as a swallow'd bait
> On purpose laid to make the taker mad;
> Mad in pursuit and in possession so;
> Had, having, and in quest to have, extreme;
> A bliss in proof, and proved, a very woe;
> Before, a joy proposed; behind, a dream.
> All this the world well knows; yet none knows well
> To shun the heaven that leads men to this hell.   (Sonnet cxxix.)

reach even to the heavens, seeing that the transcendentals of nature, or universal ideas, do in a manner reach up to divinity. And hence the famous chain of Homer (that is, the chain of natural causes), was said to be *fastened to the foot of Jupiter's throne*" (Book II., "De Augmentis," vol. iv., p. 322. "Phil. Wks.," E. & S.).

Again: "Give unto faith the things which are faith's. For the heathen themselves concede as much in that excellent and divine fable of the *golden chain;* namely, that men and gods were not able to draw Jupiter down to the earth, but contrariwise, Jupiter was able to draw them up to heaven"* (*Ib.*, p. 342).

PAN.

"Examinemus diligenter fabulas poëtarum et ingentia arcana sub iis inveniemus. Cur Pan (per quem universa natura significatur) ex 7 syringibus seu calamis fistulam composuit, per quam harmoniam dulcem edidit, nisi quia Spiritus intellectualis, qui movet cœlos, facit musicam correspondentem in his inferioribus. *Nam per compositione ex 7 fistulis significatur congregatio septem orbium planetarum et mirabili ipsorum harmonia in Cœlo et in terris*, hoc est, ubicunque natura illa universalis se extendit" ("De Naturæ Arcanis," p. 180, "Tractatus Apol.," 1617).

If we compare the above passage by Fludd with Bacon's fable of Pan, which he gives in the second book of the "De Augmentis" (p. 115, "Advancement," 1640), as one of the fables of the Poets, we find Bacon terming *Pan the universe*, and giving the same explanation of his pipe of seven reeds—the syrinx—in connection with the seven Planets—as Fludd: "The two engines which Pan bears in his hands, do point the one at harmony, the other at Empire; for the pipe of seven reeds doth evidently demonstrate the consent and harmony or discordant concord of Nature,

* "This visible and invisible fellowship of Nature *is that golden chain* so much commended, this is the marriage of heaven and riches, these are Plato's rings," &c. (p. 31, "Philosophy Reformed." Crollius, 1657).

or manifest expiations in Nature, which is caused by the motion of the seven wand'ring stars, for there are no other errors or manifest expiations in heaven save those of the seven Planets." *
Bacon writes: "Pan (ut et nomen ipsum etiam sonat) Universum, sive universitatem Rerum, repræsentat et proponit" (Lib. II., p. 522, "De Augmentis"). The reader will perceive how exactly Bacon repeats Fludd's ideas.

"In this universal subject they found the natures of all particulars, and this is signified to us by that maxim: '*Qui Proteum novit, adeat Pana*'—'He who is familiar with Proteus is on the threshold of the knowledge of Pan.' *This Pan is their Chaos, or Mercury*, which expounds Proteus, namely, the particular creatures, commonly called individuals; for Pan transforms himself into a Proteus, that is into all varieties of species, into animals, vegetables, and minerals; for out of the *Universal Nature*, or first matter, all these are made, and Pan hath their properties in himself" ("Cœlum Terræ," p. 146, Vaughan, Waite's edition).

Compare Bacon's "Fable of Pan" as Universal Nature and Chaos: "Pan, as the very name imports, represents, or layeth open the *world of things*. Concerning his original there are only two opinions that go for current. For either he came of *Mercury*, that is, the *Word of God*, which the Holy Scriptures without all controversy affirm; and the Philosophers such as were the more divine saw; *or else from the confused seeds of things*. For some of the Philosophers held that the seeds and principles of Nature were even in the substance infinite, hence the opinion of similar parts *primordial* was brought in, which Anaxagoras either invented or celebrated" (Book II., "Advancement of Learning," p. 111, 1640).

Of Proteus Bacon writes, under the title, "Proteus or Matter": "The sense of this fable relates, it would seem, to the secrets of nature and the conditions of matter. For under the person of Proteus, Matter—the most ancient of all things, next to God—

---

* This is a proof of Bacon's cabalistic tendencies.

is meant to be represented. . . . And here the story is complete, as regards Proteus free and at large with his herd. For the universe with its several species according to their ordinary frame and structure, is merely the face of matter unconstrained and at liberty, with its flock of materiate creatures. Nevertheless if any skilful Servant of Nature shall bring force to bear on matter, and shall vex it and drive it to extremities as with the purpose of reducing it to nothing, then will matter (since annihilation or true destruction is not possible except by the omnipotence of God) finding itself in these straits, turn and transform itself into strange shapes, passing from one change to another till it has gone through the whole circle and finished the period ; when, if the force be continued, it returns at last to itself" ("Wisdom of the Ancients").

ORPHEUS.

"So to sing or to play that instead of stony rocks you could draw pearls, instead of wild beasts spirits, and instead of Pluto you could soften the mighty princes of the world" ("Confessio Fraternitatis," 1615, p. 89, Waite's "Real History of the Rosicrucians").

"How indeed was that wonderful philosophical music of Orpheus created, after whose bewitching songs even the stones and rocks danced ?" (R. Fludd, p. 112, "Tractatus Apol.," 1617).

Compare Bacon's "Orpheus, or Philosophy" ("Wisdom of the Ancients," 1617).

"So great was the power and alluring force of this harmony that he drew the woods and moved the very stones to come and place themselves in an orderly and decent fashion about him."

> Therefore the poet
> Did feign that Orpheus drew trees, stones, and floods ;
> Since nought so stockish, hard and full of rage,
> But music for a time doth change his nature.
> ("Merchant of Venice," act vi.)

STRIFE AND FRIENDSHIP.

"The author therefore concludeth upon these grounds, that it is but just and reasonable, to consent unto the opinions of the two notable and famous philosophers Heraclitus and Empedocles touching this point, whereof the first hath exposed it as an infallible maxim, *Quod omnia fiant per litem et amicitiam;* That all things are made and composed of *Strife and Friendship, that is to say, of hatred and love.* The last hath pronounced it for an oracle of truth, *Quod ex quatuor elementis, et ex amicitia et lite composita sit anima;* that the soul is composed of four elements, and of peace or concord, and contention or discord" ("Mosaicall Philosophy," p. 131, Robert Fludd, 1659).

Bacon writes: "*Strife and Friendship in Nature are the spurs of Motions and the Keys of Works*" (p. 203, vol. v., Wks., E. and S.). "In the sixty-third aphorism of the First Book of the 'Novum Organum,' Bacon mentions very approvingly the philosophers of antiquity who taught this philosophy of *opposites or contraries*. The strife and friendship of Empedocles, Heraclitus' doctrine how bodies are resolved into the different nature of fire" (Spedding).

Compare Sonnet 35—

> Such civil war is in my *Love and Hate*,
> That I an accessory needs must be
> To that sweet thief which sourly robs from me.

D'Israeli, describing Fludd's philosophy, writes: "Man exists *in the perpetual opposition of sympathies and antipathies*, and the Cabalist in the human frame beheld the contests of spirits, benevolent or malign, trooping on the four viewless winds* which were to be submitted to his occult potentiality" ("Amenities of Literature," 645).

The enormous part *Sympathy and Antipathy* play in Bacon's philosophy may be diligently found in his "Natural History."

---

* The Witches in "Macbeth" are quite in keeping with this idea—personified emblems of the malign and spiritual in Macbeth's character—the grey phantoms of his own soul beckoning him on to a bloody career of crime.

"There be many things that work upon the spirit of man *by secret Sympathy and Antipathy*" (Cent. x., p. 249, Exp. 960). Again: "There are many ancient and received traditions and observations touching the Sympathy and Antipathy of Plants" (p. 119, Cent. v.) See the "Sympathy and Antipathy" of Sounds. "All *concords* and *discords* of music are (no doubt) *sympathies* and *antipathies* of sounds" (Exp. 278, p. 72, Cent. iii., "Natural History"). "The experiment of *sympathy* may be transferred from instruments of strings to other instruments of *sounds*" (Exp. 281, *Ib.*).

THE GIVING OF NAMES.

"That it was not that pure and primitive knowledge of nature, by the light whereof *man did give names to other creatures in Paradise*," &c. (Lib. I., "De Augmentis").

"For behold it was not that pure light of natural knowledge, whereby man in Paradise was able *to give unto every living creature a name according* * to his propriety, which gave occasion to the fall," &c., &c. ("Of the Interpretation of Nature," p. 219, vol iii., "Phil. Wks.," E. and S.).

Compare the Preface to the "Fama Fraternitatis," 1614.

"It is addressed to 'the wise and understanding reader.'

"'Wisdome (sayeth Solomon) is a treasure unto men that never faileth, for she is the breth of the power of God and an inherence flowing from the glory of the Almighty ; she is the brightness of the everlasting light, the unspotted mirror of the power of God, and the image of His goodness. She teacheth civility with righteousness and strength, she knoweth things of old, and con-

---

* "Quælibet ergo creatura, in creatione sua signacula habet quibus vita in ea inscribitur, et cujus actione movetur, crescit et multiplicatur, corporisque ejus substantia et figura ab alia creatura differt. Horum (inquam) signaculorum cognitione Adamus cuilibet rei creatæ nomen proprium attribuit, et earum proprietates tam occultas quam manifestas inde depromsit" ("Tract. Apol. De Characteribus Mysticis," p. 44, Pars I. Fludd, 1617).

jectureth aright what is to come ; she knoweth the subtleties of speaches and can expound darke sentences; she foreseeth signes and wonders, with the advent of seasons and times. With this treasure was our first father Adam before his fall fully indued ; hence it doth appear that after God had brought before him all the creatures of the field and the fowls under the heavens, *he gave to everyone of them their proper name, accordinge to their Nature*" (Appendix, Waite's " Real History of the Rosicrucians ").

Dr Abbott writes: "So important were names, the right names, indicating the essential natures of the things named, that to Bacon there seemed a natural connection between Adam the namer, and Adam the ruler of creatures. When fallen man should be restored to his pristine blessedness, he would regain the power of ruling, by regaining the power of naming: "*Whensoever he shall be able to call the creatures by their names, he shall again command them*" ("Bacon as a Philosopher," LXXI., Essays).

"But if things were well weighed, and this cloud of tradition removed, we should quickly find that God is more ready to give than we are to receive, for He made man (as it were) *for His playfellow*, that He might survey and examine His works" ("Anthroposophia Theomagica," p. 32, Thomas Vaughan, Waite's edition).

Compare Bacon:—"The glory of God is to conceal a thing, but the glory of the king is to find it out; as if, according to the innocent *play of children*, the Divine Majesty took delight to hide His works to the end to have them found out; and as if kings could not obtain a greater honour than to be *God's playfellows in that game*" (p. 45, Lib. I., "Advancement of Learning," 1640).

"Thou dost, perhaps, desire to know where they are at this present; believe it they have one common sepulchre, what *was once their mother is now their tomb*. All things return to that place from whence they came, and that my place is earth. If thou hast but leisure run over the *Alphabet of Nature, examine every letter, I mean every particular creature in her book.* What becomes of her grass, her coin, her herbs, her flowers? True it is both man and beast do use them, but this only by the way, for they rest not till they come to earth again " ("Cœlum Terræ ; or, the Magician's Heavenly Chaos," Thomas Vaughan, p. 128, Waite).

Compare : "Men seek truth in their own little world, and not in the great common world, for they disdain the *Alphabet of Nature* and *Primer Book* * of the Divine works, which if they did not they might perchance by degrees, and leisure after the knowledge of *simple letters* and spelling of syllables, come at last to read perfectly *the text and volume of the creatures*" ("Advancement of Learning," p. 37, 1640).

Compare :—

> Finds tongues in trees, *books in the running brooks*,
> Sermons in stones, and good in everything.
>
> ("As You Like It.")

FOUNDATIONS.

In the great "Confessio Fraternitatis R. C. ad Eruditos Europæ" of 1615, we read :

"Now concerning the first part, we hold that the meditations of our Christian father on all subjects which from the creation of the world have been invented, brought forth, and propagated by human ingenuity, through God's revelation, or through the service of Angels or spirits, or through the sagacity of understanding, or through the experience of long observation, are so great, that if all books should perish, and by God's almighty sufferance all writings and all learning should be lost, yet posterity will be able thereby *to lay a new foundation of sciences, and to erect a new citadel of truth*" (Waite's "Real History of the Rosicrucians," 89).

* "I had special and private converse with learned men, a thing most long'd for by a physician that desireth chiefly to turn over the BOOK OF NATURE" ("Philosophy Reformed," Osw. Crollius, p. 222, 1657).

This is such thoroughly Baconian language we are surprised it has not attracted attention before. For example, Bacon writes: "This one way remaineth that the business be wholly re-attempted with better preparations, and that there be throughout an *Instauration of sciences and arts*, and of all human learning raised from *solid foundations*" (Francis Verulum consulted thus, &c., "Advancement," 1640). We find in this "Confession" the Rosicrucians holding out to humanity exactly the same promise of conquest over Nature, as Bacon does. "On which work these profits will follow, that all those goods which Nature hath dispersed in every part of the earth *shall at one time and altogether be given you, tanquam in centro solis et lunæ*" ("Confessio Fraternitatis," 1615, ch. xiii., p. 97, Waite). This is what the entire Baconian philosophy is everlastingly promising and holding forth — that is, man's dominion and power over all things.

Nil nisi Parvulus.

One of the Rosicrucian doctrines concerning Natural discovery was that man must become first as *a little child*, submitting himself to be taught, and in Thomas Vaughan's " Lumen de Lumine," we find a picture of a little child, seated in an underground cave or vault, playing with pearls, and guarding a treasure with the motto, "*Nil nisi parvulus.*" Bacon repeats this idea thus: " All these idols are solemnly and for ever to be renounced, and the understanding must be thoroughly cleared and purged of them ; for the kingdom of man, which is founded in the sciences, cannot be entered otherwise than the kingdom of God—that is, in the condition of *a little child*." "Let men learn this, and becoming children again, and *infants*, not scorn to take A B C"*
(" Exp. History ").

* " Men seek truth in their own little world, and not in the great common world, for they disdain *the Alphabet of Nature, and Primer Book* of the Divine works" ("Advancement of Learning," p. 17, 1640).

SEALS.

Another favourite simile of the Rosicrucians is the Platonic metaphor to express the participation of idea with matter, as seal and impress or print. Plato uses this expression with regard to the stamp of a die or seal upon wax. We find Jacob Bœhmen working out this idea under the title "Signatura rerum." Bacon writes: "Certain it is that *Veritas* and *Bonitas* differ, but as the *seal and the print.*" In the Third Book of the "De Augmentis": "Neither are all these whereof we have spoken and others of like nature mere similitudes, as men of narrow observation may perchance conceive, but one and the very same footsteps and *seals of nature*, printed upon several subjects or matters." This image is conspicuous also in the plays and sonnets.*

> She carved thee for her *seal*, and meant thereby
> Thou shouldst print more, nor let that copy die. (Sonnet xi.).

This is prominent in the preface by Wats to Prince Charles, prefacing his translation of the "De Augmentis": "Yet with great applause he acted both these high parts of the greatest scholar and the greatest statesman of his time: and so quit himself in both, as one and the same person, in title and merit, became Lord Keeper of the Great Seal of England, and of the *Great Seal of Nature*† both at once, which is a mystery beyond the comprehension of his own times, and a miracle requires a great measure of faith in Posterity to believe it." Bacon writes at the termination of his Distribution Preface: "For God defend that

* The empress sends it thee thy *stamp*, thy *seal*.
("Titus Andronicus," act iv. sc. 2).

Bœhmen borrowed from Fludd's works entirely.

† Campanella writes: "Hic autem modus varius nascitur ex mistura ac castigatione contrariorum actiones adversas edentibus, quibus Deus Benedictus donavit agentes causas, ut instrumenta essent ad imprimendum in materia varios Ideæ primæ modos: quo in cunctis rebus ejus Bonitas elucescat. Quod forte sol non intelligit neque tellus. Sed ille solem ignemque facere cupit: hæc vero terram. Itaque debilitantur, ac res producunt proinde mistas, formatas primæ Ideæ figuris, cujus organa sunt *primaque sigilla*" ("De Sensu Rerum," p. 3, 1620).

we should publish the airy dreams of our own fancy for the real ideas of the world. But rather may he be so graciously propitious unto us that we may write the Apocalypse and true vision *of the impressions and signets* of the Creator upon the creature" (p. 38, 1640, "Advancement").

"But certainly we set the *stamps and seals** of our own images upon God's creatures" ("Exp. History").

It is well worthy attention the Rosicrucians professed (or rather furnish evidence in their writings) knowledge which in these days we should call Masonic. It seems highly probable the Mysteries (particularly the Sixth Book of Virgil as an exponent of those called by Antiquity the Eleusinian) formed one source of their hermetic knowledge. Khunrath gives as title-page engraving to his "Amphitheatrum Sapientiæ Æternæ," a portrait of two pillars (after the exact style of Bacon's title-page engraving, 1640, "Advancement"), surmounted with Sun and Moon, in evidently Masonic symbolism. Upon another engraving we find pictured the entrance to a huge subterranean passage, with the words from the Mysteries attached, "Procul, Procul este profanos." These words are to be refound in the "Chymical Marriage of Christian Rosycross," and as both these works are perfect examples of Rosicrucian literature, there can be little doubt, profound acquaintanceship with the Mysteries of antiquity was one of the secrets of the Society. Now it is very curious to find Bacon evidently possessed and saturated with this sort of knowledge, which has to a large extent entered into the style in which the Prefaces of the Instauration are penned.

Mr Waite writes: "In the third place, the Rosicrucian manifestoes contain the doctrine of the *signatura rerum*, which again is of Paracelsian origin. This is the 'magical writing' referred

* "These characters and letters, as God hath here and there incorporated them in the Sacred Scriptures, so hath He *imprinted them most manifestly on the wonderful work of creation, on the heavens, the earth, and on all beasts,* so that as the mathematician predicts eclipses, so we predict the obscurations of the Church, and how long they shall last" ("Confession of the Rosicrucian Fraternity").

to in the 'Fama,' and the mystic characters of that 'Book of Nature' which, according to the 'Confessio,' stands open 'for all eyes,' but 'can be read or understood by only a very few.' These characters are *the seal of God imprinted* 'on the wonderful work of creation, on the heavens, the earth, and on all beasts.' This '*signature of things*' is described by Paracelsus as 'a certain organic vital activity,' which is frequently 'expressed even in the exterior form of things; and by observing that form we may learn something in regard to their interior qualities, even without using our interior sight. We see that the internal character of a man is often expressed in his exterior appearance, even in the manner of his walking and in the sound of his voice. Likewise the hidden character of things is to a certain extent expressed in their outward forms. As long as man remained in a natural state, he recognised the signatures of things and knew their true character; but the more he diverged from the path of Nature, and the more his mind became captivated by illusive external appearances, the more this power became lost.' The same doctrine is developed by the most distinguished disciple of Paracelsus, the Kentish Rosicrucian, Robert Fludd. 'There are other invisible writings, secretly impressed on the leaves of Nature's book, which are not to be read or comprehended save with the eyes of understanding, being traced by the Spirit of the living God on the hidden fleshly tablets of our own hearts. . . . These internal and spiritual characters, constituting the interior writing, may also to the bodily eyes be the cause and origin of the things which do appear.' 'It is manifest,' he also remarks, 'that those vivific letters and characters impressed on the Bible and on the *great Book of Nature*,* and which we call arcane, because they are understood only by the few, are one thing, and that the dead, destroying letters of the same books, whose cortices

* Respuunt emin quasi Abecedarium Naturæ, Primumque in Operibus divinis tyrocinium; quod si non facerent, potuissent fortasse gradatim et sensim, post literas simplices et deinceps syllabas, ad *Textum et Volumen ipsum creaturarum* expedite legendum ascendere (Lib. I., p. 21, "De Augmentis," 1638).

contain the living and spiritual characters, are another" (Waite's "Real History of the Rosicrucians," p. 202).

Compare what Dr Abbott writes of "Bacon as a Philosopher" (p. 84, Introduction, "Essays"): "The similarity or analogy between different sciences is, according to Bacon, not accidental; it is as natural and as inevitable as the resemblance between the rippling surface of the sea, the ripple-marked clouds in the sky, the rippling lines on the sea-sand, and the hilly ripples of a sea-shaped undulating land—all of which are but Nature's footprints as she treads in one fashion on her various elements: for *these are not only similitudes, as men of narrow observation may conceive them to be, but the same footsteps of nature, treading or printing upon several subjects or matters.*"

"These characters and letters, as God hath here and there incorporated them in the Sacred Scriptures, so hath *He imprinted them most manifestly on the wonderful work of creation, on the heavens, the earth, and on all beasts,* so that as the mathematicians predict eclipses, so we prognosticate the obscurations of the Church, and how long they shall last" ("Confessio Fraternitatis," 1615, p. 94, Waite).

MAGNALIA, OR MARVELS.

Amongst the chief characteristics of the Rosicrucian pretensions was the claim to cure diseases. "In this, as well as in many other respects, they appear to be followers of Paracelsus, whom they profess to revere as a messenger of the divinity. Like him, they pretend to cure all diseases, *through faith and the power of the imagination,* to heal the most mortal disorders by a touch, or even by simply looking at the patient" ("Thaumaturgia," p. 359, 1835).

Compare these Rosicrucian ends proposed by Bacon,—this table being always found at the end or following "The New Atlantis" (or "Land of the Rosicrucians," according to John Heydon):—

"Magnalia naturæ præcipue quoad usus humanos." *

The Prolongation of Life.

The Restitution of Youth in some Degree.

The Retardation of Age.

The Curing of Diseases counted Incurable.

The Mitigation of Pain.

More easy and less loathsome Purgings.

The increasing of Strength and Activity.

The increasing of ability to suffer Torture or Pain."

("Sylva Sylvarum.")

The word "*Magnalia*" is borrowed from Paracelsus, and is another proof of Rosicrucian connection. The works of Paracelsus are described as found in Christian Rosy Cross' tomb or vault.

Bailey writes of the Rosicrucians: "They pretended *to protract the period of human life* by means of certain nostrums, and even to *restore youth*. They pretended to know all things. They are also called the Invisible Brothers, because they have made no appearance, but have kept themselves *incog.* for several years" (Bailey, "*Dict. in voce*"). Now it is very curious to find Bacon setting out certain claims to protract the period of human life, and even "to restore youth in some degree," in unmistakable language.

With regard to Bacon's doctrine of Spirits, which plays such a prominent part in his "History of Life and Death," and elsewhere, we find Professor Fowler writing: "It may be remarked that, though Bacon's account of 'Spirit' does not seem to be taken directly, at least without considerable modifications, from

---

* This page is to be found at the end of Bacon's "New Atlantis," and curiously carries the numbers 35, 36 as paging, these being the catalogue play number, and full number of plays in the 1623 Folio, "Troilus and Cressida" being omitted from catalogue ("Sylva Sylvarum," 1651).

Spedding writes:—"This page follows in *New Atlantis* in the original edition and concludes the volume."

The reader will see, that in connecting these *strictly Rosicrucian pretensions with the "New Atlantis," we have proof that John Heydon's "Land of the Rosicrucians" is really and not fancifully Bacon's "Atlantis."*

Paracelsus, there is much in common between the speculations of the two writers on this subject. I have not, however, thought it worth while to point this out in detail."

The curing of diseases counted *Incurable*.

Compare the King in "All's Well that Ends Well," act. ii. sc. 3:—

> *Lafen.* To be relinquisht of the Artists.
> *Par.* So I say both of Galen and Paracelsus.
> *Laf.* Of all the learned and authentic fellows.
> *Laf.* *That gave him out Incurable.*

THE LION'S WHELP.

It is evident the Rosicrucians, from the sixth chapter of their "Confession" (1615), looked to some divine event connected with the "*Lion of the Tribe of Judah.*" "But to the false and to impostors, and to those who seek other things then wisdom, we witness by these presents publikely, we cannot be betrayed unto them to our hurt, nor be known to them without the will of God, but they shall certainly be partakers of that terrible commination spoken of in our Fama, and their impious designs shall fall back upon their own heads, while our treasures shall remain untouched, till *the Lion shall arise* and exact them as his right, receive and imploy them for the establishment of his kingdom" (ch. iv., p. 92, Waite).

Bacon writes: "The blessing of Judas and Issachar will never meet, that the same people or nation should be both *the Lion's whelp*, and ass between burthens" ("Of Kingdoms and Estates"). Compare "Cymbeline":—

Sooth. [*Reads*] "When as a lion's whelp shall, to himself unknown, without seeking find, and be embraced by a piece of tender air; and when from a stately cedar shall be lopped branches, which, being dead many years, shall after revive, be jointed to the old stock, and freshly grow; then shall Posthumus end his miseries, Britain be fortunate and flourish in peace and plenty."

> Thou, Leonatus, art the lion's whelp;
> The fit and apt construction of thy name,
> Being Leo-natus, doth import so much.
> [*To Cymbeline*] The piece of tender air, thy virtuous daughter,
> Which we call "mollis aer"; and "mollis aer"
> We term it "mulier"; which "mulier" I divine
> Is this most constant wife; who, even now,
> Answering the letter of the oracle,
> Unknown to you, unsought, were clipp'd about
> With this most tender air.
>
> ("Cymbeline," last act, last scene.)

There is a passage in Ezekiel's prophecy where he represents *the church as a lofty Cedar Tree*, grown from a tender twig, so that under it "should dwell all fowls of every wing; in the shadow of the branches thereof shall they dwell."

The citation forms almost the last words of the 1623 Folio.

Madame Blavatsky writes: "'Behold the Assyrian (why not Atlantean, Initiate?) was *a cedar in Lebanon;* . . . his *height was exalted above all the trees;* . . . the cedars in the garden of God could not hide him, . . . so that all the trees of Eden . . . envied him' (Ezekiel xxxi. 3-9). Throughout all Asia Minor, the Initiates were called the 'trees of righteousness,' and the cedars of Lebanon, as also were some kings of Israel. So were the great adepts in India, but only the adepts of the left hand. When Vishnu Purâna narrates that the 'world was over-run with trees,' while the Prachetasas, who 'passed 10,000 years of austerity in the vast ocean,' were absorbed in their devotions, the allegory relates to the Atlanteans, and the adepts of the early fifth race, the Aryans" ("The Secret Doctrine," p. 494, vol. ii.).

The reader will see how curious it is to find this author connecting *Atlantis with the Cedar of Lebanon*, and thus bringing Solomon into touch historically with Bacon's fable of the "New Atlantis."

"In the little banqueting-house in the orchard at Gorhambury House, St Albans, supposed to have been built about 1565, a singular series of inscriptions exist. First, the walls have the liberal arts beautifully depicted upon them, and over them portraits of such learned men as had excelled in each, and under them verses expressive of the benefits derived from the study of them:—

> GRAMMAR.—' Lex sum sermonis, linguarum regula certa.
> Qui me non didicit cætera nulla petat.'
>
> DONATUS, LILLY, SERVIUS, and PRISCIAN.
>
> *ARITHMETIC.—'Ingenium exacuo numerorum arcano recludo.
> Qui numeros didicit quid didicisse nequit.'
>
> STIFELIUS, BUDŒUS, PYTHAGORAS.
>
> LOGIC.—' Divide multiplicis, res, explanoque latentio
> Vera exquiro falsa arguo cuncta probo.'
>
> ARISTOTLE, RODOLPH, PORPHYRY, SETON.
>
> MUSIC.—' Mitigo mærores et ecerbas lenio curas
> Gestiat ut placidis mens hilarata sonis.'
>
> ARIAN, TERPANDER, ORPHEUS.
>
> RHETORIC.—' Ille duce splendescit gratis prudentia verbis,
> Jamque ornata nitet qui fuit ante rudis.'
>
> CICERO, ISOCRATES, DEMOSTHENES, QUINTILLIAN.
>
> GEOMETRY.—' Corpora describo rerum et quo singula pacto,
> Apte sunt formis appropriata suis.'
>
> ARCHIMEDES, EUCLID, STRABO, APOLLONIUS.
>
> ASTROLOGY.—' Astrorum lustrans cursus veresque potentes
> Elicio miris fata futura modis.'
>
> REGIOMONTANUS, HALY, COPPERNICUS, PTOLEMY.

DE AMICITIA.—In amico ad monendo melius est successum quam fidem deesse. Omnia cum amico de libera: sed de ipso, prius.

DE AMORE.—Amor insane amicitia: illius affectas istuis ratio causa: et ea sola amicitia durat cui virtus basis est."

(M'Kenzie's "Masonic Cyclopædia.")

These are the *seven* liberal Arts and Sciences as illustrated in the Fellow Crafts or Second Degree in Masonry, viz.: Grammar,

---

* "ARITHMETIC.—The science of the proportion of numbers. In the lecture of the degree of Grand Master Architect, the candidate is reminded that a Mason is continually to *add* to his knowledge, never to *subtract* anything from the character of his neighbour, to *multiply* his benevolence, and to *divide* his means with a distressed brother."

Rhetoric, Logic, Arithmetic, Geometry, Music, and Astronomy. This is proof that Sir Nicholas Bacon, the father of Francis Bacon, was a Free-Mason.

"The preservation of these Arts as a part of the ritual of the Fellow-Craft's Degree, is another evidence of the antiquity of Freemasonry. These 'seven liberal arts,' as they were then for the first time called, constituted, in the eighth century, the whole circle of the sciences. The first three were distinguished by the title of *trivium*, and the last four by that of *quadrivium;* and to their acquisition the labours and studies of scholars were directed, while beyond them they never attempted to soar. Mosheim, speaking of the state of literature in the eleventh century, uses the following language : 'The seven liberal arts, as they were now styled, were taught in the greatest part of the schools that were erected in this century for the education of youth. The first stage of these sciences was grammar, which was followed successively by rhetoric and logic. When the disciple, having learned these branches, which were generally known by the name of *trivium*, extended his ambition further, and was desirous of new improvement in the sciences, he was conducted slowly through the *quadrivium* (arithmetic, music, geometry, and astronomy) to the very summit of literary fame.'"

The orders of *Architecture* follow upon all this, and it is very striking to find, that as Geometry is the science on which Masonry is founded, Architecture is the art from which it borrows the language of its symbolic instruction. In the earlier ages of the Order, every Mason was either an operative mechanic or a superintending *architect*, and something more than a superficial knowledge of the principles of Architecture is absolutely essential to the Mason who would either understand the former history of the Institution or appreciate its present objects. It is very striking, Bacon in the first part, or, as it were, the very *foundations* of his "Instauration," gives us (the first part, viz., of the "De Augmentis," "Scientiarum," or "Advancement of

Learning," 1640) a title-page, where he entitles himself the *Architect of the Sciences*, and gives us in the motto at the foot of this page a further hint to Arithmetic, Geometry, or proportion, thoroughly Masonic in its suggestions :—

> Francisci de Verulamis
> Architectura Scientiarum.
> Deus Omnia
> In mensura, et numero, et ordine disposuit.

Rosicrucian Curiosities.

"For this writing of our '*Sylva Sylvarum*' is (to speak properly) not *Natural History*, but a high kind of *Natural Magic*. For it is not a description only of Nature, but a breaking of Nature, *into great and strange works*" (Experiment 93, " Sylva Sylvarum ").

"We see how *flies and spiders*, and the like, get a *Sepulchre in Amber*, more durable than the monument and embalming of a king" (*Ib*. Experiment 100).

"Also the exudation of Rock Diamonds *and Crystals*, which harden with time : also the induration of *Bead Amber*, which at first is a soft substance; as appeareth by the *flies* and *spiders* which are found in it; and many more, but we *will speak of them distinctly*" (*Ib*. page 22, "Experiment on Induration ").

"It is manifest, that *Flies, Spiders, Ants*, or the like small creatures, falling by chance into *amber*, or the Gums of Trees, and so finding a burial in them, do *never after corrupt or rot*, although they be soft and tender bodies" (Ex. 21, p. 6, "History of Life and Death ").

Everlasting Lamps.*

"There is a tradition, that *Lamps set in Sepulchres*, will last an incredible time" (Ex. 24, p. 6, "History of Life and Death ").

* "It will be sufficient to enumerate their belief in a secret philosophy, perpetuated from primeval times, *in ever burning lamps, in vision at a distance*," &c. (Waite's "Real History of the Rosicrucians," p. 209).

In Century iv. Bacon gives (Experiments 366 to 375) much consideration to this subject. "And there are traditions of *lamps* and candles, that have burnt a very long time in caves and tombs" (374).

Thomas Vaughan writes: "Jacob makes a covenant with Laban, that all the spotted and brown cattle in his flock should be assigned to him for his wages. The bargain is no sooner made but he finds an art to multiplie his own colours, and sends his father-in-law almost a wool-gathering. 'And Jacob took him rods of green poplar, and of the hasel and chesnut-tree, and pilled white strakes in them, and made the white appear which was in the rods; and hee set the rods which he had pilled before the flocks in the gutters, in the watering-trough, when the flocks came to drink, that they should conceive when they came to drink. And the flocks conceived before the rods, and brought forth cattle ring-straked, speckled, and spotted'" ("Magia Adamica," p. 103, Waite).

> *Shy.* When Jacob grazed his uncle Laban's sheep—
> This Jacob from our holy Abram was,
> As his wise mother wrought in his behalf,
> The third possessor; ay, he was the third—
>   *Ant.* And what of him? did he take interest?
>   *Shy.* No, not take interest, not, as you would say,
> Directly interest: mark what Jacob did,
> When Laban and himself were compromised
> That all the eanlings which were streak'd and pied
> Should fall as Jacob's hire, the ewes, being rank,
> In the end of autumn turned to the rams,
> And, when the work of generation was
> Between these woolly breeders in the act,
> The skilful shepherd peel'd me certain wands
> And, in the doing of the deed of kind,
> He stuck them up before the fulsome ewes,
> Who then conceiving did in eaning time
> Fall parti-colour'd lambs, and those were Jacob's.
>   ("Merchant of Venice," act ii.)

The great English Rosicrucian, Thomas Vaughan (Eugenius

Philalethes) writes : " But most excellent and magisterial is that oracle of Marcus Antoninus, who in his Discourse to himself, speaks indeed things worthy of himself. The Nature (saith he) of the universe delights not in any thing so much, as to alter all things and then to make the like again. This is her tick tack, shee plays one game, to begin another. The matter is placed before her like a piece of wax, and shee shapes it to all formes, and figures. Now shee makes a bird, now a beast, now a flowere, then a frog, and shee is pleas'd with her own magicall performances, as men are with their own fancies. Hence she is call'd of Orpheus, 'the mother that makes many things, and ordaines strange shapes, or figures'" ("Cœlum Terræ; or the Magician's Heavenly Chaos," p. 128, Waite).

Compare this with the following of Shakespeare's supposed sonnets :—

SONNET CXIII.

Since I left you, mine eye is in my minde,
And that which governes me to goe about,
Doth part his function, and is partly blind,
Seemes seeing, but effectually is out :
For it no forme delivers to the heart
Of birds, or flower, or shape which it doth lack,
Of his quick objects hath the mind no part,
Nor his owne vision holds what it doth catch :
For if it see the rud'st or gentlest sight,
The most sweet favour or deformedst creature,
The mountaine, or the sea, the day, or night :
The Crow or Dove, it shapes them to your feature.
  Incapable of more repleat. with you,
  My most true minde thus maketh mine untrue.

The same Rosicrucian writes : " Is there anything lost since the creation ? Would'st thou know his very bed and pillow ? *It is the earth.* How many cities dost thou think have perished by the sword ? How many by earthquakes ? And how many by the deluge ? Thou dost perhaps desire to know where they are at this present : believe it they have one common sepulchre, *what was once their mother, is now their tomb.* All things return to that place from whence they came, and that very place is earth" ("Cœlum Terræ; or the Magician's Heavenly Chaos," p. 128, Waite).

Compare with the words in italics this passage from "Romeo and Juliet":—

> The earth *that's nature's mother is her tomb ;*
> *What is her burying-grave that is her womb.* *
>
> (Act ii. sc, 3.)

From long and intimate study of Lord Bacon's works, we feel persuaded he felt himself a divine instrument, and a man charged with a great message to mankind. We see this hinted at in the following words:—"For I am a trumpeter only, I do not begin the fight; perchance one of those of whom Homer:—

Καίρετε κέρυκες, διὸς "Αγγελοι ἠ' δὲ καί ἀνδρῶν"

(Book IV., p. 117, "Advancement of Learning").

Throughout Bacon's works there are interspersed hints as if he was ever looking to posterity for the realisation of some divine moment or event connected with his labours. This is most apparent in the title of one of his books only published a century after his death—"Valerius Terminus"—by which some end or finality is implied. The internal character of the work bears this out. For it deals with a "*scale*" reminding us of the fourth division of the "Instauration" missing, entitled "Scala Intellectus," or method of the mind in things exemplified. Under this section in the Distribution Preface, are introduced the Types and Platforms of Invention, in certain selected subjects worthy of remark, which we are convinced allude to the plays. We find in "Valerius Terminus," Bacon disclosing his mind upon his two methods of publishing. And we cannot believe this work was published by accident, and left in private hands without instructions, containing as it does such vital points. It seems to

---

* "For corruption is a reciprocal to generation : and they two, are as Nature two terms, or boundaries ; and the guides to life and death" ("Natural History," Century IV., Experiment 328, p. 73).

us it was intentionally reserved, that this point upon publishing privately (or reserved to a private succession of hands) might not prematurely be made known. This work is an example of the method of publishing in point to its own remarks.*

It is well worthy a passing remark that Roger Bacon (who, whether in any way connected with Francis Bacon by way of descent or not, was a remarkable character) must have exerted a powerful influence upon Bacon, inasmuch as joined to the identity of name, Roger Bacon was an experimentalist and discoverer after Francis Bacon's own heart.† Roger Bacon was a Friar, a member of the Order of St Francis, commonly called Franciscans. In "Romeo and Juliet" we find two holy *Franciscan Friars introduced*, viz., Friar Laurence and Friar John, the former playing a large part as Romeo's confessor and assistant to the lovers. The really striking part is that Friar Laurence is introduced as an Alchemist or Rosicrucian, that is if evidence is anything. For example, in the third scene, second act, with the first introduction of Friar Laurence, we find him immediately pictured as a herbalist or botanist, collecting weeds and flowers.

---

* The "Confessio Fraternitatis R. C. ad Eruditos Europæ" opens thus:—
"Whatsoever you have heard, O mortals, concerning our Fraternity by the *trumpet sound* of the Fama R. C., do not either believe it hastily, or wilfully suspect it" (1615).

Compare:—

>Let the bird of loudest lay
>On the sole Arabian tree,
>Herald sad and *trumpet* be,
>To whose sound chaste wings obey.
>
>("Phœnix and Turtle.")

† That Bacon was well acquainted with the works of his namesake Roger Bacon is certain. It has been remarked often how closely Bacon's four idols resemble the four hindrances to knowledge of Roger Bacon's "Opus Magus." But whether this was the real source of inspiration is, of course, only conjecture. But in "The History of Life and Death" we find Bacon has borrowed some stories from the "De Mirabel. Potest. Artis et Naturæ" of Roger Bacon. One of these is the story of the Lady of Formerey, or the Lady of the Wood, who, whilst seeking a white doe, met a forest ranger who had renewed his youth by means of an ointment which he had somewhere found in the forest.

SCENE III.—*Friar Laurence's Cell.*

Enter Friar Laurence, with a basket.

Fri. The grey-ey'd morn smiles on the frowning night,
Checkering the eastern clouds with streaks of light;
And flecked darkness like a drunkard reels
From forth day's path, and Titan's fiery wheels:
Now ere the sun advance his burning eye,
The day to cheer, and night's dank dew to dry,
I must up-fill this osier cage of ours,
With baleful weeds, and precious-juiced flowers.
The earth, that's nature's mother, is her tomb;
What is her burying grave, that is her womb:
And from her womb children of divers kind
We sucking on her natural bosom find;
Many for many virtues excellent,
None but for some, and yet all different.
O, mickle is the powerful grace, that lies
In herbs, plants, stones, and their true qualities:
For nought so vile that on the earth doth live,
But to the earth some special good doth give;
Nor aught so good, but, strain'd from that fair use,
Revolts from true birth, stumbling on abuse:
Virtue itself turns vice, being misapplied;
And vice sometime 's by action dignified.
Within the infant rind of this weak flower
Poison hath residence, and med'cine power:
For this, being smelt, with that part cheers each part;
Being tasted, slays all senses with the heart.
Two such opposed kings encamp them still
In man as well as herbs,—grace, and rude will;
And, where the worser is predominant,
Full soon the canker death eats up that plant.

Now, we maintain this is a complete picture of a dealer in Natural Magic, as we meet them over and over again either as Alchemists, Rosicrucians, or Occultists of the Mediæval and Renaissance periods. Baptista Porta, in his treatise on "Natural Magic," enumerates a whole catalogue of secret formulæ for producing extraordinary effects by employing the occult powers of nature. Even the magic of the ancient Chaldæans was but a profound knowledge of the power of simples and minerals. Study the lengthy passage quoted, and it will be evident the ghostly Friar Laurence is a student in this Natural Magic.

> O, mickle is the powerful grace, that lies
> In *herbs*, plants, stones, and their true qualities.
>
> In man as well as *herbs*—grace, and rude will.

And we see him gathering his "baleful weeds" in the grey dawn, before the sun has arisen, whilst the dew was on them, an essential thing, which shows the author's complete knowledge on this point. We find this repeated in "Cymbeline" by the Queen:—

> *Queen.* Whiles yet the dew's on ground, gather those flowers;
> Make haste: Who has the note of them?
>
> (Act i. sc. 6.)

It was always before dawn, or during the night, that herbs were gathered for magical purposes:—

> In such a night
> Medea gather'd the enchanted herbs
> That did renew old Æson.
>
> ("Merchant of Venice.")

The Franciscan Friar, Roger Bacon, in his treatise on the "Admirable Force of Art and Nature," devotes the first part of his work to natural facts. He gives us hints of gunpowder, and predicts the use of steam as a propelling power. The hydraulic press, the diving-bell, and kaleidoscope are all described. ("Alchemy, or the Hermetic Philosophy.") Now Francis Bacon in his "New Atlantis" completely parallels all this, giving us predictions of telephones, phonographs, explosives unquenchable in water, torpedoes, and all sorts of inventions realised since his age. Mackenzie, in his "Royal Masonic Cyclopædia," enters Roger Bacon amongst the list of Rosicrucians, and describes him thus:—

"BACON, ROGER.—A famous Franciscan friar of the eleventh century, and a believer in the philosopher's stone and in astrology. He is said to have invented gunpowder; but this is doubtful, as are also his pretensions to be considered the originator of telescopes and spectacles. He made a famous brazen head, which, artfully fitted with acoustic apparatus, gave forth oracles."

Now it is a very curious parallel that Friar Laurence is not only a *Franciscan friar*, like Roger Bacon, but (in scene vi. act 2) alludes to *Gunpowder!*

> *Friar Laurence.* These violent delights have violent ends,
> And in their triumph die; like *fire and powder*,
> Which, as they kiss, consume.

Romeo and Juliet repeatedly bring in the word ghostly in connection with Friar Laurence :—

> *Romeo.* Hence will I to my *ghostly father's* cell,
> His help to crave, and my dear hap to tell.
>
> (Act ii. sc. 3.)
>
> *Friar Laurence.* Go and pardon sin! wast thou with Rosaline?
> *Romeo.* With Rosaline, my *ghostly father?*
>
> (*Ibid.*, sc. 3.)
>
> *Juliet.* Good even to my *ghostly confessor.*
>
> (Act ii. sc. 6.)
>
> *Romeo.* How hast thou the heart
> Being a divine, a *ghostly* confessor,
> A sin absolver, and my friend profess'd,
> To mangle me with that word banished?
>
> (Act iii. sc. 3.)

It is indeed curious to find Friar Laurence constantly bringing in gunpowder in his speeches. Here it is again—

> *Friar L.* Thy wit, that ornament to shape and love,
> Mis-shapen in the conduct of them both,
> Like *powder* in a skilless soldier's flask,
> To set a fire by thine own ignorance.
>
> (Act iii. sc. 3.)

Again—

> *Romeo.* As if that name,
> Shot from the deadly level of a gun
> Did murder her.
>
> (Act iii. sc. 3.)
>
> *Romeo.* Let me have
> A dram of poison; such soon-speeding gear
> As will disperse itself through all the veins,
> That the life-weary taker may fall dead;
> And that the trunk may be discharg'd of breath
> As violently as *hasty powder fir'd*
> *Doth hurry from the fatal cannon's womb.*
>
> (Act. v. sc. 1.)

TO BACON'S WRITINGS. 353

THE PERFECT NUMBER 36.

It is a remarkable coincidence that the 1623 Folio, known by the name of Shakespeare, contains exactly thirty-six plays,* because this was the perfect number of Pythagoras. The number ONE was the point within the circle, and denoted the central fire, or God, FOUR referred to the Deity, for it was considered the *number of numbers*. It is the first solid figure; a point being 1, *a line* 2, *a superficies* 3, *and a solid* 4. It was also the TETRACTYS; a *Word* sacred amongst the Pythagoreans, and used as a most solemn oath, because they considered it the root and principle, the cause and maker of all things. Plutarch interprets this word differently. He says it is called Κοσμος, the *World, and therefore refers to the number Thirty-six* (36), which consists of the first *four odd numbers*, added into the first *four even ones*—thus :—

$$1 + 2 = 3$$
$$3 + 4 = 7$$
$$5 + 6 = 11$$
$$7 + 8 = 15$$

Total . 36

(Lecture IX., Oliver's "Signs and Symbols," p. 199. 1837.)

"The Tetractys was no other than the Glorious Tetragrammaton of the Jews. The sum of all the principles of Pythagoras is this. The *Monad* is the principle of all things. From the Monad came the intermediate *Duad*, as matter subjected to the cause *Monad*; from the Monad and the intermediate Duad, numbers; *from numbers, points ; from points, lines ; from lines, superficies ;* from superficies, solids; from these solid bodies whose elements are *four*—fire, water, air, earth; of all which transmutated and totally changed the world consists" (Stanley, "History," Phil., vol. iii., pp. 1, 100).

* "Troilus and Cressida" is strangely omitted from the catalogue of the plays in the 1623 Folio Shakespeare,—making the total number 36. This, we are convinced, was done *purposely* to give two cipher numbers, 35, 36, just as 52, 53 represent Shakespeare mathematically 1616.

Z

I here re-introduce for the benefit of readers unacquainted with my work, "Bacon, Shakespeare, and the Rosicrucians," two extracts showing the identity of John Heydon's "Voyage to the Land of the Rosicrucians" with Bacon's "New Atlantis." Line for line, and word almost for word, Heydon reproduces from beginning to end Bacon's narrative. Critics have replied by calling John Heydon a mountebank and impostor. They are ignorant of the fact *that an ideal Republic or Utopia was essentially a Rosicrucian dream*, exemplified in the "City of the Sun" by Campanella, and the "Reipublicæ Christianopolitanæ" of the Rosicrucian protagonist, John Valentine Andreas. We possess a copy of both the latter, and their resemblance to each other is striking. These Utopias are perfectly in keeping with the Reformation of Society, the Restoration of Knowledge, and the Renewal of Arts, which the Rosicrucians proposed. These were also Bacon's ends testified abundantly throughout his works. His mind was bent on *looking forward*, and we may see in the description of the scientific marvels of his "New Atlantis," anticipation of this century.

Heydon's "Voyage to the Land of the Rosicrucians."

"The morrow after our three dayes, there came to us a new man, cloathed in azure, save that his turban was white *with a small red crosse* [*] at the top. He had also a tippet of fine linnen. He did bend to us a little, and put his arms broad ; we saluting him in a very lowly manner. He desired to speak with some few of us, whereupon six onely stayed, and the

Bacon's "New Atlantis."

"The morrow after our three days were past, there came to us a new man that we had not seen before, clothed in blue as the former was, save that his turban was white, with *a small red cross on the top ;* [*] he had also a tippet of fine linen. At his coming in he did bend to us a little, and put his arms abroad. We of our parts saluted him in a very lowly and

---

[*] "We were all distributed amongst the Lords, but our old Lord and I, most unworthy, were to ride even with the King, each of us bearing *a snow-white ensign with a Red Cross*" ("Chemical Marriage of Christian Rosy Cross," 1616).

The Rosicrucian emblem was a red cross—the Red Cross of the Knight Templars, of whom they were the direct successors. See Hargreave Jennings. Emblem on title page of his book, "The Rosicrucians : their Rites and Mysteries."

rest avoided the room. He said:—
'I am by office governour of this house of strangers, and by vocation a Christian priest of the Order of the Rosie Crosse, and am come to offer you my service, as strangers and chiefly as Christians. The State hath given you licence to stay on land for the space of six weeks, and let it not trouble you if your occasions ask further time, for the law in this point is not precise.

* * *

"'We have sound-houses, where we practise and demonstrate all sounds and their generation. We have harmonies (read the "Harmony of the World") which you have not, of quarter and lesser kindes of sounds— divers instruments of musick to you unknown, some sweeter than any you have, together with bells and rings that are dainty and sweet. (See my book of "Geomancy and Telesmes.") We represent small sounds as great and deep, great sounds as extenuate and sharpe; we make divers tremblings and warblings of sounds which in their originall are entire. We represent and imitate all articulate sounds and letters (read my "Cabbala, or Art, by which Moses showed so many signs in Ægypt"), and the voices and notes of many beasts and birds. We have certain helps which, set to the ear, do further the hearing greatly. We have strange and artificiall ecchos, reflecting the voice

submissive manner, as looking that from him we should receive sentence of life or death. He desired to speak with some few of us; whereupon six of us only stayed, and the rest avoided the room. He said: 'I am by office governor of this House of Strangers, and by vocation I am a Christian priest; and therefore am come to you to offer you my service both as strangers, and chiefly as Christians. Some things I may tell you, which I think you will not be unwilling to hear. The state hath given you licence to stay on land for the space of six weeks. And let it not trouble you if your occasions ask further time, for the law in this point is not precise; and I do not doubt but myself shall be able to obtain for you such further time as shall be convenient.

* * *

"'We have also sound-houses, where we practise and demonstrate all sounds and their generation. We have harmonies, which you have not, of quarter-sounds, and lesser slides of sounds; divers instruments likewise to you unknown, some sweeter than any you have; with bells and rings that are dainty and sweet. We represent small sounds as great and deep, likewise great sounds extenuate and sharp. We make divers tremblings and warbling of sounds, which in their original are entire; we represent and imitate all articulate sounds and letters, and the voices and notes of beasts and birds. We have certain helps, which set to the ear do further the hearing greatly. We have also divers strange and artificial echos reflecting the voice many times, and as it were tossing it; and some that give back the voice louder than it came, some shriller, and some deeper; yea, some rendering the voice differing in

many times, and, as it were, to sing it, some that give back the voice louder than it came, some shriller, some deeper, some rendring the voice differing in the letters, or articular sound, from that they receive. We have also means to convey sounds in trunks and pipes, in strange lines and distances.'"

the letters or articulate sound from that they receive. We have also means to convey sounds in trunks and pipes in strange lines and distances.'"

These marvels so wonderfully realised at the present day in the speaking tube, telephone, phonograph, can hardly be called happy guesses. It is probable between Bacon's motto (attached to "Novum Organum" and "Advancement of Learning," 1640), from Daniel ("*Multi pertransibunt et augebitur scientia,*" Many shall go to and fro, and knowledge shall be increased), and these prophecies or forestalments of nineteenth century discoveries, there is a connection pointing to the end of the times. I am persuaded Bacon's "New Atlantis" is the most extraordinary realisation of modern discovery on record. Madame Blavatsky writes: "We are at the very close of the cycle of 5000 years of the present Aryan Kaliyuga; and between this time and 1897, there will be a large rent made in the Veil of Nature, and materialistic science will receive a death blow" ("The Secret Doctrine," vol. i., p. 612).

CHAPTER IV.

GENERAL REMARKS.

BACON, amongst the humours and errors of Learning, classes the opinion, "That of all sects and opinions, the best hath still prevailed." And he writes upon this, "For Time seemeth to be of the nature of a River, which carrieth down to us that which is light and blown up, and sinketh and drowneth, that which is weighty and solid" (Book I., p. 37, "Advancement"). This thoroughly agrees with what Spedding confessed to having realised, viz., Bacon's belief in some great pre-historic period, in which knowledge had been greater and more universal. The choice by Bacon of Plato's island of the New Atlantis for his ideal republic, carries this belief further out. Bacon evidently chose this site on account of its extreme pre-historic character, and with that delight in antithetic contrasts which he is so fond of, places his college of the six days upon it, and forestalls by sheer power of imagination the marvels of the scientific future. Bacon is fond of *uniting the old world to the new.* This is prominent in his ship device, whereby he imitates in the realm of science the voyages of Columbus. So we may also see in his choice of the island of the New Atlantis, as the site and field of modern discovery, the same uniting of the extremest antiquity with his ideal of man's attainments over nature in the future. Underneath all this lies dimly implied a restoration of knowledge, a returning full circle to what once he thought existed. Those who have studied Madame Blavatsky's "Secret Doctrine," will see how truly the supposed myth of the submerged island of the Atlantic is connected not only with Truth, but with secret doctrines of which the Egyptian Priests had evidently some

GENERAL REMARKS.

knowledge. It is our earnest conviction that Bacon had attained to extraordinary comprehension of Bible and esoteric, or what is called hermetic science.* We find this in the way he writes in his note-book disparagingly of the Greeks and Ægyptians, and goes back to Chaldæa † for authority. How are we to explain his statement in the preface to the "Instauration," that the "Commerce of the mind and of things might by any means be *entirely restored*"? This is exactly the language used in the Rosicrucian manifestoes, 1614. And it is remarkable that the character and plan of the "Instauration" is half divine, and borrowed from the six days of creation of Genesis. This is no fancied theory of ours. He closes his Distribution Preface with a prayer: "Wherefore if we labour with diligence and vigilance in thy works, thou wilt make us participants of thy vision and *of thy Sabbath*." ‡ This shows, closing as it does the *six divisions of the design*, that not only is the "Instauration" closely in touch with the College of the *six days* or Solomon's House of the "New Atlantis," but that Bacon's scheme was *creative*. This is very strange when we reflect, how his work appears only to be a system of Inductive Philosophy.

---

* "Nor is it, for most part, so revealed unto us, what in *Arts* and *Sciences* hath been discovered, and brought to light in diverse ages, and different regions of the world ; much less what hath been experimented, and seriously laboured by particular persons in private ; for *neither the births nor the abortions of time have been registered*" (Preface, "Great Instauration," "Advancement," 1640). By "*abortions*," Bacon means premature discoveries, before time was ripe to appreciate or accept them.

† Spedding in his preface to the Redargutio, fixing the date, by means of certain entries in Bacon's note book (Commentarius Solutus), viz., July 26th, 1608 : "Discoursing scornfully of the philosophy of the Græcians, with some better respect to the Ægyptians, Persians, Chaldees, and the utmost antiquity, and the mysteries of the poets" (Preface to the "Delineatio et Argumentum et Redargutio Philosophiarum," vol. iii., Phil. Wks., 545). So here is an independent proof, that Bacon was contemplating an address, to what he terms in his next entry "*Filios*."

"Qu. *of an oration ad filios;* delightful, sublime, and mixed with elegancy, affection, novelty of conceit, and yet sensible, and superstition" (*Ibid*).

‡ Spenser (F. Q., viii. 2):

"But thenceforth all shall rest eternally
With him that is the God of *Sabaoth* hight :
O ! that great *Sabaoth* God, grant me that *Sabaoth's* sight."

GENERAL REMARKS. 359

It is a striking feature of most of the Rosicrucian writers of note, how fond they are of the *six creative days*, as a theme or scheme for the division and treatment of their works. One of Michael Maier's celebrated works, "Septimana Philosophica," is likewise divided into *seven parts called the days*. Du Bartas' "Divine Week" is a contemporary work on the same model. Campanella's "City of the Sun" is often found bound up* with Bacon's "Atlantis," and treats of an ideal republic or commonwealth in like manner. The author was a well-acknowledged Rosicrucian. John Valentine Andreas wrote a work entitled, "Reipublicæ Christianopolitanæ"—an Utopia of exactly similar stamp. Burton, in his "Anatomy of Melancholy," classes all these three works together, in context with the Rosicrucians. A strong religious element is conspicuous in all these writings.

It is a striking point of touch between the Rosicrucians and Bacon, that they insisted upon appeal to nature by direct experiment, after the inductive method insisted on by the latter. A study of the great English Rosicrucian, Robert Fludd's works, will in a moment illustrate these points. He wrote a work on the Mosaic Cosmogony, and another work full of experiments upon Natural Science. The Rosicrucians took Solomon for their historic founder and patron. Bacon does the same in the "New Atlantis." Those who cannot realize or possibly obtain a glimmer of meaning out of what Bacon means by a "*restoration of knowledge*," may be referred to such works as "The Perfect Way" and "Clothed in the Sun," by the late lamented and extraordinary woman, Anna Kingsford. They will find there, what I take and imagine to be the lifting of the veil, and forestalments of the sort of inspired knowledge Bacon was probably in possession of, which knowledge is Hermetic and is as old as the Pyramids of Egypt. We may guess it was this sort of wisdom (which still lingers under the fossil rituals of Masonry),

---

* We possess a work entitled, "MUNDUS ALTER ET IDEM," in which Campanella's "Civitas Solis," and Bacon's "New Atlantis," are to be found side by side. The date is 1643, and the work ascribed to Bishop Hall.

that affiliates Bacon's name and his "New Atlantis," with the meeting in 1646 at Warrington of a Lodge, when his pillars were adopted, and from which the modern brotherhood date authentically their more recent history.*

Bacon's extreme predilection for quoting *Solomon* is one of the features of his "Advancement of Learning" (1605), and of the "De Augmentis" (1623). There are forty-seven citations from the "Book of Proverbs" in the 1640 Translation (see Index of "Sacred Authors"), fifteen from "*Ecclesiastes.*" Thirty-four of the *Parables of King Solomon* are not only introduced in the Eighth Book, but each is separately commented upon at considerable length, taking up twenty-six complete pages of letterpress! A glance at the catalogue of the "Sacred Authors" quoted, will show this was Bacon's favourite writer in this class of wisdom, and it is very well worthy consideration. Bacon again introduces *Solomon* as the founder of his College of the Six Days in the "New Atlantis." *Solomon was the Biblical protagonist, or patron of the Rosicrucians,*† and there is something in this fact affiliating

* "The London Freemasons *also borrowed much of their phraseology from Lord Bacon's 'Essay,'* yet fresh in men's minds, in which, adopting the idea of the 'House of Wisdom,' a technical term with the Arab Astrologers, he proposed the foundation of a 'Solomon's House,' or a learned community dedicated to experimental philosophy and the advancement of science. These philosophic and royalist plotters, in order to cloak their real object, conducted their proceedings according to the rules laid down therein; and this ceremonial and nomenclature they carefully maintain to the present day" ("The Gnostics and their Remains," King, p. 178).

† "Our philosophy also is not a new invention, but as Adam after his fall received it, *and as Moses and Solomon used it,* also it ought not much to be doubted of, or contradicted by other opinions or meanings; but seeing *the truth is peaceable,* brief, and always like herself in all things" ("Fama Fraternitatis," 1614, p. 82, Waite). Again: "Wherein Enoch, Abraham, Moses, Solomon, did excel, but especially wherewith that wonderful book the Bible agreeth. All that same concurreth together, *and maketh a sphere or globe whose total parts are equidistant from the centre*" (*Ib.*). Bacon writes: "Thus have we made as it were *a small globe of the Intellectual World*" (p. 476, Book IX., "De Augmentis") ("Jam itaque mihi videor confecisse *Globum exiguum* orbis intellectualis quam potui fidelissime.")

On pages 43, 44, 45 of the First Book "Advancement of Learning" (and "De Augmentis"), Bacon discusses Moses and Solomon.

GENERAL REMARKS.

Bacon to the Society. We read in the "New Atlantis": "There reigned in this island, about 1900 years ago, a *King*, whose memory of all others we most adore; not superstitiously, but as a Divine instrument, though a mortal man: his name was *Salomona;* and we esteem him as the law-giver of our nation." Again: "Yee shall understand (my dear friends), that amongst the excellent acts of that King, one above all hath the preeminence. It was the erection and institution of an *Order*, or *Society*, which we call *Salomon's house;* the noblest foundation (as we think) that ever was upon the earth; and the lanthorn of this kingdom. It is dedicated to the study of the works and creatures of God. Some think it bears the founder's name a little corrupted, as if it should be *Solomon's House*. But the records write it, as it is spoken. *So as I take it to be denominate of the King of the Hebrews, which is famous with you, and no stranger to us; for we have some parts of his works, which with you are lost, namely that Natural History, which he wrote of all plants, from the* cedar of Libanus, to the moss that groweth out of the wall; and of all things that have life and motion. This maketh me think, that our king finding himself to symbolise, in many things, with that King of the Hebrews (which lived many years before him), *honoured him with the title of this foundation.* And I am the rather induced to be of this opinion, for that I find in ancient records, this ORDER or SOCIETY is sometimes called Solomon's House; and sometimes the College of the SIX DAYS WORK; whereby I am satisfied, that our excellent King had learned from the HEBREWS, that God had created the world, and all that therein is, within six days; and therefore he instituting that house, for the finding out of the true nature of all things (whereby God might have the more glory in the workmanship of them, and men the more fruit in the use of them), did give it also that second name."* The extraordinary study and weight Bacon

---

* Robert Fludd introduces this passage verbatim in his "Summum Bonum," 1629. It is always repeated in the same words both by Bacon and Fludd. Bacon repeats it three times, as we have shown, and Fludd repeats it in the

attached to Solomon's writings may be further proved by reference to the "Advancement and Proficience of Learning" of 1605. There we find twenty-five more Aphorisms given and separately commented on by Bacon, which he concludes thus:—"Thus have I stayed somewhat longer upon these sentences politic of Solomon than is agreeable to the proportion of an example; led with a desire to give authority to this part of knowledge, which I noted as deficient, by so excellent a precedent; and have also attended them with brief observations, such as to my understanding offer no violence to the sense, though I know they may be applied to a more divine use: but it is allowed, even in divinity, that some interpretations, *yea, and some writings have more of the eagle than others*" (Book II. xxiii.). In a Rosicrucian Confession or Manifesto, published by Mr E. Waite, we read: "A thousand times the unworthy may clamour, a thousand times may present themselves, yet God hath commanded our ears that they should hear none of them, and hath so compassed us about with His clouds that unto us, His servants, no violence can be done; wherefore now no longer are we beheld by human eyes, unless they have received strength *borrowed from the eagle.*"

This is repeated on the last page of the poems, in that curious and mysterious threne, the "Phœnix and Turtle," which seems pretty plainly to hint at rebirth or revelation:—

> From this session interdict
> Every fowl of tyrant wing,
> Save the eagle, feather'd king:
> Keep the obsequy so strict.

That Bacon regarded the eagle in an apocalyptic sense is evident from the way he connects it with St John: "St John, an apostle of our Saviour, and the Beloved Disciple lived ninety-three years. He was rightly denoted under the emblem of the *eagle* for his *piercing sight* into the Divinity, and was a Seraph among his Apostles in respect of his burning Love" ("History of Life

"Apologeticus Tractat.," 1617. I am convinced it is a text or reference to the founder of the Rosicrucian Society, and of Solomon's House of the "New Atlantis."

and Death," 17, 18). It is plain Bacon and the Rosicrucians both allude to the eagle in the same sense. And amongst the favourite books of Scripture to which the society particularly applied themselves were the "Revelations of St John the Divine," already mentioned by Bacon. It is well worthy note that the feast of St John (Midsummer-day) is the chief festival of the Freemasons, who, according to De Quincey, Nicolai, and Murr, are lineal descendants of the Rosicrucians. In a work entitled "Aureum Seculum Redivivum, or The Ancient Golden Age, which has disappeared from the earth, but will re-appear," by Henricus Madathanus Theosophus (who styles himself "Medicus et tandem, Dei Gratia, aureæ crucis frater"), published by Franz Hartmann (Boston, 1888), we find a great deal upon the Apocalypse and the Book with seven seals. There can be little doubt the Book of Revelation is in connection with the Book of the prophet Daniel. It has generally been allowed by all writers on this subject, that the *book with the seven seals* is alluded to in the verse from Daniel: "But thou, O Daniel, *shut up the words, and seal the book, even to the time of the end: many shall run to and fro, and knowledge shall be increased*" (ch. xii. v. 4). Now this is not only Bacon's motto to both the "Novum Organum" and the "De Augmentis," 1640, but this also is the motto attached to the title-page of "Anthroposophia Theomagica," by the great English Rosicrucian, Thomas Vaughan (*alias* Eugenius Philalethes), which title-page we reproduce:—

ANTHROPOSOPHIA THEOMAGICA:

A DISCOURSE OF THE NATURE OF MAN AND HIS STATE AFTER DEATH;

GROUNDED ON HIS CREATOR'S PROTO-CHIMISTRY,
AND VERIFI'D BY A PRACTICALL EXAMINATION OF PRINCIPLES
IN THE GREAT WORLD.

BY

EUGENIUS PHILALETHES.

DAN: Many shall run to and fro, and knowledge shall be increased.
Zoroaster in Oracul.—AUDI IGNIS VOCEM.

Dr Abbott confesses Bacon wrote "*Like a priest*, like a prophet of Science, whose mission he himself describes as being to *prepare and adorn the bride chamber of the Mind and the universe*" * ("Bacon as a Philosopher," xcv.).

This language bears a certain affinity to some Rosicrucian writings, particularly the "Chymical Marriage of Christian Rosy Cross" (published by Mr Waite in his "Real History of the Rosicrucians"). This is generally understood to be a profound allegory. We cannot help thinking that this simile of Bacon's is borrowed from the *Song of Solomon*, in which is sung the Epithalamium (or marriage song) of Christ and his Church. There is good reason for believing the Rosicrucians considered Christ as the corner-stone or foundation of the world, in the light of the Logos, or Wisdom underlying the phenomenal world. That is taken in an esoteric sense, *Christ is Truth* not merely in an ethical sense, but in a philosophical and Catholic spirit, representing the marriage of man's mind to the universe. Bacon, be it observed, never separates Philosophy or science from Religion. He writes like "a priest," likes a Hermes Trigmegistus, and we take it he looked upon Religion as the frame embracing all things. The Rosicrucians borrowed much from the books of Hermes, in which the Logos doctrine is clearly enunciated as Wisdom.

CXVI.

> Let me not to the *marriage of true minds*
> Admit impediments. Love is not love
> Which alters when it alteration finds,
> Or bends with the remover to remove:
> O, no! it is an ever-fixed mark,
> That looks on tempests, and is never shaken;
> It is the star to every wandering bark,
> Whose worth's unknown, although his height be taken.

* "The explanation of which things, and of the true relation between the nature of things and the nature of the mind, is as the strewing and decoration of *the bridal chamber of the Mind and the Universe*, the Divine Goodness assisting; *out of which marriage let us hope (and be this the prayer of the bridal song)* there may spring helps to man, and a line and race of inventions that may in some degree subdue and overcome the necessities and miseries of humanity. This is the second part of the work" ("Distribntion Preface," "Advancement of Learning," p. 30. 1640).

BACON AND CAMPANELLA.

In the Second Book of the "Novum Organum" (Aphorism 36), we find Bacon enunciating the same theories held by Campanella, Telesius, and Patricius concerning the sea, viz., a rising and falling, on which Mr Ellis, "one theory, that of Telesius and Patricius, compares the sea to the water in a cauldron, that is to say, it rises and tends to boil over when its natural heat is called forth under the influence of the sun, moon, and stars, and then after subsides" (Ellis and Spedding, vol. iii., p. 41). Mr Fowler, in his notes to his edition of the "Novum Organum," calls attention to this (p. 463). Bacon has followed or imitated Telesius more than anybody else. "Bacon derived more ideas from him [Telesius] than from any other of the novelists, as he has somewhere called the philosophical innovation, and has written a separate treatise on three systems of philosophy, of which his is one" (Works, i., 564, footnote). But Campanella was a disciple of Telesius. Professor Fowler: "To Telesius, whom he [Bacon] calls the best of the novelists, Bacon refers, perhaps, more than to any other modern writer" ("Novum Organum," p. 312). Again: "Campanella, *whose name is frequently coupled with that of Bacon by the German writers of the seventeenth century, and who was celebrated in his time as the disciple of Telesius*" (Introduction, "Novum Organum," p. 95).

This is most important evidence, for it bears out the declaration of Tobias Adami * (Campanella's editor), prefixed to the

* This is what we read in the 1640 "Advancement": "Tob. Adami, in his preface to the 'Realis Philosophia' of that excellent philosopher Campanella, speaks his opinion thus: 'We erect no sect, establish no placits of Heresy, but endeavour to transcribe universal and ever veritable philosophy out of the ancient original copy of the world: not according to variable and disputable speculations, but according to the conducture of sense and irrefragable depositions of the *Architect* himself, whose hand in works differs not from his word in writing. And of the 'Great Instauration' of the deep mining philosopher Fra. Bacon, Lo. Verulam, Chancellor of England, a work of high expectation, and most worthy, as of consideration, so of assistance, be brought to perfection, *it will perchance appear that we pursue the same ends, seeing we tread the same footsteps in tracing, and, as it were, hounding nature by sense and experience.*'"

judgments upon Bacon, printed in Wat's translation of the "De Augmentis," 1640. There can be no doubt, from the evidence of the striking resemblance of Campanella's "City of the Sun" to Bacon's "New Atlantis," there was some secret connection of philosophic aim or collaboration of brotherhood between them. It is our opinion Telesius, Campanella, Severinus, and Bacon were all members of the fraternity of Rosicrucians. The comparison of Bacon to Campanella is most frequent in writers upon Bacon's works. Leibnitz: "Interea feliciter accidit ut consilia magni viri Francisci Baconi, Angliæ Cancellarii, de augmentis scientiarum, et cogitata excitatissima Cardani et Campanellæ et specimina melioris philosophiæ Kepleri et Galilei et Cartesii ad manus pervenirent" ("Opera Philosophica," Erdman, p. 91). He then felt as if transported to another world. "At si ille Bacono, hic Campanellæ comparetur, apparet illos humi repere; hos magnitudine cogitationum, consiliorum, immo destinationum assurgere in nubes, ac pene humanæ potentiæ imparia moliri. Illi ergo tradendis principiis, hi conclusionibus ad usum insignibus eliciendis meliores." Professor Fowler remarks: "It is curious so frequently to find the name of Bacon coupled by German writers with that of Campanella" (Introduction, "Novum Organum," p. 109).

Perhaps this continual coupling of names by German writers has some source in the fact that the Rosicrucian Manifestoes took rise in Germany. We find Burton, in his "Anatomy of Melancholy," coupling Bacon's "New Atlantis" with Campanella's "City of the Sun." For example, "Utopian parity is a kind of government to be wished for rather than effected, *Respub. Christianopolitana, Campanella's City of the Sun, and that 'New Atlantis,'* witty fictions but mere chimeras" (p. 60, Democritus to the Reader, 16th edition, "Anatomy of Melancholy"). And in a footnote we read, (appended to Respub. Christianopolitana), "JOHN VALENTINE ANDREAS, LORD VERULAM." Now John Val. Andreas, was supposed by De Quincey, to have been the author of the Rosicrucian Fraternity and Manifestoes. It is therefore striking to find Burton, who, as we shall show, knows more than he openly writes, thus coupling Bacon and Andreas together. For example, as to Burton's knowledge of the real founder of the Order of Rosie Cross, and the mythical history of its founder: "I should here except some cynics—Menippus, Diogenes, that Theban Crates, or to descend to these times, that omniscious, only wise fraternity of the Rosie Cross, those great theologues, politicians, philosophers, physicians, philologers, artists, &c., of whom St Bridget, Albas Joacchimus, Leicenbergius, and such divine spirits, have prophesied, and made promise to the world, if at least there be any such, (Hen. Neuheusius makes a doubt of it, Valentinus Andreas, and others), or an Elias Artifex, their Theophrastian master; whom, though Libavius and many deride and carp at, yet some will have to be *the Renewer of all Arts and Sciences, reformer of the world and now living;* for so Johannes Montanus Strigoniensis (that great patron of Paracelsus) contends, and certainly avers, *a most divine man* (Divinus ille vir, auctor notarum in ep. Rog. Bacon, ed. Hambur., 1608), and the quintessence of wisdom, wheresoever he is; for he, his fraternity, friends, &c., are all betrothed to wisdom, if we may believe their disciples and followers. I must needs except Lipsius and the Pope, and expunge their names out of the catalogue of fools: for beside that parasitical testimony of Dousa,—

> A sole exoriente Mæotidas usque paludes,
> Nemo est, qui justo se æquiparare queat.

Lipsius saith of himself, that he was *humani generis quidam pædagogus voce et stylo*, a grand signior, a master, a tutor of us all: and for thirteen years, he brags how he sowed wisdom in the Low Countries (as Ammonius the philosopher did in Alexandria), *cum humanitate literas et sapientiam cum prudentiâ: antistes sapientiæ*, he shall be *sapientum octavus*" (p. 72, "Democritus to the Reader"). In a footnote we read (attached to the description of the founder of the Rosicrucians "*now living*"), "*omnium artium et scientiarum instaurator."* This can only apply to Francis Bacon. For he repeatedly alludes to his own work, as a renewal or restoration of knowledge, of *Arts and Sciences,* and the actual title of his great work is the *Great Instauration.* Burton wrote this in 1621, and this proves that what both De Quincey and Mr Waite have affirmed as to the mythical history of the society being a fraud, is true.

We find Bacon in his Instauration Preface writing: "Restabat illud unum ut res de integro tentetur melioribus præsidiis, utque fiat *scientiarum et artium atque omnis humanæ doctrinæ in universum instauratio,* a debitis excitata fundamentis." Here we have almost Burton's words,—"*Instauration of Arts and Sciences.*" But see in how many points the description given by Burton of the founder of the Rosicrucians agrees with what we know of Bacon. To begin with, he was at the time Burton wrote a "grand signior," Lord Keeper of the Seal (1617), Baron Verulam, and in 1621 Viscount St Albans. "*Antistes Sapientiæ*" means a Great Lawyer, an Oracle of the Law (Ainsworth, "Latin Dictionary"). We find Bacon's "New Atlantis" cited side by side with the "Resp. Christianopolitanæ" of the great Rosicrucian protagonist, Valentine Andreas. To confirm this evidence, we have John Heydon, a Rosicrucian Apologist, reproducing, word for word, without any alteration of note or importance, the entire text of Bacon's "New Atlantis," and entitling it "*The Land of the Rosicrucians*"! Critics have replied by classing Heydon impostor and mountebank. If Heydon's evidence stood singly this retort might have weight. But was Burton also an impostor? Is Nimrod an impostor, who deliberately calls Campanella a member of the brotherhood or gang (as he writes) of the Rosie Cross? And do we not find Professor Fowler calling attention to the strange coupling of Bacon's name with Campanella's by German writers? The date of Campanella's "Civitas Solis" is 1623, the date of the publication of the Folio plays known as Shakespeare's, and the "De Augmentis." The internal evidence of Campanella's "City of the Sun" is to place it side by side in the same category of Utopian works as Bacon's "New Atlantis." Both are portraits of an ideal Republic. And have we not in the fact that Valentine Andreas wrote a work of this class, positive evidence afforded that such Utopian or ideal scheme for the reformation of Society was one of the Rosicrucian dreams? The first Rosicrucian Manifesto, reproduced almost literally from Boccalini's "Ragguagli di Parnasso," presents us with exactly the same end or aim. We are introduced to the Seven Wise Men of Greece, who severally propose ideas for the bettering of society. The Rosicrucians termed themselves a college.

> Quid vis? Collegium nostrum est Acadæmia quædam,
> Doctrinæ studiis cum pietate sacra.
> ("John Valentine Andreas," Berlin, 1619.)

Bacon's "New Atlantis" is called the "*College* of the Six Days." Bacon writes in the Preface to the "Advancement of Learning," 1640: "This one way remaineth, that the business be wholly re-attempted with better preparations, and that there be throughout an *Instauration of Sciences and Arts*, and of all human learning raised from solid foundations." These words are but Burton's over again, and in the Second Book of the "Advancement" (78, 79) Bacon again introduces the subject of *Arts and Sciences* in context with *foundations and Colleges*. In the great Rosicrucian Manifesto, published at Cassel in 1614, and Frankfort-on-the-Main, 1615, occur these words: "He shewed them new growths, new fruits and beasts, which did concord with old philosophy, and prescribed them new Axiomata, *whereby all things might fully be restored*." This refers to Father Rosy Cross, the founder of the society. Now compare Bacon's statement prefacing the *Instauratio* : "Francis of Verulam . . . being convinced that the human intellect makes its own difficulties, not using the true helps which are at man's disposal soberly and judiciously ; thought all trial should be made, whether that commerce between the mind of man and the nature of things, which is more precious than anything on earth, or at least than

GENERAL REMARKS.

anything that is of the earth, might by any means *be restored to its perfect and original condition*" (Latin text: "*restitui posset in integrum*"). Dr Abbott, in his Introduction to the "Essays" writes of Bacon: "He seems to believe that in some happier original condition of Mankind, the Mind and Nature were once wedded, but are now divorced. He aims *at restoring to its perfect and original condition that commerce between the Mind of Man and the Nature of Things, which is more precious than anything on earth*" (Works, vol. iv. p. 7, "Bacon as a Philosopher," LXVII.). There can be no doubt Bacon did believe in some prehistoric period, when knowledge was profounder, for Spedding even acknowledges this. Bacon writes: "The Græcians were, as one of themselves sayeth, *You* Græcians are ever children! They knew little antiquity; they knew, except fables, not much above five hundred years before themselves. They knew but a small portion of the world" (Bacon's "Note Book").

In the "Magia Adamica" of Thomas Vaughan (Eugenius Philalethes) we find him repeating this: "Most apposite then was that check of the Ægyptian to Solon: *O Solon, Solon! Vos Græci semper pueri estis, nullam antiquam habendes Opinionem, nullam disciplinam tempore canam.*" "You Græcians (said he) are ever childish, having no ancient opinion, no discipline of any long standing" (p. 91, Waite's "Magical Writings of Vaughan").

It is very curious to find the Rosicrucian founder presenting his society with "*New growths, new fruits* *—and prescribed them *new Axiomata*," because this is thoroughly Baconian language, as every student will immediately recognise. In Bacon's "Natural History" we read, "Our experiments we take care to be (as we have often said) either *Experimenta, Fructifera, or Lucifera*—either of use or of discovery." And as for "*Axiomata*," it is a

---

* Page 69, "Fama Fraternitatis," Waite's "History of the Rosicrucians." Rawley writes (Preface to the Reader, "Sylva Sylvarum"): "And for use, his Lordship hath often in his mouth, the two kinds of experiments, *Experimenta Fructifera, and Experimenta Lucifera.*"

GENERAL REMARKS.

word repeatedly employed by Bacon in the "Novum Organum" of any general proposition. In Aphorism 103, "*Axiomata*" are contrasted with "Opera" and "particularia." In Aphorism 104 he speaks of "*axiomata generalissima*" (*qualia sunt principia quæ vocant artium et rerum*), "*axiomata media,*" and "*axiomata minora*" or "*infima.*" So frequently does Bacon introduce this word that it really constitutes a great feature of the "Novum Organum," namely the discovery of *new axioms or axiomata*. "For our road does not lie on a level, but ascends and descends; *first ascending to axioms, then descending to works.*" . . . Again, "But from the *new light of axioms*, which, having been educed from these particulars by a certain method and rule, shall in their turn point out the way again to new particulars" (Aphorism 103, "Novum Organum," Book I.). In short, the "Novum Organum" is largely made up of a system of establishing axioms by forms of Induction.

CAMPANELLA'S "CITY OF THE SUN."

I cannot do better than transcribe here Nimrod's description of Campanella's "City of the Sun" (Civitas Solis) from his "Discourses of History and Fable." Nimrod was a profound student of this class of literature, and the attentive reader will recognize many points reflected in Bacon's writings. "It is impossible for me to pass under silence the name of Thomas Campanella. He was a Dominican friar of Calabria, endowed with great talents, but addicted to atheism and magic. Being accused of those errors, he was confined in the inquisition at Rome; and afterwards banished to a convent at Stilo, his native town. He declared that St Bridget,[*] Joachim of Calabria, Savonarola, and

[*] The learned author of Nimrod seems to think that the Rosicrucians belonged to the order of Mandaïtian Sabaites. Mandaite from Javar Mando di heye or Herald of Life. The Jardeno, or mystic Jordan of the Mandaites, is interpreted by them *a stream of red water*, and derived from ourdà *a rose*. Giordano Bruno says that all wisdom, Divine, Mathematical, and Natural, *proceeds from the intelligible sun* ("Spaccio de la Bestia," p. 215). His doctrine is

even St John the Evangelist, had prophesied concerning him, and he caused himself to be announced as *The Messiah that was to come* (Giannone, 'History di Napoli,' p. 311). Campanella is said to have undergone atrocious tortures, but he escaped the capital punishment to which his dupes were condemned, by shamming madness in the depositions which he made. However he remained in prison from 1600 to 1626. He was the author of a romance entitled '*Civitas Solis Idea Reipublicæ Philosophicæ*,' which is a production running on all fours with Inchoffer's '*Monarchy of the Solipses*,' except that the former is a serious panegyric, and the latter a severe satire, upon the same thing. In a dialogue between a Genoese navigator and the Grand Master of the Hospitallers, the former describes the City of the Sun in Taprobane. (T. Camp. Civ. Sol. annexed to Philos. Real., p. 417, &c., ed Franc. 1623, *date of Folio Shakespeare*). Its description coincides minutely with the scheme of that ancient city called Babel or Troy, as heretofore explained by me. It is built with four gates to the four cardinal points, and it is, *distincta in septem gyros ambitusve ingentes a septem planetis nominatos*, each enclosure being strongly fortified. In the centre of all a mount ascends from the plain, and upon its summit there is a temple constructed with wonderful art.

"The temple is round and supported upon columns, without walls. It has a roof or dome upon which all the stars are delineated. Upon the altar *there is nothing but a large globe representing earth, and another representing heaven.*" We pause in the description, to call attention to the parallel presented by the title-page engraving of Bacon's "Advancement of Learning," 1640, to the words placed in italics. For Bacon's entire "Advancement of Learning" he calls the "Intellectual Globe," and, indeed, in an intermediate sketch of the "De Augmentis," afterwards abandoned, written in 1612, shows us he had once the intention of

that of the Eastern Sabianism, and the same as are contained in Julian the apostate's writings. "The Rosy Cross look upon Apollonius as their tutelary deity" ("Naudè la Rose-Croix," p. 42).

GENERAL REMARKS.

entitling the "De Augmentis" by this name. Bacon concludes eight books of the "De Augmentis" with the words, "And now (most excellent king) we have with a small bark, such as we were able to set out, sail'd about the universal circumference of the *old as the new World of Sciences*" (ch. i. Book IX.). Again in the eighth book, "Deinde et ad perfectionem literarum hoc ipsum spectat, quia legitimæ inquisitionis vera norma est, *ut nihil inveniatur in globo materiæ, quod non habeat parallelum in globo crystallino sive intellectu*" (772. Phil. Works, I., Spedding). To wit —"This kind of wisdom much respects the perfection of Learning; because it is the right rule of a perfect inquiry that nothing be found in the Globe of Matter, that hath not a parallel in the Crystalline Globe or the Intellect"* (Book VIII., p. 59, "Advancement of Learning"). Remark Bacon's "Description of the Intellectual Globe," written in 1612, opens with his tripartite division of History, Poetry, and Philosophy (as in the Second Book Advancement 1605 and 1623), and deals largely with the *heavens and astronomy.* The reader may see on the title-page referred to, the two globes portrayed—or hemispheres, one entitled the *Visible* world, the other the *invisible* world; the former plainly the old world, the latter dotted out only. It is to the last that his ship emblem is bound on an intellectual voyage of discovery. And this should be paralleled with the fact, the "New Atlantis" is an island placed mid the ocean of the new world, like Prospero's magic island in "The Tempest."

Miranda. O brave *New World !*

That this is no imaginary theory is proved by Bacon's language in his "Distribution Preface," where, speaking of the Prætermitted Parts, entitled "*A New World of Sciences*" (marked by stars), he writes:—"Wherefore we will not neglect to ride along

---

* "Dr Thompson, the Master of Trinity College, Cambridge, has pointed out to me that the origin of Bacon's 'globe of matter' and 'globe of crystal or form' is probably the σφαῖρος αἰσθητός and the σφαῖρος νοητός of Empedocles as interpreted by Proclus. See Proclus in Timæum, p. 160 D, and Simplicius in Physica, p. 7 b." (Wright, "Advancement of Learning").

(as it were in passage) the *coasts* of accepted Sciences and Arts—for these are found in the *Intellectual Globe*, as in the terrestrial soils, improved and deserts." We continue our description of the "City of the Sun":—"The citizens are governed by their high priest, whom in their language they call SOL, and designate by the symbol ⊙, but whom we might properly call Metaphysicus. *They have all their possessions in common*, and the dispensation of them appertains to magistrates." We must again beg the reader's indulgence to point out an unquestionable and important Rosicrucian parallel, which attracted the attention of the author of Nimrod, who writes (p. 517) further on:—"The Christianopolis, Uranopolis, or Eleutheropolis of Andreæ (John Val. Andreas, to whom De Quincey attributes the entire Rosicrucian hoax, as he considers it) has a *certain similitude* to the Civitas Solis. He desired to *abolish property and establish community of goods*" ("Rep. Christ.," c. xv., p. 48; "Myth Christ.," L. vi. c. 7, p. 285). This is a strong point, showing how these works are affiliated. But the astonishing parallel furnished by the play of "The Tempest," in the words of Gonzalo, finds extraordinary point, seeing Prospero's magic island,* like the island of the "New Atlantis," is evidently a dream or Utopian paradise.

> *Gon.* Had I plantation of this isle, my lord,—
> *Ant.* He'd sow't with nettle-seed.
> *Seb.* Or docks, or mallows.
> *Gon.* And were the king on't, what would I do?
> *Seb.* 'Scape being drunk for want of wine.
> *Gon.* I' th' commonwealth I would by contraries
> Execute all things; for no kind of traffic
> Would I admit; no name of magistrate;
> Letters should not be known; riches, poverty,
> And use of service, none; contract, succession,

* Bacon writes:—"For 'tis an immense Ocean that surrounds the island of Truth" (p. 58, vol. ii., Shaw's Edition, 1733).

Compare—"So to live in one place that neither the people which dwell beyond the Ganges could hide anything, nor those which live in *Peru* might be able to keep their secret, their counsel from thee" (ch. iv., "Confessio R. C."):—

Bacon's "New Atlantis"—"We sailed from *Peru* (where we had continued by the space of one whole year)."

> Bourn, bound of land, tilth, vineyard, none;
> No use of metal, corn, or wine, or oil;
> No occupation; all men idle, all;
> And women too, but innocent and pure;
> No sovereignty;—
>   *Seb.*   Yet he would be king on't.
>   *Ant.* The latter end of his commonwealth forgets the beginning.
>   *Gon. All things in common nature should produce*
> Without sweat or endeavour: treason, felony,
> Sword, pike, knife, gun, or need of any engine,
> Would I not have; but nature should bring forth,
> Of its own kind, all foison, all abundance,
> To feed my innocent people.
>   *Seb. No marrying 'mong his subjects?*
>   *Ant.* None, man; all idle; whores and knaves.
>   *Gon.* I would with such perfection govern, sir, to excel the golden age.
>   ("Tempest," act ii. sc. 1.)

Critics have joined issue with Sebastian and Antonio in declaring the author of the plays, intended to turn into ridicule Gonzalo's speech. But they forget that Sebastian and Antonio are the wicked scoffers, who fall under Prospero's especial displeasure, and they overlook the fact Prospero loves Gonzalo, and terms him his "*true preserver.*" On the contrary, it may be seen in the reproof Gonzalo brings upon the disbelievers in the matter of *Tunis being identical with Carthage*, and the incredulity this is met with by the same characters, the author's intention was to make the seemingly impossible and miraculous *the real*, and by art to mock us as we laugh with the cynics in the play. The reader may see Campanella's ideas and Andreas' reproduced in the line—

> All things in common—.

Campanella writes: "*The community of women* is likewise one of their institutions." Compare—

> No marrying 'mong his subjects.

There can be no doubt that these words [*] of Gonzalo's point to

---

[*] *Gonzalo.* I would with such perfection govern, sir;
   T' excel the *golden age.*
This is the key to the passage. The Rosicrucians believed in the Golden Age or Millennium, and its return with the end of the Times.

these literary Utopias or Philosophical Republics we cite. And it is curious Campanella's "City of the Sun" was published 1623, the same date as the Folio plays and the "De Augmentis."

The fact that Bacon's last work, published in 1627, the year after he died, presents us with the ideal portrait of an island placed mid-ocean, and that the last play written and placed first in the 1623 Folio *also is laid upon an island*, carries a certain amount of evidence by parallelism along with it. Prospero deals in just that sort of magic which Disraeli maintains is Rosicrucian. And there is the further parallel given by John Heydon, who identifies Bacon's "New Atlantis" with the "Land of the Rosicrucians." We have already found that the author of "The Tempest" was thinking of the Rosicrucian Utopias of Campanella and John Valentine Andreas, when he puts in Gonzalo's mouth the description of an ideal Republic, already cited by us. It is perfectly true Gonzalo's speech reads like satire rather than truth. But we must again remember Prospero terms him his "*true preserver.*"

> Holy Gonzalo, honourable man,
> Mine eyes even sociable to the show of thine
> Fall fellowy drops.
> O good Gonzalo
> *My true preserver and a loyal sir*
> *To him thou follow'st.*
>
> ("Tempest," act v. sc. 1.)

It is our conviction Gonzalo is introduced as an emblem of faith and miracle. He utters *seeming extravagances*, but the evident intention of the poet author was to contrast his ideal utterances and longings *favourably against the sceptics and incredulous scoffers who laugh at him.*

Ad. Widow Dido said you? You make me study of that;
She was of Carthage, not of Tunis.
Gon. This Tunis, sir, was Carthage.
Ad. Carthage?
Gon. I assure you Carthage.
Ad.. His word is more than the miraculous harp.
Seb. He hath raised the wall and houses too.
Ant. What impossible matter will he make easy next?

Seb. I think he will carry this island home in his pocket, and give it his son for an apple.

Ant. And sowing the kernels of it in the sea, bring forth more islands.

Gon. Ay.

(Act ii. sc. 1.)

We see Gonzalo is right upon *the matter of Tunis having been Carthage!* And this suggests the poet's intention was to show Gonzalo being right on one point, *is right in all his utterances.* It may be observed Gonzalo's critics are the unbelievers who gradually are brought under the power of Prospero's wrath and self-disclosure. Those who, like ourselves, perceive a miraculous element foreshadowed in Bacon's art, of a planned revelation accompanying cipher discovery, will recognise in the portrait of Gonzalo and his critics a parallel akin to the present position of the Bacon Shakespeare problem in England.

The year Bacon died (1626), Ben Jonson wrote a Masque called "The Fortunate Isles," * which was designed for the Court on Twelfth Night of that year. Both the title and the internal evidence point to the play of "The Tempest." In introducing one Johphiel, *an airy spirit*, it is certain Ben Jonson *is parodying Ariel.* That Prospero holds some sort of affinity to Jupiter, must be patent to those who reflect upon the introduction of the classical Masque with Ceres, Juno, and Iris, or the speech where he says "He has rifted the stout oak with Jove's own bolt"—

Enter, running, JOHPHIEL, *an airy spirit, and (according to the Magi) the intelligence of Jupiter's sphere: attired in light silks of several colours, with wings of the same, a bright yellow hair, a chaplet of flowers, blue silk stockings, and pumps, and gloves, with a silver fan in his hand.*

> *Johp.* Like a lightning from the sky,
>   Or an arrow shot by Love,
> Or a bird of his let fly ;
>   Be't a sparrow, or a dove :
> With that winged haste, come I,
>   Loosed from the sphere of Jove,
>   To wish good-night
>   To your delight.
>
> ("The Fortunate Isles," act 1.)

* "The Fortunate Isles, and their Union, celebrated in a Masque designed for the Court, on the Twelfth-Night, 1626."

In the following extract there is a parallel to Gonzalo's speech, upon his ideal Commonwealth, or Utopia, already quoted by us:—

> *Por.* No intermitted wind
> Blows here, but what leaves flowers or fruit behind.
> *Cho.* 'Tis odour all that comes !
> And every tree doth give his gums.
> *Pro.* There is no sickness, nor no old age known
> To man, nor any grief that he dares own.
> There is no hunger here, nor envy of state,
> Nor least ambition in the magistrate.
> But all are even-hearted, open, free,
> And what one is, another strives to be.
> *Por.* Here all the day they feast, they sport and spring,
> Now dance the Grace's hay, now Venus ring:
> To which the old musicians play and sing.
> *Sar.* There is Arion, tuning his bold harp,
> From flat to sharp,
> *Por.* And light Anacreon,
> He still is one !
> *Pro.* Stesichorus there too,
> That Linus and old Orpheus doth outdo
> To wonder.
>
> ("The Fortunate Isles," act 1.)

I think nobody, who carefully reads this masque, will fail to perceive, that Ben Jonson had the play of "The Tempest"—the magic island of Prospero—in his mind's eye when he wrote "The Fortunate Isles," in 1626. The above is the description of an *ideal terrestrial paradise.* And this idea is reflected in the play of "The Tempest" in many points and touches.

> *Ferdinand.* Let me live here ever ;
> So rare a wonder'd father and a wife,
> *Make this place Paradise.* ("Tempest.")

This is no chance metaphor, as we may find the following parallel pointing to Virgil's Vth book of the "Æneid":—

> Come unto these *yellow sands*
> And then join hands, &c., &c.

—which evidently is plagiarized from Virgil's description of *Paradise or the Elysian fields.*

> Pars in gramineis exercent membra palæstris
> Contendunt ludo, et *fulva luctantur arena.*
>
> (Book VI., "Æneid.")

GENERAL REMARKS. 379

The opening of the Heavens by Prospero in the presentation of the masque proves our case, for this was just the heavenly side of the Mysteries—the initiate being first led through a symbolical death into Tartarus or Hell, and afterwards presented with a sight of the Gods of Olympus. All this is represented by Virgil in his sixth book of the " Æneid," which, ever since Warburton's " Divine Legation," has been accepted as a description of initiation into these shows. Why should Bacon imitate all this? The reply is not far to seek. He treads in the footsteps of Virgil and Dante. And it is just these Ancient Mysteries, circling round the origins of the Drama, which constitute the particular fountain lore, of societies like the Rosicrucians, and to which even modern Freemasonry traces back its history. We maintain the island of "The Tempest" is one of the Fortunate Isles, described by Lambertus Floridus as *" Paradisus insula in oceano in oriente,"* or of Olympiodoms (MSS. Commentary on the " Gorgias " of Plato), which he calls the Islands of the Blessed—of the emancipated soul —that is, of *Truth and Light*.

The curious part is that this masque is full of the Rosicrucians, whom Ben Jonson *identifies with the players*.

> *Merefool.* I do like their show,
> And would have thanked them, being the first grace
> The company of the Rosy-cross hath done me.
>   *Johp.* The company o' the Rosy-cross, you widgeon !
> The company of [the] players. Go, you are,
> And will be still yourself, a Merefool, in :
> And take your pot of honey here, and hogsgrease,
> See who has gulled you, and make one.   [*Exit* Merefool.

It is quite a mistake to think Jonson introduces the Rosicrucians only to make fun of them. He makes fun of one Merefool, who is seeking to enter their ranks. But in *hogsgrease* * is there no reference to *Bacon?*

* Lord Bacon adopted during his lifetime the crest of *a boar, or Hog*, which may be seen upon the cover of the " Novum Organum," 1620. This shows he entered perfectly into the joke of the play upon his name Bacon.
        Hang Hog is Latin for Bacon.
                    ("Merry Wives of Windsor.")

>   *Sar.*   And Amphion ! he is there.
>   *Por.*   Nor is Apollo dainty to appear
> In such a quire ; although the trees be thick.
>   *Pro.* He will look in, and see the airs be quick,
> And that the times be true.
>   *Por.*   Then, chanting.
>   *Pro.*   Then,
> Up with their notes, they raise the Prince of Men.
>   *Sar.* And sing the present prophecy that goes.
> Of joining the bright Lily and the Rose.

The lily and the rose are the two Rosicrucian flowers. We have already found Heydon identifying Bacon's "New Atlantis" with the land of the Rosicrucians. But the Atlantis, according to all the Ancients, was Ogygia, the Isle of the Hesperides, in short, *one of the Fortunate Isles*, placed in the West, and supposed to be the birth-place and home of Jupiter, and other gods of Olympus. How is it Jonson introduces *the Rosicrucians in connection with the Fortunate Isles?* For the Island of Atlantis has been abundantly identified with not only Avalon, or the Grass Green Island of Apples (another name for the Hesperides), but with the Paradise and Infernal Regions of the Ancients. We find in the names of the Shakespeare Theatres titles which are strangely Rosicrucian—the Rose, the Swan, the Phœnix, the Curtain (or Veil), the Globe ; and, moreover, we find in the "Confession of the Rosicrucian Fraternity" of 1615, that "*one of the greatest impostors being a stage player, a man with sufficient ingenuity for imposition.*" The fact that a religious society like the Rosicrucians should call attention *to the stage, or to an actor upon it*, is pregnant with profound evidence if carefully considered at all. There is only one conceivable type of impostorship connected with a *stage player* outside his profession, and *that is authorship*. Shakespeare was both actor and reputed author.

CHAPTER V.

BACON'S "HOLY WAR."

ONE of the titles by which the Rosicrucian Fraternity was known was the "*Valley of Peace*."* In the 1614 "*Fama Fraternitatis*" we read: "Truth is *peaceable*, brief, and always like herself in all things." Eugenius Philalethes attaches the following address to the Rosicrucians to the first chapter of his "Anthroposophia Theomagica":—"To the Most Illustrious and truly regenerated brethren R. C., to the *peace-loving* apostles of the church in this contentious age, salutation *from the centre of peace*" (Waite's edition, "Magical Writings of Thomas Vaughan," Eugenius Philalethes). Bacon is fond of several times introducing in his writings the following:—"And as Alexander Borgia was wont to say of the expedition of the French for Naples, that they came with chalk in their hands to mark up their lodgings, and not with weapons to fight; so I like better *that entry of truth which cometh peaceably with chalk* to mark up those minds which are capable to lodge and harbour it, than that which cometh with pugnacity and contention" (Redargutio). Very curiously this forms again the thirty-fifth aphorism of the first book of the "*Novum Organum*," and this is the number of the plays in the 1623 Folio Catalogue. In a letter to Sir Thomas Bodley he writes: "*If you be not of the lodgings chalked up.*" The connection

---

* "There is a somewhat remarkable document in the Latin language professing to be the record of a masonic meeting of the period, but discovered recently in Germany, along with Lodge minutes of the Hague, dated 1637, and styled 'Lodge of the Valley of Peace.' This document is called the 'Charter of Cologne.' It has been printed in English, and is to be found in Dr Burne's 'History of the Templars'" (*The Freemasons' Quarterly* (1840), *The Freemasons' Magazine* (1859), &c.)

of *peace and war*—that is, soldiers who do not actually fight except with chalk in their hands—is eminently suggestive of a *peaceable crusade*, or reformation, and as it appears one of the titles of the Rosicrucians was *Militia Crucifera Evangelica*. In 1598 there was a meeting of them at Lunenburg (*vide* De Quincey's Essay). We have the authority of John Val. Andreas that the society was formed "*out of the ruins of the Knight Templars.*" Like the latter, they aimed at rebuilding the Temple. "*Ascendamus ad montem rationabilem et œdificemus domum Sapientiæ*" ("Summum Bonum," Fludd, 1629). If the student will read Bacon's "Holy War" with this in his mind, he will see that Bacon's idea of a crusade carries out this idea. And he will, I think, easily perceive Bacon does not seriously propose *a real war with swords, but rather one with pens.* "For I am of opinion, that except you could bray Christendom in a mortar, and mould it *into a new part, there is no possibility of a Holy War.*" The *possible* and the *impossible* are wonderfully discussed in this tract. Bacon gives a sort of hint when he says: "Except they had the gift of Navius that they could, *hew stones with pen-knives.*" *Martius*—one of the six characters of the dialogue—is introduced thus: "But let us, if you think good, give Martius leave to proceed in his discourse; for methought he spake like a *Divine in Armour.*" The reader may perceive by the title (Holy War) and a number of such hints that, Bacon is thinking of the Crusades and the Templars. The great motto of Constantine, who gave the order the red cross, is introduced thus: "Yet our Lord that said on earth, to the Disciples, *Ite et prædicate*, said from Heaven to Constantine, *In hoc signo vinces.* What *Christian soldier* is there that will not be touched with a Religious emulation, to see an *order of Jesus*, or of *Saint Francis*, or of *Saint Augustine* do such service, for enlarging the Christian borders; and an order of *Saint Iago*, or *Saint Michael*, or *Saint George*, only to robe and feast and perform rites and observances ?" Mark how all these *Orders* are introduced in context with *Christian soldiers!* The motto, "*In hoc signo vinces,*" may be refound in the "Marriage of Christian Rosy Cross," 1616. This motto went with the sign seen by Constantine in the heavens, the fiery Cross. And in Bacon's "New Atlantis," we read: "The morrow after our three days were passed, there came to us a new man that we had not seen before, clothed in blue as the former was, save that his turban was white, *with a small red cross on the top*." * This "New Atlantis," John Heydon identifies line for line, word for word, with the "*Land of the Rosicrucians!*" In my opinion Bacon's "Holy War," written in 1622, and *placed at Paris*, is a profound hint for the *Militia Evangelica Crucifera*, or Rosicrucians, whom we hear of at Paris, next year (1623), at a meeting, the numbers being curiously thirty-six, or the number of the plays in the 1623 Folio. All this, if coincidence only, is very curious. Why does Bacon lay this dialogue at Paris? The style of the writing is at the commencement *Alchemical*—a profound hint worthy note. "Here be four of you, I think were able to make a good world; for you are as differing as the *four elements*, and yet you are friends. As for *Eupolis*, because he is temperate, and without passion, he may be the *fifth Essence*. If we five (*Pollio*) make the *Great World*, you alone may make the *Little*" (page 1). The reader perceives the reference here to the *Macrocosmos* and *Microcosmos*—the Great and Little Worlds—which was one of the Rosicrucian tenets (see Fludd's works *passim*). This tract is full of Masonic allegory and hints from beginning to end. And here let us remark, it is not a satire. Bacon writes in the letter to Lancelot Andrews, Bishop of Winchester, prefixed to it: "But revolving with myself my writings, as well those I have published as those which I had in hand, methought they went all into the City, and none into the *Temple;* where because I have found so great consolation, I desire likewise to make some poor oblation.

---

* "We were all distributed amongst the Lords, but our old Lord and I, most unworthy were to ride even with the king, each of us bearing a snow-white ensign *with a Red Cross*" ("Marriage of Christian Rosenkreutz," 1616).

"Having replied that I was a Brother of the *Red Rosie Cross*, &c. " (Ibid., p. 111).

"The Templars were the famous *Red Cross Knights* whom Spenser has taken in his Faery Queen to typify perfect holiness or the Church."

Therefore I have chosen an argument, *mixed of Religious and Civil* considerations, and likewise mixed between *Contemplative and Active*. For who can tell whether there may not be an *Exoriere Aliquis?* Great matters (especially if they be Religious) have (many times) small beginnings, *and the Platform may draw on the Building*" ("Dedicatory Epistle").

The reader may see by the allusion to the *Temple and its building*, that Bacon is referring to the *House of Wisdom*—the Temple of Solomon! He writes of the Princes of the World: "For they have made a great path in the seas, unto the ends of the world; and set forth ships and forces of Spanish, English, and Dutch enough to make China tremble. And all this for pearl, or stone, or spices; but for the pearl of the Kingdom of Heaven, or the stones of the heavenly Jerusalem, or the spices of the Spouse's Garden, not a mart hath been set up." It may be perceived by this hint of *Contemplative and Active* arguments what he really means. Upon page 38 he writes: "I was ever of opinion that the *Philosopher's Stone* and an *Holy War* were but the *rendez-vous of cracked* brains." By Bacon's saying that he comes "*with chalk in his hands to mark up lodgings peaceably,*" he shows how adverse he was to any forcible entry of Truth, by means of pugnacity or contention. It is therefore necessary to examine this tract apart from the serious or surface proposition for a new crusade. It seems to us that in this Advertisement is hidden some society of a reforming or religious character.

The first striking thing that calls our attention is the marked way Bacon, in this "Holy War," preserves the true *anti-infidel* spirit, in his denouncement of the Ottomans or Turks, which we shall show is also a Rosicrucian feature. "But let me recall myself; I must acknowledge that within the space of fifty years (whereof I spake) there have been three noble and memorable actions upon the infidels, wherein the Christian hath been the invader. For where it is upon the defensive, I reckon it a war of nature, and not of piety. The first was that famous and fortunate war by sea, that ended in the *Victory of Lepanto;* which hath put a hook into the nostrils of the Ottomans to this day" (p. 34). This battle, which decided the fate of Europe, was fought in 1572, the same year as the Massacre of Saint Bartholomew, and it was this year the star or comet appeared in Cassiopea which has been by some supposed to be the star of Bethlehem. Bacon again writes of the Turks (in this "Holy War"): "So that if things be rightly weighed, *the Empire of the Turks* may be truly affirmed, to be more barbarous than any of these. A cruel tyranny, bathed in the blood of their Emperors, upon every succession: a heap of vassals and slaves: no nobles, no gentlemen: no free-men, no inheritance of land, no stirp or ancient families: a people that is without natural affection, and as the Scripture saith, that regardeth not the desires of women: and without piety or care towards their children: a nation without morality, without letters, arts, or sciences; that can scarce measure an acre of land, or an hour of the day: base and sluttish in buildings, diets, and the like: and in a word, a very reproach of human society: and yet this nation hath made the garden of the world a wilderness; for that as it is truly said, concerning the *Turks: Where Ottoman's horse sets his foot, people will come up very thin*" (p. 37). "I confess that it is my opinion that a war upon the Turks is more worthy than upon any other gentiles, infidels, or savages, that either have been, or now are, both in point of religion and in point of honour." Directly we turn to the Rosicrucian "Confession" of 1615, we find the same *anti-papal* and *anti-Mahomet* spirit displayed as by Bacon, "Although we believe ourselves to have sufficiently unfolded to you in the *Fama*, the nature of our order, wherein we follow the will of our most excellent father, nor can by any be suspected of heresy, nor of any attempt against the commonwealth, we hereby do condemn the *East* and the *West* (meaning the *Pope and Mahomet*) for their blasphemies against our *Lord Jesus Christ*" (chapter i., "Confessio Fraternitatis R. C., ad. Eruditos Europæ"). Again, in the "Advertisement" we read: "And as we do securely call the Pope Antichrist, which was formerly a capital offence in every place, so we know certainly that what we here keep secret, we shall in the future thunder forth with uplifted voice, the which, reader, with us desire with all thy heart that it may happen most speedily." Again: "What think you, therefore, O Mortals, seeing that we sincerely confess Christ, *execrate the pope*," &c. (chap. xiii., "Confessio," 1615).

Bacon shows throughout his writings the most intense antipapal spirit. Dr Abbott writes: "The Essay on *Religion* in 1612 is nothing but a protest against the crimes perpetrated in the name of the Roman superstition; and even in the ampler and graver Essay of 1625, on the Unity of Religion, Bacon can suggest no means for procuring Unity, except the *damning and sending to Hell for ever those facts and opinions that tend to the support of such crimes as Rome had encouraged*" (Bacon as a Theologian, p. cxi., "Essays").

Again: "The genuine and intense hatred felt by Bacon for Romanism is well illustrated by the letter he wrote to Toby Matthew on hearing that the latter had been converted to the Church of Rome: '*And I entreat you much sometimes to meditate upon the extreme effects of superstition in this last Powder Treason, fit to be tabled and pictured in the chambers of meditation as another Hell above ground, and well justifying the censure of the heathen that superstition is worse than atheism; by how much it is less evil to have no opinion of God at all than such as is impious towards His Divine Majesty and Goodness.' Good Mr Matthew receive yourself from these courses of perdition*" (Introduction, p. cxii., *Ib.*).

Again: "What Duessa is in the Faery Queen, that is Rome in Bacon's policy. Wherever in the Essays he writes the word 'superstition,' we may take it for granted that he is thinking of Rome" (*Ib.*, cxiii.).

Bacon writes in the "Advertisement for a Holy War":— "This Pope is decrepit, and the bell goeth for him. Take order, that when he is dead there be chosen a Pope of fresh years, between fifty and threescore; and see that he take the name of Urban, *because a Pope of that name did first institute the Cruzada,* and (as with an holy trumpet) did stir up the voyage for the Holy Land." This is a reference direct to the Crusades, and no doubt a key to the entire "Advertisement of a Holy War." "The Rosicrucians," according to Valentine Andreas, "were formed out of the ruins of the *Knight Templars* by one faithful brother." It seems to us the style Bacon's "Holy War" is written in is full of hints, half cabbalistical and half hermetic, the general spirit being anti-papal and against the Turks.

There is little doubt the Rosicrucian idea of a General *Reformation* of Society, was a secret or underground movement to carry on the work of the Great Reformation (begun by Luther and Melancthon), by means of a secret brotherhood or fraternity, in the same way that Free Masonry aims at the purification of society by means of a private appeal to all that is best, noblest, and most unselfish in man, stimulating the interest by a certain amount of mystery, secrecy, and symbolism. Not only this title —" *Reformation* of the whole Wide World" recalls the Great Reformation, but their emblem, a cross surmounted by a rose, *was the heraldic device of Luther.** And to strengthen this evidence, we find their secret crusade or Reformation was also (like Luther's) anti-papal. Amongst their privileges, powers, and declarations, Naudé enumerates:—

"That by their means the triple crown of Peter will be ground into the dust.

"That they confess freely and publicly, with no fear of repression, that the Pope is Anti-Christ.

"That they denounce the blasphemies of East and West, meaning Mahomet and the Pope, and recognise but two sacra-

* "They bore the Rose and Cross as their badge, not because they were Brethren of the Concocted and Exalted Dew, not because they had studied the book called Zohar, not because they were successors and initiates of the ancient Wisdom-Religion and the sublime hierarchies of Eld, but because they were a narrow sect of theosophical dissidents, because the monk Martin Luther was their idol, prophet, and master, because they were rabidly and extravagantly Protestant, with an ultra-legitimate violence of abusive Protestantism, because, in a single word, the device on the seal of Martin Luther was a Cross-crowned heart rising from the centre of a Rose" (p. 242, Waite's "Real History of the Rosicrucians").

ments, with the ceremonies of the early Church, renewed by their congregation" (Waite's "Real History of the Rosicrucians," p. 399).

Germany and England were the two countries in Europe where the Reformation first took hold, and it is not surprising if the visit of the Rosicrucian Michael Maier to England should have had results. The Rosicrucians were a protestant, religious society, thoroughly in harmony with Christian doctrines, which is further proved by Robert Fludd's explanation of their emblem, the Rose mounted on a Cross:—

"In England the pseudonymous author of the 'Summum Bonum,' who is supposed to be Robert Fludd, gives a purely religious explanation of the Rose Cross symbol, asserting it to mean 'the Cross sprinkled with the rosy blood of Christ.' All authorities are agreed upon one important point in the character of Andreas, and that is his predilection in favour of secret societies as instruments in the reformation of his age and country. According to Buhle, he had a profound and painful sense of the gross evils and innumerable abuses which afflicted the German fatherland, and which were revealed, not eradicated, by the lurid fire-brand of Luther's reformation. These abuses he sought to redress by means of 'secret societies'" (Waite's "Real History of the Rosicrucians").

I have assumed Bacon's mind was bent upon self-sacrifice. It is certainly a most remarkable thing, both the "Advancement of Learning," in Two Books (first published 1605), and the more stately "De Augmentis" of 1623, *commence and end* with the idea and allusion of *Sacrifice*. "There were under the law (excellent King) both daily *sacrifices* and free-will offerings" (opening of First Book, *both* 1605 and 1623). "But the errors I claim and challenge to myself as mine own. The good, if any be, is due *Tanquam, adeps sacrificii* to be incensed to the honour, first of the divine Majesty, and next of your Majesty, to whom on earth I am most bounden." These are the actual words concluding the work of the "Proficience and Advancement of

Learning," 1605. Now it is very striking that the "De Augmentis" of 1623 (which constitutes an enlargement of the Second Book of the "Proficience" into eight books) terminates with the same allusion, though the context is dissimilar. "Notwithstanding, seeing the greatest matters are owing unto their principles, it is enough to me that I have *sown unto Posterity and the immortal God*, whose divine Majesty I humbly implore through his son and our Saviour, that he would vouchsafe graciously to accept these and such *like sacrifices of humane understanding, seasoned with religion as with salt, and incensed to his glory*"* (Book IX., the end, p. 477, 1640 "Advancement"). These final words are placed in italics. There was evidently some particular association in Bacon's mind between the "De Augmentis" and *Sacrifice*. For in a letter to Sir Thomas Bodley upon sending this book, he writes: "My labours I have dedicated to the King; desirous if there may be any good in them, it may be as the *fat of a sacrifice*." This idea of *sacrifice* is closely connected with the simile of *sowing seed*. In a letter to Dr Playfer, requesting him to translate the book of the "Advancement of Learning" into Latin:—"I have this opinion, that if I had sought mine own commendation, it had been a much fitter course for me, to have done as gardeners used to do, by taking their *seeds and slips*, and rearing them first into plants, and so uttering them in pots, when they are in flower, and in their best state. But for as much as my end was merit of the state of learning *and not glory;* and because my purpose was to excite other men's wits than magnify my own; I was desirous to prevent the uncertainness of my own life and times by uttering rather *seeds* than plants; nay,

* "They that sow in tears shall reap in joy. He that goeth forth and weepeth, bearing precious seed, shall doubtless come again with rejoicing, bringing his sheaves with him" (Psalm cxxvi. 5, 6).

> Who sows in tears shall reap in joy,
>   The Lord doth so ordain;
> So that his seed be pure and good,
>   His harvest shall be gain.
>
> (Bacon's translation.)

and further (as the proverb is) by sowing with the basket rather than with the hand." This passage refers entirely to the "Advancement of Learning" or "De Augmentis." It is remarkable to find the Sixth Book treating of Secret Ciphers and Delivery, opening with again this simile of *sowing and harvest.* "For there a book is found entitled FORMICARIUM ARTIUM; we have indeed accumulated a little heap of small dust, and laid up many *Grains of Arts and Sciences* therein, whereto ants may creep and there repose a while, and so betake themselves to new labours. Nay, the wisest of the kings sends the slothful, of what rank or quality soever, unto the ants; and those we define to be slothful, whose only care is to live upon the main stock, but not to improve it *by sowing the ground of sciences over again and reaping a new harvest** (Book VI., 258, 1640). The impression this opening passage leaves upon our minds is that this Art of Tradition or Delivery Bacon thus introduces has something in common with the simile of the ants, seeds, and underground store Bacon propounds. It seems to us Bacon has presented us this simile to suggest not only *resurrection* of his own art, or of his name, but that it is for us to develop these underground seeds, to till the garden of his Theatre, and make a proper use of the hints and directions contained and obscured purposely in this work. The aforesaid passage quoted from his letter to Dr Playfer is pregnant with *self-suppression* and not *self* "*glory,*" as he writes of his style of delivering the "Advancement." And we must take the hint he gives us of his "*purpose to excite other men's wits,*" which is evidently part of the object he has in view connected with this particular work—"*sowing with the basket rather than with the hand,*"—as if to say this work was pregnant with the sowings for posterity he concludes it with.

* This emblem of *seed and sowing* is typical of the Rosicrucian Fraternity. Fludd: "Nos docet Apostolus ad mysterii perfectionem vel sub *Agricolæ* vel *Architecti* typo pertingere"—either under the image of a *husbandman who cultivates a field*, or of an architect who builds a house. Bacon adapted both types, for in his "Advancement of Learning," 1640, he styles himself Architectura Scientiarum.

Upon page 96 (Book II.) he writes in context with the subject of *Lost Names:* "But such swans are rare in our age; and although many men more mortal in their vigilancies and studies than in their bodies *despise the memory of their names as if it were fume or air, animæ nil magnæ laudis egentes:* namely, whose philosophy and severity spring from that root, *Non prius laudes contempsimus quam laudanda facere descivimus.*" We cannot doubt that this is written in application to himself. (There are ninety-five words upon this page in italics; and the ninety-fifth word all counted from the top of the page is "*Poets*"). In the above passage quoted we find the self-confession of a great mind despising praise, and again the suggestion of effacement and self-sacrifice with regard to a name.* That Bacon held the ends he proposed to himself, and their results before all things first and himself as nothing is certain. "Francis Verulam consulted thus, and thus concluded with himself; the publication whereof he conceived did concern the present and future age." The conclusion of these motives of Bacon's to his Instauration of sciences, concludes: "Truly he estimated other ambition whatsoever, *inferior to the business he had in hand;* for either the matter in consultation, and thus far prosecuted, is nothing; or so much as the conscience of the merit itself *ought to give him contentment without seeking a recompense from abroad.*" Belief in this theory of sacrifice can only be accepted upon the grounds that Bacon was throughout actuated by deep religious feelings

---

* The Rosicrucian doctrines were closely connected *with sacrifice,* Christ being their divine pattern, and their jewel a crucifix and rose. Robert Fludd in his "Summum Bonum" and "*Sophiæ cum Moriâ certamen*" explained the symbols of the Rose and the Cross as meaning "*the Cross sprinkled with the rosy blood of Christ.*" Again Fludd writes: "Eadem mens sit in vobis quæ est in Jesu," *i.e.,* "May the same mind dwell in you as in Jesus." We find throughout the Rosicrucian writings, and particularly Fludd's, Christ identified as the Corner Stone of the invisible Temple of Wisdom: "Concludimus igitur quod Jesus sit templi humani lapis angularis; atque ita, ex mortuis, lapides vivi facti sunt homines pii; idque transmutatione reali ab Adami lapsi statu in statum suæ innocentiæ et perfectionis, *i.e.,* à vili et leprosâ plumbi conditione in auri purissimi perfectionem" ("Summum Bonum," p. 37).

of extraordinary character. Nobody acquainted with his works will doubt that. And as far as is permitted for human art to parallel Divine Art, I believe Bacon has approximated creation. We have the parallel of the six days and the six divisions of the "Instauration," terminating (in the Distribution Preface) with a prayer: "Wherefore if we labour with diligence and vigilance in thy works, thou wilt make us participants of thy vision and of thy sabbath."* The inspired character of Bacon's "Advancement" is a particular feature of its own, and should be duly remarked. This work contains one hundred and fifty quotations or allusions to Sacred Scripture, and this is sufficiently curious in itself.

Another important point to register upon this subject, is Bacon's repeated appeal to posterity and far off ages. It cannot be explained upon the accepted understanding he refers to his Inductive System of Philosophy only. For during Bacon's life-time Galileo, Harvey, Gilbert, and others were successfully applying experiment and induction to Nature, and nobody knew that better than Bacon. Let those who wonder at this assertion read the dialogue carried on between Spedding and Ellis in the preface to the *Parascere*. They will find Ellis declaring the Baconian Philosophy "*has yet to come*," and that Bacon's extravagant claims for his peculiar system cannot be explained upon any as yet received hypothesis. One of Bacon's promises were *Examples* to illustrate his system in practice. The second part of the "Instauration" was to be applied to the fourth, which was to exemplify the method of the mind in the comprehension of things upon models, as by a scale or ladder. Bacon writes in the most confident terms upon these examples which were apparently never completed, or if completed, withheld. This fourth part of the "Instauration" (as likewise the fifth and sixth) is missing. Yet in some posthumous writings published at Amsterdam by Gruter, 1653, he speaks of two of the parts as

* See Preface, "Instauration": "And by the protection and assistance of the Divine Power have borne up and encouraged ourselves" (p. 15).

if they existed, and in none of his writings explains or apologises for their absence. The entire Baconian philosophy is bound up with these missing parts, or second half of the "Instauration." The fact that there is no sketch, no hint of what these platforms, types, and models were to be, or are (beyond what we adduce as to the paging 35, 36, and the 71 capital words on these pages *) in his Preface yet confidently alluded to as completed, requires some explanation and is sufficiently suspicious. I adhere to Delia Bacon's intuitive theory that the plays belong to this series.

"Our Lord at His solemn manifestation to the Gentiles when the inquiry of the Greeks who came saying, 'We would see Jesus,' was answered by the voice from heaven, *spoke of himself as the* CORN (OR SEED) *of* wheat which dying should arise, and bring forth much fruit." The Hebrew New Testament translating "corn" by the same word used as "seed" in Genesis iii. 13. I am convinced the sacrifice implied in Bacon's authorship of the plays, and his constant comparison of *Poetry to Seed*, and his conclusion of the "De Augmentis" with the words, "*I have sowen unto posterity and the immortal God,*" have a profounder relationship to the founder of Christianity than we can at present form any idea of. It is striking that almost the last words in the Folio, 1623—the last act of Cymbeline—*refer to Christ and the Church.* For the "*Lion's Whelp*" is "*the Lion of the tribe of Judah*," the Messiah (Rev. v. 5). It is noteworthy the Rosicrucians entirely based their doctrines upon the Bible. Their advent upon the stage of Europe is connected with the star of Bethlehem, 1572, and the spirit of their writings is anti-papal. In the description of the vault of Christian Rosy Cross, given in the "Fama Fraternitatis," we find this description: "In the midst, instead of a tombstone was a round altar covered with a plate of brass, and thereon this engraven:—

A. C. R. C. *Hoc universi compendium unius mihi sepulchrum feci.*
Round about the first circle or brim stood—

Jesus mihi omnia."

* In my last work, "Hermes Stella," pages 103, 104, 105.

All this should be compared with Bacon's extraordinary knowledge of Scripture, which is reflected in the plays known as Shakespeare's.

The type of "*Agricolæ*," or husbandmen, which Robert Fludd ascribed for the Rosicrucian Fraternity, is a strong parallel pointing to this parable of *self-sacrifice and seed*. The Rosicrucians evidently took *Christ's sacrifice in the sense of buried seed or corn*, promising future harvest, and it is striking Bacon joins hands with them in this point. I am convinced *the sacrifice of name, with respect to the authorship of the plays known as Shakespeare's*, is closely connected with all this, being part of their self-renunciative doctrines reflected by their head and founder, Francis Bacon, the King Solomon of their House of Wisdom.

De Quincey writes: "I shall now sum up the results of my inquiry into the origin and nature of Free-masonry, and shall then conclude with a brief notice of one or two collateral questions growing out of popular errors on the main one.

"I. The original Free-masons were a society *that arose out of the Rosicrucian mania*, certainly within the thirteen years from 1633 to 1646, and probably between 1633 and 1640. Their object was *magic* in the cabbalistic sense, *i.e.*, the *occult wisdom* transmitted from the beginning of the world, and matured by Christ; to communicate this when they had it, to search for it when they had it not; and both under an oath of secrecy.

"II. This object of Free-masonry was represented *under the form of Solomon's Temple*—as a type of the true Church, whose corner-stone is Christ. This temple is to be built of men, or living stones; and the true method and art of building with men it is the province of *magic* to teach. Hence it is that all the masonic symbols either refer *to Solomon's Temple*, or are figurative modes of expressing the ideas and doctrines of *magic* in the sense of the Rosicrucians, and their mystical predecessors in general."

I consider, if this last conclusion of De Quincey's as to *Solomon's Temple is to be accepted as true, then it is certain Bacon's* "*New*

Atlantis" is in connection with Free-masonry through Rosicrucianism. Bacon's calls his "College of the Six Days" *Solomon's House*, and Tenison, in his "Baconiana," terms the entire "Instauration" "Domus Sapientiæ," or the House of Wisdom.* My theory is Lord Bacon was the representative Solomon of the Society, and anyone reflecting upon the repeated introductions by Bacon of this writer's name and his works, must see that Bacon had a special object in repeating so often, "'The glory of God *is to conceal a thing,* but the glory of the King is to find it out;' as if,

* "The London Free-masons also borrowed much of their phraseology from Lord Bacon's Essay, yet fresh in men's minds, in which, adopting the idea of the 'House of Wisdom,' a technical term with the Arab astrologers, he proposed the foundation of a 'Solomon's House,' or a learned community dedicated to experimental philosophy and the advancement of science. An important point is the fact that the Rosicrucians are acknowledged even now amongst the Free-masons as a *degree* or class, although disclaimed as the parent stock, a truth which, if allowed, were utterly incompatible with the fraternity's claim to immemorial antiquity" ("The Gnostics and their Remains," King, pp. 178, 179).

"'Do any of you know that the Ashmolean Masonry is altogether ignored on the Continent of Europe?' the Surgeon inquired.

"'Brother Frederick Nicolai has given it a decided contradiction,' the Skipper replied. 'He says that the object of the meeting at Warrington, so far from being Masonic, was simply for the purpose of carrying out a philosophical idea which had been promulgated by Lord Bacon in his "New Atlantis" of the model of a perfect society, instituted for the secret purpose of interpreting nature, and of producing new arts and marvellous inventions for the benefit of mankind, under the name of Solomon's House, or the College of the Six Days' Work, which, in plain language, was intended to be an ideal society for the study of natural philosophy. *The persons present at these meetings are said by Nicolai to have been Rosicrucians,* and we know this to be true of Ashmole himself. He asserts, further, that these men erected, in their Lodge, two Great Pillars, which they called the Pillars of Hermes, in front of Solomon's House, and they used a chequered pavement, a ladder of seven staves or rounds, and many other secret symbols'" ("Discrepancies of Freemasonry," Oliver).

Professor Buhle affirms as the "main thesis" of his concluding chapter, that "Freemasonry is neither more nor less than Rosicrucianism as modified by those who transplanted it into England." This is De Quincey's opinion also: "For I affirm, as the main thesis of my concluding labours, THAT FREE-MASONRY IS NEITHER MORE NOR LESS THAN ROSICRUCIANISM AS MODIFIED BY THOSE WHO TRANSPLANTED IT UNTO ENGLAND" ("Hist. Critico-Inquiry," chap. v., De Quincey).

according to the innocent play of children, the Divine Majesty took delight *to hide His works, to the end to have them found out; and as if kings could not obtain a greater honour than to be God's playfellows in that game.*"

This is the chief text and key-note of Bacon's mind,—concealment and reserve. It quite falls in with his other observations. "*Let great authors so have their due, as we do not derogate from Time, which is the Author of Authors and Parent of Truth*" (p. 35, "Advancement," 1640). Or this: "*Another error induced by the former is, a suspicion and diffidence, that anything should now to be found out, which the world should have missed and passed over so long time*" (p. 36, "Advancement," 1640).

Both these passages are upon pages numbered 35 and 36, which agree with the thirty-five plays in the 1623 Folio Catalogue, and if we add "Troilus and Cressida" (*omitted from the Catalogue expressly, probably to give two play numbers*), the thirty-six plays known as Shakespeare's.

CHAPTER VI.

HERMES STELLA.

BACON'S MYSTERIOUS ASTROLOGICAL MSS. NOTES, 1603, WITH STRANGE PARALLELS FROM THE ROSICRUCIAN ROBERT FLUDD.

SPEDDING, in his "Note to Preface to Valerius Terminus," describes certain writing in Bacon's hand found at the bottom of the title page of "Valerius Terminus," and which he reproduces in facsimile.

Facsimile

OF

THE TITLE PAGE OF THE MANUSCRIPT

OF THE

VALERIUS TERMINUS.

See pp. 205 and 213, vol. iii., "Phil. Wks.," Spedding.

At the bottom of the title page of "Valerius Terminus of the Interpretation by Nature," with the annotations of Hermes Stella, we find in Bacon's hand :—

Spedding endeavoured to throw what light he could upon what he considered these to be astronomical figures, with the date 1603 attached to them. In a footnote he writes:—" The writing in the original is on the outside of the last leaf, which is in fact the cover. The front cover, if there ever was one, is lost. The ink with which the line containing the symbols is written corresponds with that in the body of the MS.; and the line itself is placed symmetrically in the middle of the page near the top. The two lower lines are apparently by another hand, probably of later date, certainly in ink of a different colour, and paler. The word 'Philosophy' is in Bacon's own hand, written lightly in the upper corner at the left, and is no doubt merely a docket inserted afterwards when he was sorting his papers. What connexion there was between the note and the MS. it is impossible to say. But it is evidently a careful memorandum of something, set down by somebody when the MS. was at hand; and so many of the characters resemble those adopted to represent the planets and the signs of the zodiac, that one is led to suspect in it a note of the positions of the heavenly bodies at the time of some remarkable accident;—perhaps the plague, of which 30,578 persons died in London, during the year ending 22nd December 1603. The period of the commencement, the duration, or the cessation of such an epidemic might naturally be so noted. Now three of the characters clearly represent respectively Mercury, Aquarius, and Sagittarius. The sign for Jupiter, as we find it in old books, is so like a 4, that the first figure of 45 may very well have been meant for it. The monogram at the beginning of the line bears a near resemblance to the sign of Capricorn in its most characteristic feature. And the mark over the sign of Aquarius *appears to be an abbreviation of that which usually represents the Sun.* (The blot between 1603 and B is nothing; being only meant to represent a figure 6 blotted out with the finger before the ink was dry.) Suspecting therefore that the writing contained a note of the positions of Mercury and Jupiter in the year 1603, I sent a copy to a scientific friend, and asked him if from such data he could determine the month indicated. He found upon a rough calculation (taking account of mean motions only) *that Jupiter did enter the sign of Sagittarius about the 10th of August* 1603, and continued there for about a twelvemonth; that the Sun entered Aquarius about the 12th or 13th of January 1603-4; and that Mercury was about the 16th or 17th of the same month in the 26th or 27th degree of Capricorn:—coincidences which would have been almost conclusive as to the date indicated, if Capricorn had only stood where Aquarius does, and vice versa. But their position as they actually stood in the MS. is a formidable, if not fatal, objection to the interpretation.

"According to another opinion with which I have been favoured, the first monogram is a *nota bene;* the next group may mean *Dies Mercurii* (Wednesday) 26*th January* 1603; *and the rest refers to something not connected with astronomy.* But to this also there is a serious objection. The 26th of January 1603-4, was a Friday; and it seems to me very improbable that any Englishman would have described the preceding January as belonging to the year 1603. Bacon himself invariably dated according to the civil year, and the occasional use of the historical year in loose memoranda would have involved all his dates in confusion. I should think it more probable that the writer (who may have been copying a kind of notation with which he was not familiar) miscopied the sign of Venus into that of Mercury; in which case it would mean *Friday*, 26th January 1603-4. But even then the explanation would be unsatisfactory, as leaving so much unexplained. Those however who are familiar with old MSS. relating to such subjects may probably be able to interpret the whole."

We have a strange astronomical parallel to point out in connection with this date 1603, and the entry of Jupiter into the sign Sagittarius. And we discovered it this way. We were reading Robert Fludd (the great English Rosicrucian) in his reply, 1617, to the attacks of Libavius upon the assertions of the Fraternity of the Rosy Cross, written in a little work entitled

"Tractatus Apologetici," when we came upon Chapter V. of the First Part, in which Fludd explains how the appearance of new stars were taken by the society as a sign of God's will to them (the Rosicrucian Society), indicating a restoration of the world and an augmentation of the Order. The title of the chapter runs, " Quod voluntas Dei ejusque ordinationes characteribus magni libri Naturæ et signaculis novarum stellarum declarari possit."

Tex. *Dei mundum restauraturi voluntas signaculis novarum stellarum et characteribus magni libri naturæ declarata est* (ch. v., pars. i.).

That the Will of God and His Providence through the characters of the great book of Nature, and through new stars can be made manifest. The Will of God in the reformation, amelioration (or restoration) of the world has been declared through the signs of new stars, and through the characters of the great book of Nature.

Fludd proceeds now to indicate what these stars and signs are, and at the end of the chapter gives a Horoscope, with the date 20th of December 1603, which is the year attached to Bacon's mysterious annotations. Fludd tells us that new stars have appeared in Serpentarius and Cygnus, and this last star we find Bacon [*] also noting in his works.

It may be seen Spedding, in his note, assumes one of Bacon's figures in the facsimile given of the title page of the manuscript is meant for Jupiter and Sagittarius. Now it is an excessively strange and striking parallel that Fludd, in the chapter we allude to, lays the greatest stress upon Jupiter entering Sagittarius on the 20th December 1603 in conjunction with Saturn. Fludd writes: "Anno Dom. 1603, die 20 mensis. Decemb. secundum novam computationem, hora Meridiana percepi, quod Saturnus in gra. 8

---

[*] Etiam conspici nuper cœpit stella nova in pectore Cygni, quæ jam per duodecim annos integros duravit, ætatem cometæ (qualis habetur) longo intervallo supergressa, nec adhuc diminuta aut adornans fugam. (P. 752, vol. iii., "Phil. Works," E. and S.)

et 39 min. Saggittarii moveret. Similiter quod Jupiter grad. 8 et 39 min. 58 secund. ejusdem signi eodem ferè instante sibi vendicaret " (p. 70, pars. i.). ("In the year 1603, the 20th December following, new style, at midday, Saturn in 8 degrees, 39 seconds, entered Sagittarius. Likewise, Jupiter nearly at the same moment, in 8 degrees 39 seconds, entered the same sign—Sagittarius.")

In the "Confession of the Rosicrucian Fraternity addressed to the learned of Europe," which appeared in 1615, reproduced by Mr Waite in his "Real History of the Rosicrucians " (p. 93), we read : " God, indeed, hath already sent messengers which should testifie His will, to wit, some new stars which have appeared in *Serpentarius* * and *Cygnus*, the which powerful signs of a great Council show forth how for all things which human ingenuity discovers, God calls upon His hidden knowledge, as likewise the Book of Nature, though it stands open truly for all eyes, can be read or understood by only a very few."

I propose to give here the entire chapter from Fludd verbatim. The reader will find it sufficiently curious, and is begged to note the reference to Solomon at the beginning, and remember Solomon is the founder of Bacon's "College of the Six Days " in the " New Atlantis." Also that Fludd alludes to the star of Bethlehem, which appeared in 1572 in Cassiopea, and with the advent of *which the Rosicrucian Society is intimately connected.* It was with the appearance of this star that Paracelsus wrote: " Quod utilius Deus patefieri sinet, quod autem majoris momenti est, vulgo adhuc latet usque ad Eliæ Artistæ adventum, quando is venerit." " God will permit a discovery of the highest importance to be made, it must be hidden till the advent of the artist Elias." Again : " And it is true, there is nothing concealed

---

* The Rhodians, who had a special veneration for the sun, as their magnificent solar Colossus attests, recognised in SERPENTARIUS, Phoibas, a hero who had exterminated the serpents which formerly infested their country. The Rhodians, or Rose-worshippers, or Rosycrucians, never embarked on any maritime expedition without offering sacrifice to Phoibas " ("Enoch," vol. ii., Kenealy).

which shall not be discovered, for which cause a marvellous being shall come after me, who as yet lives not, and who shall reveal many things" (Waite's "Real History of the Rosicrucians," p. 34). On the next page the same author writes: "The comet of 1572 was declared by Paracelsus to be "the sign and harbinger of the approaching revolution." It was this comet or star which shone upon Bacon's freshmanship at Cambridge, when he was twelve years old, and when he first began to question the philosophy of Aristotle. *This star* is expected to reappear again either this year or at least shortly, its period varying slightly over three hundred years.*

There can be no question the Rosicrucians connected their advent closely with this event. They took Christ with His self-sacrifice, mystery, and atonement, as an emblem for their own secret ends. We see this in their jewel, a crucified rose on a cross—we find it in their typical allusions to themselves as husbandmen (Agricolæ), and in their religious aims to aid the Reformation and combat the papacy.

It is for some astronomer versed in these matters to decipher Bacon's notes, and declare whether they refer to the same conjunction of stars that Fludd calls attention to in 1603. The year is the same in both cases. If, as I firmly believe, Bacon's notes refer to Jupiter and Saturn, with Venus or other stars entering Sagittarius, it will be easy to discover whether there were two such conjunctions the same year 1603. It is a highly suspicious fact that Fludd connects this conjunction with the Rosicrucian Fraternity. Bacon thought it evidently of some importance, else he would not have attached the words "Hermes Stella," which means *a secret star*. That it all is connected with some cipher is suggested by the *false paging implied in the words*—

> Libri dimidium est pagina 34
> Pagellarium numeri veri.

This proves Bacon *mispaged purposely*, as Mr Donnelly has

---

* This star lasted till 1574, which same year Robert Fludd was born; died 1637, buried Bearsted Church, Kent.

already said of the 1623 Folio, and which is again evidenced in the 1640 "Advancement of Learning," where we find the first false paging 52 (upon true page 50), and the second false paging 53 (upon true page 55), these two numbers 52, 53 constituting Shakespeare's full age, 1616, and the year he had just entered when he died. The sum of these figures 52 and 53 is 105, and if it is coincidence, it is a very strange one, to find Bacon commences the subject of Poetry upon page 105 of this same work. Our firm conviction is that 52 and 53 are mathematical portraits of (in the frame paging) Shakespeare, 1616. I give the German translation as it stands from the text Adamah Booz, 1782.

Das sechste Kapitel.

Daß der Wille Gottes und seine Verordnungen durch Bezeichnungen des großen Naturbuches, und durch neue Sternbilder angezeiget werden könne.

Text: Der Wille Gottes in der vorzunehmenden Verbesserung der Welt ist durch neue Sternbilder, und durch Bezeichnungen des großen Naturbuches angedeutet worden.

In den vorhergehenden ist bewiesen worden, daß die geheimen Bezeichnungen den Sternen am vierten Tage von Gott eingedruckt und eingezeichnet worden sind, durch deren Ordnung und Stellung auf den himmlischen Seiten des großen Naturbuches geheime Sinnbilder hervorgebracht werden, und in deren Innersten große und wunderbare Naturgeheimnisse begriffen sind. Das Leben, Wesen und alle Eigenschaften der Sterne bestehen also im Worte; weil sie und die Himmel durchs Wort des Herrn gemacht sind. Ohne der wesentlichen Kenntniß, Lesen und wahren Bedeutung dieser Bezeichnungen und geheimen Sinnbilder, ist alle Weltweisheit nichts anders als wahre Thorheit und Unwissenheit, und die Astrologie ist für eine eitele und abergläubische Wissenschaft zu halten, deren Vorhersagungen (meistens) ungewis und lügenhaft befunden werden. Denn wem die Kenntniß dieser geheimen Sprache und Schrift, und der verborgenen Bezeichnungen, von Gott verliehen ist; der wird auch die wahren Naturen, Veränderungen und Eigenschaften der Gestirne, und alle ihre Würkungen und Verrichtungen, gleichsam mit erleuchteten Augen lesen und verstehen können. Aber diese Wissenschaft der Bezeichnungen und geheimen himmlischen Sinnbilder ist cabalistisch, und eine ohne Denkmale der Buchstaben geschehene mündliche Fortpflanzung vom Vater auf den

Sohn. Unter diese Art der Cabala scheint die Kosmologie, oder Weltlehre, mit begriffen zu seyn, in welcher besonders von den Geheimnissen des Buches der Natur gehandelt wird, indem durch eine vollkommene Einsicht dieser Wissenschaft der irrdischen und himmlischen Dinge Kräfte und Eigenschaften erkläret werden. In dieser Art der Wissenschaft soll Salomon sich für allen andern hervorgethan, und den Schlüssel dieser geheimen Schreibart besessen haben, weil er der obern und untern Dinge Naturen verstand, und in aller Art der wahren Weisheit unterrichtet und auf eine bewundernswürdige Weise geübt war. Vielleicht ist eben diese Art der Cabala den Brüdern der Gesellschaft vom Rosenkreutze von ihrem Vater Rosenkreutz nach Art der Juden übergeben worden; denn es scheint als ob sie dieses (wiewohl nicht mit ganz deutlichen Worten) in ihrer Fama und Confeßion bekenneten. Wenn dem also ist; ist es dann wohl unmöglich, daß sie eben dasjenige durch diese Kunst leisten, was unsere Vorfahren, die dieses Geschenk ursprünglich von Gott selbst empfangen, damit verrichtet haben? Welche nach dem Zeugnisse Josephs und anderer glaubwürdigen Schriftsteller in der Kenntniß und Beobachtung der Bezeichnungen und Beschaffenheiten der Sterne dergestalt erfahren gewesen sind, daß sie kein Bedenken trugen, aus dem einsichtsvollen Anschauen der gestirnten Himmel voraus zu sagen: was Gott alles für Befehle durch die Sterne, gleichsam als durch seine Diener, hierunten wolle ausgerichtet haben. Ja es scheint, als ob Josephus eingesehen hätte, daß diese Kunst dem Adam zuerst geoffenbaret worden sey, als welchem, wie schon oben erwähnet worden ist, durch diesen göttlichen Unterricht alle Eigenschaften aller Geschöpfe, auch auf ihren ersten Anblick, bekannt, und vermöge der ihnen durchs Wort eingedruckten göttlichen Bezeichnungen, deutlich und offenbahr waren. Es trägt sich zwar bisweilen zu, daß auch Afterastrologen, denen die Geheimnisse der wahren Astrologie, oder Sterndeuterkunst, unbekannt sind, durch ihre betrügerische und ungewisse Kunst etwas gewisses vorherstellen und bestimmen, jedoch ohne die natürlichen Bezeichnungen der himmlischen Seiten zu wissen; eben so, wie die gemeinen Gesichts=und Händewahrsager, nachdem sie (aus den vorher angesehenen Lineen und Durchschnitten des Gesichts oder der Hand) die Anlagen und Anneigungen der Menschen betrachtet haben, die natürlichen Bezeichnungen derselben aber gänzlich vernachläßigen, oder vielmehr nicht verstehen, bisweilen etwas gewisses vorher und wahr zu sagen pflegen, so, daß sie einigermaßen bisweilen von Veränderungen der Luft, Geburtsstellungen, Diebstählen, Wahlen und dergleichen mehr, etwas vorhersagen können; aber doch so, daß ihr Urtheil und zukünftige Stellung sehr mangelhaft, fehlerhaft, und mit vielen Zweifeln und Ungewisheiten vermischt ist; weil diese ihre Wahrsagung bloß aus der Würkung und Erfahrung hergenommen ist, nicht aber aus ihrem Ursprunge, nämlich aus einer wahren Einsicht der Bezeichnungen der himmlischen Natur. Sie nehmen also ihre Beweise aus der Erfahrung her, wo gemeiniglich viel Betrug mit unterläuft, und nicht aus Vernunftgründen, als auf welchen alle ungezweifelte Wahrheit beruhet. Es ist also offenbahr, daß es nicht schwer seyn kann, aus den erkannten Bezeichnungen des großen Naturbuches von den Würkungen der theils seit der Schöpfung her vorhandenen, theils erst neulich erschienenen, Sterne richtig und gleichsam mit offenen Augen zu urtheilen. Und doch fragt Dr Libavius: wie es möglich seyn könne, den göttlichen Willen aus neuen Sternbildern voraus zu sagen? Dem wir hierauf ferner antworten, daß dieses nicht anders geschehe, als wie die Verordnungen aus ihren Ausführungen, oder die Ursachen aus ihren Wirkungen, oder der Grundsatz aus seinem Endzwecke, erkannt werden. Denn die Weisen bezeugen, daß aus dem Endzwecke einer jeden Absicht ihr Grundsatz erhelle. So beweisen die zur Ausführung dieser oder jener Sache fertigen Diener die Absicht des Befehlhabers. So bedeuten die gesehenen und von den Weisen erkannten und verstandenen Bezeichnungen und Eindrücke einer Anordnung auf dem himmlischen Papiere den auszuführenden Willen des Obersten. Und so wie ein neuer Stern, als etwas seltenes in der Natur, für ein Wunderwerk zu halten ist, so zeigen auch die in ihm gesehenen oder bemerkten Bezeichnungen die erstaunenden und wunderbaren Würkungen des göttlichen Willens an. So vernahmen die Magi oder Weisen aus dem Morgenlande aus den vom Morgen sich bewegenden neuen Sternbilde den Willen Gottes: daß nämlich der König der Juden, ein göttlicher und über alle andere erhabener Mann, in Judäa gebohren sey. Denn sie sahen, lasen und erkannten mit ihren Augen die Bezeichnung Christi in dem Sterne. Wo (fragen sie Matth. ii. 2) ist der neugebohrne König der Juden? Wir haben seinen Stern gesehen im Morgenlande, u. s. w. Das heißt: einen Stern, in welchem die Bezeichnungen Christi eingegraben sind. Denn sie wurden nicht etwa eines ungewissen, sondern eines Christo allein eigenen Sternes gewahr, nicht anders, als wenn sie den göttlichen und unaussprechlichen Namen dieses Königs mit geheimen Bezeichnungen hineingeschrieben gesehen hätten. Ja sie wußten aus den wunderbaren Bezeichnungen des Sterns vorher, daß der gebohrne Christus kein gemeiner, sondern ein geistlicher und anbetungswürdiger König sey, daher sie ihn aufsuchten, und (wie einem Gotte) göttliche Ehre erwiesen. Hieraus sehen wir also, daß nicht bloß den Juden, sondern auch ausländischen Weisen, nämlich Persern, der verborgenste und geliebteste Wille Gottes durch Bezeichnungen eines neuen Sterns offenbaret worden sey. Die erstere Ankunft Christi ist also durch Bezeichnungen eines neuen Sterns der Welt angekündigt worden; es wird daher auch nichts unmögliches seyn, daß seine letztere Zukunft, und andere wunderbare Verrichtungen, aus den Bezeichnungen neuer Sterne zu unsern Zeiten durch mündliche Prophezeyungen angezeiget werden können, zumal da dieser Meynung der Prophet Joel ii. 28-30 beyzupflichten scheint, wo Gott spricht: Ich will meinen Geist ausgießen über alles Fleisch, und eure Söhne und Töchter sollen weissagen; eure Aeltesten sollen Träume haben; und eure Jünglinge sollen Gesichte sehen. Auch will ich zur selbigen Zeit beyde über Knechte und Mägde meinen Geist ausgießen. Ich will Wunderzeichen geben im Himmel und auf Erden u. s. w. Dasjenige aber heißet ein Wunderwerk oder Wunderzeichen, was sich in der Natur selten zuträgt, daher war der den Weisen aus Morgenlande, erschienene Stern ein Wunder in der Natur. So sind auch die zu unsern Zeiten sichtbar gewordenen Sterne im Schlangenträger und Schwane, für Wunder in der Natur zu halten. Und wenn wir die Natur desjenigen Zeichens, oder derjenigen Länge des Thierkreises am Himmel, in welcher die sinnbildliche Figur des Schlangenträgers, oder des Serpentarius oder Ophiuchos, begriffen ist, auf eine bloß gemeine astrologische Art betrachten, und die Himmelsgestalt nach der Lage und Stellung der Länge dieses Zeichens untersuchen wollen; so werden wir in die Gegend des Schützen und in das Haus oder Wohnung des Jupiters kommen, und, nach einer bloß auf gemeine Art angestellten Beobachtung der Natur dieser Stelle, finden: daß sie nicht wenig zur Verherrlichung der Brüderschaft, und zur Wahrheit ihrer Prophezeyungen beytrage. Denn nach der natürlichen Aufeinanderfolgung der Zeichen, wenn wir vom Widder zu zählen anfangen, (in welchem Zeichen sich die Sonne bey Entstehung der Welt zuerst bewegt haben soll) wird ihr das erste Haus der Himmelsgestalt zugeeignet; das andere dem Stiere: das dritte den Zwillingen, u. s. f. Wir werden also finden, daß der Schütze seinen natürlichen Stand im neunten Hause habe, welches Religion, Weisheit, Träume, wahre Gesichte anzeiget; daher die Araber dieses Haus die Religion und Gott selbst genennet haben. Es ist einigermaßen durch die Erfahrung bestätiget, daß wegen der Wahrsagung, welche Jupiter natürlicherweise in dieser Stellung bedeutet, Prophezeyungen, Wahrsagungen und Erzählungen künftiger Dinge angezeiget werden. Daher es wahrscheinlich ist, daß diejenigen, welche die geheimen Bezeichnungen der in dieser Länge des Thierkreises neulich entdeckten Sterne zu lesen und zu verstehen die Geschicklichkeit besitzen, auch ohne Zweifel viele und wunderbare Sachen von dem Wachsthume der Weisheit, von der Wahrsagung durch Gesichte, von Voraussagungen zukünftiger Dinge, und dergleichen mehr, der Welt werden verkündigen können. Desgleichen kann der neulich im Schwane sichtbar gewordene Stern, in so ferne er in der Länge des Steinbocks angetroffen wird, dem in der natürlichen Reihe der Zeichen der zehnte Theil der Himmelsgestalt zugeeignet wird, Würde und Erhöhung der Welt, durch eine Erneuerung, d. h. Veränderung derselben aus dem schlechtern ins bessere, anzeigen und vorherbedeuten. Denn das zehnte Haus verspricht Herrschaft, Würde, Verbesserung und Erhöhung. Ja es ergießet sich aus der beständigen Quelle seine Kraft mit sehr glücklicher und zunehmender Ausübung der Künste. Ob also gleich (wie in dem vorhergesagten bewiesen worden ist) ein jeder Stern eine geheime Bezeichnung durchs Wort (Werbe) bey seiner Schöpfung ihm eingedruckt empfangen hat, welche gleichsam das Siegel seines Lebens ist; so kann doch bisweilen selbst ein Weiser und in den Bezeichnungen der Natur sehr geübter, aus Mangel eines oder des andern, zur vollkommenen Zusammensetzung einer sinnbildlichen Schrift erforderlichen, Sterns, eben sowohl irren, als derjenige, welcher ein gewöhnliches Wort lieset, in welchem irgend ein Buchstabe entweder gänzlich fehlet, oder zugleich mit verstanden wird; so, daß dadurch der Wortverstand und Natur geändert werde: wie z. B. die Wörter anus und annus, desgleichen anus und manus, in welchen aus Mangel eines Buchstabens, nämlich des n oder m, der Sinn der Schrift oder des Worts geändert wird, so, daß der Leser dadurch irre gemacht, und vom wahren Verstande abgeführet wird. Auf die nämliche Weise kann durch einen oder den andern zu den himmlischen Sinnbildern hinzugefügten Stern; (welchen Gott den Menschen vor der gesetzten und von ihm bestimmten Zeit nicht hat entdecken wollen) der Sinn der sinnbildlichen Schrift des Himmels, nunmehro endlich den Menschen völlig offenbahret werden, da er vorher unvollständig, zweifelhaft und ungewis war. Und das ist vielleicht der Sinn der Brüderschaft in diesen Worten: der Wille Gottes wegen Erneuerung und Verbesserung der Welt ist durch neue Sternbilder und Bezeichnungen des grossen Naturbuches angezeiget worden.

Nunmehro will ich endlich auch anzeigen, was ich aus der Rosenkreutzerbrüderschaft ihren Prophezeyungen, Verbesserungen der Künste, und ihrer durch alle Welt bekannten Weisheit für Schlüsse gezogen und gesammlet habe. Da Weissagung, Glaube, Religion, Gottheit, Träume, Gesichte, Weisheit, und dergleichen mehr, durch das neunte Haus der Himmelsgestalt angezeiget werden, in dessen Länge der Schlangenträger, als das Behältniß der neuen Sterne, angetroffen wird: desgleichen weil dieses Haus, in der natürlichen Aufeinanderfolgung der Zeichen, dem Schützen zugeeignet wird, welcher das Zeichen Jupiters ist, und daher diese neunte Himmelsabtheilung das Haus Jupiters genennet wird; so habe ich den Jupiter, seine Natur, Veränderungen und Würkungen aufs genaueste untersuchet, als welche am stärksten und deutlichsten bemerket werden in der unter allen Planeten am stärksten zwischen den beyden obern, nämlich dem Saturnus und Jupiter, sich ereignenden Zusammenkunft, wenn sie körperlich, d. h. in einerley Grade und Minute zugleich zusammen kommen. Ich habe öfters die Astrologen von den mannichfaltigen Würkungen dieser Zusammenkunft verschiedentlich sprechen hören. Denn einige (unter welchen ich den Ptolemäus und Cardanus nennen will) haben diese Zusammenkunft deswegen für die stärkste gehalten, weil sie in Gesetze, Staaten und Religionen einen Einfluß hat. Meszahalah hat auf Veranlassung dieser merkwürdigen Zusammenkunft, eines gewissen grossen Propheten Ankunft verkündigt. Alboazen Haly hat auch aus ihrer Eigenschaft von Geschäften der Fürsten und hohen Dingen, desgleichen von Propheten geweissaget. Guido Bonatus hat aus dieses Aspecten Gegenwart wundervolle Begebenheiten, und der Welt bevorstehende wunderbare Dinge vorhergesaget. Aller dieser Meynungen gehen dahin, daß nämlich ein in der Zusammenkunft starker und herrschender Planete, wenn er ein unglücklicher (nämlich Saturnus) ist, der Welt Unglück und Nachtheil; hingegen wenn er ein glücklicher (nämlich Jupiter), Glück und Vortheil verschaffe. Wenn wir dieses fleißig erwägen; so werden wir unsere Absicht auf folgende Art erreichen. Im Jahre 1603 den 20 Decembr. nach dem neuen Stil, in der Mittagsstunde, bewegte sich Saturnus im 8. Grade und 39 Minuten des Schützen. Desgleichen stand Jupiter, fast in eben dem Augenblicke, im 8 Grade 39 Min. und 58 Secunden des nämlichen Zeichens. Ich verfertigte also die Himmelsgestalt für diesen Tag und Stunde, nach der Polhöhe von 38 Graden, unter welcher Sardinien liegt, das ist gleichsam die uns bekannte Hälfte nördlicher Breite, wenn wir vom Aequator bis zum 76sten Erhöhungsgrade zählen, weil die Würkung dieser Zusammenkunft allgemein ist, und fand den Himmel auf folgende Art gestellet. In der Spitze des zehnten Hauses beobachtete ich den 27 Grad des Schützen. Im 29 Grade desselben traf ich die Venus an. Der 16 Grad des Steinbocks nahm die Spitze des eilften Hauses ein, so, daß der vordere Theil dieses Zeichens zugleich seine natürliche Stelle behauptete. Der zwölfte Theil des Wassermannes war nach der Spitze des zwölften Hauses gerichtet. Der 24 Grad der Fische durchschnitt die Spitze des ersten Hauses, oder des Horoscops, gleich wie der 9te Grad des Stieres unten im andern, und der 7te Grad der Zwillinge im dritten Hause anzutreffen waren. So, daß wir durch den Gegenschein der Zeichen finden, daß der 27 Grad der Zwillinge zu gleicher Zeit ins vierte Haus eingerückt sey. So bewahrte der 16 Grad des Krebses den Anfang oder die Schwelle des fünften Hauses, gleichwie der 12te Grad des Löwen das sechste, der 24ste Grad der Jungfrau das siebende, der 9te Grad des Scorpions das achte, und endlich der 7de Grad des Schützen das neunte Haus inne hatten. Hernach merkte ich den Stand und die Beschaffenheit der Irrsterne in dieser Himmelsfigur an, und fand, daß die Sonne in der Spitze des zehnten Hauses im 27 Grade des Schützen war, Saturnus aber und Jupiter im 8 Grade und 39 Min. des Schützen im neunten Hause zusammenkamen. Ich bemerkte auch, daß Merenrius den Eingang dieses Hauses bewachte, und Mars durch den vierten Grad der Wage mitten im siebenden Hause zog, gleichwie der Mond durch den 24 Grad der Krebses im fünften Hause gieng, und das Drachenhaupt den 14 Grad des Scorpions, so wie der Drachenschwanz den entgegengesetzten Stand, nämlich den 24 Grad des Stiers im andern Hause einnahm. Dieses war also die ganze Himmelsbeschaffenheit zur Zeit dieser großen sich neuerlich ereigneten Zusammenkunft, welche ohne Zweifel große und erstaunende Dinge in Ansehung der Ankunft der Propheten, der Aenderung alter Sitten, der Verbesserung der alten verderbten Religion, und der vielleicht gänzlichen Austilgung, oder wenigstens Verminderung der päbstlichen und muhamedischen Hoheit, u. s. w. nach der Brüder Vorhersagung, anzuzeigen und vorzubedeuten scheinet. Desgleichen scheinet sie verwunderungswürdige Dinge von Verbesserung und Erhöhung der alten Künste und Wissenschaften, von Offenbahrung der wahren Weisheit, und dergleichen mehr, zu verkündigen. Wir wollen also den Stand und Beschaffenheit dieser Planeten untersuchen, und aufs fleißigste nachforschen, welcher von ihnen mächtiger oder beglückender sey. Wenn wir nun dieses ernstlich erwägen, so finden wir, daß Jupiter mächtiger sey, als die übrigen Planeten; weil er auf mehrere Beweise seiner Stärke Ansprüche macht, als die übrigen. Denn er befindet sich in seinem Hause, wo er fünf Würden erhält; überdies wird er in seiner Freudigkeit angetroffen weswegen er noch vier andere Würden bekömmt, und eben so viele, in so ferne er die Herrschaft in dem Horoscop, oder im Aufgange erhalten hat, und noch zwo Würden scheint er zu erhalten, weil er sich in seiner Grenze befindet. Daher unstreitig Jupiter die Herrschaft über den ganzen Himmel damals gehabt hat. Ueberdies war Saturnus in seiner Triplicität, wodurch er drey Würdigkeiten erhält: beyde gehen auch vor Aufgang der Sonne auf, und sind von der Sonne nicht verbrannt, welches an den drey obern Planeten ein gutes Zeichen ist. Beyde sind vor sich gehend, und wegen dieses geraden Laufes im Epicycle oder Nebenkreise stärker. Beyde sind, weil sie sich vorwärts, nach der Ordnung der Zeichen, gegen Morgen, bewegen, schnellen Laufes; beyde stehen im männlichen Grade; und beyde sind endlich Tagezeichen. Woraus erhellet, daß diese Planeten in ihrer Zusammenkunft sowohl an wesentlichen als zufälligen Würdigkeiten ganz vorzüglich sind. Wiewohl Jupiter an Ehre und Würde viele Grade über den Saturnus (aus schon angeführten Ursachen) erhoben zu seyn scheinet. Es ist also offenbahr, daß diese beyden Planeten glücklich und sehr gut constelliret sind. Wir merken daher nach der Meynung der gelehrtesten Astrologen an: daß Saturnus in einer guten Constellation verehrungswürdige, tiefnachdenkende und schwere Künste erlernende, ernsthafte, wichtige und beschwerliche Thaten ausübende, verschwiegene und eingezogene Leute mache. Jupiter aber in seiner glücklichen Constellation bringe gerechte und ehrbare, gute und wohlthätige, religiöse und verständige und sich liebende Menschen hervor. Und unter den Würden bedeutet er: Propheten, Bischöffe, Vorsteher der Religion, Richter, Künstler und Rechtsgelehrte. Denn wenn wir die natürliche Beschaffenheit des Jupiters untersuchen, welche warm und feuchte, luftig und sanguinisch ist; so finden wir, daß er nicht nur allen untern Dingen, wegen Gleichheit seiner natürlichen Anlage, zugethan, sondern auch über die Sterne selbst Richter sey; daher es kommt, daß die Menschen durch seine Einflüsse gehorsam, gottesfürchtig, und gerecht erfunden werden: gleichwie Saturnus in der guten Constellation einen standhaften, tiefsinnigen, ernsthaften, und mit wichtigen oder geheimen Dingen beschäftigten Menschen anzeiget. Weil sie aber beyde im neunten Hause zusammenkommen, und weil der Schütze, welcher selbiges bewohnet, die natürliche Wohnung des Jupiters ist, der zugleich auch, in Ansehung der Zeichenfolge, sich in seiner natürlichen Behausung befindet; so müssen wir die Natur des neunten Hauses sowohl, als auch des Schützen, fleißig erwägen. Wir wissen aber aus der Lehre der Alten (wie auch oben erwähnet worden ist), daß dieses Haus seine Benennung von Gott und der Religion führe, und Religion, Treue und Glauben, lange Reisen, die Gottheit, Gesichte, Träume, Prophezeyungen, Weisheit, Weissagung, oder Erzählung zukünftiger Dinge, Weltweisheit, Wissenschaft, u. s. w. bezeichne. Wie dieses Mesehella, Aomar, Alkindus, Zael, Albenair, Dorotheus, Ptolemäus, Sconerus, und andere, sowohl ältere als neuere, bezeugen. Der Schütze ist ein Aufgangs-und Tagezeichen, feurig und männlich, und bedeutet an den Menschen eine Geneigtheit zum Frieden, zur Klugheit, zur Wiederherstellung verwüsteter Staaten und verlorner Künste und zum geselligen ehrbaren Vergnügen. Nachdem wir nun die in der Länge des Jupiterzeichens, im Schlangenträger, wie auch die im Schwane angetroffenen Sterne untersuchet haben; so wollen wir nun auch die Zusammenkunft des Jupiters und des Saturnus, um die Zeit ihrer Erscheinung, und nicht viel vor Bekandtwerdung dieser Brüderschaft vom Rosenkreutze betrachten, an welcher wir bemerken, daß sie mit den Absichten und Versprechungen der Brüderschaft gänzlich übereinstimmen. Denn Jupiter, welcher kräftiger als Saturnus, ist für die Welt eine gute Vorbedeutung, nämlich der Ankunft der Propheten, sowohl nach der natürlichen Beschaffenheit des Hauses, als auch vermöge der glücklichen Zusammenkunft, welche, nach dem Messahalah, eines oder mehrerer Propheten Ankunft bedeutet, und zwar keiner falschen, betrügerischen, oder bösen, sondern guter, nach den Eigenschaften der zusammengekommenen und gut constellirten Planeten; daher sie, dem Einflusse des Saturnus zu Folge, als ehrwürdige, tiefsinnige, als Lehrer schwerer Künste, als solche, die wichtige Thaten unternehmen, als arbeitsame, verschwiegene und eingezogene verheißen werden. Daß dieses aber die Eigenschaften dieser Brüderschaft sind, bezeugen ihre Fama und Confeßion. Nach dem Einflusse des

Jupiters aber wird ihnen Gerechtigkeit, Frömmigkeit, Gütigkeit, Religion, Gunst, Klugheit und die Gabe der Weiffagung zugeeignet. Aus der Beschaffenheit des neunten Hauses, in welchem die Zusammenkunft geschahe, wird ihnen Treue und Glaube, Weisheit, Weiffagung, Religion, Prophezeyung, Weltweisheit und Kenntnifz der Wissenschaften zugestanden. Vom Schützen und Jupiter zugleich erhalten sie Friedfertigkeit und Klugheit, und das Vermögen, den in Verfall gerathenen Künsten wieder aufzuhelfen. Da überdies Jupiter die Herrschaft nicht nur über den ganzen Himmel überhaupt führet, sondern auch insbesondere der Herr sowohl des neunten Hauses, in welchem er angetroffen wird, als auch des Aufgangswinkels selbst, oder des ersten Hauses, ist, indem in desselben Spitze die letztere Hälfte der Fische sich befindet; so bedeutet er wahre Prophezeyungen, wahre Träume, wahre Künste und Secten, wie solches Dorotheus bezeuget. Weil aber das aufsteigende Zeichen der Fische ein nächtliches Haus ist; so zeiget dieses an: daſz diese Brüder, die sich zwar jetzo noch versteckt halten, sich täglich mehr ausbreiten und vermehren werden, und daſz ihr Glanz und Morgenröthe, wie nach dem Grauen des Tages, plötzlich hervorbrechen, und sich täglich mehr und mehr veroffenbahren und verherrlichen werde. Und das um so viel mehr, weil es ein fruchtbares Zeichen ist, welches dasjenige, was von seinem Herrn angezeiget wird, vermehret. Daher Jupiter im neunten Hause eine Menge und Vermehrung der Propheten, und Zunahme der Weisen, u. d. m. bedeutet. Auch Mercurius, als gleichsam der Wächter dieses Hauses der Zusammenkunft, zeiget fürtrefliches Genie, Religion, Weltweisheit, Mathematik, Weiffagung, und zukünftige Erfindung neuer Künste an. Und weil auch die Sonne in das neunte Haus eingetreten ist, jedoch so, daſz sie, zur Zeit der Zusammenkunft, durch die Spitze des zehnten Hauses vorübergieng, und das Zeichen des Jupiters einnahm; so wird auch ihre Kraft mit den günstigen Würkungen des Jupiters vereinigt, daher sie eine Erhöhung und Erneuerung der Dinge aus einem schlechten in einen bessern Zustand, und eine verbesserte Ausübung der Künste anzeiget. Mars, mitten im siebenden Hause, nämlich im vierten Grade der Wage, bedeutet Neid wider des Jupiters Würkungen, und daſz die verheißenen Propheten oder Weisen Feinde haben werden, welche desto neidischer und zäntischer seyn werden, weil er im Gesichte und in der Triplicität des Saturnus, als welcher neidisch macht, angetroffen wird. Weil aber der böse Einfluſz des Saturnus sowohl durch die guten Eigenschaften des Jupiters, als auch durch dessen glückliche Constellation, verbessert wird; so werden zwar diese Neider wie Hunde bellen, aber keinesweges beißen können. Denn obgleich Mars an einem zänkischen Orte steht, nämlich im siebenden Hause, so kann er doch, weil er aller wesentlichen Würde beraubet ist, nichts böses wider die günstigen Würkungen des Jupiters, nämlich: die Prophezeyungen, Wahrsagungen, Verbesserungen der Künste, und dergleichen, ausrichten; ausgenommen daß ihm bisweilen etwas wider desselben Würkungen schwatzhafterweise auszustoßen verstattet wird. Was endlich der Mond im fünften Hause zum Nachtheile eines gewissen alten Propheten, als des Muhameds, verkündige; und was der der Spitze seines Hauses, nämlich der im dritten Hause sich befindenden Zwillinge, gerade gegenüberstehende Mercurius, als welcher ehemaligen Glauben und Religion bedeutet, von dem Verfalle eines gewissen königlichen Bischofs anzeige, will ich hier übergehen, weil es nicht zu unserm Vorhaben gehöret, und bloß dieses berühren: daß Jupiter in Ansehung der wahren Religionslehre und Erklärung, der Verbesserung gemeiner Künste, und der Erneuerung und Wiederherstellung der Sittlichkeit, viel zu versprechen scheine. Hieraus erhellet also, daß die wunderbaren Würkungen dieser Planetenzusammenkunft, in so ferne sie die Brüderschaft betreffen, auch in der gemeinen Sterndeuterkunst ausgeleget, und daß ihre Religion, Glaube, Weisheit, Wissenschaft und neue Weltweisheit, Prophezeyung, Verbesserung gemeiner Künste, Ehrbarkeit, Ansehen, Tiefsinnigkeit, geheimen Künste, Treue, Gerechtigkeit, u. d. m. am Himmel auch von Afterastrologen, durch Betrachtung dieser Zusammenkunft, vorhergesehen und verkündigt werden können. Und ich behaupte steif und fest, daß man in vielen Jahrhunderten keine schicklichere und wahrscheinlichere Planetenzusammenkunft für die Vergrößerung der Prophezeyung, Religion, Weltweisheit und Weisheit, antreffen wird, als diese, welche sich in oben angeführten Jahre, Monate, und Tage ereignete. Außerdem daß die an eben den Orten dieser Himmelsgestalt beobachteten neuen Sterne und ihre geheime Schriften uns ohne Zweifel noch weit höhere und wichtigere Dinge und Begebenheiten entdecken wurden, wenn uns (wie wir schon erinnert haben) die wahre Kenntniß der geheimen Bezeichnungen nicht verborgen wäre. Ich mache also den Schluß, daß diese Gesellschaft hierinnen nichts ungereimtes behauptet hat: daß der Wille Gottes durch Zeichenbilder neuer Sterne und durch Bezeichnungen des großen Naturbuches offenbaret werde, und daß er beschlossen habe, die Anzahl dieser Brüderschaft zu vermehren, und daß die Brüder zuverläßig wissen, daß die Zeit kommen wird, wo, was jetzo noch verborgen ist, offenbahr, und öffentlich mit lauter Stimme und ausdrücklichen Worten bekannt werden wird; und dieses soll geschehen sowohl durch wiederhergestellte Uebereinstimmung der ganzen Welt, als auch durch Erscheinung neuer Sterne im Schlangen=

träger und Schwane. Dieses bestätiget auch das Haus Jupiters, die Fische im Aufgange, welches ein Zeichen der Fruchtbarkeit und der Vermehrung der von seinem Herrn angezeigten Dinge, wie schon oben angezeiget worden, ist. Desgleichen zeiget der Mond in seinem Hause, und indem er den fünften Theil des Himmels durchläuft, wo er die süßeste Würkung des Kinderzeugens zu haben pfleget, die Vermehrung der Brüder, und das Zunehmen der Weisheits= söhne, oder der Würkungen Jupiters, an. Wie denn auch selbst Jupiter in seiner guten und glücklichen Constellation die verheißene Vermehrung und Frucht der schwangern Minerva beschleuniget. Endlich ist zu merken: daß das Zeichen des neunten Hauses bey dieser großen oben beschriebenen Planeten= zusammenkunft eben so beschaffen gewesen sey, wie bey der ersten Sonnenbewegung zur Zeit der Schöpfung. Denn nach des Abts Trithemius und anderer geschickten Weltweisen und erfahrner Astrologen Beurtheilung geschah die erste Erscheinung der Sonne, welche den vierten Tag nach der Schöpfung ausmachte, im Widder, weil dieses Zeichen des Thierkreises sich am Morgen dieses Tages im ersten Hause, oder Horoscop, befand, so wie der Stier im andern u. s. f. (wie schon gesagt worden ist). Woraus augenscheinlich erhellet: daß der Schütze (das Zeichen und Haus Jupiters) in der natürlichen Reihe der Zeichen damals das neunte Haus oder Abschnitt des Thierkreises inne gehabt hat. Ich habe also gefunden, daß zur Zeit dieser großen neuerlich sich ereigneten Zusammenkunft, nicht nur der Zustand des neunten Hauses und seines Zeichens der nämliche gewesen sey, wie damals, zur Zeit der Schöpfung, sondern auch, daß der Planete desselbigen Zeichens, nämlich Jupiter, in selbigem als in seinem eigenen und Tagehause, mit günstiger und glücklicher Bestralung aufgenommen worden sey. Ja, daß es sogar den Saturnus, als einen, für allen übrigen, bösen und unglücklichen Planeten, in seinen Palast aufgenommen, regieret, verbessert, und dessen rohe Sitten und wilde Natur, durch seine guten Eigenschaften und glücklichen Einfluß, gemildert und zahmer gemacht habe. Eben daraus haben (nach meiner Einsicht) die Brüder die sittliche Erneuerung und Wiederherstellung der Welt, das heißt, die Erneuerung, Verbesserung und Erhöhung der Sitten, Wissenschaften und Künste, und die Freyheit und Erleuchtung der in der Sclaverey und Irrthum lebenden Menschen, und den hellglänzenden Schein der schon lange verfinsterten Wahrheit, mit gänzlicher Verweisung und Ausrottung der Unwahrheit, desgleichen die Zurückbringung und durch vereinigte Kräfte zu befördernde Erneuerung des goldenen Zeitalters, (zu dessen Anfange Adam in seiner Unschuld das Paradies bewohnet haben soll) nicht unschicklich vorher= kündigt, indem sie an einem Orte ihres Bekenntnisses sagen: daß die Welt eine Erneuerung bedürfe; und an einem andern Orte: daß der Wille Gottes in Ansehung der Weltverbesserung durch die Bezeichnungen im grossen Naturbuche bekannt gemacht worden sey. Ferner wird die

Wiederherstellung der Sitten, Verbesseung der Künste und Beförderung der Wissenschaften durch die Bemühungen gewisser der Welt verheißenen Propheten oder Weisen, augenscheinlich bewiesen; weil ein Theil des Schützen, der das ganze neunte Haus inne hatte, auch die Spitze des zehnten Hauses einnahm. Woraus gefolgert wird, daß alle vom Herrn des neunten Hauses angegebene Würkungen (als: Weisheit, Weltweisheit, Gesetze, Religion, Gerechtigkeit, Propheyung, Künste und Wissenschaften, und dergleichen mehr, das vorher schon angeführet worden ist) zur Erhöhung abzwecken, das heißt, zur Versetzung aus einem schlimmern und geringern, in einen bessern und edlern, Zustand; weil das zehende Haus mit Staaten, Würden, Ehrenstellen, Erhöhungen der auszuübenden Künste und Wissenschaften zu thun hat, und dieses um desto mehr, weil die Sonne, als ein königlicher Planete und Beförderer der Wissenschaften, in diesem Hause in Gesellschaft der Venus angetroffen wird, welche freygebig, wohlthätig, angenehm und sinnreich ist. Und auf diese Art habe ich dem doppelten Zweifel des Dr Libavius: wodurch nämlich die Brüder ihre Vorhersagungen aus neuen Sternen und Zeichenbildern des Himmels beweisen wollen; und worinne die Erneuerung und Verbesserung der Welt bestehen solle? hinlänglich (wie ich glaube) und überflüßig begegnet.

Eine wahre Abbilduug der oben angeführten Himmelsgestalt, welche die Natur und Beschaffenheit des Himmels, wie sie zur Stunde der letzten großen Planeten-zusammenkunft war, erkläret. Sie ist aus dem Tagebuche des Martinus Everhardus von Brügge genommen nach der Polhöhe von 38 Graden.

Die Ursache, warum ich den Grad dieser Polhöhe für alle andere erwählet habe, ist oben kürzlich und mit einem Worte gleichsam angezeiget worden.

Anmerkung.

Die Sonne, die Venus, der Saturnus und Jupiter werden in das Haus oder Tagezeichen des Jupiters, nämlich in den Schützen, zugleich aufgenommen, mit welchem Ophiuchos, oder der Schlangenmann, mit seinen neuen Sternen aufsteiget. Desgleichen wird Saturnus vom Jupiter in seinen Palast günstig aufgenommen; dieses Zeichens oder' Hauses, nämlich des Steinbocks, Vorbertheil (mit welchem der Schwan mit seinen neuen Sternen aufsteiget) wird im zehenden Hause angetroffen.

Die Sonnenerhöhung ist mitten am Himmel. Der Mond nahet sich dem Saturnus im Gedrittscheine in der eilften Nachmittagsstunde, und die Venus dem Monde in der drey und zwanzigsten Stunde. u. s. w.

Ende des ersten Theils.

Bacon writes: "But this is that which will indeed dignify and exalt knowledge, if contemplation and action may be more nearly and straitly conjoined and united together than they have been; *a conjunction like unto that of the two highest planets, Saturn, the planet of rest and contemplation, and Jupiter, the planet of civil society and action*" (p. 26 (*bis*), "Advancement of Learning," 1605; p. 40, "Advancement of Learning," 1640).

This shows Bacon had noted the conjunction of Saturn with Jupiter, Fludd adduces in this chapter from his "Apologus." The reader may also see in the fact, Fludd's apology was published 1617, proof it was written 1616, *the year of Shakespeare's death*. I find in many of Maier's works the date 1617 upon the title-page, and 1616 in the Preface as date of writing, the discrepancy arising from the publisher's date and the author's date, or interval of time taken in setting up the copy. In the 1623 "De Augmentis," the above quotation is to be found upon page 38, *mispaged* 46. The reader will also note the coincidence that it is upon page 26 of the *First Edition* of the 1605 "Proficience and Advancement of Learning" the citation occurs, and that we find 26 as the first figure of Bacon's Annotations to "Hermes Stella." 1603 is also the date of "Valerius Terminus."

THE STAR OF BETHLEHEM.

In the 1879 edition of *Zadkiel's Almanac* a treatise on the Star of Bethlehem, by the late Mr Wm. Hutton, was published, in which it was stated that the re-appearance of the new star in Cassiopeia, which was observed in A.D. 945, 1264, and 1572, might be expected in 1887. Down to the time of writing (July 1889) the star has not re-appeared. It will be observed that the exact period of its recurrence is uncertain, for the two periods given by the years before-mentioned are unequal—319 and 308 years respectively. But if we take the longer period, and apply it to 1572, we have 1891 as the approximate year of its re-appearance.

In Chaldæan astrology the constellation Cassiopeia was termed Nin-makh, "mighty lady," one of the twelve stars presiding over Martu, the West, Syria or Phœnicia. Nin-makh is one of the various developments of Ishtar (the Moon or Venus in the sign *Taurus* or *Virgo*). The same constellation was also termed "the woman with child" (Eratu), because it brings forth, every 300 and odd years, the brightest and most remarkable new star, its child. In the Chaldæo-Greek legend, Cassiopeia boasted that her child was fairer than all the Nereids.

This beautiful star appearing in Cassiopeia, and its line of right ascension falling in the second decanate of *Aries*, the sign ruling Judea, was held by the Magi to be the symbol of Christ.

A graphic account of the appearance of this star in 1572 was given by Tyco Brahe, the renowned astronomer and astrologer, some extracts from which will be found in Humboldt's "Cosmos." The star continued from November, 1572, to March, 1574,* or

* Robert Fludd, the great Rosicrucian, was born in 1574.

seventeen months. It was brighter than Sirius, and rivalled Venus. Its colour was successively white, yellow, red, and white again, and it remained stationary all the while in the position which it occupied when discovered. It was seen by some persons in the daytime, about noon.

Doctor Kenealy writes: "The blazing star, Iliaster, which appears in the Masonic lodges, which these gentlemen call the Star of Bethlehem: truly enough, for this was also the star of the Naros" (p. 154, vol. ii., "Enoch"). It was in connection with this star Paracelsus wrote that the Bird Phœnix is the soul of the great Iliaster ("De Vita Longa," c. 2), meaning, evidently, the periodic re-appearance of this star.

"The only sect or association with which the Rosicrucians may be pertinently compared, and which we hear of before the year 1610, is the *Militia Crucifera Evangelica*, which assembled at Lunenburg in 1598 under the auspices of the mystic and theosophist, Simon Studion. Its proceedings are reported in an unprinted work from his pen, entitled 'Naometria, seu nuda et prima libri, intus et foris scripti, per clavem Davidis et calamum (virgæ similem) apertio; in quo non tantum ad cognoscenda tam S. Scripturæ totius, quam naturæ quoque universæ, mysteria, brevis fit introductio—verum etiam Prognosticus (stellæ illius matutinæ, Anno Domini 1572, conspectæ ductu) demonstratur Adventus ille Christi ante diem novissimum secundus per quem homine peccati (Papâ) cum filio suo perditionis (Mahomedo) divinitus devestato, ipse ecclesiam suam et principatus mundi restaurabit, ut in iis post hac sit cum ovili pastor unus. In cruciferæ militiæ Evangelicæ gratiam. Authore Simone Studione inter Scorpiones. Anno 1604'" (p. 213, Waite's "Real History of the Rosicrucians").

Spedding writes: "In the 'Cogitationes de Naturâ Rerum,' of which the date is unknown, we find, '. . . mutationes in regionibus cœlestibus fieri, ex cometis quibusdam satis liquet; iis dico qui certam et constantem configurationem cum stellis fixis servarunt; qualis fuit ille qui in Cassiopeâ nostrâ ætate apparuit.' This star in Cassiopeia appeared in 1572. But another of the same kind, and no less *remarkable, appeared in September* 1604. It is said to have been brighter, when first seen, than Jupiter, and though its brightness diminished afterwards, it was distinctly visible for more than a year. In the 'Descriptio Globi Intellectualis,' which we know to have been written about the year 1612, the passage which I have just quoted appears in a new form. 'Id enim [sc. admirandas in cœlo accidere mutationes atque insolentias] perspicitur in cometis sublimioribus, iis nimirum qui et figuram stellæ induerunt absque comâ, neque solum ex doctrinâ parallaxium supra lunam collocati esse probantur, sed configurationem etiam certam et constantem cum stellis fixis habuerunt, et stationes suas servarunt, neque errones fuerunt ; quales ætas nostra *non semel* vidit ; primo in Cassiopeâ, *iterum non ita pridem in Ophiucho.*' "

(Ophiuchus and Serpentarius are identical.)

"*The bright star which appeared between Cepheus and Cassiopeia in the years* 945, 1264, *and* 1572, *the last time being observed by Tycho, the great Danish astronomer, is considered to have probably been the same star at its periodical return of about three hundred years.* That which appeared in 1604, in the constellation Ophiuchus, was observed by Kepler. He even conjectured that it might have been the star of Bethlehem ; but it was not vertical over Jerusalem and Bethlehem, which the star in Coma was. The star of Kepler was near the ecliptic, being just over the planets Jupiter and Saturn, then in conjunction " (Mazzaroth).

Allowing for the difference of old and new style computation, this evidently is 1603, viz., Fludd's conjunction of Jupiter and Saturn.

APPENDIX.

I INTRODUCE here an important proof of cipher connection between Bacon's "History of King Henry the Seventh" and the Folio plays of 1623. The reader will find the numbers 52, 53 against *Stage-play*, counted from the bottom of the page upwards, and 268 down. The numbers 52, 53 are Shakespeare's full years, and year he had entered (1616) when he died. 268 is the number of the word Bacon, page 53, " Merry Wives of Windsor," counted down the column. What is really suggested by these figures is Shakespeare (52), Bacon (268), *Stage-play*. The critic can test these figures in Bacon's " History of King Henry the Seventh," either 1622 or 1641 edition.

(Pages 19, 20.)

TABULATED TABLE of Page 21, Bacon's "History of King Henry the Seventh," 1622.

word	a	b	c	d	word	e	f	g
Education ;		1		320	in		46		275
or		2		319	his		47		274
in		3		318	infancy,		48		273
fit		4		317	known		49		272
answers		5		316	to		50		271
to		6		315	few ;		51		270
questions,		7		314	but		52		269
or		8		313	a		53		268
the		9		312	*youth*	2	54	24	267
like,		10		311	that		55		266
any		11		310	till		56		265
ways		12		309	the		57		264
to		13		308	age		58		263
come		14		307	almost		59		262
near		15		306	of		60		261
the		16		305	ten		61		260
resemblance		17		304	years		62		259
of		18		303	had		63		258
him		19		302	been		64		257
whom		20		301	brought		65		256
he		21		300	up		66		255
was		22		299	in		67		254
to		23		298	a		68		253
represent.		24		297	*court*	3	69	23	252
For		25		296	where		70		251
this		26		295	infinite		71		250
Lad	1	27	25	294	eyes		72		249
was		28		293	had		73		248
not		29		292	been		74		247
to		30		291	upon		75		246
personate		31		290	him.		76		245
one,		32		289	For		77		244
that		33		288	King		78		243
had		34		287	EDWARD	4	79	22	242
been		35		286	touched		80		241
long		36		285	with		81		240
before		37		284	remorse		82		239
taken		38		283	of		83		238
out		39		282	his		84		237
of		40		281	brother		85		236
his		41		280	the		86		235
cradle,		42		279	*Duke*	5	87	21	234
or		43		278	of		88		233
conveighed		44		277	*Clarence's*	6	89	20	232
away		45		276	death,		90		231

APPENDIX.

would		91		230	person	12	143	14	178
not		92		229	that		144		177
indeed		93		228	knew		145		176
restore		94		227	particularly		146		175
his		95		226	and		147		174
son		96		225	familiarly		148		173
(of		97		224	EDWARD	13	149	13	172
whom		98		223	PLANTAGENET	14	150	12	171
we		99		222	had		151		170
speak)		100		221	a		152		169
to		101		220	hand		153		168
be		102		219	in		154		167
Duke	7	103	19	218	the		155		166
of		104		217	business,		156		165
Clarence	8	105	18	216	from		157		164
but		106		215	whom		158		163
yet		107		214	the		159		162
created		108		213	*priest*	15	160	11	161
him		109		212	might		161		160
Earl	9	110	17	211	take		162		159
of		111		210	his		163		158
Warwick,	10	112	16	209	aim.		164		157
reviving		113		208	That		165		156
his		114		207	which		166		155
honour		115		206	is		167		154
on		116		205	most		168		153
the		117		204	probable,		169		152
mother's		118		203	out		170		151
side,		119		202	of		171		150
and		120		201	the		172		149
used		121		200	precedent		173		148
him		122		199	and		174		147
honourably		123		198	subsequent		175		146
during		124		197	acts,		176		145
his		125		196	is		177		144
time,		126		195	that		178		143
though		127		194	it		179		142
RICHARD	11	128	15	193	was		180		141
the		129		192	the		181		140
Third		130		191	*Queen*	16	182	10	139
afterwards		131		190	*Dowager*,	17	183	9	138
confined		132		189	from		184		137
him.		133		188	whom		185		136
So		134		187	this		186		135
that		135		186	action		187		134
it		136		185	had		188		133
cannot		137		184	the		189		132
be,		138		183	principal		190		131
but		139		182	source		191		130
that		140		181	and		192		129
some		141		180	motion.		193		128
great		142		179	For		194		127

APPENDIX.

certain		195		126	thinking		242		79
it		196		125	her		243		78
is,		197		124	daughter,		244		77
she		198		123	as		245		76
was		199		122	the		246		75
a		200		121	King		247		74
busy		201		120	handled		248		73
negotiating		202		119	the		249		72
woman,		203		118	matter,		250		71
and		204		117	not		251		70
in		205		116	advanced		252		69
her		206		115	but		253		68
withdrawing-Chamber	18	207	8	114	depressed : and		254 255		67 66
had		208		113	none		256		65
the		209		112	could		257		64
fortunate		210		111	hold		258		63
conspiracy	19	211	7	110	the		259		62
for		212		109	*book*	21	260	5	61
the		213		108	so		261		60
King		214		107	well		262		59
against		215		106	to		263		58
King		216		105	prompt		264		57
RICHARD	20	217	6	104	and		265		56
the		218		103	instruct		266		55
Third		219		102	this		267		54
been		220		101	*Stage*	22	268	4	53*
hatched ;		221		100	*Play*	23	269	3	52
which		222		99	as		270		51
the		223		98	she		271		50
King		224		97	could.		272		49
knew,		225		96	Nevertheless		273		48
and		226		95	it		274		47
remembered		227		94	was		275		46
perhaps		228		93	not		276		45
but		229		92	her		277		44
too		230		91	meaning,		278		43
well ;		231		90	nor		279		42
and		232		89	no		280		41
was		233		88	more		281		40
at		234		87	was		282		39
this		235		86	it		283		38
time		236		85	the		284		37
extremely		237		84	meaning		285		36
discontent		238		83	of		286		35
with		239		82	any		287		34
the		240		81	of		288		33
King,		241		80	the		289		32

* Mark 53 against *Stage*, and 52 against *Play*. It is upon page 53, "Merry Wives of Windsor," and page 52 (mispaged 54) " I King Henry IV.," *we find three entries of the word Bacon.*

APPENDIX.

better		290		31	should		306		15
and		291		30	possess		307		14
sager		292		29	the		308		13
sort		293		28	*Crown,*	25	309	1	12
that		294		27	but		310		11
favoured		295		26	at		311		10
this		296		25	his		312		9
enterprise		297		24	peril		313		8
and		298		23	to		314		7
knew		299		22	make		315		6
the		300		21	way		316		5
secret,		301		20	to		317		4
that		302		19	the		318		3
this		303		18	over- }		319		2
disguised		304		17	throw }		320		1
idol	24	305	2	16					

It may be seen the words "*this Stage-Play*" are the 267, 268, and 269th words down the page. Upon page 53, " Merry Wives of Windsor " (col. 106), these numbers give :—

this	267 }	For	267 }	p. 53.
{ *Stage-*	268 }	Bacon	268 }	" M. W.
{ *Play*	269 }	I	269 }	W."

It may be seen *Play* is the 23rd word in extraordinary letterpress, not only pointing to Richard III., which is the 23rd play in the 1623 Folio, but possibly to the date 23—1623.

APPENDIX.

(Page 23.)

TABULATED TABLE, Page 23, "History of King Henry the Seventh," 1641.

word		#		#	word		#		#
his		1		307	upon		44		264
escape,		2		306	the		45		263
the		3		305	bruit		46		262
cunning		4		304	of		47		261
Priest	1	5	27	303	*Plantagenet's*	4	48	24	260
changed		6		302	escape.		49		259
his		7		301	But		50		258
copy,		8		300	yet		51		257
and		9		299	doubting		52		256
chose		10		298	that		53		255
now		11		297	there		54		254
PLANTAGENET	2	12	26	296	would		55		253
to		13		295	be		56		252
be		14		294	too		57		251
the		15		293	near		58		250
subject		16		292	looking		59		249
his		17		291	and		60		248
Pupill	3	18	25	290	too		61		247
should		19		289	much		62		246
personate,		20		288	*Perspective*	5	63	23	245
because		21		287	into		64		244
he		22		286	his		65		243
was		23		285	disguise,		66		242
more		24		284	if		67		241
in		25		283	he		68		240
the		26		282	should		69		239
present		27		281	show		70		238
speech		28		280	it		71		237
and		29		279	here		72		236
votes		30		278	in		73		235
of		31		277	*England*	6	74	22	234
the		32		276	he		75		233
people,		33		275	thought		76		232
and		34		274	good		77		231
it		35		273	(after		78		230
pieced		36		272	the		79		229
better,		37		271	manner		80		228
and		38		270	of		81		227
followed		39		269	*scenes*	7	82	21	226
more		40		268	in		83		225
close		41		267	*Stage-* }	8	84*	20	224
and		42		266	*Plays* }	9	85	19	223
handsomely		43		265	and		86		222

* If we add the paging 23 to 83, 84, we get 106, 107, and it is upon columns 106, 107 of the Comedies and Histories, 1623, we find the words Bacon and *Francis* (22 times).

APPENDIX.

Maskes)	10	87	18	221	least		139		169
to		88		220	intermingled		140		168
shew		89		219	persons		141		167
it		90		218	of		142		166
a		91		217	whom		143		165
farre		92		216	he		144		164
off;		93		215	stood		145		163
and		94		214	assured,		146		162
therefore		95		213	as		147		161
sailed		96		212	he		148		160
with		97		211	should		149		159
his		98		210	have		150		158
scholar		99		209	done,		151		157
into		100		208	since		152		156
Ireland,	11	101	17	207	he		153		155
where		102		206	knew		154		154
the		103		205	the		155		153
affection		104		204	strong		156		152
to		105		203	bent		157		151
the		106		202	of		158		150
House		107		201	that		159		149
of		108		200	country		160		148
Yorke	12	109	16	199	towards		161		147
was		110		198	the		162		146
most		111		197	House		163		145
in		112		196	of		164		144
height.		113		195	YORKE,	16	165	12	143
The		114		194	and		166		142
King		115		193	that		167		141
had		116		192	it		168		140
been		117		191	was		169		139
a		118		190	a		170		138
little		119		189	ticklish		171		137
improvident		120		188	and		172		136
in		121		187	unsettled		173		135
matters		122		186	state,		174		134
of		123		185	more		175		133
Ireland,	13	124	15	184	easy		176		132
and		125		183	to		177		131
had		126		182	receive		178		130
not		127		181	distempers		179		129
removed		128		180	and		180		128
Officers	14	129	14	179	mutations		181		127
and		130		178	than		182		126
Chancellors,	15	131	13	177	*England*	17	183	11	125
and		132		176	was.		184		124
put		133		175	But		185		123
in		134		174	trusting		186		122
their		135		173	to		187		121
places		136		172	the		188		120
or		137		171	reputation		189		119
at		138		170	of		190		118

APPENDIX.

his		191		117	and		243		65
Victories		192		116	plotted		244		64
and		193		115	before		245		63
successes		194		114	hand.		246		62
in		195		113	Simon's	22	247	6	61
England	18	196	10	112	first		248		60
he		197		111	address		249		59
thought		198		110	was		250		58
he		199		109	to		251		57
should		200		108	the		252		56
have		201		107	Lord		253		55
time		202		106	Thomas	23	254	5	54
enough		203		105	Fitzgerald,	24	255	4	53
to		204		104	Earl	25	256	3	52
extend		205		103	of		257		51
his		206		102	Kildare,	26	258	2	50
cares		207		101	and		259		49
afterwards		208		100	deputy		260		48
to		209		99	of		261		47
that		210		98	Ireland,	27	262	1	46
second		211		97	before		263		45
Kingdom,		212		96	whose		264		44
Wherefore		213		95	eyes		265		43
through		214		94	he		266		42
this		215		93	did		267		41
neglect,		216		92	cast		268		40
upon		217		91	such		269		39
the		218		90	a		270		38
coming		219		89	mist		271		37
of		220		88	by		272		36
Simon	19	221	9	87	his		273		35
with		222		86	own		274		34
his		223		85	insinuation,		275		33
pretended		224		84	and		276		32
Plantagenet	20	225	8	83	by		277		31
into		226		82	the		278		30
Ireland	21	227	7	81	carriage		279		29
all		228		80	of		280		28
things		229		79	his		281		27
were		230		78	youth		282		26
prepared		231		77	that		283		25
for		232		76	expressed		284		24
revolt		233		75	a		285		23
and		234		74	natural		286		22
sedition,		235		73	Princely		287		21
almost		236		72	behavour		288		20
as		237		71	as		289		19
if		238		70	joined		290		18
they		239		69	perhaps		291		17
had		240		68	with		292		16
been		241		67	some		293		15
set		242		66	inward		294		14

APPENDIX.

vapours	295	13	*Earl's*		302	6
of	296	12	own		303	5
ambition	297	11	mind,		304	4
and	298	10	left		305	3
affection	299	9	him		306	2
in	300	8	fully		307	1
the	301	7				

We reproduce here a facsimile reduced lithograph of page 265, Bacon's "Advancement of Learning," 1640, whereby the strange system of italicising words in this work may be studied. If the reader will count the words in italics upon this page, he will find they are fifty-three in number, counting the words "*non-significants*" as two words. This number fifty-three bears a quintuple relationship to the paging 265.

$$53 \times 5 = 265.$$

This evidently bears out the assertion of the text, and is an example of Bacon's words on this page with regard to this cipher he invented at Paris. "It containeth the *highest degree of cipher*, which is to signify *omnia per omnia*, yet so as the *writing infolding* may bear a quintuple proportion to the *writing infolded*."

Page 32 of this 1640 "Advancement of Learning" has also 53 words in italic words upon it. Also page 32 of Preface.

Page 91, 52 italic words upon it.

Page 97, 52 italic words upon it (subjects, *Relations and Poetry*).

Page 104, 53 italic words upon it.

Page 124, 52 italic words upon it.

Page 173, 53 italic words upon it.

This cannot be chance. These two numbers, 52, 53, represent Shakespeare's age, viz., full years, and the year he had just entered when he died, April 1616, according to the Stratford monument. The mispaging in this work also commences with *a false number* 52 and *a false number* 53, thus in sequence from page 49 (taken from twelve copies we have examined). Pages :—

	False.					False.
49	52	51	52	53	54	53

"Advancement of Learning," 1640.

Upon pages 105, 106, 107 we first come upon the subject of Poetry, the Drama, and Stage Plays :—

| 105 | 106 | 107 |
| Poetry. | Drama. | Stage Plays. |

Let the reader note that the sum of 52 and 53, *the two false pagings*, point to Poetry, p. 105, as if to point to the 1623 Folio columns.

$$52 + 53 = 105.$$

The double of 53 is 106, and upon this page or column in the 1623 Folio Plays, page 53, "Merry Wives of Windsor," we find the word "*Bacon.*" We also find the word "*Bacon,*" page 53, "1 King Henry IV.," and twice upon page 52 (mispaged 54) of this same play. So that the only four entries of the word "Bacon" in the Plays called Shakespeare's, are always to be found upon pages bearing the numbers 53, 52, or Shakespeare's age in 1616 when he died. All this bears out our evidence in the Introduction with regard to the extract upon pages 52, 53, "Confessio Fraternitatis," 1617, relating to an impostor styled a *Stage-Player or Comedist*. It is by mathematics this cipher is constructed. I am convinced the paging bears a *portrait in the frame* * by *figures, of Shakespeare and of Bacon at important epochs or dates like* 1616, 1623.

Upon page 29 of the first part of the 1671 "Resuscitatio" there is the following suspicious passage relating to *Lord Henry Howard* (Earl of Northampton), of whom Bacon writes: "Wherein he said, that he would not put his credit *upon ciphers and dates.*" It was in Northumberland House, which formerly belonged to the same Earl of Northampton, that a manuscript was found, on which was scribbled passages connecting Bacon's name with the play of "Love's Labour's Lost." It is to this same Lord Henry Howard Bacon writes: "For your Lordship's love, rooted upon good opinion, I esteem it highly, because I have tasted the fruits of it; *and we both have tasted of the*

---

* Bacon writes: "For it came into our mind, that in MATHEMATHICS *the frame standing,* the demonstration inferred is facile and perspicuous; on the contrary, without this accommodation and dependency, all seems involved and more subtle than indeed they be" (p. 36, "Advancement," 1640).

best waters in my accompt to knit mind's together" (p. 84, Part I., "Resuscitatio," 1671). This evidently is an allusion *to the waters of Parnassus; or of Poetry, viz., Helicon.*

"In 1867 there was discovered in the library of Northumberland House in London, a remarkable MS. containing copies of several papers written by Francis Bacon. It was found in a box of old papers which had long remained undisturbed. There is a title page, which embraces a *table of contents* of the volume, and this contains not only the names of writings unquestionably Bacon's, but also the names of plays which are supposed to have been written by Shakespeare. But only part of the manuscript volume remains, and the portions lost embrace the following pieces enumerated on the title leaf:

> *Orations at Graie's Inns revells*
> . . . . *Queen's Mat*^{s} . . . .
>   *By Mr. Frauncis Bacon*
> *Essaies by the same author.*
> *Richard the Second.*
> *Richard the Third.*
> *Asmund and Cornelia.*
> *Isle of Dogs frmnt.*
>   *By Thomas Nashe, inferior places.*

How comes it that the Shakespeare plays, "Richard II." and "Richard III.," should be mixed up in a volume of Bacon's manuscripts with his own letters and essays and a mask written by him in 1592? Judge Holmes says: "And then, the blank space at the side and between the titles is scribbled all over with various words, letters, phrases, and scraps of verse in English and Latin, as if the copyist were merely trying his pen, and writing down whatever first came into his head. Among these scribblings, beside the name of Francis Bacon several times, *the name of William Shakespeare is written eight or nine times over.* A line from *The Rape of Lucrece* is written thus: 'Revealing day through every crannie peeps and,' the writer taking *peeps* from the next couplet instead of *spies*. Three others are *Anthony comfrt. and consort* and *honorificabilitudino* and *plaies* [plays]. . . . The word *honorificabilitudino* is not found in any dictionary that I know of, but in 'Love's Labour's Lost'" ("The Great Cryptogram," Donnelly, 282, vol. i.).

Now this Northumberland House where this paper was found belonged to Lord Henry Howard, Earl of Northampton, who, with Bacon and the Earl of Salisbury, shared chief honours in the administration of James the First's Government. Before discovering this last curious coincidence of the finding of this paper, I had long had suspicions that Lord Henry Howard was in some literary connection with Bacon. The thirty-fifth Apophthegm is repeated *twice* in the collection of the 1671 "Resuscitatio," which can hardly be the result of accident, and introduces this same Earl of Northampton.

Michael Maier, who visited England in 1617, and who was the friend of Robert Fludd, the great English Rosicrucian and Apologist of the Order, contributes, in his "Symbola Aureæ Mensæ" (Frankof., 1617), the following Ænigma in poetry connected with the centre of the Rosicrucians (page 296). It will be seen that Apollo figures as protagonist again, and that there is some implied hint to an island in the west.

> Ænigmata A ix. Musis et
> Apolline de Collegio Germanorum
> Philosophorum R. C. eorumque loco,
> ipsis discutienda, honoris gratia
> proposita.

1. ÆNIGMA CALLIOPES.*

Longus in HESPERIO *protenditur æquore tractus*
Ad septem lato prospectans axe TRIONES,
In medio nunc terra jacet, quæ fertur ADELPHA
Nomine dicta, virum magnæ virtutis alumna,
Parvo licet spacio passus vix mille pererret
Circuitu immensi præ fluctibus INSULA PONTI
Non est tuta satis, cujus prope littora PROTEUS
Qui Deus in varias mutat se corpore formas,
Sæpe die, radios sole emittente serenos,
Visitur: hic captus per multas denique curas
Artis et ingenii, se fatur, ad æqua paratum
Reddere quæsitis responsa, nec edere falsi
Velle aliquid, Quæ sint, fuerintve, futurave restent,
Se callere, sed hæc cunctis prædicere nolle:
Ergo lubens, inquam posco quâ littoris orâ
Conveniant cælo genitus, Dea Cypris et illa
Quam peperit Latona simul, ne ferre recuset:
Hæc est summa mei, quod ei committo negoti:
Annuit ille, sonis et talibus ora resoluit, &c.

(P. 297, " Symbola Aureæ Mensæ, 1617.)

---

* This work bears date 1617—the year following Shakespeare's death! All the Rosicrucian literature of importance appears with Shakespeare's death, 1616, when Fludd first publishes.

Is there no sly reference to Fludd's name in the word "*Fluctibus*," his Latin name, which he adopted being *Robertus di Fluctibus?* We have reproduced the text exactly as it is printed in the original, the words HESPERIO, TRIONES, ADELPHA, INSULA PONTUS, PROTHEUS, being in large Roman type, and evidently being accented thus to indicate hints of importance. It seems to us Atlantis is pointed at *or an Island of the Ocean, situated to the West and North.* The previous year —1616—(this work was printed 1617), Maier, the author, was in England on a visit to Robert Fludd. This island may be the "New Atlantis."

The Church of St Michael's, where Lord Bacon is buried, was originally founded by Abbot Ulsinus, and is dedicated to St Michael the Archangel. Parts of a painted ceiling in wood which covered the chancel still exist, and are shown to the visitor who inquires to see this curious fragment, on which is depicted the Day of Judgment, with the Archangel Michael and bodies rising out of their coffins. Evidently this was a painted emblem or representation in harmony with the name of the church—St Michael. It is remarkably curious and striking to find Bacon alluding to St Michael in his Apophthegms as follows, and evidently thinking of this painted ceiling with which he must have been so familiar:—

23. "Queen Elizabeth being to resolve upon a great officer, and being by some, that canvass'd for others, put in some doubt of that person, whom she meant to advance, called for Mr Bacon; and told him *she was like one with a Lanthorn seeking a man;* and seem'd unsatisfied in the choice she had of a man for that place. Mr Bacon answered her that he had heard that in old time, there was usually *painted in the Church Walls the Day of Doom, and God sitting in judgment and Saint Michael by him, with a pair of balances;* and the soul and the good deeds in the one balance, and the faults and the evil deeds in the other; and the soul's balance went up far too light. Then was our Lady painted with a great pair of beads; who cast them into the light balance, and brought down the scale; so he said place and authority which were in her majesties hands to give, were like our Ladies beads, which though men through any imperfections, were too light before, yet when they were cast in, made weight competent" (p. 226, "Resuscitatio," 1671, Part I.).

A still more curious and extraordinary parallel is now to be adduced by us. In the Sonnets we find one which undoubtedly alludes to Saint Michael (*rebel powers*) and to a tomb.

146.

> Poor soul, the centre of my sinful earth,
> Fool'd by those *rebel powers* that thee array,
> Why dost thou pine within, and suffer dearth,
> Painting thy outward walls so costly gay?
> Why so large cost, having so short a lease,
> Dost thou upon thy fading mansion spend?
> Shall worms, inheritors of this excess,
> Eat up thy charge? Is this thy body's end?
> Then, soul, live thou upon thy servant's loss,
> And let that pine to aggravate thy store;
> Buy terms divine in selling hours of dross;
> Within be fed, without be rich no more:
>   So shalt thou feed on Death, that feeds on men,
>   And, Death once dead, there's no more dying then.

CHYMISCHE HOCHZEIT CHRISTIANI ROSENCREUTZ. Erstlich Gedruckt zu Strassburg, Anno M.DC.XVI.

I am in possession of the above work, first edition. It is to be noted this work was published the year Shakespeare died, 1616. I find in this original first edition, a great number of ENGLISH WORDS interlarded with the German text, which shows the author knew English, or perhaps translated the work from English into German. For example, pages 52, 53 (Shakespeare's two ages), I find the words "*Combination, Execution, Interpretation*," which is very curious. It must be remembered that in 1616 very few German writers were acquainted with the English language. Upon page 57 I find the English word *Inscription;* p. 60, *Dedication;* p. 62, *Solution, Question;* p. 79, *Vocal Music;* p. 81, *Disputation;* p. 88, *Intercession;* p. 6, *Calculation;* p. 19, *Compass;* p. 21, *Instruction;* p. 33, *Perturbation;* p. 39, *Perfection, Inquisition;* p. 44, *Reputation,* &c., &c. Perhaps these are cipher key words. In this Romance there are several strange ciphers given. Breithaupt, in his "Ars Decifratoria" (1737), writes: "Tandem omnium novissime inter Germanos scientia artis decifratoriæ inclaruit NICOL SEELAENDERUS, Hannoveranus, qui occultas istas scripturas, quæ in CHRISTIANI ROSENCREUTZERI *nuptiis Chymicis* inveniuntur, solvere, et quænam sub iis arcana naturæ lateant, detegere annisus est, uti haud ita pridem ex relationibus Hamburgensibus de rebus eruditis percepimus." (*Vid.* Hamburg *Berichte von gelehrten Sachen de anno* 1736, num. xlvi. et num. lxxxiii. p. 748, *seqq.*)

I should like here to point out that the "Chemical Wedding" is divided into the *Days of the Week*, which is a feature we refind peculiar to Bacon's "*College of the Six Days.*" Indeed a distinct affiliation may be traced between this work and Bacon's "New Atlantis," revealed in trifling details such as the description of the three lofty *Cedars*, described in the margin as *three Temples*. An old man is introduced on the seventh day, who in the original text is sometimes called Atlas, sometimes *Atlantis*. "*Auff des Atlantis Oration machet sich unser Alter herfür*," &c. (p. 134, Chymische Hochzeit, 1616). In Michael Maier's "Arcana Arcanissima," I find him describing ATLAS, in the second book of his Hieroglyphics, the word ATLAS being placed in extraordinary capitals in the margin, and in this respect a singular feature in the work, p. 80. He writes: "*Atlas* enim Hesperi frater, quia ad Hesperi occasum Ægypti et Græciæ respectu situs sit; Hinc et *Mercurius* Atlantiades dicitur, quia à quibusdam in Atlante genitus æstimatur." Again, "*Per Hesperum ejusque;* filias eadem montana loca Atlantis intelligimus," p. 81. I think it highly probable Maier is hinting at *the Island of Atlantis* in the Ænigma poem by him, entitled, "Ænigma Calliopes," for the word *Hesperio* is printed by itself in capitals, and Atlas was brother to this Hesperio, who was Lord of the Hesperides or Islands of the West. Madame Blavatsky writes: "The myth of Atlas is an allegory easily understood. Atlas is the old continents of Lemuria and Atlantis, combined and personified in one symbol. The poets attribute *to Atlas as to Proteus* a superior wisdom and an universal knowledge, and especially a thorough acquaintance with the depths of the ocean; because both continents bore races instructed by Divine masters, and because both were transferred to the bottom of the seas where they now slumber until their next re-appearance above the waters" ("Secret Doctrine," vol. ii. p. 762). The reader will find in Maier's enigma poem the word *Proteus* in capitals. This was the *Saturnian Kingdom*, where the golden age once reigned. Maier writes: "De *Aurea ætate* receptum est, quod aliquando acta sit *sub saturno rege*" (p. 91, "Arcana Arcanissima"). In the margin we find against this, "*Lapis in Helicone positus.*" The reader will see here is a connection between the origin of the R. C. Society and Helicon, Saturn being again found in the poem in capital letters.

Nimrod, in his Alchymus (vol. iv. p. 557, "History and Fable"), writes: "Two flowers of Harpocrates, the Red and the White, blossom in the garden of the Knights Templar." To this he adds a footnote: "See Part I., 'Henry VI.,' act ii. sc. 4." This is a striking hint, because we do find the author of the play in question has laid *the scene of plucking the red and white roses in the Temple garden*. The Rosicrucians were not merely fancifully affiliated to the Templars, but their *direct successors*, a relationship every writer on the subject, from Andreas to Hargreave Jennings, acknowledges.

www.ingramcontent.com/pod-product-compliance
Lightning Source LLC
Chambersburg PA
CBHW031247230426
43670CB00005B/78